Agency in Archaeology

Agency in Archaeology is the first critical volume to scrutinize the concept of human agency and to examine in depth its potential to inform our understanding of the past.

Theories of agency recognize that humans make choices, hold intentions and take action. Their use offers archaeologists the means to move beyond broad structural or environmental explanations of culture change and instead to consider the individual and the group. As such, the concept of agency has gained influence in every variety of archaeology, from post-processualism to evolutionary ecology. However, there has been little consensus among archaeologists on what "agency" actually means, and specifically how it can be used in studying the pre-modern past.

Agency in Archaeology brings together nineteen internationally renowned scholars who have very different, and often conflicting, stances on the meaning and use of agency theory in archaeology. The volume is composed of five position statements and nine case studies, drawing on regions from North America and Mesoamerica to western and central Europe, and ranging in subject from late Pleistocene hunter-gatherers to the restructuring of nineteenth-century gender relations in the northeastern US.

This groundbreaking collection will be required reading for advanced undergraduates, postgraduates and scholars of archaeological theory and material culture studies.

Agency in Archaeology

Edited by Marcia-Anne Dobres
and John E. Robb

London and New York

First published 2000 by Routledge
11 New Fetter Lane, London EC4P 4EE

Simultaneously published in the USA and Canada
by Routledge
29 West 35th Street, New York, NY 10001

Routledge is an imprint of the Taylor & Francis Group

Typeset in Goudy by Curran Publishing Services Ltd
Printed and bound in Great Britain by TJ International Ltd, Padstow, Cornwall

British Library Cataloguing in Publication Data
A catalogue record for this book is available from the British Library

Library of Congress Cataloging in Publication Data
Agency in archaeology / edited by Marcia-Anne Dobres, John Ernest Robb.
288 pp. 24.6 x 17.4 cm
Includes bibliographical references and index.
1. Archaeology – Philosophy Congresses. 2. Social archaeology Congresses. 3.
Agent (Philosophy) Congresses. 4. Human ecology Congresses. 5. Social
ecology Congresses. I. Dobres, Marcia-Anne. II. Robb, John E.
CC72.4.A35   2000   99–44275
930.1'01—dc21   CIP

ISBN 0–415–20760-6 (hbk)
ISBN 0–415–20761–4 (pbk)

Contents

Figures

Tables

Contributors

John C. Barrett is a Reader in Archaeology at the University of Sheffield. He has taught at the Universities of Leeds and Glasgow, undertaken fieldwork widely in Britain, and is the author of *Fragments from Antiquity*. His research interests cover later prehistory and the archaeology of the early Roman period. He is also actively engaged in developing the theoretical and methodological framework for field archaeology within the context of commercial archaeology in Britain. He is currently working on a new book, *Archaeology after Theory*.

Elizabeth M. Brumfiel is the John S. Ludington Trustee's Professor at Albion College and chair of the Anthropology and Sociology Department. She has directed archaeological investigations at Aztec-period sites in central Mexico. She focuses on two research questions: how social inequality has been and is being constructed along the lines of class, gender and ethnicity, and how struggles for status within human groups sometimes lead to social change. She has edited four books: *Production and Power at Postclassic Xaltocan*; *Factional Competition and Political Development in the New World* (with John W. Fox); *The Economic Anthropology of the State*; and *Specialization, Exchange and Complex Societies* (with Timothy K. Earle).

John Chapman is a Reader in Archaeology at the University of Durham and specializes in archaeological theory and method, social archaeology, landscape archaeology, and the later prehistory of central and eastern Europe. He has completed major fieldwork projects in Dalmatia and Hungary and is soon to start a landscape project in Moldavia. His most recent book is *The Changing Face of Dalmatia* (with R. Shiel and S. Batovic) and he has a book in print entitled *Fragmentation in Archaeology: People, Places and Broken Objects*.

John E. Clark is Associate Professor of Anthropology at Brigham Young University and director of the New World Archaeological Foundation. He has carried out fieldwork in the American southwest and Mexico. His publications include work on lithic analysis and typologies, replication experiments, workshops, craft specialization, early ceramics and figurines, obsidian exchange, political economy, the transition to sedentary agriculture, ethnohistory, early government, origins of rank societies, and the evolution of Mesoamerican civilizations. His current projects include, in addition to the above, early Mesoamerican sculpture, Aztec moral and political philosophy, natural law and private property, kingship, Folsom technology, the phenomenology of selfhood, Mesoamerican gods, the theoretical justification of replication experiments, and philosophies of action and free will.

George L. Cowgill studied in Moscow (Idaho), holds degrees in physics, taught for thirty years at Brandeis University, and is currently a Professor of Anthropology at Arizona State University. He has worked in the southern Maya Lowlands and, since 1964, at Teotihuacan, Mexico, where he was a member of René Millon's Mapping Project. He has been associated with Saburo Sugiyama and Rubén Cabrerain excavations at the Temple of Quetzalcóatl and the Moon Pyramid. His principal interests are in ideational and political aspects of complex societies, quantitative methods in archaeology, and understanding contemporary human fertility changes in poor nations.

Marcia-Anne Dobres is a Research Associate with the Archaeological Research Facility, University of California at Berkeley, and currently teaches at the University of South Carolina. Her research in Europe and South Africa focuses on Palaeolithic hunter-gatherer technology, gender, art, and symbolism. Her interests also include the history and sociopolitics of archaeological practice, and the relationship between popular culture, archaeology, and systems of representation. She is author of *Technology and Social Agency: Outlining a Practice Framework for Archaeology*, and senior editor of *The Social Dynamics of Technology: Practice, Politics, and World Views* (with Christopher R. Hoffman).

Joan M. Gero is now teaching at American University in Washington, D.C., after a recent move from the University of South Carolina. She serves as senior North American representative to the World Archaeological Congress. During the 1980s, she directed excavations at the early administrative center of Queyash Alto in Peru, and her current co-directed project in the Argentinean Andes involves Early Formative household economies. Her interests include the problem of how best to demonstrate the contingent nature of archaeological practice in knowledge production. She has written about the origins of complex society, feminist interpretations of prehistory, and the sociopolitics of archaeology. Her publications include *Engendering Archaeology: Women and Prehistory* (co-edited with Margaret Conkey).

Ian Hodder now teaches in the Department of Cultural and Social Anthropology at Stanford University. He is a Fellow of the British Academy and until recently was Professor of Archaeology at Cambridge University. His main interests are in method and theory, and in the Neolithic of Europe and the Near East. He currently directs the long-term excavation project at Çatalhöyük in Turkey. His publications include *Symbols in Action*; *Reading the Past*; *The Domestication of Europe*; *Theory and Practice in Archaeology*; and *The Archaeological Process*.

Matthew Johnson is a Professor of Archaeology at the University of Durham, UK. His research interests center on England and Europe AD 1200–1800, especially domestic architecture and landscape history. He has written on theoretical issues in historical archaeology and changing notions of landscape and identity. His publications include *Housing Culture: Traditional Architecture in an English Landscape*; *An Archaeology of Capitalism*; and *Archaeological Theory: An Introduction*. He is currently working on a book entitled *Building Histories: Castles at the End of the Middle Ages*.

Arthur A. Joyce is Assistant Professor of Anthropology at the University of Colorado at Boulder. His research focuses on the problem of state formation in Mesoamerica, especially the relationship between agency, ideology, power, interpolity action, and the development of complex societies. He is also interested in the social and ecological effects of human impact on Pre-Columbian landscapes. He has conducted fieldwork in the Oaxacan highlands, Belize, and eastern North America, and for the past twelve years has directed an interdisciplinary archaeological project in the lower Río Verde Valley, Oaxaca, Mexico. His publications include: "Ideology, Power, and Urban Society in Prehispanic Oaxaca" (*Current Anthropology*; with M. Winter); "Prehispanic Human Ecology of the Río Verde Drainage Basin" (*World Archaeology*; with R. G. Mueller); "Ideology, Power, and State Formation in Oaxaca" (in *Emergence and Change in Early Urban Societies*); "Interregional Interaction and Social Development on the Oaxaca Coast" (*Ancient Mesoamerica*; with M. Winter and R. G. Mueller); and "Arqueología de la costa de Oaxaca: Asentameintos del periodo Formativo en el valle del Río Verde Inferior" (*Estudios de Antropología e Historia*).

Lisa J. Lucero is an Assistant Professor of Anthropology at New Mexico State University at Las Cruces. Her interests include the development of complex societies, Mayan archaeology, and ceramic analysis. At present she is researching how early Mayan leaders appropriated traditional and domestic ritual to acquire power.

Henrietta L. Moore is Professor of Anthropology and Director of the Gender Institute at the London School of Economics. Her interests include east and west Africa, and the anthropology of gender. Her most recent books include *A Passion for Difference* and *The Future of Anthropological Knowledge*. She is also author of *Space, Text, and Gender: An Anthropological Study of the Marakwet of Kenya* and *Feminism and Anthropology*.

Timothy R. Pauketat is an Associate Professor of Anthropology at the University of Illinois. He previously taught at the University of Oklahoma and the State University of New York, and was recipient of the Lower Mississippi Valley Survey's C. B. Moore Award (1995). His research interests lie in understanding the historical relationships between tradition, production, and inequality. His field research focuses on the Mississippian period in central and southeastern North America, particularly around the famous Cahokia site. His numerous publications include *The Ascent of Chiefs* and *Cahokia: Domination and Ideology in the Mississippian World* (with Thomas Emerson).

John E. Robb is Lecturer in Archaeology at the University of Southampton, UK. He is currently excavating Neolithic sites in Calabria, southern Italy, and studying human skeletons from Italy, England, and other places. He has published various articles on skeletons, symbols, Neolithic social life, and Indo-Europeans, and is editor of *Material Symbols* and co-editor of *Social Dynamics of the Prehistoric Central Mediterranean*.

Kenneth E. Sassaman recently joined the anthropology faculty of the University of Florida after eleven years with the Savannah River Archaeological Research Program of the South Carolina Institute of Archaeology and Anthropology. He works primarily in the southeastern United States on issues of hunter-gatherer technology, social organization, and regional integration. He is currently completing a popular synthesis of Stallings prehistory, while implementing a long-term research project in the St Johns River valley of northeast Florida.

Paul A. Shackel is Assistant Professor of Anthropology at the University of Maryland. He served as park archaeologist at Harpers Ferry National Historical Park where he directed a long-term interdisciplinary project. He is currently working on archaeological co-operative agreements with the National Park Service at Manassas National Battlefield Park and at Petersburg Battlefield Park. He has written more than forty articles, and his books and edited volumes include: *Material Culture: An Archaeology of Annapolis, Maryland, 1695–1870*; *Culture, Change and the New Technology: An Archaeology of the Early American Industrial Era*; *Historical Archaeology of the Chesapeake* (with Barbara J. Little); *Annapolis Pasts: Contributions from Archaeology in Annapolis* (with Paul Mullins and Mark S. Warner); and "An Archaeology of Harpers Ferry's Commercial and Residential District" (*Historical Archaeology*; with Susan E. Winter).

Anthony Sinclair is Lecturer in Archaeology at the University of Liverpool. His research interests include the social nature of stone tool production in France and Spain during the last glacial maximum, and the social construction of landscape and technology during the later Palaeolithic in Europe. He is also now investigating the nature of Middle Pleistocene behavior in Makapansgat, South Africa. In addition, he is completing a fieldwork project examining elite material culture in eighteenth-century Britain.

H. Martin Wobst is Professor of Anthropology at the University of Massachusetts at Amherst. An "archaeologist of the pen," his interests lie in theory in archaeology, in the theory of method, and in the implications for theory from archaeological practice. He is also interested in the implications of archaeological practice for non-archaeologists, whether indigenous folk, administrators, state governments, other scientists, or "the public." His work in Europe (particularly east and southeast Germany) and, more recently, Australia and South Africa, includes studies of Palaeolithic (and ethnographic) hunter-gatherers, rock art, and style. His present work focuses on typology and classification in archaeology, and how they help to construct classified people, and make class society easier to imagine in both the past and the present. He is fighting a lone battle against "the classified world" and artifactual "virtual realities," of which people (past and present) may or may not be aware. Most recently, he is interested in thinking locally, acting locally, and alliancing globally.

William H. Walker is an Assistant Professor of Anthropology at New Mexico State University at Las Cruces. He specializes in the study of ancient religions. He is currently co-director with James Skibo of a project exploring the ritual organization of the Casas Grandes Interaction Sphere, as part of the La Frontera Archaeological Program.

Preface

This volume has its origins in an impromptu conversation about agency between the two editors in New Orleans in 1996, which quickly developed into a symposium organized for the 1997 Society for American Archaeology meetings in Nashville. We wish to thank David Anderson, Bill Lipe, and Tobi Brimsek for help in organizing that symposium, and the SAA Program Committee for sponsoring it. The Royal Society, the University of Southampton, and the School of American Research kindly assisted with logistic support and travel assistance. The participants in that session as well as the audience created the stimulating dialogue that is continued in this volume. We would especially like to thank Richard Blanton and Meg Conkey, who participated in the Nashville symposium but were unable to contribute to this volume.

Routledge has supported this project from the outset. In seeing the manuscript through production, Vicky Peters and her staff at Routledge have provided encouragement and advice, and we especially thank Catherine Bousfield, and Chris Carr of Curran Publishing Services, for their diligence. We also extend our thanks to Garth Bawden, Randy McGuire, and a third (anonymous) reviewer for their astute comments and suggestions on the prospectus. We have also benefited greatly from the advice and ideas of a number of colleagues; Marcia-Anne takes this opportunity to thank Laura Ahearn, Val Carnegie, Chris Hoffman, Ann Kingsolver, Vern Scarborough, and Brad Weiss. For a variety of technical and administrative help in preparing the manuscript, we are grateful to the Department of Anthropology and Office of Instructional Support (University of South Carolina), and to the Department of Archaeology (University of Southampton). Finally, Sophia Jundi helped edit the manuscript carefully and efficiently.

Editors' note

Rather than ask the contributors to conform to a single dating system, we have chosen to have each chapter employ its author's preferred notation: BP, BC/AD, BC (cal.), and so forth.

Marcia-Anne Dobres
John E. Robb

Acknowledgments

Figure 7.2, San José Mogote Monument 3, is redrawn from an original in K. V. Flannery and J. Marcus, "The Growth of Site Hierarchies in the Valley of Oaxaca: Part 1," in *The Cloud People: Divergent Evolution of the Zapotec and Mixtec Civilizations*, ed. K. V. Flannery and J. Marcus, Academic Press, New York (1983).

Figure 7.3, Late formative *danzante* portraits from Monte Albán, is redrawn from an original in J. F. Scott, *The Danzantes of Monte Albán. Part II: Catalogue*, Dumbarton Oaks, Studies in Pre-Columbian Art and Archaeology no. 19, Washington, D.C. (1978).

Figure 7.5, Building J conquest slab from Monte Albán, is redrawn from an original in A. Caso, "Calendaria y Escritura de las Antiguas Culturas de Monte Albán," *Obras Completas de Miguel Orthón de Mendizábal* 1: 116–13 (1947).

Figure 9.2, an aerial view of Monks Mound, Cahokia site, is reproduced with permission from Cahokia Mounds State Historic Site.

Figure 9.3, an excavation profile of the upper stages of Monks Mound, is adapted from Figure 5 in N. A. Reed, J. W. Bennett, and J. W. Porter, "Solid Core Drilling of Monks Mound: Technique and Findings," published in *American Antiquity* 33 (1968).

Figure 10.5, a schematic of Barton Ramie housemound depositional history, is based on Figure 11 in G. R. Willey, W. R. Bullard, J. B. Glass, and J. C. Gifford, *Prehistoric Maya Settlements in the Belize Valley*, Peabody Museum of Archaeology and Ethnology Papers, vol. 54, published by Harvard University, Cambridge, Mass. (1965).

Figure 10.6,. Profile of North Acropolis, Tikal, is reproduced by courtesy of the University of Pennsylvania Museum, Philadelphia.

Table 15.1, ceramic vessels by refined ware for two master armorer households, is taken from page 8.15 of M. T. Lucas, "Ceramic Consumption in an Industrializing Community," in *Interdisciplinary Investigations of Domestic Life in Government Block B: Perspectives of Harpers Ferry's Armory and Commercial District*, Occasional Report no. 6, ed. P. A. Shackel, published by the US Department of the Interior, National Park Service, Washington, D.C. (1993).

Part 1
Editors' introduction

1 Agency in archaeology

Paradigm or platitude?

Marcia-Anne Dobres and John E. Robb

The cat's pajamas or the Emperor's new clothes?

Agency has become the buzzword of contemporary archaeological theory. In processual archaeology, the agency concept is fast encroaching into the theoretical vacuum left by the collapse of high-level systemic models, while in post-processual circles, theorists of all kinds are concerned to understand how acting, feeling, and relating subjects constituted themselves under circumstances beyond their full comprehension or direct control. Unlike other key concepts, some version of agency is endorsed by theorists across the spectrum, from phenomenology to evolutionary ecology. The result is the apparent, if not genuine, possibility of a theoretical consensus unparalleled perhaps since the 1960s. If popularity implies theoretical soundness, it is clear that agency is a Good Thing.

Yet, surprisingly, there has been little direct scrutiny of the concept of agency. Most archaeological applications of agency theory are just that: *ad hoc* appeals to the concept to make sense of a particular problem or situation. The implication here, bolstered by citations of the ambiguous, often incomprehensible but incontrovertibly high-brow writings of Bourdieu, Giddens, and Foucault, is that the idea of agency in itself is inherently sound: it is only our *use* of the concept that needs to be worked out. The result is that there is little consensus about what "agency" actually means. Few authors are explicit in their use of the term, nor has there been sustained consideration of basic methodological and epistemological issues so as to make it applicable and appropriate to the premodern past. This absence of a theoretical critique adds to the slippery imprecision with which "agency" is currently used, and its ubiquity masks deep divides among archaeologists invoking the concept. An especially thorny issue here is the relationship between agency theory and our common-sense views of the world. Agency views have spread so rapidly and with so little critical examination that one sometimes suspects they have been used as a bridge to get "beyond" theory and do "real" archaeology. The flip side of common-sense applications of agency theory has been for some archaeologists to dismiss it as mere "hand-waving" which adds little to our understanding of ancient politics and culture.

As things stand, then, agency in archaeology is not a theoretically sophisticated paradigm, but rather a lingua franca – an ambiguous platitude meaning everything and nothing. We regard this as a problematic state of affairs. If the agency concept is useless, it should be deconstructed rather than invoked superficially and discarded when the theoretical winds shift to another quarter. But if it has merit, it deserves deeper consideration and more extensive theoretical elaboration. In the history of archaeology, theoretical movements that have made a lasting contribution to how we view the past have been those that have been subjected to multiple generations of scrutiny, often emerging in a very different form than they began. Without searching critique, current interest in agency is likely to do little more than peak, fade, and provide future historians with a horizon marker for archaeological works dating to the 1990s. If agency theory really is to become useful in understanding ancient people and their contribution to large-scale processes of cultural change – if we are to avoid simply slapping agency onto the past like a fresh coat of paint – we must integrate theoretical discourse, archaeological practice, analytic methodologies, and concrete case studies.

The goal of this book is to create a dialogue among archaeologists interested in agency, archaeologists critiquing it, and archaeologists for whom the jury is still out. Rather than arguing for a single view of agency, we have tried to collect as wide a variety of views as possible. Readers will have still other views. The goal is, someday, to do justice to our common interest: the worlds of the past.

Where does "agency" come from? A brief historical overview

Questions about personhood, volition, self-determination, and the nature of consciousness and reasoning can be traced back to Greek philosophy, especially Aristotle. They were central themes in the eighteenth-century writings of John Locke, David Hume, Jean-Jacques Rousseau, Adam Smith, and the nineteenth-century theorist John Stuart Mill, who together articulated the individual-centered philosophies of free-will, choice, intentionality, and the "purposeful activity of thrifty individuals" that still serve as the ideological basis of Western democracy. The very cornerstones of the social sciences are built on the question of how social institutions and self-determination – structure and agency – drive social reproduction (Archer 1988).

Durkheim's normativism and Parsons' functionalist and formalist theories dominated sociological discussions of agency for much of this century. Parsons (1949), in particular, stressed a utilitarian rationality underlying human decision-making and emphasized – perhaps over-emphasized – institutions as pervasive top-down constraints on individual choice (Giddens 1979; Halperin 1994). By the 1960s, this view was codified in the notion of "methodological individualism," which was an attempt to explain the causal relationship between macroscale (constraining) institutions and microscale individual decision-making (choice), based on nomothetic principles of maximization, optimization, and practical rationality (see Clark, this volume). Thus, at about the same time that archaeologists began embracing neo-evolutionary theory and cultural ecology, many sociocultural and economic anthropologists were embracing methodological individualism, especially in the study of contemporary non-capitalist social formations (Halperin 1994).

It is really only in the last two decades that anthropologists have seriously begun to rethink these concepts. Recent agency theory stems in large measure from Garfinkel's pioneering work on ethnomethodology in the 1960s (Garfinkel 1984), and from the writings of Giddens (1979, 1984) and Bourdieu (1977). These foundational works were subsequently taken in a variety of directions by Archer (1988, 1995), Sztompka (1991, 1994a), Storper (1985), Heritage (1987), Cohen (1987), Bryant and Jary (1991), and Kegan Gardiner (1995), among others. According to these theorists, and in contrast to previous paradigms, social agents are viewed not as omniscient, practical, and free-willed economizers, but rather as socially embedded, imperfect, and often impractical people. Agency theorists also talk of a much more interactive (or dialectic) relationship between the structures in which agents exist and, paradoxically, which they create.

In large measure, this shift toward a more humanized and dynamic picture of the negotiations taking place between individuals, communities, and institutions has been enabled by a focus not so much on agency and agents, as on practice (Ortner 1984; Turner 1994: 43). Indeed, the roots of contemporary practice theory can be traced back to two of Marx's most of-quoted passages:

> men [sic] make their own history, but they do not make it just as they please, they do not make it under circumstances chosen by themselves, but under circumstances directly encountered, given and transmitted from the past.
>
> (Marx 1963: 15 [orig. 1869])

> As individuals express their life, so they are. What they are, therefore, coincides with their production, both with what they produce and with how they produce.
>
> (Marx and Engels 1970: 42)

All of the core elements of contemporary practice theory are here:

- society is a plurality of individuals who exist only by virtue of the relationships they create during everyday material production (*praxis*)
- humans produce their cultural histories through *praxis*, which highlights the processual nature of social reproduction
- individual (or group) free-will and volition are explicitly disavowed, in part because people do not choose the conditions within which they live
- these structural conditions have a strong material basis
- institutional settings and conditions constitute a material world that is made, experienced, and perceived (that is, symbolized and made meaningful) by those living in it (which prefigures agency theories of embodiment, discussed later)
- society exists as the result of antecedent conditions, which gives time and history prominent roles in shaping social formations and the particular practices constituting them.

Marx's focus on *praxis* was essentially a theory of knowledge concerning people's practical engagement with the world, while his emphasis on production linked material and experiential activity to society, thought, and beliefs (Dobres in press; Tilley 1982).

In the late 1970s and early 1980s, Giddens (1979, 1984) reconstituted these elements as part of his critique of the formalism long dominant in sociology. Through his "duality of structure," he argued that people create the conditions and structures in which they live, largely as a result of the unintended consequences of their actions. Structure-building is an ongoing and recursive process between actors and forces beyond their control that is never really completed (cf. Archer 1995; Sztompka 1994b). Parallel to these claims, Bourdieu, once a devout structuralist (e.g., 1973), began questioning how social practice shapes society by concentrating on the taken-for-granted routines of daily life, or habitus, within which people create and become structured by institutions and beliefs beyond their conscious awareness or direct control (Bourdieu 1977).

Thus, by the early to mid-1980s, the question of practice and the dialectic of agency-structure had moved to the mainstream of socio-cultural anthropology (as in Moore 1986; Sahlins 1981; Scott 1985; overview in Ortner 1984). This reconfigured interest in the interplay of actors and structures was also being explored (independently) in philosophy (e.g., Brand 1984; Turner 1994), and feminist and gender studies (overview in Kegan Gardiner 1995; see also Gero, this volume). At the same time, the Annales School was rethinking the temporal relationship between large-scale institutions and small-scale social practices. Braudel's (1980) tripartite division of time into long-term structures, medium-term cycles, and short-term events underlined two especially vexing questions: first, how do structures outlive the agents who create, move through, and change them?; and second, how do short-term events contribute to longer-term processes? (cf. Bintliff 1991; Knapp 1992a).

Agency in archaeology: the theoretical landscape

The first self-proclaimed and epistemologically self-reflective theoretical revolution in modern archaeological theory was the New Archaeology, whose founding charter was laid in 1962 with Binford's article "Archaeology as Anthropology." The New Archaeologists argued that archaeology should be based explicitly on anthropological theory. By anthropological theory, they meant the social evolutionism of Service, Sahlins and Fried, often combined with the concept of ecological adaptation. Culture was conceptualized as a self-regulating and internally integrated system (e.g. Clarke 1968). Significantly, a central tenet of their manifesto was that archaeologists should be ambitious: with the development of new theoretical questions, methodological techniques, and epistemological safeguards, virtually all aspects of ancient social life could be investigated.

The New Archaeology's theoretical manifesto could have led in many theoretical directions, and it is a fascinating question why some, such as agency, became the roads not taken. For example, at the outset of the New Archaeology, Binford (1962) underlined behavioral links between individual political process, symbols, and material culture, and pointed out that people "differentially participate in culture" (Binford 1965), while Redman (1977) suggested that it could be analytically useful to comprehend the "smallest interaction group" possible and to understand how "analytical individuals" contributed to larger-scale social processes such as craft specialization, the organization of large-scale distributive networks, and the rise and fall of complex social formations. In retrospect, theoretical concerns that could have been linked to the question of agency were, instead, equated with the devalued empirical search for the archaeological signatures of individuals. For better or worse, processual archaeologists made "systems" their problem, and agents were encased in a "black box" of no analytic or explanatory importance (cf. Brumfiel 1992; Hodder 1986; Trigger 1989). Archaeologists who did deal with the social roles of individuals, primarily in often very sophisticated discussions of the dynamics of chiefdoms and early inequality, tended to assume political actors motivated by a uniform, commonsense ambition for power.

By the early 1980s, intellectual movements outside the discipline had begun to influence archaeologists who were increasingly frustrated by the "faceless blobs" (Tringham 1991) peripheralized in mainstream accounts of the past (see also Cowgill 1993; Marquardt 1992; Peebles 1992; Shanks and Tilley 1987). It was among an odd mixture of "post" processualists (among them Marxists, structuralists, symbolists, and feminists) that an explicit concern with agents and agency began to coalesce. Various Marxist agendas emerged for understanding the historical relationship between institutional structures (economic and ideological, especially), sociopolitical movements, conflicts among individuals and groups, and large-scale transformations (as in Leone 1986; Miller and Tilley 1984; Spriggs 1984; Tilley 1982). Meanwhile, other researchers began to turn their attention to structures and symbols "in action" (e.g. various essays in Hodder 1982a, 1982b), although explicit links to structuration, habitus, and the dialectic of event and structure were not obvious until later (see Wobst 1997). What in hindsight can be seen as a move toward agency-oriented questions was also developing through gender research, starting as early as the late 1970s (especially Fedigan 1986; Rapp 1977; Silverblatt 1988; cf. Conkey and Gero 1997). Still more recently, agency has been explicitly taken up by scholars influenced by the Annales school (e.g., Duke 1991; Bintliff 1991; Knapp 1992b).

The common ground among these disparate approaches to "theorizing the subject" was the claim that historical contexts of social and material interaction, along with non-discursive perceptions of the world, served as the proximate boundary conditions within which ancient people negotiated their world, while simultaneously creating and being constrained by it. As Hodder summed it up:

> since societies are made up of individuals, and since individuals can form groups to further their ends, [then] directed, intentional behavior of individual actors or ideologies can lead to structural change. Indeed, societies might best be seen as non-static negotiations between a variety of changing and uncertain perspectives.
>
> (Hodder 1987a: 6)

Throughout the 1980s and 1990s, interest in agency intensified in at least four distinct areas of archaeological inquiry. The first concerned gender. Researchers interested in ancient gender dynamics (Conkey and Spector 1984; Silverblatt 1988) and those concerned with the gendered nature of archaeological practice (Gero 1983, 1985) began calling for new approaches to theorizing the subject and of the imperative to understand such microscale contributions to the macro-structuring of ancient cultures and culture change. Today, the diversity of theoretical standpoints and research questions among archaeologists concerned with gender and agency in both theory and practice is striking (Conkey and Gero 1997). Among these, feminist challenges to mainstream discourse about the body are leading to a reconfigured interest in the embodiment of individual and collective subjectivity (see Gero, this volume).

A second area of debate in which the question of agency played a part concerns the significance of material culture variation, a topic that was again pursued in parallel among several conceptually distinct lines of research. Over several decades, debates about style had finally led archaeologists to recognize that an increasingly complex variety of (possibly endless) meanings could be read into material patterns. Thus meanings were not only context-dependent (Hodder 1987b), but necessarily sensitive to an actor's social personae and situatedness (e.g. Carr and Neitzel 1995; overview in Hegmon 1992). What began as a concern with formal and functional variability in material culture patterning developed into a host of questions about social contexts and arenas of and for action and structuration through what Wobst (this volume) calls material culture "interferences."

Third, a number of archaeologists began connecting agency and material culture via other theoretical bridges, primarily through phenomenology and/or Giddens' structuration theory. Barrett's (1994) pioneering *Fragments from Antiquity* examined the phenomenological experience of megalithic monuments, and parallel works by Tilley (1993, 1996), Thomas (1991), Parker Pearson and Richards (1994), and others have focused on the social construction of the actor's subjectivities within a constructed environment. Clearly such approaches pose complex questions for archaeology. Specifically, if structures and society are always "in process" rather than fixed and static, and if there is a continually negotiated "conversation" taking place between historically constituted agents and the long-term structures they create and live within, then what does this suggest about the causes and consequences of material culture patterning and variation (cf. in this volume Wobst, Sassaman, Chapman, Sinclair, and Shackel; also Dobres 1995, 1999a, in press).

A fourth hotbed of agency-oriented explanations has been in studies of emerging inequality (e.g., Clark and Blake 1994; Price and Feinman 1995). In contrast to the premises of gender research (e.g. Silverblatt 1988), this line of research has focused on how the strategic pursuit of prestige or power can lead to large-scale social change, for example, how individual foragers competing for personal status through feasting may have adopted agricultural practices to further their personal interests (as in Hayden 1995). Hallmarks of this approach include an interest in long-term social change, exemplified perhaps in Marcus and Flannery's (1996) theoretically understated but monumental synthesis of Zapotec prehistory, and a general assumption that actors are usually and fundamentally motivated by a desire for power and prestige (see Clark, Walker and Lucero, Joyce, this volume; Gero provides a critique).

Among other recent approaches exploring individual interests and actions and their contribution to long-term, large-scale social transformations have been optimal foraging models, varieties of game theory, as well as Darwinian and evolutionary ecology models.

Some controversial issues

Probably the most basic and contentious issue in recent agency theory is: what exactly is agency?

Agency is a notoriously labile concept (Sewell 1992), but most agency theorists, whatever their stripe, would subscribe to at least four general principles similar to those proposed by Marx (see pp. 6–8): the material conditions of social life, the simultaneously constraining and enabling influence of social, symbolic and material structures and institutions, habituation, and beliefs; the importance of the motivations and actions of agents; and the dialectic of structure and agency. Most would probably also agree that agency is a socially significant quality of action rather than being synonymous with, or reducible to, action itself.

This general framework, however, bears as tight a relationship to actual agency interpretations as the Sermon on the Mount does to the different Christianities of warlike Crusaders and pacifist Quakers. Table 1.1 lists some of the interpretations of agency and practice that have been proposed in the last decade or so.

Clearly these views are not mutually exclusive, and in a given situation agency may be construed in many of these senses. For example, let us imagine a Hopi man making a mask for a kachina dance. In doing so, he is reproducing the basic cosmological beliefs of his society, experiencing the effective performance of a technical procedure, and validating the ritual system of Hopi society and the social relations created through it. Inasmuch as the social organization of ritual may have suppressed overt economic inequality between clans while the competing performance of roles may have legitimated a disguised form of it (Levy 1992), his ritual preparation may have unwittingly perpetuated a hegemonic situation; and if he belonged to a poor clan, his contribution to reproducing Hopi social relations through this ritual dance would have contradicted any discursive ambitions of manifesting or bettering his own situation through such performance. He is also practicing and performing technological tasks such as carving and painting, perhaps with some identity-reinforcing discussion of how to do so with his peers. Indeed, by enacting the physical requirements to make the mask, and through the thoughts he must hold in order to do it properly, he is also

Table 1.1 What is " agency"? circa 1980–90

The replication of unconscious cognitive structures (as in Bourdieu's [1977: 78] "generative principles of regulated improvisations").

The social reproduction of system-wide power relations via cultural actions (as in Gramsci's (1971) idea of " hegemony" and Althusser's (1990) idea of the "ideological state apparatus;" cf. Pauketat, this volume).

Resistance or challenge to system-wide power structures through direct or indirect individual or collective action (cf. Chapman, Shackel, this volume).

The constitution of individual subjectivity through diffuse power relations (as in Foucault (1994); cf. Leone 1995).

The constitution of the individual as a psychological entity (cf. Cowgill, this volume).

The experience of individual action in creating a life story (cf. Hodder, Johnson, this volume).

The imposition of form on material via socially situated creative activity (cf. Wobst, Sassaman, Sinclair, this volume).

A process of intersubjective engagement with the material and social world (e.g. Barrett 1994; Dobres in press; Thomas 1996; cf. Barrett, this volume).

The creation of formal and social distinctions through expressive activity (Carr and Neitzel 1995; cf. Clark, Joyce, Walker and Lucero, this volume).

The successful deployment of discursive and non-discursive technological knowledge and skill (e.g. Dobres 1995, 1999b, in press; cf. Sinclair, this volume).

The strategic carrying out of intentional plans for purposive goals (as in models of actors rationally pursuing prestige or power; cf. Cowgill, Clark, Walker and Lucero, this volume).

The strategic carrying out of an intentional plan in accordance with a specific culturally constructed idea of personhood (cf. Johnson, this volume), class (cf. Shackel, this volume), or cosmos (cf. Joyce, this volume).

becoming a certain kind of person, possibly even developing a number of overlapping social personae. But most of these are rarely conscious goals (except when dedicated social critics arm themselves with revolutionary practical consciousness). His discursive intentions may be more immediate: to prepare for a ritual that will confirm his claim or ambition to be a ritual participant or leader, to gain, assert or reconfirm his social authority and prestige, to promote the interests of his clan or ritual society, or to fulfill a debt or impose an obligation on someone else.

In this simplified example, there seems little contradiction between different construals of agency, leaving us free if we wish to adopt the "eclectic" view that agency has many simultaneously operative qualities. But the range of activity outcomes sometimes identified as "agency" often directly contradict each other (for instance, when one chooses to express one's dissent with a situation through the very institutions that ultimately recreate it). In such cases, it is often difficult to choose which aspect of agency is the most relevant and which can be "explained away." In other instances, it is the contradiction between different aspects of agency that may be the real dynamic we need to understand.

Basically, then, we can take one of two approaches to the problem of understanding agency. The "eclectic" strategy is to recognize that agency operates in many ways at once, and that, in a given situation, contradiction among its different dimensions is far more typical and interesting than concordance. In archaeological accounts, according to this view, what really matters is which aspects of agency one highlights, or, better yet, how one grapples with their ambiguities and contradictions without reductionism (cf. Gero, this volume). However, this strategy may over-generalize the use of the term agency so far that it renders it practically useless. How helpful is it to see agency as a quality, a process, a conscious intention, an action, an unintended consequence, and a descriptive category all at the same time? Moreover, though focusing on ambiguity and contradiction is often compelling, the "eclectic" approach may ultimately be more of an evasion rather than a real resolution of certain theoretical difficulties.

The second alternative is to define agency more narrowly and clearly, perhaps through a restricted working definition relevant to the particular question at hand. However, what should this restricted definition be? What are the critical issues to resolve? And, by reducing the multiple, overlapping, and contradictory qualities of agency down to a narrow elemental few, do we risk losing whatever makes agency useful, interesting, and relevant to understanding real social situations?

There are no easy answers to these questions. Our goal in this volume is not to force some common ground (we leave the reader to decide if such even exists), but to demonstrate the need for clarity. Given the variety of agency definitions and approaches now available, it is no longer enough simply to invoke human actors and pay homage to Bourdieu and Giddens. Archaeologists have now to make a case not only for why the agency concept is useful, but also why their particular approach is more appropriate than others.

Among other difficult issues raised by the concept of agency, there are five that compel particular attention: intentionality and social reproduction; scale; temporality and social change; material culture; and the politics of archaeological practices.

Intentionality and social reproduction

Probably the biggest divide among agency enthusiasts is between those who stress agency as the intentional actions of agents and those who stress its non-discursive qualities. Particularly in studies of political behavior and the development of social inequality, there is a strong tradition of arguing that the way individual actors consciously pursue what they want is a driving force in social change. In contrast, other theorists (notably McCall 1999) contend that what actors want or intend is often irrelevant to the real social consequences of their actions. McCall points out that the unintended consequences of action are not merely what happens when an actor's plan goes awry, but rather include the unwitting reproduction of all the social contexts within which the actor's intentions and strategies make sense, and that this is really their most important effect. Several other theoretical watersheds parallel the intentional/unintentional distinction in agency theory. For instance, are an actor's motives and behaviors rational or part of some cultural, gender-specific, or other form of "palaeopsychology"? To what extent do the symbols (such as ideologies) manipulated by actors also help constitute them? (Robb 1998, 1999). These issues are explored in this volume, particularly in Cowgill's examination of the role of reason, rationality, and psychology in agency, in Joyce's and Clark's discussions of agency and the possible motivations of incipient elites, and in Pauketat's argument that the unintentional outcomes of agents' self-interested actions often contribute to their own subordination.

Scale: individual agency, multiple agencies, and the agency of groups

Is agency exercised only by individuals or can groups exercise agency? We see this, in part, as an issue of phenomenological scale, but it also conjures up the specter of methodological individualism. The majority tradition in Anglo-American archaeology has certainly been to associate agency with individuals (whether analytical or real). This is most often seen in top-down models of political relations, in which power is exercised by those in command. Challenges to this paradigm come from a number of directions. For example, the post-modern deconstruction of the individual implies that agency and power work through individuals, rather than being co-opted and exercised by them. In effect, society constructs a situation in which people act; it is less relevant who pulls the trigger and why they think they are doing so. Other theorists, however, have argued that agency is less about the intentional exercise of personal interests and more about a cultural process *through* which person-hood and a sense of "groupness" are constructed, negotiated and transformed. Thus, rather than conflating agency with individuals, should we instead focus explicitly on the agency of social collectivities? Finally, is it enough to talk vaguely about generic actors and agency (those "faceless blobs" again), or do we need to consider multiple styles or varieties of agency within a society, such as those associated with gender, age, race, class, or other culturally recognized forms of subjecthood?

In this volume, Wobst asks us to consider group-level agency, while Hodder and Johnson concentrate on individuals as real historical agents. In substantially different ways, Pauketat, Sassaman, Shackel, and Chapman all deal with the paradox of overlapping but contradictory self- and group-level agencies. What is striking is how differently these case studies work through the problem of multiple phenomenological scales. In contrast, Walker and Lucero focus on the agency and effects of one particular group (ritual leaders) and its conscious attempts to appropriate the beliefs and practices of the community as a whole.

Agency and social change

If agency is important in understanding society in the short run, it must be included in explanations of social change over long time spans, but this poses a number of controversial implications. Among the most difficult is the question of which aspects of agency help shape long-term cultural change: intentional, strategic actions? the unintended environmental and economic consequences of such actions, which might be imperceptible at any given moment but which accumulate irrevocably over generations? the unintended reproduction of social and cultural structures? Is long-term, group-level agency simply individual agency at a larger scale, or does the game change at different phenomenological scales? Do different kinds of causality, or does a different balance between structure and agency, operate over different temporal and spatial scales? Is the interplay of agency and structure different in different kinds of society (as suggested by interpretations emphasizing the conservatism of "traditional" societies)? Can an agency theory developed for modernity be applied to premodern societies, for instance, to investigate not why things change but why they appear to remain the same over the unimaginably long periods evident in much of prehistory? If agency can be useful outside the arena in which the idea was developed, then how should contemporary agency theory be modified to deal with issues unique to archaeology?

In one way or another, practically every contributor in this volume deals with these issues, and this in itself may attest to the usefulness of agency in understanding social transformations. For example, Shackel asks how gender-specific consumer choices helped to create a working-class consciousness in the nineteenth century. Similarly, in the case of archaic hunter-gatherers, Sassaman explores the relationship between gender ideologies, marital rules of residence, and divisions of labor that, in this situation, contributed to long-term and collective resistance to social differentiation; he identifies, in other words, a change towards sameness. More generally, Hodder, Barrett, and Johnson address the question of how to write about microevents and the real, meaningful lives of past people without falling prey to archaeological meta-narratives. Gero does this as well, but takes a radically different stance (which we discuss later).

Agency and material culture

Analyzing agency through archaeological remains poses undeniable challenges. Most anthropologists would agree that a ritual mask could bear any or all of the motivations and meanings proposed in the Hopi example above. Many archaeologists, finding such a mask (or its non-perishable parts) might balk at proposing more than a couple of the possible interpretations, perhaps favoring those felt to be the most empirically demonstrable. What, then, are the most appropriate ways to use artifacts to analyze agency in the past?

Discussions of agency have traditionally centered on those archaeological cases where we can discern or postulate individuals doing material things: making pots, holding feasts, burying the dead, and so forth. It has also been suggested that understanding how artifacts were used in expressing or defining an agent's interest is more important than determining what the artifacts' practical or symbolic functions may have been, how they were produced, and by whom. But a counter-view, that to inquire into the dialectic of artifact variability, individuals and groups, and social structure need not deteriorate into a search for the traces of individuals, was proposed more than twenty years ago (Redman 1977), and has recently been re-elaborated from a number of theoretical standpoints (Dobres 1995, 1999a, in press; Mithen 1990; Shennan 1989). Individual- and group-oriented approaches to agency have barely scratched the surface in understanding the ways in which material culture reproduces, promotes and thwarts agency.

Theorists also dispute the relationship between people and material culture, and these lines of argument closely parallel those discussed above under "intentionality." At one end of the theoretical spectrum, those who believe that agency is about intentionality also tend to argue that the material world is created and manipulated by more or less freely acting individuals. Hence material artifacts and patterns can be viewed as essentially inactive traces, residues, or correlates of particular kinds of human activity and agency. At the other end of the spectrum are theorists who argue that meanings and values, histories and biographies, even personhood and agency can be attributed to material things. Hence material culture must be viewed as not only actively constructing the world within which people act, but also the people themselves.

The studies in this volume pursue a range of analytic methodologies for understanding agency in the past. Sinclair uses technical *chaîne opératoire* analysis to identify valued qualities in Solutrean knapping skill that would have made stone tool production a form of self-expression. Chapman's innovative study of Neolithic and Copper Age burials interprets them not as a static, timeless assemblage of bodies and grave goods but as a time-ordered sequence of self-referential statements. Walker and Lucero reconstruct depositional sequences that relate to the ritual actions of incipient leaders. By arguing that artifacts are active "interferences" in people's lives, Wobst asks us to reconsider how we think about material culture generally. In one way or another, then, the chapters in this volume follow suit in developing arguments about the role and significance of material culture in agency studies.

Agency and the political context of archaeological practice

Agency is a political concept. As a general way of understanding how people act in society, it must derive in part from our views on how we think people in our own society should or do act. Agency theories can thus be peculiarly insidious tools for populating the past with "actors" whose situated experiences and activities do little more than recreate those of the theorist (see Brumfiel, this volume). If we are not careful, an unconsidered version of agency can be used to reproduce, and indeed naturalize, the political forms of relations and dominations within which we now live. For this reason, current agency theory has been challenged on the grounds that it is problematically androcentric and essentialist in its very conception (cf. Gero, this volume). To date, most postulated actors of the past are middle-aged adults; in truth, some archaeological reconstructions of agency seem to deal exclusively with adult male heads of households, leaving the majority of society relegated to invisible, passive non-agenthood.

Other biases can be more subtle. Bender (1993: 258) points out that in current anthropology and archaeology, "the emphasis on the autonomy of the individual and on individual agency mirrors contemporary western politics." Agency accounts of strategic competition in the past often unwittingly reflect the essentially middle-class experiences of most academics acting as agents in social arenas where they are neither inherently privileged nor categorically denied privileges, but where they are clearly rewarded for competitive performance. These (and other) possible biases are not limited to one strain of agency theory, however. Many recent post-processual studies, for instance, have envisioned individuals needing to construct their own identities by forging links to landscapes, by performing rituals, by adopting ethnicities, by enacting genders, and so on. But the pervasive need to construct and reaffirm personal identity is a prevailing theme of post-modern culture, and archaeological work focusing on it may, therefore, reflect our understandings of our own society more than they do any particular past era.

Thus, a particularly controversial question for potential agency theorists is how agency theory in archaeology can be used for purposes other than legitimizing modern social relations by uncritically projecting them back in time. In decided contrast to all other contributors in this volume, Gero draws her inspiration from explicitly politicized sources outside anthropology and archaeology: feminist political economists, third-world activists, and culture critics whose explicit agendas are to show how contemporary gender and race ideologies influence the global economic realities of women and other disenfranchised groups. Gero points out how such ideological influences feed into the political economy of academic knowledge, but she leaves it to the reader to consider for themselves how such arguments are to be applied as correctives to the biased interpretive frameworks archaeologists may employ. This is an important argument, for it suggests that we may be able to use agency theory not only to understand the past, but also to trace out and correct at least some of the more insidious political effects of contemporary practice (Gero 1985).

Conclusions

Agency studies in archaeology are beginning to pass the "add actors and stir" stage; agency now needs to be problematized critically and productively in much the same way that gender studies were after the first rush to identify women in the archaeological record. Some key theoretical issues we believe warrant sustained consideration are discussed earlier: issues of definition, intentionality, scale, temporality, material culture, and politics. One real litmus test for the success of this endeavor will be how we answer the question, does thinking about agency change the way we do archaeology, not merely in how we dig or survey, but also in how we understand artifacts, sites, and landscapes within our representations of the past?

We also need to acknowledge the hard-learned lesson of history: that archaeology has been colonized by too many theoretical empires originating in disciplines with standpoints and agendas very different from our own. Rather than being content to borrow concepts of agency wholesale, we need to address how contemporary agency theory should be modified to fit archaeological research interests, archaeological scales of inquiry, and the unique qualities of archaeological data. We should also return to a cardinal lesson of early New Archaeology: archaeology does not have to be the intellectual poor cousin of anthropology, gratefully and uncritically accepting hand-me-down concepts and theories. Archaeologists often study societies, practices, and processes of social change unknown in the modern world, and we have a uniquely long temporal vision. Moreover, we deal with material culture far more seriously and innovatively than do most social scientists, and material culture is clearly central to creating agents and expressing agency. Studies of the long-term, studies of societies different from the present, and studies recognizing the centrality of material culture are sorely lacking in contemporary agency theory, thus archaeological concepts have something important to say beyond our own disciplinary walls.

Bibliography

Althusser, L. 1990. *For Marx*. Verso, London.

Archer, M. S. 1988. *Culture and Agency: The Place of Culture in Social Theory*. Cambridge University Press, Cambridge UK.

—— 1995. *Realist Social Theory: The Morphogenetic Approach*. Cambridge University Press, Cambridge UK.

Barrett, J. C. 1994. *Fragments from Antiquity: An Archaeology of Social Life in Britain, 2900–1200 BC*. Blackwell, Oxford.

Bender, B. 1993. "Cognitive Archaeology and Cultural Materialism." *Cambridge Archaeological Journal* 3(2): 257–60.

Binford, L. R. 1962. "Archeology as Anthropology." *American Antiquity* 28(2): 217–25.

—— 1965. "Archeological Systematics and the Study of Culture Process." *American Antiquity* 31(2): 203–10.

Bintliff, J. 1991. "The Contribution of an Annaliste/Structural History Approach to Archaeology," in *The Annales School and Archaeology*, ed. J. Bintliff, pp. 1–33. Leicester University Press, London.

Bourdieu, P. 1973. "The Berber House," in *Rules and Meanings*, ed. M. Douglas, pp. 98–110. Penguin, Baltimore.

—— 1977. *Outline of a Theory of Practice*, trans. R. Nice. Cambridge University Press, Cambridge UK.

Brand, M. 1984. *Intending and Acting: Toward a Naturalized Action Theory*. MIT Press, Cambridge Mass.

Braudel, F. 1980. "History and the Social Sciences: The *Longue Durée*," in *On History*, pp. 25–54. University of Chicago Press, Chicago.

Brumfiel, E. M. 1992." Distinguished Lecture in Archaeology: Breaking and Entering the Ecosystem: Gender, Class, and Faction Steal the Show." *American Anthropologist* 94(3): 551–67.

Bryant, C. and D. Jary (eds) 1991. *Giddens' Theory of Structuration: A Critical Appreciation*. Routledge, London.

Carr, C. and J. E. Neitzel (eds) 1995. *Style, Society and Person: Archaeological and Ethnological Perspectives*. Plenum, New York.

Clark, J. E. and M. Blake 1994. "The Power of Prestige: Competitive Generosity and the Emergence of Rank Societies in Lowland Mesoamerica," in *Factional Competition and Political Development in the New World*, ed. E. M. Brumfiel and J. W. Fox, pp. 17–30. Cambridge University Press, Cambridge UK.

Clarke, D. 1968. *Analytical Archaeology*. Methuen, London.

Cohen, I. 1987. "Structuration Theory and Social Praxis," in *Social Theory Today*, ed. A. Giddens and J. H. Turner, pp. 273–308. Stanford University Press, Stanford.

Conkey, M. W. and J. M. Gero 1997. "Programme to Practice: Gender and Feminism in Archaeology." *Annual Review of Anthropology* 26: 411–37.

Conkey, M. W. and J. D. Spector 1984. "Archaeology and the Study of Gender." *Advances in Archaeological Method and Theory* 7: 1–38.

Cowgill, G. L. 1993. "Distinguished Lecture in Archaeology: Beyond Criticizing New Archaeology." *American Anthropologist* 95(3): 551–73.

Dobres, M-A. 1995. "Gender and Prehistoric Technology: On the Social Agency of Technical Strategies." *World Archaeology* 27(1): 25–49.

—— 1999a. "Of Paradigms and Ways of Seeing: Artifact Variability As If People Mattered," in *Material Meanings: Critical Approaches to the Interpretation of Material Culture*, ed. E. Chilton, pp. 7–23. University of Utah Press, Salt Lake City.

—— 1999b. "Technology's Links and *Chaînes*: The Processual Unfolding of Technique and Technician," in *The Social Dynamics of Technology: Practice, Politics, and World Views*, ed. M-A. Dobres and C. R. Hoffman, pp. 124–46. Smithsonian Institution Press, Washington, D.C.

—— in press. *Technology and Social Agency: Outlining a Practice Framework for Archaeology*. Blackwell, Oxford.

Duke, P. 1991. *Points in Time: Structure and Event in a Late Northern Plains Hunting Society*. University of Colorado Press, Niwot.

Fedigan, L. 1986. "The Changing Role of Women in Models of Human Evolution." *Annual Review of Anthropology* 15: 25–66.

Foucault, M. 1994. "Two Lectures," in *Culture/Power/History*, ed. N. Dirks, G. Eley, and S. B. Ortner, pp. 200–21. Princeton University Press, Princeton.

Garfinkel, H. 1984. *Studies in Ethnomethodology*. Polity Press, Cambridge UK.

Gero, J. M. 1983. "Gender Bias in Archaeology: A Cross-Cultural Perspective", in *The Socio-Politics of Archaeology*, ed. J. M. Gero, D. Lacey and M. Blakey, pp. 51–7. Research Reports no. 23, University of Massachusetts, Amherst.

—— 1985. "Socio-Politics and the Woman-at-Home Ideology." *American Antiquity* 50: 342–50.

Giddens, A. 1979. *Central Problems in Social Theory: Action, Structure, and Contradiction in Social Analysis*. University of California Press, Berkeley.

—— 1984. *The Constitution of Society: Outline of a Theory of Structuration*. University of California Press, Berkeley.

Gramsci, A. 1971. *Selections from the Prison Notebooks*. International Publishers, New York.

Halperin, R. H. 1994. *Cultural Economies Past and Present*. University of Texas Press, Austin.

Hayden, B. 1995. "Pathways To Power: Principles for Creating Socioeconomic Inequalities," in *Foundations of Social Inequality*, ed. T. D. Price and G. Feinman, pp. 15–86. Plenum, New York.

Hegmon, M. 1992. "Archaeological Research on Style." *Annual Review of Anthropology* 21: 517–36.

Heritage, J. 1987. "Ethnomethodology," in *Social Theory Today*, ed. A. Giddens and J. H. Turner, pp. 224–72. Stanford University Press, Stanford.

Hodder, I. (ed.) 1982a. *Symbolic and Structural Archaeology*. Cambridge University Press, Cambridge UK.

—— (ed.) 1982b. *Symbols in Action: Ethnoarchaeological Studies of Material Culture*. Cambridge University Press, Cambridge UK.

—— 1986. *Reading The Past*. Cambridge University Press, Cambridge UK.

—— (ed.) 1987a. *Archaeology as Long-Term History*. Cambridge University Press, Cambridge UK.

—— (ed.) 1987b. *The Archaeology of Contextual Meanings*. Cambridge University Press, Cambridge UK.

Kegan Gardiner, J. (ed.) 1995. *Provoking Agents: Gender and Agency in Theory and Practice*. University of Illinois Press, Urbana.

Knapp, A. B. 1992a. "Archaeology and Annales: Time, Space, and Change," in *Archaeology, Annales, and Ethnohistory*, ed. A. B. Knapp, pp. 1–21. Cambridge University Press, Cambridge UK.

—— (ed.) 1992b. *Archaeology, Annales, and Ethnohistory*. Cambridge University Press, Cambridge UK.

Leone, M. P. 1986. "Symbolic, Structural, and Critical Archaeology," in *American Archaeology Past and Future: A Celebration of the Society for American Archaeology 1935–1985*, ed. D. J. Meltzer, D. D. Fowler and J. A. Sabloff, pp. 415–38. Society for American Archaeology, Washington, D. C.

—— 1995. "A Historical Archaeology of Capitalism." *American Anthropologist* 97: 251–68.

Levy, J. 1992. *Orayvi Revisited: Social Stratification in an "Egalitarian" Community*. School of American Research, Santa Fe.

Marcus, J. and K. V. Flannery 1996. *Zapotec Civilization: How Urban Society Evolved in Mexico's Oaxaca Valley*. Thames and Hudson, London.

Marquardt, W. H. 1992. "Dialectical Archaeology." *Archaeological Method and Theory* 4: 101–40.

Marx, K. 1963 [orig. 1869]. *The Eighteenth Brumaire of Louis Bonaparte*. International Publishers, New York.

Marx, K. and F. Engels 1970 [orig. 1846]. *The German Ideology*. International Publishers, New York.

McCall, J. 1999. "Structure, Agency, and the Locus of the Social: Why Post-Structural Theory is Good for Archaeology," in *Material Symbols: Culture and Economy in Prehistory*, ed. J. E. Robb, pp. 16–21. Center for Archaeological Investigations, Southern Illinois University, Carbondale, Illinois.

Miller, D. and C. Tilley (eds) 1984. *Ideology, Power, and Prehistory*. Cambridge University Press, Cambridge UK.

Mithen, S. 1990. *Thoughtful Foragers: A Study of Prehistoric Decision Making*. Cambridge University Press, Cambridge UK.

Moore, H. L. 1986. *Space, Text, and Gender: An Anthropological Study of the Marakwet of Kenya*. Cambridge University Press, Cambridge UK.

Ortner, S. B. 1984. "Theory in Anthropology Since the Sixties." *Comparative Studies in Society and History* 26(1): 126–166.

Parker Pearson, M. and C. Richards (eds) 1994. *Architecture and Order: Approaches to Social Space*. Routledge, London.

Parsons, T. 1949 [orig. 1937]. *The Structure of Social Action*. Free Press of Glencoe, New York.

Peebles, C. 1992. "Rooting Out Latent Behaviorism in Prehistory," in *Representations In Archaeology*, ed. J.-C. Gardin and C. Peebles, pp. 357–84. Indiana University Press, Bloomington.

Price, T. D. and G. M. Feinman (eds) 1995. *Foundations of Social Inequality*. Plenum Press, New York.

Rapp, R. R. 1977. "Gender and Class: An Archaeological Consideration of Knowledge Concerning the Origins of the State." *Dialectical Anthropology* 2: 309–16.

Redman, C. 1977. "The 'Analytical Individual' and Prehistoric Style Variability," in *The Individual in Prehistory: Studies of Variability in Style in Prehistoric Technologies*, ed. J. Hill and J. Gunn, pp. 41–53. Academic Press, New York.

Robb, J. E. 1998. "The Archaeology of Symbols." *Annual Review of Anthropology* 27: 329–46.

—— 1999. "Secret Agents: Culture, Economy, and Social Reproduction," in *Material Symbols: Culture and Economy in Prehistory*, pp. 3–15. Center for Archaeological Investigations, Southern Illinois University, Carbondale, Illinois.

Sahlins, M. 1981. *Historical Metaphors and Mythical Realities: Structure in the Early History of the Sandwich Islands Kingdom*. University of Michigan Press, Ann Arbor.

Scott, J. 1985. *Weapons of the Weak: Everyday Forms of Peasant Resistance*. Yale University Press, New Haven.

Sewell W. H. Jr. 1992. "A Theory of Structure: Duality, Agency, and Transformation." *American Journal of Sociology* 98(1): 1–29.

Shanks, M. and C. Tilley 1987. *Re-constructing Archaeology*. Cambridge University Press, Cambridge UK.

Shennan, S. 1989. "Cultural Transmission and Cultural Change," in *What's New? A Closer Look at the Process of Innovation*, ed. S. E. van der Leeuw and R. Torrence, pp. 330–46. Unwin Hyman, London.

Silverblatt, I. 1988. "Women in States." *Annual Review of Anthropology* 17: 427–60.

Spriggs, M. (ed.) 1984. *Marxist Perspectives in Archaeology*. Cambridge University Press, Cambridge UK.

Storper, M. 1985. "The Spatial and Temporal Constitution of Social Action: A Critical Reading of Giddens." *Environment and Planning D: Society and Space* 3: 407–24.

Sztompka, P. 1991. *Society in Action*. University of Chicago Press, Chicago.

—— (ed.) 1994a. *Agency and Structure: Reorienting Social Theory*. Gordon and Breach, Switzerland.

—— 1994b. "Society as Social Becoming: Beyond Individualism and Collectivism," in *Agency and Structure: Reorienting Social Theory*, ed. P. Sztompka, pp. 251–82. Gordon and Breach, Switzerland.

Thomas, J. 1991. *Rethinking the Neolithic*. Cambridge University Press, Cambridge UK.

—— 1996. *Time, Culture and Identity*. Routledge, London.

Tilley, C. 1982. "Social Formation, Social Structures and Social Change," in *Symbolic and Structural Archaeology*, ed. I. Hodder, pp. 26–38. Cambridge University Press, Cambridge UK.

—— 1993. *Interpretative Archaeology*. Berg, Oxford.

—— 1996. *An Ethnography of the Neolithic*. Cambridge University Press, Cambridge UK.

Trigger, B. 1989. *A History of Archaeological Thought*. Cambridge University Press, Cambridge UK.

Tringham, R. E. 1991. "Households With Faces: The Challenge of Gender in Prehistoric Architectural Remains," in *Engendering Archaeology: Women and Prehistory*, ed. J. M. Gero and M. W. Conkey, pp. 93–131. Blackwell, Oxford.

Turner, S. 1994. *The Social Theory of Practices: Tradition, Tacit Knowledge, and Presuppositions*. University of Chicago Press, Chicago.

Wobst, H. M. 1997. "Towards an 'Appropriate Metrology' of Human Action in Archaeology," in *Time, Process, and Structured Transformation in Archaeology*, ed. S. E. van der Leeuw and J. McGlade, pp. 426–48. Routledge, London.

Part 2
Thinking agency

2 Agency and individuals in long-term processes

Ian Hodder

Introduction

Archaeological data raise the issue of scale in a most extreme form. On the one hand, the processes observed by archaeologists stretch out over spans of time which are difficult or impossible for individual actors to comprehend or perceive. These are the processes of the long term, the rise and fall of complex political systems, the slow transformation of subsistence technologies, the *longue durée* of *mentalités*, the battle-ship curves of styles, and so on. Archaeological emphasis on the long term is reinforced by patterns of survival and recovery. From many periods and areas, few sites survive or few have been excavated with modern scientific techniques. Thus, there is little choice but to talk of the large scale, the generalized, the gross patterning. There are also sociopolitical reasons for the archaeological focus on the long term. For example, archaeology grew in Europe as an inherent part of nationalism, to provide a long-term basis for the nation state, and reference to the long-term archaeological past is an integral part of many indigenous claims to territory today. Within the Western academy, archaeology identified itself as a separate field of inquiry by opposing its concern with the long term to the shorter spans dealt with in sociocultural anthropology (in the United States) and in history (in Europe).

On the other hand, archaeological understanding of the long term is built up from traces of the smallest and least significant of acts. Our data are produced by the dropping and breaking of a pot and the kicking or tossing of its sherds. They are produced by the discard from meals, the knapping of flint or the scratching on clay. True, there are also the walls of houses and temples protected in tells and the monuments built to last in open landscapes. But even these we increasingly understand as constructed at particular moments in time for specific historical purposes; the social meanings of these temples and monuments do not stay the same. Again, there are sociopolitical factors involved. Archaeologists in Europe defined themselves as different from historians by their concentration, not on elite texts, but on the mundane practices and residues of daily life.

These radical differences in scale inherent within archaeological data and within the archaeological discipline, might be supposed to have encouraged theories which deal fully with the relationships between individual events and large-scale process. On the whole, however, and especially over recent decades, in both processual and postprocessual archaeology, archaeologists have eschewed the small scale in favor of long-term trends. It was particularly in traditional culture-historical archaeology that attempts were made to conceive of the "Indian behind the artifact," for example in identifying the individual "hand" of the painter of a Greek vase (Hill and Gunn 1977), or in discussions of the intentionality of Caesar crossing the Rubicon (Collingwood 1946). But since the 1960s, the emphasis has shifted to the "system behind the Indian behind the artifact." Despite the rhetoric of many recent theoretical perspectives in archaeology, in what follows I argue that insufficient attention has been given to the role of small-scale events and processes within the long term. I argue that archaeologists have come to focus on agency and on the *construction* of individuals, selves, and subjects. I argue, following Meskell (1996; Knapp and Meskell 1997) that this constructivist position is inadequate, and particularly inappropriate for dealing with the particularity of archaeological data: the radical differences of scale. I argue that there is a need to shift from agency and the construction of social beings, to individual narratives of lived lives and events.

Agency

In my view, the early uses of the term "agency" in postprocessual archaeology have to be understood in terms of an opposition that was being made with the term "behavior." The use of the latter term, even if not associated specifically with behaviorism, was seen by critics as implying a passive stimulus–response view of human action, and as implying the description of events from an external, distanced point of view: "her arm was raised" as opposed to the agency-centered view that "she raised her arm."

The notion that material culture was active derived from a critique of the view of social systems as peopled by actors who respond predictably to events and produce material culture as by-products of those responses. It could be shown that individual actors actively used material culture (Hodder 1982) in their competing, contradictory and changing strategies. An emphasis was thus placed on intentionality, and it was this that became central to discussions of agency (Hodder 1986; Shanks and Tilley 1987). While in my own early texts on this subject there was much discussion of individuals, no attempt was made to identify them specifically. Rather, the reason for foregrounding individuals was to make a theoretical point: that we needed to consider how people were actively pursuing specific actions and intentions. "The individual" was at that point a theoretical prop to the emphasis on intentionality.

Another reason for the early emphasis on the individual was to foreground indeterminacy. Rather than large-scale systems and processes in which individuals were caught and determined, the theoretical focus on the individual underlined the idea that human beings were able to monitor the effects of their actions and act in novel, creative ways. So again, it was not a matter of identifying individual agents but of emphasizing at a theoretical level the move away from behavioral and deterministic perspectives.

If early work on agency was couched in terms of intentionality and indeterminacy, the concept soon came to be overtaken by a very different view: that agency amounted to "the power to act." In my view, this shift reflects the long-standing inability of the discipline to cope in theoretical terms with the individualized and with the small-scale. And indeed, the effect of this shift was that the emphasis on individuals was lost, a trend noted by Johnson (1989).

Agency thus came to be seen in terms of the resources needed in order to act (Miller and Tilley 1984; Shanks and Tilley 1987). These resources were both material and symbolic (informational). The control of prestige goods or esoteric knowledge was seen as the basis of power, both power *to* and power *over* (ibid.). An example of a study in which power is related to resources without explicit consideration of individuals is provided by Walker and Lucero (this volume). Many such perspectives on agency derived from Foucault and Giddens (Miller and Tilley 1984), and they have increasingly been subject to criticism in the social sciences (e.g., Turner 1994), mainly because they do not in the end provide an adequate theory of the subject and of agency. Despite an apparent emphasis on the duality of structure and agency, Giddens is criticized for leaving little room for transformative action.

We can see the limits of the structurationist view in many of its applications in archaeology. Agency appears in these applications to be routinized, and materially and objectively structured. A good example in archaeology is provided by the "big men aggrandizers" discussed by Hayden (1990). There is perhaps an androcentric aspect to the focus on power (Meskell 1996). There is little emphasis on intentionality as individualized, small-scale and transformative.

For example, Barrett (1994) provides one of the clearest and most successful sustained applications of structuration theory in archaeology. It is clear, however, that he wishes to get away from specific moments of intentionality and from accounts of meaningful and transformative action (but see also Barrett, this volume). He argues that "we have not uncovered what those monuments meant" (Barrett 1994: 1). In discussing Neolithic and Bronze Age monuments in Britain, practices sometimes appear to become separated from mind. "Monumentality originated in neither the idea nor the plan but rather in the practice and in the project" (ibid.: 23). This seems to be denying discursive intentionality, idea and plan too completely. Perhaps as a result, Barrett's agents seem caught in long-term structures with a materialist bent. For example, Barrett argues that in the British early Neolithic the use of monuments and landscapes is generalized. Thus, a wide range of activities occur at "ancestral sites." This pattern is linked to long fallow agricultural systems and generalized rights to community land. In the later Neolithic and early Bronze Age a shorter fallow system implies closer links to the land, the closer definition of inheritance and tenure, and the clearer marking of burial locations on the landscape. Barrett's emphasis is on the practical mastery of material and symbolic resources within routines and locales. He foregrounds practices and their material structuring. There is discussion of how "people" control and respond to the choreography of place, but no account of individual lived lives. Agency is seen in terms of resources: what is available to allow action to take place, rather than in terms of individual forward-looking intentionality and creativity.

Subjects and selves

Notions of individuality and individual creativity have become highly suspect within many of the social sciences. It is clear that many of our contemporary Western notions derive from historically specific concepts of individuality and intimacy (Giddens 1992). In particular, Foucault (1977) has demonstrated the way in which discourses emerged in the late eighteenth and nineteenth centuries associated with the identification, surveillance and disciplining of persons as individuals. In more recent times, new information technologies and new global production, distribution and consumption processes have emphasized the fragmentation and individualization of time, space and product (e.g., Castells 1996). The individual is increasingly seen as a particular historical product of capitalism and, in particular, of late capitalism.

However, the concept of the individual self has been rescued by anthropological and historical perspectives which chart changing concepts of self and the body across time and space. For example, Moore (1994) provides a discussion of how in different ethnographic concepts different conceptions of the body boundary can be found. In Western societies we tend to see the outer skin as the boundary of body and self. In other societies, the boundary of self may extend to include objects in the world around. The way is open to explore cultural variation in the factors which lead to different constructions of the self and of subjectivity. In archaeology a relevant study is that by Treherne (1995). Treherne discusses changing concepts and practices of the self and the body during the European Bronze Age. Why do toilet articles such as tweezers and razors appear at a particular moment in European prehistory? Treherne shows that such articles are related to evidence for increasing individualism: warfare, bodily ornament, horses and wheeled vehicles, the hunt, and the ritual consumption of alcohol. While all these activities are related to the rise and transformation of a male warrior status group, Treherne argues that the key is a changing aesthetics of the body. He describes the "warrior's beauty" and his "beautiful death." This aesthetics is a framework of meaning linked to a set of practices which is quite specific historically and which is part of a distinctive form of self-identity. This life-style crystallized across Europe in the mid-second millennium BC out of roots in the previous few millennia. The institution of the warrior elite was to survive into, and in part give rise to an aspect of, the later feudal order in Europe.

Elegant as such accounts are, the aim is not to examine agency in terms of the forward-looking intentionality of individual lives. Rather, the focus is on the social construction of subjectivities as part of the unfurling of long-term processes. This constructivist view of bodies, selves and subjects is also seen in recent applications of phenomenological approaches in archaeology. For example, Thomas (1996), Gosden (1994) and Tilley (1994) have all looked to Heidegger and his idea of "being in the world" (also Barrett, this volume). These authors use phenomenology to focus on how the subject experiences the world though the body. In particular, they explore how subjects experience monuments and landscapes as they move through them and carry out practices in them.

These phenomenological approaches are important in that they attempt to break away from approaches which foreground structures and systems binding people into particular modes of behavior over time. They seek to undermine the notion of universal oppositions between culture and nature, mind and body, meaning and practice, structure and agent. Rather they place emphasis on the local and the personal: the lived experiences of individuals inhabiting monuments and landscapes. They also show that the sites and monuments never had one single meaning. Rather the meanings were continually changed through time (Bradley 1993). The site or monument is not a static structure but the product of a long cycle of reordering and renegotiating.

For example, Thomas (1996) describes the ways in which Neolithic Linearbandkeramik houses were centers of experience of the self and of the environment. The daily practices of cutting down trees, moving earth, respecting older houses, living in and using the buildings created a sense of place. People came to "know" a place as part of "being-in-the-world." The similarities of form of Linearbandkeramik houses and megalithic long tombs over vast areas are not seen in terms of a common meaning. Indeed, Thomas argues that the houses or tombs did not have a common meaning. All that was shared in northwest Europe was a "material vocabulary" (ibid.: 135).The similarities are presumably produced by the routinization of practices. But why did people keep doing the same thing with their house plans and tomb plans? And why these specific plans?

The answers to these questions are again often given in terms of the organization of material resources and in terms of the social construction of subjectivities within power strategies. For example, Tilley (1994) argues that the placing of prehistoric monuments in the landscape is related to material factors. The need to control and fix meanings in the landscape is linked to herding and the control of animals, migratory routes and pastures. Treherne makes a related point in relation to Thomas' (1996) work:

Thomas' attention is given to the manipulation of individual bodies, and concomitant notions of subjectivity, through the dominant interpretations of built or acculturated space fixed by hegemonic groups. . . . What he is really concerned with is an external process of subjectification.

(Treherne 1995: 125)

So once again, the lived experiences of individual bodies located in a particular time and place are not explored, despite claims to the contrary. There is too little emphasis on subjectivity and self as constructed by individual agents.

Individual lives

I have argued so far that a notion of agency as involving intentionality and indeterminacy has become overshadowed in recent debates by a perception of agency in terms of the availability of resources and of the structuring of lives within long-term and large-scale processes. There is little room in such accounts for the individual construction of events and processes. An adequate account of agency needs to supplement structurationist and phenomenological accounts with dimensions of experience which can be gained from an examination of individual lives.

There is, however, a different tradition in archaeology which points towards a less constructivist position. This is work influenced by feminist and Queer theory. Feminist archaeologists have for some time been concerned with the general ideas of "peopling" the past and of putting faces on the "faceless blobs" which seem, according to most archaeological accounts, to have inhabited much of prehistory (e.g., Gero and Conkey 1991; Tringham 1991). But it is particularly radical notions of difference and the performativity of sexual identities (Butler 1990) which have led to detailed attempts to reconstruct the individuality of past lives (e.g., Knapp and Meskell 1997; Meskell 1998).

Within these more radical notions, emphasis is often placed on the ways in which the same subject can take on different identities. Indeed, an "individual" is itself a larger whole constructed from individual events. We cannot assume that the acts of a subject will always amount to "an individual," that is a distinctive pattern of behavior associated with a single body. The potential exists to build up evidence of individual characteristics in archaeology. For example, the artist's "hand" is identified by repeated peculiarities of style or technique. Individual variation in the knapping of flint has been recognized from the refitting of cores. Repeated physical movement can be identified from the examination of skeletons (Molleson 1994). For example, certain bodies are found to have repeatedly sat in certain positions while grinding, or to have repeatedly used their teeth to clean fibres and so on.

So rather than starting with "individuals" we need to see how "individuals" and other wholes such as sites, cultures and exchange networks are constructed, not solely by large-scale processes and hegemonic groups, but through the intentionality within particular and individual events.

Any construction of individual lived lives involves starting off with the traces of individual events. The evidence excavated by archaeologists is usually the result of a palimpsest of individual events. Certainly the individual events can sometimes be extracted from the palimpsest (the breaking of a pot identified from refitting within a general spread of pottery, the digging of a particular post hole within a pattern of post-holes, etc.). It is often possible to work out the intentionality and decision-making involved in individual event sequences, as in work on *chaînes opératoires*, without relating those sequences to a particular embodied individual. In other cases, as discussed below, it may be possible to link individual events and individual sequences of events together as the products of a particular person. It is necessary to attempt to build up from the former (events and event sequences) to the latter (embodied individuals) so that the construction of the individual in a particular society can be approached. It is rare that archaeologists can identify named individuals; it is rare that they can piece together anything approaching a full account of an individual life. Yet we routinely have evidence of fragments of lives. The challenge is to build up these fragments into the fullest possible accounts of individual lived lives, by grouping together events and sequences of events wherever possible.

The focus on the individual event is important for a number of reasons. First because of the indeterminacy of levels, that is, that events are not determined by the structures within which they are embedded. Structure and system can never be fully instantiated in the moments of daily action except provisionally and partially. In the practice of the lived moment it is impossible for all the abstractions and constraints of systems and structures to be present except in the simplest of terms and most provisional of ways. This is because of the complexity and size of the system, unacknowledged conditions and incomplete knowledge held by actors, different perspectives and interpretations of appropriate action, and an inability to predict all its consequences.

There must, then, always be a disjunction between event and structure. One can never adequately explain one level by another; the systems, structures and events are simply not equivalent. If there is not a determinate relationship between large-scale and small-scale, macro- and micro-scales, then it cannot be sufficient to focus all archaeological endeavor on the large-scale. To do so is to treat all variability as "noise," as indeed it has been treated through recent decades in archaeology. Despite the New and processual archaeological emphasis on variability, the aim was always to reduce variability to "trend + noise." As already noted, the emphasis on general trends has continued in most postprocessual archaeology. Rather than treating variability in these terms it can be approached as the situated construction of difference.

Another reason for the need to describe individual actions and lives at the microscale, is that it is at the human scale that contradictions and conflicts are worked out, lived through and resolved. A full explanatory account cannot remain at the level of the interaction of variables. In fact these variables interact through the lives of individuals, in the compromises they made and the solutions they found. The structures are worked out and reproduced in the bodies of historical lives.

This is why it is not enough merely to identify individual events and persons. The inadequacy of such an approach is evident in the studies of prehistoric "bog bodies" in northern Europe (Coles and Coles 1989; Glob 1977). The detail which can be gained of the last moments in the lives of these individuals is remarkable. Their last meals can be described, and the processes of their death inferred. Their hair style and clothing can be clearly seen, and the state of their fingernails gives an indication of the mode of life they had lived. Yet, the very isolation of these bodies in wetland areas means that we understand very little of the social contexts in which the individuals lived and died. We still do not understand why the deaths occurred, whether they had a ritual or penal or other character. We can say little about how these individuals fitted into or reacted against the structures that surrounded them.

Individual lives: the example of "the Ice Man"

In some such cases there is more potential for placing well-preserved bodies and the specific instances of the deaths into a wider and transforming social structure. For example, I have suggested that the evidence regarding the "Ice Man" found in the Austrian Alps (Spindler 1993), both allows a window into an individual life, and provides an opportunity to explore how that life dealt with and contributed to the contradictions generated by large-scale processes (Hodder 1999).

The body was dated to 3300 – 3200 BC, and the man, who was between thirty-five and forty years old, was associated with a wide range of equipment and clothes. These artifacts and the body itself allow Spindler to argue that the Ice Man had, in his life, been both connected to and disconnected from wider lowland society. The man was clearly integrated into exchange networks and had recently been travelling through lowland agricultural areas. Lowland communities may have depended on him as a metal trader, hunter or shepherd. On the other hand, the man was obviously highly self-sufficient. He carried an extraordinary amount of equipment with him which allowed him to travel and survive in upland and cold conditions. There is evidence of independence and self-sufficiency, and a concern with the care and healing of his own body.

The clothes and the food of the Ice Man thus suggest an independence and an experience of surviving in a harsh and dangerous environment. Yet he had close contact with other groups and his existence depended on lowland communities. Lowland groups in turn depended on him and his like for the exploitation of upland environments. We see an individual threading a life together, one involving contradictions between dependency and self-sufficiency. We sense the duality in his commitment to and need for long-term social relationships with lowland groups, and his need to break away from such dependencies to live on his own.

Looked at on another scale, we can see the Ice Man and the contradictions which ran through his life as part of larger-scale processes. Large parts of Europe at this time were undergoing a shift from societies based on a corporate sense of lineage towards societies in which individuals and small groups competed for access to exchange goods (Thomas 1987). An important part of this change was the spread of the use of secondary animal products and the greater exploitation of upland areas (Sherratt 1981). In terms of symbolic change, I have argued there was a shift from the corporate group symbolized by the domestic hearth to individualized groups associated with hunting, warring and exchange (the *agrios*; see Hodder 1990).

These large-scale transformations in economy, society and ideology could only be achieved through the actions of individuals as they worked through the dichotomies between older systems and the practical world in which they lived their daily lives. In the Ice Man's life we see him struggling, even to his death, with contradictions which translated in his context into an opposition between upland and lowland. The lowland groups to which he had access may still have practiced collective burial and thus were part of the older system in Europe (Barfield 1994). His own life-style became necessary as people increasingly went into the mountains to obtain stone and ores, to herd sheep or to hunt. These new developments ushered in a life of independence, harshness and individual opportunity. The Ice Man found individual solutions. He found a way of carrying embers in a birch bark container. He had his own "medicine kit" in the form of two pieces of birch fungus attached to his left wrist. He got someone to make tattoos on him to protect him or to heal a strain or wound. We see in all this the intentional creation of a new world, breaking away from but dependent on the corporate. We see the small-scale drama within the large-scale movement of millennia.

An example from Çatalhöyük

Another example I wish to provide deals not with long-term change but with long-term stability. One of the most remarkable characteristics of the early Neolithic mound sites in central Anatolia such as Asikli Höyük and Çatalhöyük is that the buildings, streets and internal settlement organisation stay very stable over millennia. How were the structures behind these continuities reproduced? How did individual action make sense of the structures and regenerate them? I want to attempt to answer these questions by considering a case from the recent excavations at Çatalhöyük (Hodder 1996).

In Building 1 on the North part of the East mound (Figure 2.1), over sixty burials were found beneath the floor. The floor and wall plaster resurfacings suggest that the building was used for about forty years. It is therefore assumed that those buried in the building had lived in this and adjacent or other buildings. Examination of the skeletal evidence suggests some family resemblances amongst the bones (Theya Molleson and Peter Andrews; see http: //catal.arch.cam.ac.uk/catal/catal.html). The last burial in the building was distinctive in a number of respects. This was of an older male but with the head missing (Figure 2.2). The specific removal of the head was not observed in the other burials, but head removal is known from depictions in the Çatalhöyük art. "Vultures" are shown picking the flesh from headless corpses. Since excarnation does not seem to be indicated by the human bones from the site so far examined in the new excavations, it seems likely that the practices associated with death in the art refer to mythology. Alternatively or additionally, head removal was restricted to individuals of special and/or ritual status.

The special character of the headless burial was confirmed by his association with an

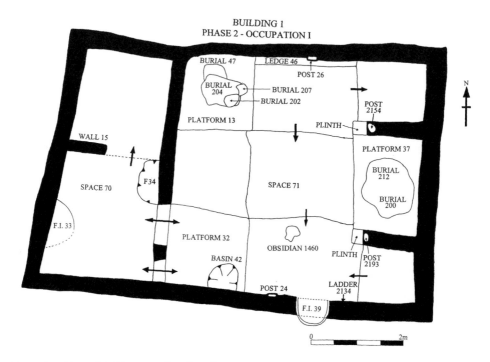

Figure 2.1 Plan of Building 1 at Çatalhöyük

unusual object, a small bone worn as a pendant. This bone proved to be the deformed penis bone of a small weasel-like creature (Figure 2.3).

The special status of this individual was thus implied by the removal of his head, by the penis bone, and by the fact that his burial was the last to occur in the building before abandonment. In addition he was buried under what seems to have been the main platform, centrally placed, within Building 1.

Figure 2.2 Headless male burial from beneath the eastern platform in Building 1

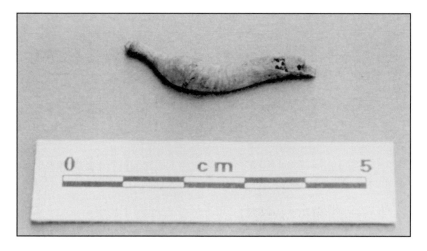

Figure 2.3 Probable deformed penis bone of mustelid with traces of wear from the burial shown in Figure 2.2

Note: Preliminary identification by Nerissa Russell

What else can we say about this individual and the way that he lived his life? Examination of the human bones from beneath Building 1 has suggested the possibility that the forty-year life-cycle of this house follows the life-cycle of the extended family buried beneath its floors. The early burials include high proportions of young individuals; indeed, as the building grows older, so only old individuals are buried within it. This suggests that the building was first founded by a young family head. His and/or her children then either died or moved away, until only older individuals were left and finally the building was abandoned. When the building was abandoned it was purified by burning and intentionally filled in. Soon afterwards, however, someone dug down into Building 1 to remove a bull sculpture from the main internal wall.

It is reasonable to argue from the special treatment of the last burial, the headless man, that it was his death which finally led to the abandonment of the building. He may well have been the individual who founded the building and became the family head. If so, we can say something about this particular man's death and life. His death led to the removal of the great ancestral sculpture from inside the house. In his life, he would have witnessed the deaths of many of his siblings, cousins and children. The infant and child mortality rate for those buried in the house is very high. It is not too difficult to argue that the penis bone worn by this elder had something to do with fertility. Perhaps this man came to use such symbols and other special powers to protect the family and help it to deal with the death of so many of its children.

Indeed, we have increasingly come to argue at Çatalhöyük that much of the "art" may have been involved in protection, mediation with ancestors and reproduction. The personal and individual solution found by the elder in Building 1 was perhaps part of a pattern which assured the continuity of an art devoted to dealing with loss and instability. In terms of the interaction of variables over the long term, we can see that the symbolism and "art" created links to the ancestors, that it mediated with the spirit world. And we can see that behavior of this type was necessary in the context of early agriculture and large settled communities. It is through the individual life that these interactions take place. We can get a surprisingly full picture of the elder of Building 1. We can look at the hearth he must have known so well, crawl through the same entry ways he must have used. But we can also see how he dealt with tragedy and loss, and how his particular solution carried his family through forty years and many deaths. The use of symbolic representation to deal with ancestors and spirits was part of a long-term structure, but we glimpse its working in individual circumstances.

Narrative windows

It is clear in the examples given above that the details even of prehistoric individual lives can to some extent be put together. But accounts of such lives seem to demand a rhetoric rather different from that associated with log-normal curves and input–output diagrams. An intriguing link has begun to emerge in recent literature between the discussion of individual lives and the writing of narratives. In terms of the history of archaeology a fine example is provided by Joyce (1994). In historical archaeology, Spector (1993) has created an evocative narrative of the lives of individuals at the moment of early contact between colonial and Native American groups.

In my view, the switch to a different narrative mode may often be an integral component of a commitment to the small scale. Because of the indeterminate relations between the long term and the individual act, it is inadequate to describe and reconstruct individual lives and events in terms of macro-processes using the rhetoric of the distanced observer. It is not enough to describe the interaction of variables. Rather, the aim is to capture the way these variables are understood and dealt with (including the contradictions) in the practices and concepts of individual experiences. How do people struggle with the forces which appear to enclose them? A narrative account is needed because the macro-processes do not fully account for what is being observed at the small scale. There is a difference between causal and interpretive statements. Causal explanation deals with the interrelationship of variables at a distance, in the abstract, removed from the specificity of events. Interpretation in the form of thick description (Geertz 1973; see also Sinclair, this volume) attempts to include accounts of the contingent and historical specificity of events.

This emphasis on narrative is also important because of the public interest in the human scale of the past. The popularity of Spindler's book on the Alpine Ice Man is remarkable. It demonstrates the public fascination with the detailed and the individualized. It demonstrates the public need to sense a human scale in the vast expanses of archaeological time. The narrative windows which we construct around individual events and lives create a point of entry into the long term for the non-specialist.

Conclusion

For much of its data, archaeology can only give a general systemic view; it can describe the flow of cultures or systems, the rise of complexity, the collapse of states and interregional networks of exchange. The data are often too scanty to allow anything else, and the ability of archaeologists to paint grand syntheses with a broad brush is impressive (for a recent argument in favor of "grand narrative," see Sherratt 1995). But there are moments in archaeology which capture the public imagination when very rich and detailed information is found: an Ice Man, a Pompeii, a Shang tomb or a Tutankhamun. We should not scoff at this: the popularization derives from a fascination we all share. It invites narrative. It provides a window into the workings of the grand systems which we so painstakingly monitor for so much of our archaeological lives.

It is not only the sensational finds which allow windows into the fine grain of temporal sequences, however. Indeed, it could be argued that archaeologists are better equipped at studying specific moments and daily rhythms than larger scale processes. Archaeologists can reconstruct in great detail the sequences of actions behind the knapping of a flint nodule. Knowledge of the sequences involved in making and firing a pot may be understood down to a few minutes. Seasonal activities may be constructed from tooth growth or shell middens. Medieval archaeologists may be able to reconstruct the daily routes from house to field, and the weekly passages from house to church and back again. In many ways, it is the human scale which is the stuff of archaeology; it is the larger scale which is more distanced from archaeological material.

I would argue, however, that few approaches in archaeology adequately recognize that different types of account are needed at different scales. Archaeologists have developed effective techniques for dealing with the large scale and the long term. When it comes to individuals and events, there have been few successful studies. Rather than abstract mathematical modelling of diversity and contingency, attention must be paid to lived experience. Rather than focusing on agency in terms of the resources (symbolic and material) needed to act and on the hegemonic control of action, attention can be directed to the intentionality and uncertainty of daily life. Rather than accounts of "being" which remain materialist, dichotomous and disembodied, narrative interpretations are needed of the specificity of meaningful action (Gero 1991; Kus 1992). Grand syntheses of the long term may not be commensurable with small narratives of lived moments (Marquardt 1992), but both are needed in an archaeology which accepts roles for intentionality, uncertainty and individual creativity in human behavior.

Bibliography

Barfield, L. 1994. "The Iceman Reviewed." *Antiquity* 68: 10–26.

Barrett, J. 1994. *Fragments of Antiquity*. Blackwell, Oxford.

Bradley, R. 1993. *Altering the Earth: The Origins of Monuments in Britain and Continental Europe.* Society of Antiquaries of Scotland, Edinburgh.

Butler, J. 1990. *Gender Trouble: Feminism and the Subversion of Identity*. Routledge, New York.

Castells, E. 1996. *The Rise of the Network Society*. Blackwell, Oxford.

Coles, B. and J. Coles 1989. *People of the Wetlands*. Thames and Hudson, London.

Collingwood, R. G. 1946. *The Idea of History*. Oxford University Press, Oxford.

Foucault, M. 1977. *Discipline and Punish*. Vintage, New York.

Geertz, C. 1973. *The Interpretation of Cultures*. Fontana, London.

Gero, J. M. 1991. "Who Experienced what in Prehistory? A Narrative Explanation from Queyash, Peru," in *Processual and Postprocessual Archaeologies*, ed. R. Preucel, pp. 126–89. Southern Illinois University, Carbondale.

Gero, J. M. and M. W. Conkey (eds) 1991. *Engendering Archaeology: Women and Prehistory*. Blackwell, Oxford.

Giddens, A. 1992. *The Transformation of Intimacy*. Stanford University Press, Stanford.

Glob, P. V. 1977. *The Bog People*. Faber, London.

Gosden, C. 1994. *Social Being and Time*. Blackwell, Oxford.

Hayden, B. 1990. "Nimrods, Piscators, Pluckers, and Planters: The Emergence of Food Production." *Journal of Anthropological Archaeology* 9: 31–69.

Hill, J. and J. Gunn 1977. *The Individual in Prehistory*. Academic Press, New York.

Hodder, I. (ed.) 1982. *Symbols in Action*. Cambridge University Press, Cambridge UK.

—— 1986. *Reading the Past*. Cambridge University Press, Cambridge UK.

—— 1990. *The Domestication of Europe*. Blackwell, Oxford.

—— (ed.) 1996. *On the Surface*. British Institute of Archaeology at Ankara and McDonald Institute, Cambridge UK.

—— 1999. *The Archaeological Process*. Blackwell, Oxford.

Johnson, M. 1989. "Conceptions of Agency in Archaeological Interpretation." *Journal of Anthropological Archaeology* 8: 189–211.

Joyce, R. 1994. "Dorothy Hughes Popenoe: Eve in an Archaeological Garden," in *Women in Archaeology* ed. C. Claassen, pp. 51–66. University of Pennsylvania Press, Philadelphia.

Knapp, A. B. and L. Meskell 1997. "Bodies of Evidence in Cypriot Prehistory." *Cambridge Archaeological Journal* 7(2): 183–204.

Kus, S. 1992. "Toward an Archaeology of Body and Soul," in *Representations in Archaeology*, ed. J.-C. Gardin and C. S. Peebles, pp.168–77. Indiana University Press, Bloomington.

Marquardt W. H. 1992. "Dialectical Archaeology." *Archaeological Method and Theory* 4: 101–40.

Meskell, L. 1996. "The Somatisation of Archaeology: Institutions, Discourses, Corporeality." *Norwegian Archaeological Review* 29: 1–16.

—— 1998. "Intimate Archaeologies: the Case of Kha and Merit." *World Archaeology* 29: 363–79.

Miller, D. and C. Tilley (eds) 1984. *Ideology, Power and Prehistory*. Cambridge University Press, Cambridge UK.

Molleson, T. 1994. "Can the Degree of Sexual Dimorphism Provide an Insight into the Position of Women in Past Populations?" *Dossier de Documentation Archéologique* 17: 51–67.

Moore, H. 1994. *A Passion for Difference: Essays in Anthropology and Gender*. Polity Press, Cambridge UK.

Shanks, M. and C. Tilley 1987. *Reconstructing Archaeology*. Cambridge University Press, Cambridge UK.

Sherratt, A. 1981. "Plough and Pastoralism," in *Pattern of the Past* ed. I. Hodder, G. Isaac and N. Hammond, pp. 261–305. Cambridge University Press, Cambridge UK.

—— 1995 "Reviving the Grand Narrative. Archaeology and Long-Term Change." *Journal of European Archaeology* 3: 1–32.

Spector, J. D. 1993. *What this Awl Means: Feminist Archaeology in a Wahpeton Dakota Village*. Minnesota Historical Society, Minneapolis.

Spindler, K. 1993. *The Man in the Ice*. Weidenfeld and Nicolson, London.

Thomas, J. 1987. "Relations of Production and Social Change in the Neolithic of North-West Europe." *Man* 22: 405–30.

—— 1996. *Time, Culture and Identity*. Routledge, London.

Tilley, C. 1994. *The Phenomenology of Landscape*. Berg, London.

Treherne, P. 1995. "The Warrior's Beauty: the Masculine Body and Self-Identity in Bronze-Age Europe." *Journal of European Archaeology* 3: 105–44.

Tringham, R. E. 1991. "Households with Faces: The Challenge of Gender in Prehistoric Architectural Remains," in *Engendering Archaeology: Women and Prehistory*, ed. J. M. Gero and M. W. Conkey, pp. 93–131. Blackwell, Oxford.

Turner, B. S. 1994. *Orientalism, Postmodernism and Globalism*. Routledge, London.

3   Troubled travels in agency and feminism

Joan M. Gero

Let me open by referring to Nancy K. Miller's wry comment: "When I hear agency, I think bureaucracy, [but] I'd like to think *travel!*" (cited in Ahearn 1995). Briefly here I want to take advantage of the *travel agency* associations to visit three known sites where notions of agency intersect with issues of gender. As tour guide on these travels, I shall want to point out how, at each site, the relationship between feminism and agency is complex, troubled, and mutually subverting, so that at each site examining agency raises profound questions about feminism, and examining feminist theory raises critical issues about agency. There is no attempt in this short piece to apply my musings to archaeological situations, but I hope the many archaeological case studies in the rest of this volume will make it possible to evaluate my tour guide cautionary notes against a variety of contexts.

First site: the gender of the agent

The first gender/agency site we visit is marked by the fact that the concept of agency is used not as a qualifying adjective but as an emphatic noun; agency is something one "has" (or doesn't have), and different individuals apparently have more or less of it, and in general men appear to have more of it than women. Although the "social agent" is nominally gender neutral or without gender, the contexts in which "agentic" action is taken are deeply associated with male actions and activities (public, authorized leadership roles, mastery over the environment, initiating alliances and trade), and precisely what is valorized in agency is masculinist: seizing the moment, launching new undertakings, asserting oneself and one's priorities and self-interests. Thus, the admired action figure of contemporary social theory, the "social agent," is gendered male by association (first) with traditional western male behaviors emphasizing "action," and (second) with western male-associated personal qualities emphasizing decisiveness and assertiveness.

Moreover, like Superman, the theorized classic liberal agent acts alone and autonomously, unaided (unhindered) by webs of relationship and social networks, discounting intimate relationships, participatory decision-making, or negotiation (Code 1991: 76). As a solitary social actor, the "agent" denies the fundamental social interconnectedness and interdependence of personhood, prescribing by his actions a course of atomistic self-interest. It is not only feminist accounts that might notice this: the action figure/agent is drawn almost as a caricature of the not-asking-directions side of males, going it alone, independent and self reliant! In the end, the agent as we encounter him in much social theory seems depressingly prescriptive of a masculinist model for how life is to be lead in the society of late capitalism: pursuing one's atomistic goals with single-minded actions (ibid.: 80).

We can also attend here to what these notions of agency preclude. In its rejection of passivity, agency downplays or devalues other critical social moves such as building community and consensus, averting conflict, preserving social and economic balances, or restricting and controlling self-interested expressions of power. Privileging *agency* as a significant locus of social change forefronts certain social moves while obscuring or ignoring others; it values some human abilities and dismisses others (I think of such critical non-agentic abilities as being able to identify and define significant goals, or access information efficiently, foresee outcomes, enjoy and sustain caring relationships with others, or even empathize!). What other modes of being might play important roles in substantiating or changing the social order, and why, once again, are we examining an issue that is so often associated with active males? Why agency and not empathy?

Subtly or blatantly, consciously or implicitly, most "agents" of social theory – and the values they act upon – are gendered male. In privileging agency as an explanatory virtue in archaeological social theory, we risk promoting and reiterating the deep divide between active males and passive females, already depressingly familiar to us in archaeology from the earliest writings on gender by Conkey and Spector (1984) and discussed again by authors like Watson and Kennedy (1991).

Feminist theory has taught us to be wary of terms that favor men and preclude or disadvantage women, to inspect carefully what it is that such terms measure and authorize, and to observe who is doing the authorizing and measuring. Many years ago bell hooks suggested that we must "talk about the way we see the struggle to assert agency – that is, the ability to act in one's best interest – as a male thing" (cited in Gardiner 1995: 6). If we move forward with agency, we must be sure to do so on terms that feminists help to define.

Before leaving this first gender/agency site, it is also interesting to turn 180° from our view of agency, and look briefly back at feminist theory from the vantage point of agency. Here we note that feminist theory, as though agreeing that women initiate actions less successfully than men, has sometimes responded by asserting "victimhood" as the female-gendered counterpart of agency, advancing a superior moral value for women in place of their capability to act. In conjunction with this position – or in response to it – are the various strands of psychoanalytic feminist theory that explain why women raised in patriarchal society fail to hold more agentic power (Chodorow 1997; Cixous 1980; Irigaray 1985). But ultimately neither victimhood nor psychoanalytic disadvantage are satisfactory responses to the value placed on action rather than on mediation or on understanding or on virtue.

The issues, then, of how agency is gendered, who is rewarded for having it, and why we grant it primacy, are all features of the first site on this tour.

Second site: feminist praxis and the "right" agent

The second gender-agency site on this tour involves the identification of a model of agency that is specifically useful for achieving the practical and political goals of feminism. Feminist theory-making has always been explicitly invested in producing change, and notions of agency are both central to this programme and vulnerable to being derailed by other agendas. In archaeology, for example, the feminist agenda has drawn on prehistoric gender relations and, more specifically, on prehistoric women's experiences in order to problematize everyday assumptions of interpretation and to open up the possibility of using new categories that admit women's experience more centrally (e.g., Conkey and Gero 1991; Dobres 1995; Joyce 1998; but see Conkey and Gero 1997 for how these agendas can be derailed). At the same time, feminists in archaeology have examined the dynamics of the professional community to insist on and work towards gender equality in the values and structures of the archaeological workplace (e.g., Nelson, Nelson, and Wylie 1994). How do we theorize such taking of action in feminist programmes, and at what level is feminist agency appropriate? Which agency models – and what kind of ideal agent – serves best, or is capable of serving at all, the practical and goal-oriented ends of emancipatory change required by feminism? Before following the path of this idea, we consider some background notions.

Most pressingly, we must confront an apparent central paradox of feminism and agency: the fact that although feminism is defined in part by its commitment to change, it also depends, by some definitions, on the recognition that women are circumscribed in their ability to take meaningful action (Wylie 1997). Feminism is posed in a fundamental tension with agency, not because of feminism's reluctance to grant primacy to the individual, but because the limits to women's actions (the limits of androcentrism, of patriarchy) define some (essentialist) versions of feminism (cf. *Hypatia* 1997 for further recent discussions of essentialist issues in feminism).

This paradox suggests that arguments around a feminist notion of agency must confront how feminists conceive of the nature of the subject (using here a less theoretically loaded term than "agent"): the action-taker or effect-producer, victim, knower, facilitator or resister. Gardiner (1995: 2–8) points out that feminism has sustained a long-standing debate and devoted considerable attention to examining the degree of stability and independence of this knowing and acting subject, arguing either for the enduring identity of a liberal, free-willed individual – the Cartesian constituting subject (or the "I do" view) – *versus*, in the postmodern view, the subject as decentered and of constantly shifting identity, the product of prevailing discourses, or the constituted subject (the "shit happens" view) (ibid.: 7). And while this debate on the nature of the subject certainly isn't limited to feminist discussions, the problem in feminism is particularly critical to feminist praxis, and particularly conflicted in terms of political ends; as already suggested, the multiple voices of women have to be seen as shaped by a context of domination. Indeed, to avoid identifying patriarchy as a strong source of feminist voices would be to ignore social context and to legitimate the status quo. On the other hand, following Stephanie Riger's argument, to assume that women have no voice other than the echo of prevailing discourses denies agency and risks repudiating the possibility of social change (cited in ibid.: 8–9). So within feminist theory-making, the idea of agency has become a fundamental and prerequisite query around which other concepts are defined.

What kind of agent, then, can we trust to put into practice the political agenda that is central to the project of feminism (and one, also, whom we'd trust to produce outcomes in prehistory)? There is good reason to be suspicious of the essentialized, abstracted and universalized agent; we have already confronted some of the questions that arise from adopting an unsubstantiated subject (surreptitiously gendered male) who is generally evoked when action is called for, and we will come back to him anyway at the third site. Haraway puts the problem this way: "We need the power of modern critical theories of how meanings and bodies get made, NOT in order to deny meanings and bodies, but in order to build meanings and bodies that have a chance for life" (cited in Hekman 1995: 200). What is needed is a heterogeneous subject, and again Haraway puts it best: "The knowing self is partial in all its guises, never finished, whole, simply there and original; it is always constructed, situated together imperfectly, and therefore able to join with another, to see together without claiming to be another" (ibid.: 201).

Ever since First Wave feminism recognized sisterhood as powerful, the practical feminist aims of "sisterhood" have all too easily suggested the adoption of a model of agency on the supra-individual level, that is, "collective agency" or "social agency" or "interpersonal agency." But Haraway leads us in another direction: towards an individual active subject who is constructed or constituted by discursive formations but who is also capable of action. Two versions of such a heterogeneous, partial knowing and acting subject/agent are available in the literature. The first of these has been called the "*dialectical* subject" (Hekman 1995: 197); this subject is conceived to have access to an "inner world" untainted by context, a presocial "self" that is capable of authentic modernist agency, while much of her "external" reckoning is constituted by social discourse. In this subject, we have replaced "supra-individual agency" with a complex agent whose motivations and actions are formulated by different internal selves. We arrive at something that might be called "sub-individual agency": agency that takes place below the level of the individual, perhaps on the level of the "dividual!" (McKim Marriott, cited in Ahearn 1995), which helps us account for internal dialogs or for how we sometimes feel "torn" (ibid.). All the time that the dialectical agent is defined by the winds of the moment there is also alive within her a steadfast cognitive subject who tacks back and forth between discourse and self-directed knowledge.

But Susan Hekman (1995), troubled by the binarism of this dialectical subject, proposes an alternative "*discursive* subject" for whom agency and construction are not antithetical. In Hekman's account, the discursive subjects do not require a *pre*discursive "I" on the inside, but instead find agency within the discursive spaces open to them in their particular historical moments. Agency is thus not a thing but an *opportunity to act*, and not a homogenous or invariant opportunity but a mosaic of chances determined mutually and reflexively by agent and by discourses. This discursive mix of context, capability, timing, and a "taking up of the tools" denies any simple opposition of a constituting subject divorced from discursive forces. "Construction is not opposed to agency," insists Judith Butler; "it is the necessary scene of agency, the very terms in which agency is articulated and becomes culturally intelligible" (cited in ibid.: 203).

The agent required by feminism, then, is not necessarily herself gendered male or female; that is hardly the point. Rather, the agent of feminist action constitutes and is constituted by both the moment of action and her capabilities, the tools at hand. These defining considerations and possibilities are required in the juxtaposition of feminism and agency, following inexorably from fundamental tensions between the collective interests/actions of "women" and the inherently individualized notion of agency, and resolving the paradox of producing change out of the paralysis of patriarchy.

Third site: agency universalized and decontextualized

Lastly, let's spend a brief moment visiting a third meta-issue, one more site where gender meets agency, where I can play devil's advocate and ask whether the very concept of agency is not just another homogenizing, meta-MANeuver to fit nuanced and gendered human experience into pre-determined, categorical masculinist modes of thought. Although the binary-blasting, feminist notion of discursive agency avoids the worst of the pitfalls, most connotations of the "thing" we call agency, that which all "agents" are said to "have," is at some level conceptualized as a quality that can be universalized over time, space and gender. Once again we confront a concept that is put into service to reduce the infinitely diversified ways in which humans take action – and interact with structure – to a unidimensional mode, one that flattens motivation and sensibility, omits cognition and meaning, and ignores sensory experience. All human action is expressed as a single (suitably vague) dynamic, divorced from context, content and condition, and agents in any single socio-historic moment are made to be roughly equivalent to agents in any other. As such, agency is applied to grossly comparative and acontextual ends, where gendered humans and the lives they construct are secondary to theoretical frameworks, modern perspectives and research trajectories.

Perhaps the (related) point on which to conclude our tour, then, asks about gender and the modern, scholarly "agency" that is supported by adopting this term in archaeological research. One common sense argument declares that agency theory has been adopted as a corrective reaction to the rigid constraints of the ecosystem theory and its monolithic, homogenizing and dehumanized approach to social systems (Saitta 1994). But it is not at all clear that the universalizing and homogenizing problems of viewing societies as tightly integrated wholes (ibid.), the very ideas that were to be undone in the new turns of theory, are avoided or resolved by defining a notion like agency as though it were a single mono-lithic ability or characteristic. We may have replaced environmental factors with active humans, but they are timeless, featureless, interchangeable and atomistic individuals, untethered to time or space.

Perhaps what our "agents," our active players at the center of archaeological reconstructions, are ultimately in place to do in archaeology today is to show that we as social scientists are ourselves not merely products of discursive flows, but control and manipulate data to make it say what we think it means. The agents we insert into prehistoric reconstructions mirror and demonstrate that archaeologists themselves must take action to show meaning. At this level, we must even more fervently interrogate who the agents are behind the popularity of the term today, and ask whether issues of feminist agency make any sense or hold importance in archaeological research.

Acknowledgments

Sincere thanks to Marcia-Anne Dobres and John E. Robb for their invitation to participate in this volume and for their on-target editorial comments; my conflicted feelings about agency would never have been formalized without their provoking questions and stimulating forum. I also owe warm thanks to Laura Ahearn for her generous and supportive help in providing references, sharing ideas, and offering her "Opening Remarks" from her 1995 AAA Agency Panel.

Bibliography

Ahearn, L. M. 1995. *Opening Remarks*. Paper presented at the 94th Annual Meeting of the American Anthropological Association, Washington, D.C.

Chodorow, N. 1997. "The Psychodynamics of the Family." Reprinted in *The Second Wave: A Reader in Feminist Theory*, ed. L. Nicholson, pp. 181–97. Routledge, New York.

Cixous, H. 1980. "The Laugh of the Medusa," in *New French Feminism: An Anthology*, ed. E. Marks and I. De Courtivron, pp. 245–64. University of Massachusetts Press, Amherst.

Code, L. 1991. *What Can She Know? Feminist Theory and the Construction of Knowledge*. Cornell University Press, Ithaca.

Conkey, M. W. and J. M. Gero 1991. "Tensions, Pluralities and Engendering Archaeology: An Introduction to Women and Prehistory," in *Engendering Archaeology: Women and Prehistory*, ed. J. M. Gero and M. W. Conkey, pp. 3–30. Blackwell, Oxford.

—— 1997. "Programme to Practice: Gender and Feminism in Archaeology." *Annual Review of Anthropology* 26: 411–37.

Conkey, M. W. and J. D. Spector 1984. "Archaeology and the Study of Gender." *Advances in Archaeological Method and Theory* 7: 1–38.

Dobres, M-A. 1995. "Gender and Prehistoric Technology: On the Social Agency of Technical Strategies." *World Archaeology* 27: 25–49.

Gardiner, J. Kegan 1995. "Introduction," in *Provoking Agents: Gender and Agency in Theory and Practice*, ed. J. Kegan Gardiner, pp. 1–20. University of Illinois Press, Urbana.

Hekman, S. 1995. "Subjects and Agents: The Question for Feminism," in *Provoking Agents: Gender and Agency in Theory and Practice*, ed. J. Kegan Gardiner, pp. 194–207. University of Illinois Press, Urbana.

Hypatia: A Journal of Feminist Philosophy 1997 Special Issue: *Third Wave Feminism*, vol. 12 (Summer).

Irigaray, L. 1985. *This Sex Which Is Not One*. Cornell University Press, New York.

Joyce, R. A. 1998. "Performing the Body in Pre-Hispanic Central America." *RES: Anthropology and Aesthetics* 33: 147–65.

Nelson, M. D., S. M. Nelson and A. Wylie (eds) 1994. *Equity Issues For Women in Archeology*. Archeological Papers of the American Anthropological Association no. 5. American Anthropological Association, Washington, D.C.

Saitta, D. 1994. "Agency, Class and Archaeological Interpretation." *Journal of Anthropological Archaeology* 13: 201–27.

Spector, J. D. 1993. *What this Awl Means: Feminist Archaeology in a Wahpeton Dakota Village*. Minnesota Historical Society, Minneapolis.

Watson, P. J. and M. C. Kennedy 1991. "The Development of Horticulture in the Eastern Woodlands of North America: Women's Role," in *Engendering Archaeology: Women and Prehistory*, ed. J. M. Gero and M. W. Conkey, pp. 255–75. Blackwell, Oxford.

Wylie, A. 1997. "Good Science, Bad Science or Science as Usual?; Feminist Critiques of Science," in *Women in Human Evolution*, ed. L. Hager, pp. 29–55. Routledge, New York.

4   Agency in (spite of) material culture

H. Martin Wobst

Points of departure

Not long after "behavior" in archaeology had become enshrined in a "behavioral archaeology" a generation ago (Schiffer 1972, 1976), many archaeologists began to feel concerned that behaviorism was too narrowly construed. They felt that archaeology and the study of people should be about more than functional exigency. One should not be able to theorize people exhaustively as if they had been rats in mazes of insurmountable constraint (Hodder 1982a, 1982b; Miller and Tilley 1984; Tilley 1982, 1984). Early in the 1980s many began to see the very term "behavior" as a red flag, indicative of an overly mechanistic treatment of past humans. For example, at the 1982 Theoretical Archaeology Group Meetings in Durham, England, presenters engendered intense reaction if they unthinkingly let the term "behavior" slip into their remarks.

It was at this point that the "action" concept entered archaeology. In contrast to the "behavior" of behaviorist archaeologists, the term "action" did not seek uniformitarian stimulus and response. It promised instead to document the informed choices of sentient humans in context. The concept was derived from Anthony Giddens (1979, 1984): humans are envisioned as entering contexts informed by experience and by their knowledge of history and social structure; they are taken to have a sense of what is or is not habitual, appropriate, opportune, painful, or rewarding in those contexts, and their actions are assumed to be informed by this sense. Such actions, in turn, help to shape social structure: they change the distribution of precedents for others in the social field. In that sense, any action changes social structure, whether its intent was to change it or to explicitly preserve it; in either case, actions modify our knowledge and the distribution of precedents that inform it. This makes for a very dynamic concept; structure is forever in process (but never there). Actions are informed by structure but they also change it, in a never-ending process that Giddens labels "enstructuration."

"Action" promised to get archaeologists out of their "behaviorist" straight-jackets. Armed with it, archaeologists began to talk about people actively constructing their futures. In the anglophone world of the eighties, such talk was always tempered with the proviso that the actors themselves were "socially constituted" (to contrast them with the yuppies, the Stakhanovites of the Reagan years, whom the popular literature depicted as entirely free-willed, self-made and ego-centric). Many archaeologists at the time considered the liberation from behaviorism to be as empowering as the revolution experienced by the preceding generation. In that previous transformation, explicit and "new" "Science" had claimed to break the perceived "History" mold of the archaeological forebears, as expressed, for example in Binford (1968), in the image of White (1949). As their predecessors had done after 1962, many well-known archaeologists revised their paradigms. And, like a generation earlier, many did this not only to deal more sensitively with the people of the past, but also to challenge with archaeological data what they perceived to be social pathologies in the present (cf. Wobst 1989).

I participated in both of these apparent transformations of archaeology. In the early seventies, I had indeed talked about "behavior" – that is, about humans so constrained in their room to move that only a very narrow range of "behavioral" outcomes seemed conceivable – for example in my simulations of human mating systems (Wobst 1971, 1974). Many other people at that time (quite appropriately, even by present standards) talked about "behavior" when they specified mechanical or physical processes, as for example in analyzing the fracture mechanics of flint (Speth 1971, 1972).

In the 1980s and 1990s, my interest gradually shifted toward "action." With hindsight, I think this occurred for three reasons. First, action allowed me to talk more sensitively about humans: culture did not exist without them, they were the "operators" of culture (to mix paradigms), and our theories needed to take them into account. I found it increasingly diffi-cult to make sense of the past or the present without reference to the folk who had produced them. Second, action allowed me to talk about more complex contexts and theo-retical questions than could be modeled mechanistically. I was becoming interested in histories and contexts as differentiating humans, rather than as cloning machines. Last, but not least, action gave me more room to include social contradictions, disjunctures, and competing interests into my understandings of contexts, and thus to keep the emerging pictures of the past more dynamic and more in process.

At the same time, I did not paradigmatically close my eyes to "behavior," that is, to contexts for action in which there was so little room to maneuver as to leave people no choice but to "run the maze." Thus, while I myself prefer to talk about humans as "acting" I am quite tolerant of people who do research on "rats" that (are forced to) "behave." Of course, even under the most severe constraints, when humans "act" they are informed by (and contribute to) context, history, and social structure. It is that latter trinity, rather than the material artifacts themselves, that make material constraints "do the trick." But human circumstance varies by class, race, and gender, and between mazes and palaces. To under-stand the human condition, we need to keep that entire range in our field of vision. Context by context, we need to know what makes the mazes work as much as we need to define the differential ranges for action from one end of society to the other. The action concept is theoretically appealing precisely because it allows us to think about humans as variable, and to investigate what broadens and what constrains that ability to vary.

Action and artifacts

It might sound almost oxymoronic to wed the "action" concept (ostensibly as full of motion as "action" movies) with "artifacts" (the epitome of the "unmoving" at the usual scales that archaeologists interact with them). But we have the same relation with artifacts in the present: we act in the face of artifactual precedent (and forever generate artifactual products). Many artifacts do not move much more than prehistoric ones when and where we interact with them. Nevertheless, they form reference points in our choice of how to act appropriately. Our life continuously and, on average, successfully negotiates this relation-ship with inanimate "artifacts." We do this with scientific knowledge, that is, with knowledge that we experimentally or experientially validate for ourselves.

For a long time now, I have referred to artifacts as material products of, and material precedents for, human action (Wobst 1978: 303, 307). While this definition might be mechanically appropriate, it seems to convey too passive an image: the artifacts are just there, affording action; or action takes place and artifacts rain down as a result (almost like the input and output *vis-à-vis* the black boxes of systems engineers). To better harmonize with the action concept, and to acknowledge artifacts more explicitly in their intimate articulation with human agency, I have begun to refer to human artifacts as "material interferences," or as "material intentions to change." That is, I see artifacts as linked to peoples' intentions to change something from what it was to what they thought it should be (Wobst 1997), or to prevent change that would take place in the absence of those artifacts. The term "interference" emphasizes that people entered artifacts into contexts they wanted to change (or that would change in undesirable directions if artifacts did not interfere). Humans artifactually interfere where they cannot or choose not to accomplish (or prevent) change by other means. "Other means" are non-artifactual ones: speech and other sounds, gestures and other motions, odors, and touch (Wobst 1997, 1999).

The term "interference" helps me to talk about yuppies and rats, and about good, bad, and ugly things perpetrated by human agency via artifacts. It even helps me to squeeze a dose of function into an action kind of paradigm. Agency via artifacts is an interference that helps us imagine individuals and groups as more than mechanistic robots. It produces the templates for visualizing practical and impractical reason, utopias, metaphysics, and morals. Material interferences engender, envision, constitute, contest, and contain the agent, and they help reify subject and object alike.

Action, artifacts and the Palaeolithic

Artifacts take time, space, personnel, matter, and energy: if one could get by without them, why not? After all, there is always the option of interacting and acting without artifactually interfering at all. Moreover, we should consider how intensively we are interfering with artifacts in each others' lives. Today, human material interference has become all pervasive: it ranges from portable to non-portable artifacts. Humans are the major variable in the age and sex distributions of many animals, and their presence is visible in any pollen-spectrum; humans even are increasingly responsible for the distribution of matter and elements. Given the ubiquity of this material interference in peoples' lives, we actually know very little about what governs the various ways artifacts interfere in human life today or have done in the past; we remain ignorant about what is responsible for changes in the intensity and pervasiveness in which we allow artifacts to interfere in each others' lives (cf. Miller and Tilley 1996). We do not know much at all about what determines the range of intensity of this interference from different people and milieux, from people who consciously avoid artifacts as interferences (e.g. hermits), to others who would be unthinkable without them (e.g. police officers), and from contexts that are explicitly zoned to evade material interference (e.g. nudism), to others that are almost baroque in their material exuberance (e.g. inaugurations). Even today, in a society that must be at the peak when it comes to material interference in human lives, there is a tremendous range in the intensity of those interferences. For example, consider the contrast between a wilderness area and a brown-coal open pit mine, between transcendental meditation and Macy's Parade, or between a hermit's hovel and Bill Gates' residence.

Of course, animals also materially impact animals, plants, and matter, and some even use artifacts for this purpose. Many of the artifact uses that we had considered uniquely human have since been shown to be shared with some of our primate relatives (see, for example,

McGrew 1992; Wrangham 1994). On present evidence, it appears that where modern humans differ most from animals is in the intensity with which they interfere with other humans via artifacts, and in the reverberation and pervasiveness of these artifactual impacts. We do not quite know yet if these are qualitative or quantitative differences. To resolve the question, we need to know more about the material record of our ancestral primate relatives, and about the variation in artifact usage in our own past and present. I devote the remainder of this essay to helping us think about those questions.

I want to look here at the Palaeolithic. I do this not because I consider the Palaeolithic simple or primitive. Nor do I consider human material interference with humans particularly progressive or "modern"; it must be as modern to attempt to minimize material interferences with each other. The Palaeolithic appeals to me because it is a particularly rich constellation of contexts to think about artifacts as material interventions in society.

For example, by its very term, Palaeolithic contains the hominid "starting gate" for materially interfering with each other. Thus, it must contain scenarios that made such interference reasonable, rewarding or unavoidable and other scenarios that had opposite pushes and pulls. Especially during its "middle" and "upper" parts, the Palaeolithic is rich in variance in "artifactuality" within and between populations, through time and space. Later, contemporaneous Palaeolithic populations often score at opposite ends of the human range when it comes to the intensity of their material interferences, and populations in the same historic trajectory rapidly changed their materiality, along that range from near avoidance of materiality to baroque artifactuality. The Palaeolithic is thus a laboratory for exploring what circumstances, historic trajectories, and social and environmental contexts articulate with broadening or narrowing ranges for human action via artifact interferences, what brings about conditions that make humans look more like rats than like sentient beings, and what differentiates or homogenizes the material interferences of humans in the lives of other humans, within and between social contexts and historical trajectories.

Why has there been so little action in the Palaeolithic?

"Action" has only been whispered in Palaeolithic circles. Virtually all of the early illustrations of action paradigms in archaeology have been with historic or ethnoarchaeological data (for example, Hodder 1982a, 1982b; Leone 1984). Prehistoric applications of the action concept tend to cluster near the end of prehistory (the Bronze and Iron ages), and become increasingly rarer the more one approaches earlier hunter-gatherer populations (but see Sinclair, Sassaman, this volume; also Dobres 1995a, 1995b; Handsman 1987; Roveland 1989; Volmar 1992). Apparently, there seems to be a notion that the more the human mind is implicated in the data, in the activity, in the context, or in their interpretation under consideration, the more difficult the theorizing and the more one is dependent on the spoken or at least the written work. In this way, people revalidate Hawkes' (1954) ladder of inference and archaeological difficulty, from subsistence (easy) to the mind (hard). If neither writing nor spoken words are available to aid the archaeologist, then the most descriptively rich and complex data are sought, often places that are assumed to be rich in presumed "ritual" data and contexts, as for example in Hodder's earliest archaeological illustrations, Neolithic Orkney (Hodder 1982b: 218–28, or in his recent focus on Çatalhöyük in Hodder 1998). Palaeolithic data, those mere fragments of stones and bones, are rarely considered sufficiently rich and complex to permit us to think about agency in the archaeological record. Thus, "action" approaches have avoided them.

All Palaeolithic sites have (at least some) lithic remains. It is thus not surprising that lithics have become the currency for Palaeolithic interpretation. The study of Palaeolithic lithics has made rapid advances in the last forty years, and we now know much more about their sources, dates, use wear, experimental replication, and manufacture, and a host of other topics. Those advances have been achieved in behavioralist-like paradigms that delineate stimulus and response, and constraints narrowing down the range of action, if they are not altogether about material physics, chemistry and mechanics. (This is not necessarily true for French archaeology with its *chaîne opératoire* concept, which often is interested in making statements about cognitive matters, although not necessarily in agency terms; beginning explicitly with Sackett 1977, 1982).

In terms of artifacts as interferences, Palaeolithic explanations have concentrated on how lithics interfere with natural variables (raw materials, environmental contexts, material worked on, and so forth) and have sought to define the natural, mechanical, or material constraints that result in predictable outcomes. Such a research emphasis goes hand in hand with broadly shared scientific assumptions and popular stereotypes about the evolutionary status of foragers, particularly with the notion that they are closer to nature than other populations and thus subject to tighter constraints from their environments. This program does not leave much room for action, for the history and context of the range of choices actually taken, nor have intra- and intercultural variability and variation in material action found much of a place in this behavioral paradigm (Dobres 1999; Dobres and Hoffman 1994).

With Palaeolithic data, specifically, there have been very few attempts to theorize about lithics as interferences in the social field, beyond attempting to formalize the traditional concept of archaeological cultures (i.e., artifacts and artifact attributes that are formally similar "reflect" interaction within social groups; and difference in artifacts and artifact attributes "reflect" lack of interaction and thus absence of social boundaries), as for example in Sackett's papers (1977, 1982), and even earlier in Bordes (1968) (but see Sinclair, Sassaman, this volume).

The main reason action approaches have avoided the Palaeolithic is that there has been a dearth of theorizing about how to make "action" visible in one's material data in general, regardless of the specific time period (Dobres and Hoffman 1994). Of the early approaches that claimed to be illustrative of "action" in archaeology, most were so structuralist as to make "action" actually invisible in the presentation of the data (Wobst 1996). Moreover, since Palaeolithic data are usually considered to be poor and simple, archaeologists have not been tempted very often even to tell structuralist stories about them (such as those by Conkey 1978; or Leroi-Gourhan 1965).

Thus, Palaeolithic hunter-gatherers have been presented as if they had no agency. All artifact production was forced upon them by hostile nature, and all of it was directed toward these hostile forces of nature (or they merely followed their mental templates). This text-book caricature of our Palaeolithic ancestors essentially presents them as "rats" running mazes and leaves little if any room for their unfolding humanity (see also Hodder 1986: 102).

Working edges as social interference

Let us rethink Palaeolithic artifacts as interferences in society and begin with lithic working edges. Working edge form rarely occupies more than a small part of Palaeolithic artifacts, and there is not much change in working edges throughout the Palaeolithic: there is a finite number of shapes and cross-sections, concave, convex, steep, not so steep, and so on. The shape of these active ends is not that much different between Oldowan and Upper Palaeolithic artifacts, nor at a given time across space.

I am all for discovering and formalizing the general equations that functionally link edge form with matter, such as "to get A out of matter B, with stone type C, working edge form D is best." But, *a priori*, such a relationship does not necessarily help us in understanding Palaeolithic contexts of agency, for even with all of these functions worked out, we are dealing with a social field larger than artifact physics or mechanics. Artifacts employed in ordinary tasks alter more than the descriptive attributes of matter; they also interfere with humans, via perception and cognition. Even if the makers had in mind only ways of interfering with matter and nature, functionally appropriate artifacts establish lasting templates for what is thought practical. Functionally appropriate artifacts are also reference points for actors to grade themselves and others in terms of their competence, adherence to group standards, or approximation of cognized optimality (Dobres 1995a). In these ways, social action and mechanics are inseparably imprinted and interwoven, even on something as tritely "functional" as Palaeolithic stone tools (see Sinclair, Sassaman, this volume).

Where interference with matter is the obvious intent, agents may choose, or be compelled, to use lousy working edges. They may choose to make working edges that are too small, large, fickle, or otherwise dysfunctional. They may satisfice rather than optimize or maximize, or they may want their working edges to signal that they don't particularly care one way or the other. In the divergent histories and contexts of the Palaeolithic there must be significant differences in how closely Palaeolithic foragers approximated the functional ideal and we might be able to establish that *post facto*. There must be significant measurable differences in how much deviation was acceptable in a given context and how noticeably each artifact production, use, or discard event interfered with it.

From context to context and historic trajectory to historic trajectory, there must have been significant differences between the various "normal" activities, varying for different raw materials, food stuffs, social groups, age groups, and the spatial ranges over which work was carried out. The "pure function" of the working edge thus turns into a rich arena for social action, observable in changing variances of measurements between activities, contexts, agents, and so on. Where have these ever been reported as social variables in the Palaeolithic?

The degree to which lithic working edges are bounded conceptually from their functional and meaningful alternatives also varies within and between populations and through time. Is working edge form continuous from one archaeologically defined tool type to the next, across most of the intervening production possibilities? Or does it cluster into modes not linked by intervening pieces? Are some working edges bounded because their measurements do not intergrade into the measurements of other types of working edges, while others intergrade without any hiatus? How does material interference along this axis help to differentially constitute Palaeolithic actors and society?

Another interesting social dimension is the degree to which working edge form is tied to given contexts. What particular actions are tied to a given working edge (let's assume the association of a certain type of scraper with a certain species or part of plant or animal being processed)? Which contexts are worked non-dogmatically, with different kinds of working edges? In what circumstances do we have one, the other, or both? Since such variation in material associations manipulates the rule-boundedness of the given society and helps to define what is considered "natural" or "functional," variation in action along this dimension helps to materially negotiate and reify the potential for, or the evasion of, a classified world (see also Dobres 1999). Of course, there is bound to be temporal, spatial and contextual variation in the relative importance of interferences in the social field. But *a priori*, there is no reason to assume which if any part of an artifact's variability and variation is primary and which can be considered residual. Ultimately, the ways in which the artifact interferes with matter and with the social field are discursive with one another. They are both virtually inseparably evidence of agency. They help to constitute the stage and the language for the play that establishes how matter, utility, artifacts, and society are constituted.

The social frames around working edges

Once all is said and done about working edges, they vary considerably less across Palaeolithic time and space than the social frames in which they were embedded: that is to say, the material modifications that surrounded and staged them, but were not themselves necessary for the task. For example, Clactonian or Levallois flakes, blades or microblades might all have the same size notch. Functionally equivalent knives may be made on local or wildly exotic stone; their handles may be of stone, bone, ivory, or wood, decorated, or left blank; and their backing might have been left natural, or modified by a careful and elaborate series of careful retouching steps.

If we have correctly identified the working edge of an artifact, that is, the end that was designed to have impact on materials, and understood the structural demands such work might place on the remainder of the piece (such as sufficient thickness, size, and geometries), then the proportion of the piece that is not the working edge or specified by those demands is usually significantly larger than the working edge itself. In the course of the Palaeolithic, it is those parts that vary significantly more than the working edges themselves, and, so far, we have not even begun to record, much less to assess, what variables invite intense social action on these parts of pieces, and which ones don't.

Many interesting social questions are raised by variation along this axis of working edge to non-working edge portions of a stone tool, and there is a huge reservoir of observations on Palaeolithic action for the observer to record and analyze. For example, are the "frames around the working edge" that go with a given working edge designed to look similar or are they allowed to vary in the given context? Which frames are similar across different working edges? Which are different? Is use-wear more or less common on the more impressive looking frames? Do all working edges have labor intensive frames, or only a few? Are there breaks in time or space in the distribution of the frames, but not the working edges? How would society look different without this material interference in its social structure? How does action on the non-working portions of the artifact in this social field help to constitute an individual's individuality? Or a group's groupness? A subject's begging to differ? Or a leader's material control over social fission? Do some working edges come in and go out simply because more or less frame surface was desirable for interfering with people?

Action within and between artifact categories

A whole dimension of Palaeolithic artifactual interferences is invisible because interpretation is compartmentalized by artifact category; flaked stone is taken to be self-referential with flaked stone, bone with bone, and so on, with each such material class analyzed by different researchers. Yet because these different classes of materials were probably worked by the same laborers, these different arenas are in reference, in tension, and in tune with one another. Interference in one occurs with an awareness of the construction, contrast, contradictions, and logical tensions of the other artifact categories. Thus we can ask: "how does stone form interfere with other areas of Palaeolithic thought, and which other axes are in cahoots with or disrupt the allocation of form and effort in flaked stone?" This point has been well explored by Gero (1983) for lithics in South American complex society.

Actions of individuation and group affiliation

Where individuals want to constitute themselves as individuals or as members of a group, where leaders want to prevent or promote fission, or where egalitarian principles are under threat of increasing differentials, agents need to figure out who behaves how, and what is regular and what is unusual for the given individual and for all. Without artifact interferences, this calls for the long-term observation of individuals, or short-term observations of many individuals simultaneously. Artifacts help materialize, constrain, and afford those actions, in sharp contrast with our closest primate relatives. Without artifact interferences, that would put a definite limit on the size of the group or on the length of time a group could be held together (which in turn would make the required observations more difficult). It would also impede social classifications, social positions, statuses, and categories.

In their social role as material interferences in the social field, artifacts are designed to influence how people interact and come to know about each other. They bring about change in how people evaluate each other and themselves. They provide individuals with a "tool" to change the reading of individual intent, and they provide group members with material scales to evaluate the individualization or "groupification" efforts of their cohort members. Such material interferences are always placed into a context to change it (be that matter or people or people's perceptions of people or matter), or to modify the inherited readings. For, if the system would have ticked on without artifactual intervention, why waste time, space, personnel, and material?

Where there are artifacts, they are fossilized evidence of peoples' action in trying to intervene in history (in addition to and inseparably intertwined with interfering with matter). Thus, I suggest that where there are artifacts, things were in contest rather than "there," and becoming rather than complete. Artifacts are a testimony of contest, not resolved social structure. Consider the different contextual reading one gets if one applies this argument explicitly:

1   Cloned lithic form across space or time would not, by itself, be evidence of the resolved self-understanding of ethnicity (*sensu* Bordes and Sackett), but of a contested understanding that needed shoring up by material precedents, referents, and thinking aids. Shapes are shared because there was a problem with holding things together without such interference.

2   Massive structures such as those on the Central Russian Plain (Soffer-Bobyshev 1984) would not be evidence that Palaeolithic group size was such and such, but of material action to get a social unit of that size established, in a contested stream of precedents. The situation would have been viewed as sufficiently dubious to warrant the massive expenditures of time, personnel and material to affect or effect group size.

3   Painted cave walls interfere with the spacing action of people and with their ability to transmit, or get access to, knowledge. They would thus bespeak attempts at social control, of power in contest, and of resistance (Bender 1989). The more cave art, the more things would have been in contest, the stronger the social control to be constituted by this material interference, and the stronger the potential for resistance (and thus for mutual interferences in each other's social actions).

Artifacts do not tell stories: they create and modify stories. If stories could be told without artifacts, they would be. If gravity and nature were reigning plain and simply, there should be few Palaeolithic artifacts, and they all should look Oldowan.

In the Palaeolithic, artifacts significantly changed the ability of people to interfere with each other and their external world. Artifacts liberated individuals from physical constraints on their ability to interfere with each other and exposed them to material interference from others. This enabled human exploitation at scales otherwise inconceivable. On the other hand, this ability to interfere materially in the social field set in motion an incredible increase in the possibility to differ from others. Material interferences also afforded the possibility of resistance, revolution, and sabotage (see Shackel, this volume). That disequilibrium, which I believe was set in motion sometime in the Lower Palaeolithic, is still unstable and has not been resolved.

Yet, to avoid as much as possible materially interfering in other people's lives has always been modern human action also (though pushed into a corner lately). Such strategies are observable today, distributed differentially across and within societies, and varying by context, class, and gender among others. By attempting to evade materiality and its potential social effects, they offer to be less destructive of natural resources, and less supportive of materially underwritten social hierarchies. They tend to lend themselves to social entities significantly different from the ones on center stage today. We need to learn more about how these strategies work. What better data to learn about them than archaeological ones, and particularly those from the Palaeolithic that got me started on this exercise. The Palaeolithic record, in its variability and variation in time and space, is the richest reservoir of agency in the archaeological record.

This set of considerations about human agency and artifacts as social interferences turns even Palaeolithic lithics into arenas that were centrally implied in social change and variation. These arenas are pleasingly dynamic, rather than nature-bound and repetitive, and they ennoble even the lowly lithic working edge as having been a major player in Palaeolithic agency and society.

Acknowledgments

I would like to thank my students at the University of Massachusetts, especially those in Prehistoric Cultural Ecology and Theory and Method in Archaeology. If I had not been able to talk with them about the topics addressed in this paper, my head would never have gotten that high up into the clouds. Discussions with Amy Gazin-Schwartz and Angele Smith have been especially helpful. They should not be blamed, however, for my shortcomings in this chapter.

Bibliography

Bender, B. 1989. "Roots of Inequality," in *Domination and Resistance*, ed. D. Miller, M. Rowlands and C. Tilley, pp. 83–95. Unwin and Hyman, London.

Binford, L. R. 1968. "Some Comments on Historical versus Processual Archeology." *Southwestern Journal of Anthropology* 24(3): 267–75.

Bordes, F. 1968. *The Old Stone Age*. World University Library, New York.

Conkey, M. W. 1978. *An Analysis of Design Structure: Variability among Magdalenian Engraved Bones from North Coastal Spain*. Unpublished Ph.D. dissertation, Department of Anthropology, University of Chicago.

Dobres, M-A. 1995a. "Gender and Prehistoric Technology: On the Social Agency of Technical Strategies." *World Archaeology* 27(1): 25–49.

—— 1995b. *Gender in the Making: Late Magdalenian Social Relations of Production in the French Midi–Pyrénées*. Ph.D. dissertation, Department of Anthropology, University of California, Berkeley. University Microfilms, Ann Arbor.

—— 1999. "Technology's Links and *Chaînes*: The Processual Unfolding of Technique and Technician," in *The Social Dynamics of Technology: Practice, Politics, and World Views*, ed. M-A. Dobres and C. R. Hoffman, pp. 124–46. Smithsonian Institution Press, Washington, D.C.

Dobres, M-A. and C. R. Hoffman 1994. "Social Agency and the Dynamics of Prehistoric Technology." *Journal of Archaeological Method and Theory* 1(3): 211–58.

Gero, J. M. 1983. *Material Culture and the Reproduction of Social Complexity: A Lithic Example from the Peruvian Formative*. Unpublished Ph.D. dissertation, Department of Anthropology, University of Massachusetts, Amherst.

Giddens, A. 1979. *Central Problems in Social Theory: Action, Structure, and Contradiction in Social Analysis*. University of California Press, Berkeley.

—— 1984 *The Constitution of Society: Outline of the Theory of Structuration*. Polity Press, Cambridge UK.

Handsman, R. G. 1987. "Stop Making Sense: Toward an Anti-Catalogue of Woodsplint Basketry," in *A Key into the Language of Woodsplint Baskets*, ed. A. McMullen and R. G. Handsman, pp. 144–64. American Indian Archaeological Institute, Washington, Conn.

Hawkes, C. 1954 "Archaeological Theory and Method: Some Suggestions from the Old World." *American Anthropologist* 56: 155–68.

Hodder, I. (ed.) 1982a. *Symbolic and Structural Archaeology*. Cambridge University Press, Cambridge UK.

—— 1982b. *Symbols in Action*. Cambridge University Press, Cambridge UK.

—— 1986. *Reading the Past*. Cambridge University Press, Cambridge UK.

—— 1998 (principal investigator) *Çatalhöyük excavations*. Website: http: //catal.arch.cam.uc/catal. catal.html (June 1998).

Leone, M. P. 1984. "Interpreting Ideology in Historical Archaeology: Using the Rules of Perspective in the William Paca Garden in Annapolis, Maryland," in *Ideology, Power and Prehistory*, ed. D. Miller and C. Tilley, pp. 25–35. Cambridge University Press, Cambridge UK.

Leroi-Gourhan, A. 1965. *Treasures of Prehistoric Art*. Abrams, New York.

McGrew, W. C. 1992. *Chimpanzee Material Culture: Implications for Human Evolution*. Cambridge University Press, Cambridge UK.

Miller, D. and C. Tilley 1984. "Ideology, Power and Prehistory: An Introduction," in *Ideology, Power and Prehistory*, ed. D. Miller and C. Tilley, pp. 1–15. Cambridge University Press, Cambridge UK.

—— 1996 Editorial. *Journal of Material Culture* 1: 5–14.

Parker Pearson, M. 1982. "Mortuary Practices, Society and Ideology: An Ethnoarchaeological Approach," in *Symbolic and Structural Archaeology*, ed. I. Hodder, pp. 99–103. Cambridge University Press, Cambridge UK.

Roveland, B. 1989. *Ritual as Action. The Production and Use of Art at the Magdalenian Site, Goennersdorf*. Unpublished M.A. thesis, Department of Anthropology, University of Massachusetts, Amherst.

Sackett, J. M. 1977. "The Meaning of Style in Archaeology." *American Antiquity* 42: 369–80.

—— 1982. "Approaches to Style in Lithic Archaeology." *Journal of Anthropological Archaeology* 1: 59–112.

Schiffer, M. B. 1972. "Archeological Context and Behavioral Context." *American Antiquity* 37: 156–65.

—— 1976. *Behavioral Archeology*. Academic Press, New York.

Soffer-Bobyshev, O. 1984. *The Upper Palaeolithic of the Central Russian Plain: A Study of Fluctuational Trajectories of Culture Change*. Unpublished Ph.D. dissertation, Department of Anthropology, City University of New York.

Speth, J. D. 1971. *Technological Basis of Percussion Flaking*. Unpublished Ph.D. dissertation, Department of Anthropology, University of Michigan, Ann Arbor.

—— 1972. "Mechanical Basis of Percussion Flaking." *American Antiquity* 37(1): 34–60.

Tilley, C. 1982. "Social Formation, Social Structures and Social Change," in *Symbolic and Structural Archaeology*, ed. I. Hodder, pp. 26–38. Cambridge University Press, Cambridge UK.

—— 1984. "Ideology and the Legitimation of Power in the Middle Neolithic of Southern Sweden," in *Ideology, Power, and Prehistory*, ed. I. Hodder, pp. 26–38. Cambridge University Press, Cambridge UK.

Volmar, M. A. 1992. *The Conundrum of Effigy Pestles*. Unpublished M.A. thesis, Department of Anthropology, University of Massachusetts, Amherst.

White, L. A. 1949. *The Science of Culture*. Grove Press, New York.

Wobst, H. M. 1971. *Boundary Conditions for Palaeolithic Cultural Systems: A Simulation Approach*. Unpublished Ph.D. dissertation, Department of Anthropology, University of Michigan, Ann Arbor.

—— 1974. "Boundary Conditions for Palaeolithic Social Systems: A Simulation Approach." *American Antiquity* 39: 149–78.

—— 1978. "The Archaeo-Ethnology of Hunter-Gatherers, or the Tyranny of the Ethnographic Record in Archaeology." *American Antiquity* 43: 303–9.

—— 1989. "A Socio-Politics of Socio-Politics in Archaeology," in *Critical Traditions in Archaeology*, ed. V. Pinsky and A. Wylie, pp. 136–40. Cambridge University Press, Cambridge UK.

—— 1996. "Toward an 'Appropriate Metrology' of Human Action in Archaeology," in *Time, Process, and Structured Transformation in Archaeology*, ed. S. E van der Leeuw and J. McGlade, pp. 426–48. Routledge, London.

—— 1997. "Material Authenticity and Autochthony, Before and After Markets," in *Fulbright Symposium: Indigenous Cultures in an Interconnected World*. Pre-printed papers, non-paginated, Museum and Art Gallery of the Northern Territory: Darwin, Australia.

—— 1999. "Style in Archaeology, or Archaeologists in Style," in *Material Meanings: Critical Approaches to Material Culture*, ed. E. S. Chilton, pp. 118–32. University of Utah Press, Salt Lake City.

Wrangham, R. W. (ed.) 1994. *Chimpanzee Cultures*. Harvard University Press, Cambridge, Mass.

5 "Rationality" and contexts in agency theory

George L. Cowgill

When I was asked to discuss issues concerning agency and archaeology, my first reaction was that I had no very specific views; only a general notion that the agency concept was a Good Thing. I felt that in trying to respond I would be like an electron satisfied with a comfortably fuzzy and spread-out wave function, maybe here or maybe there, or almost anywhere, hit by an experimental probe and forced to collapse its wave function and decide matters hitherto left vague. But I soon realized that in fact I already had some quite sharp and strong opinions. I present some of them here, with special emphasis on the thorny issue of "rationality," and suggestions for clarification of the sometimes vague concept of "context."

Agency theory seems less a tool than a paradigm, almost a worldview. The Giddensian concepts of structuration, duality of patterning, and of individuals whose actions are *in relation to* circumstances (but not mechanically determined by circumstances) and which in turn have *effects on* circumstances (though usually not very large effects) seem to me the only way of thinking about present or past social phenomena that makes any sense.

If that were all there was to it, an "agency" outlook would be useful because it gives us some clear ideas of things to avoid. One is the notion that there are any human societies in which people normally follow custom unthinkingly, without often confronting situations that call for conscious choice. Another (beloved of old-line processualists) is that the adaptive response of societies to external stress is the key explanatory concept. A third is that individuals are not merely agents, but *free* agents, who can, at least in the social sphere, make just about anything they choose happen in their lives (a view especially vulnerable to feminist criticism; see Gero, this volume). Problems with all these ideas have been extensively discussed and I see no need to say much about them here. A view that does require comment is that something much like biological natural selection is the key explanatory concept.

Limits of Darwinian approaches

Approaches labeled "Darwinian" are very diverse (e.g. Barton and Clark 1997; Maschner 1996), and some may be compatible with agency approaches (see Clark, this volume). Under some circumstances, especially when a fairly large number of small politically autonomous societies coexist in a region, there can be a "cultural selection" process, in which some social/cultural/technological types of society become increasingly prevalent while others become less prevalent, in spite of strong intentions on the part of their members to socially reproduce their type. What Boone and Smith (1998) call evolutionary ecology does not seem wrong, but I think it is needlessly limited because it pays too little attention to, "undertheorizes" if you will forgive the term, individual agents.

However, I am highly critical of the "strict selectionist" version, associated especially with Robert Dunnell and his students (e.g., chapters in Teltser 1995). Key concepts of strict selectionism, taken from biological evolution where they have been very productive, include *variation* and *selection* operating on variation. A crucial aspect of strict selectionism is that individual intentions have no explanatory value, at least not on the scales appropriate for archaeology. This is diametrically opposed to my view. On short-term time scales of a century or two, the intentions of individuals are important because they are an important source of variation, even if they are not the sole source. The source of biological variation is genetic mutation, and mutations are independent of selection pressures. This is emphatically not the case with human intentions as a source of sociocultural variation, because these intentions are significantly related to the contexts and perceived interests of individuals. The mind-set of strict selectionism diverts attention from contexts, resources, and interests, but that is exactly where attention should be focused, at least for short- and medium-term phenomena. Conflicting interests, conditioned by the different contexts of different individuals, are a major factor in intentions to reproduce or to alter existing sociocultural contexts. Many might go further and frame the matter in terms of dialectical tensions that drive change (e.g., McGuire 1992).

It could still be argued that, in the longer run, over millennia, it doesn't matter whether the sources of variation are random or structured by sociocultural contexts; selection will operate to favor some sociocultural types more than others. But social reproduction is an active process, and this means that perceptions of interests and the intentions that flow from these perceptions are constantly recreated. The fact that a particular type of situation may tend to generate some intentions more than others provides, in itself, in Darwinian terms, a form of selection, because it affects the relative frequencies with which different sociocultural phenomena are reproduced. These recurrently produced intentions are not necessarily the only source of selection, but there is no reason why they should be overridden by other sources. Even in the long term, recurrent intentions, conditioned by recurrent diverse situational interests, continue to count.

Focusing agency

Even if we avoid all these errors (action is overwhelmingly constrained by custom, action is virtually unconstrained, societal adaptation is the key, or selection is the key), we are still left with very vague ideas about what we should do instead. There are many varieties of agency theory, and some are better than others. To me, one key concept is that most people most of the time behave "sensibly" in regard to their perceived interests, in the circumstances in which they find themselves. Things do not happen just because someone wants them to happen, yet individual human intentions are at the root of both persistence and change in sociocultural forms. Furthermore, although sociocultural phenomena are not simply the sums of individual intentions, processes operating at supra-individual levels do not obliterate the effects of individual intentions and do not render intentions irrelevant to explanations.

In some discussions of agency, it is considered a property that only some individuals possess, or that is possessed to greatly varying degrees. I find this terminology unhelpful, and I prefer to think more about agents than agency. Every human is an agent. The same applies to the term "social actor," which sometimes seems to be used as if only a few people get to be actors and, as it were, the rest of us are stagehands or maybe just audience. I would rather speak of *each* of us as a social actor. None of this is to say that we are all equal. On the contrary, individual differences in resources, power, prestige, authority, and what might be called "social leverage" are critical, as are differences in personality and other psychological traits. This is so even in very small-scale societies. Resources, power, prestige, authority, dominance, resistance, and social leverage already seem perfectly good words for aspects of inequality. I think that to speak of agency in this sense is redundant at best, and may actually confuse issues.

Insights from demographic anthropology

One especially problematic variety of agency theory that is probably the real target of many critiques tends to equate agency theory with individualism and economic rationality approaches. These found particularly clear formulations in the works of Adam Smith and other Western economists and philosophers of the late 1700s to mid-1800s, and they survive (indeed, flourish) in the thought of many contemporary economists, although there are refreshing exceptions, such as Robert Frank (1988). In the economic literature I see a whole other conceptual world, and I often feel myself on the other side of a mental gulf as profound as that which separates me from creation scientists. Our bedrock assumptions, even our ideas of what counts as real, often seem too different to allow any fruitful synergy.

This attitude toward economic models is grounded in my personal experience. After an early start in physics, I shifted to anthropology in the 1950s, concentrating in archaeology. I did not do this because I found physics objectionable (as long as I wasn't directly involved in developing weapons), but because I enjoyed archaeology more and felt I was better at it. I did have a vague feeling that applications of physical science discoveries were creating or exacerbating sociocultural problems, and while there seemed to be no shortage of physical science research, there did seem to be a shortage of social science research that might help us to deal with the sociocultural problems. By the 1970s I was worried about environmental and social problems connected with the immense increase in human numbers, and this led to an interest in demography. This had the not unwelcome side-effect that I learned some palaeodemography, but the main motivation had little to do with archaeology (which I did not then see as closely related to present day issues of ethics and right action), and I saw demography mainly as something very different from archaeology – like gaining skills in topics as disparate as Rumanian and mining engineering (Leacock 1930) – that I could find time to do and that would ease my conscience.

In fact, what I learned had unexpected payoffs for my thought about archaeological issues. I found out more than I liked about how wrong-headed economic demographers could be, and how effective their institutions and practices are at perpetuating this wrong-headedness. There is a strong tendency drastically to under-imagine differences in contexts. Lots of numbers about lots of people are accepted without paying enough attention to their validity, while qualitative data on a few people, no matter how valid, are dismissed as "anecdotal" and of little value. Johansson (1993), Hammel (1990), and Greenhalgh (1990) provide excellent discussions of these issues. Mamdani (1972), though a little overdrawn in places, is an early and entertaining exposé of the cluelessness of well-intentioned but anthropologically naive interventions. Sociologically-trained demographers tend to be better, but even they (e.g. Caldwell *et al.* 1987) emphasize ethnographic methods for collecting better data, and make less use of anthropological theory (cf. Hammel 1990).

I also found wonderfully instructive anthropological accounts of real people negotiating, planning, weighing alternatives, honoring or not honoring obligations, striving to maintain or improve their social standings, trying to reduce risks, seeking satisfactions, and so on, in the situations in which they found themselves, and by means of the resources at their disposal. These studies concern behavior that is relevant for fertility rates, though not usually behavior calculated to achieve some target family size. Greenhalgh (1995) and Kertzer and Fricke (1997) are important recent edited volumes on anthropological demography. As a single outstanding example, Caroline Bledsoe and Fatoumatta Banja (1997) discuss how rural women in The Gambia (West Africa) perceive pregnancies as impairing their well-being and reducing their capacity for future child-bearing, whether they result in miscarriage, still birth, or live birth. This is especially so when a woman perceives her current physical condition as inopportune for pregnancy. What might look to an uninformed observer like a "natural pattern" of unregulated fertility is in fact the outcome of very conscious planning and reasoned efforts to conserve health and child-bearing capacity, to space and time pregnancies so as to maximize the number of living children. Thus, the issues are very different from those taken for granted in much of traditional demographic theory, such as whether another child can be afforded and the balance of drains and inputs children make on or to household finances. These other issues are also important to women in The Gambia, but the relevant context will be fundamentally misunderstood if one lacks knowledge of the sort that Bledsoe and Banja provide.

Refining rationality

Jenkins (1992) sensibly argues that Bourdieu is excessively critical of Rational Action theorists such as Jon Elster. Nevertheless, we must define "rationality" less narrowly, freed of the baggage that accompanies "rationality" in the senses used by economists and game theorists. In this broader sense, most people behave rationally most of the time, but we all have the experience of reflecting on past behavior and deciding that we have acted irrationally. Fatigue can impair judgement; strong emotions can override reason, often in rather patterned ways (overcome by rage, hunger, or sexual desire, we behave in ways we consider foolish and/or morally wrong; overcome by panic, we may flee a situation it would be more rational to face). It is interesting that, in English, the very term "overcome" implies that there is some normal, proper, rational way of behaving that is there to be overcome. I wonder how similar other languages are in this regard. In other cases, we can be inspired, by the examples and often the rhetoric of others, to be braver, more generous, or more aggressive than we would otherwise consider rational. A great deal more is going on in our minds than just "being rational" about things. Attempts to explain or understand sociocultural phenomena are hopelessly flawed if they do not take into account individuals and our propensity to make what we think are rational choices most of the time, but they will also be seriously incomplete if we do not give other mental phenomena their due. This is one of the reasons why developments in psychology are of such great potential importance for archaeologists (and all other students of social phenomena).

Palaeopsychology

Palaeopsychology never should have been derided. If agency is important we need to learn much more about agents, and this means learning much more about how human brains and minds work. This is a tremendously active field, in neuroscience, cognitive psychology, and evolutionary psychology, with notable contributions by archaeologists (e.g., Mithen 1996). There are many strongly-held views, often at odds with one another. However, I am sure that archaeologists will be missing something of major importance if we do not keep up with developments in this field. I am also sure that many inbuilt capacities and propensities will be found; old models of the inexperienced human mind as a blank slate that passively absorbs inputs (e.g., Locke) are hopelessly inadequate. This does not mean that mental activities are rigidly specified, but it does mean that some kinds of mental things are much easier to learn and easier to do than others (and harder to unlearn or avoid doing). It is also highly likely that the human brain – the organ that produces the activities we call "mind" (mislabelling a set of processes as a thing) – is fairly modular, yet has a high capacity to link across modules. A tremendous amount remains to be learned about the number and nature of these modules. This new knowledge will enrich our ideas about ancient agents.

Reasoning

We must be extremely careful about what aspects of rationality are universally applicable, and which aspects are more context-specific. It is hard to avoid a definition that does not boil down to "thinking about it the way I would," or "getting the 'right' answer." There is a fairly distinct kind of mental activity (though with the usual fuzzy borders) that can be called "reasoning," and it means things like weighing alternatives, and trying to figure out the likely consequences of doing this or doing that. It contrasts with other kinds of mental activity, such as reflex reactions, feeling physical sensations, feeling emotions, arousing emotions, noticing things and not noticing things, any of which may go on concurrently with reasoning. What I mean by "rationality" is "using reasoning as a major factor influencing action." The reasoning may involve assumptions that I (and probably you) consider faulty, and/or what I (and probably you) consider mistakes in logic. The hallmark of reasoning is not the "correctness" of the method or the result, but the type of mental activity involved.

I believe reasoning-type mental activity is a human universal and, while I think I see signs of rather simple reasoning in my cats, I think highly developed reasoning abilities are a distinctively human mental capacity. Furthermore, although I have been careful not to define reasoning and rationality in terms of getting the correct answer, I believe that reasoning, for most people most of the time, in situations that are not too unfamiliar to them, leads them to a pretty good answer. That is, it is helpful to them in making choices that improve their chances of attaining something close to their conscious goals and furthering their perceived interests. I am not a sociobiologist, yet I don't think that we would have evolved elaborate reasoning abilities if they did not tend to increase biological fitness for our ancestors. This implies that there are some common denominators to human reasoning. There is a rough analogy with speaking; speech is a human universal, while what we talk about and the languages we use vary widely. So with reasoning; we all reason, but what we reason about and the procedures we use may differ greatly. The allegedly universal rationality assumed by "economic man" models is shown by anthropological knowledge to be the very opposite. Its image of highly individualistic actors whose *only* important mental processes are reasoning in relation to explicit goals, is, in fact, exceptionally culture-specific and ethnocentric. It is probably also highly androcentric, which is one basis for claims that agency approaches are androcentric (see Gero, this volume).

The problem with so-called universal rationality lies less in the emphasis on reasoning than in the belief that it is decontextualized when in fact it is exceedingly context-specific; specific to certain western (and perhaps male) contexts. The women discussed by Bledsoe and Banja are probably not being less (or more) rational than capitalist CEOs; they are being rational in regard to different perceived issues, in relation to different contexts, different experiences, and different knowledge.

Perceived interests

"Perceived interest" is another key concept. I stress "perceived" to emphasize that, although there is a universal core of interests connected with sheer survival, further interests are largely socially constructed, and even those interests closest to sheer animal well-being are conceived in ways that can be strongly structured culturally. Equally important is that no two individuals will have quite the same perceived interests, although members of particular class, gender, and factional categories may have many in common (as emphasized by Brumfiel 1992). To the extent that individuals in such a category engage in coordinated action based on perceived common interests, it is probably sometimes useful to think of the whole category as a sort of "super-agent." In such cases, research might focus on how coordinated action is brought about and maintained, and the extent to which the interest group can hold together and avoid defectors (cf. Hechter 1987 on differences between party discipline in British and US politics).

Contexts

Contexts have physical and sociocultural aspects. By "physical" I mean the natural environment and the technological means for interacting with it – the sorts of topic archaeology has focused on especially and which remain important – not superseded by a focus on individual actors. There has been some tendency to overemphasize socially constructed aspects of contexts, as if what you don't see or don't believe can never be important. I am a philosophical realist. Very different attitudes toward and concepts of phenomena such as time, life, death, procreation, landscapes, food, and so on must be recognized, yet we cannot disregard aspects of these phenomena that are real, whether or not any minds are there to perceive them.

By "sociocultural" aspects of context I mean all the social institutions and ideas in which an individual finds himself or herself situated. This includes Bourdieu's "habitus" and, I think, "structures" in Giddens' sense. They are historically contingent but fairly widely shared among an age, gender, and status category in some particular time and place. One's actions are not simply dictated by these institutions and ideas, but one unavoidably acts with regard to them, obeying, questioning, resisting, manipulating, or whatever.

A third aspect of context is the specific individuals and material circumstances with which one interacts. For example, concepts of what is right and proper and also what is likely or unlikely to occur are part of the sociocultural aspect of context, as are notions about relations between older and younger sisters. The fact that I as an individual have two older sisters and one younger, each with such-and-such characteristics, is part of this third aspect of context, which might be called one's *situation*.

Another way of sharpening thought about context is to distinguish between external and internal. External contexts exist outside persons, but an important part of one's internal context is one's perceptions and feelings about the external context.

Relations between individuals and their contexts are often considered difficult to theorize. I am a little uneasy about this. In the abstract, it seems dead simple: individuals' perceived interests are strongly affected by their contexts, yet individuals must still make choices, and the outcomes of action based on these choices, intended or not, will affect the context. People are affected by their contexts and people have effects on their contexts.

Explaining change

Moving down from this grand abstract level to understand or explain specific cases of socio-ocultural change (or the lack of it) seems, at present, more an *ad hoc* matter of trying to reconstruct what happened in specific cases and suggesting reasons that seem to make sense in terms of individual/context interactions. Further theorizing about the relationship seems unproductive except in the light of such case studies.

Lack of change needs explaining as much as does change. If received cultural rules are never so strong as to prohibit choosing and maneuvering in the light of one's perceived interests, then lack of change cannot be explained as "cultural inertia." There is *always* active cultural reproduction. Sociocultural changes, especially rapid ones, often happen when individuals or a group with enough influence *intend* to make change, even though the results are often not, or not just, those intended. Change also happens for other reasons, including slow change that is merely the result of imperfect replication of received traditions. Also, some change really is due to outside factors; we should not over-react against attempts to explain all change as exogenous.

Absence of change also has to be produced, and it implies that incentives for keeping things the same, or disincentives for change, are repeatedly created and *re*-created over many generations. Since individuals in different situations have different incentives, lack of change implies that, for a long time, the efforts of those who dissent from the status quo, or actively work against it, may cause disturbances but lead to no structural changes; resistance for sure, rebellions perhaps, but not revolutions.

It is undesirable to label a lack of change "stability" or "stagnation." The former smacks of systems models and has a baggage of positive value appraisal. The latter implies a "progress" model and has pejorative overtones. Both divert attention from the point that sociocultural reproduction is always an active process, whether or not the received form is reproduced almost exactly or with considerable change.

How can archaeologists apply the concept of rationality?

So, how does any of this actually apply to archaeology, especially to prehistory? Nothing I have said about individuals reasoning sensibly in regard to their perceived interests and contexts depends on the use of written records (though writing provides new techniques for reasoning and enlarges the scope for rationality). Therefore, it is just as applicable to the past (at least the last 30,000 years) as to the present (e.g. see Wobst, Sinclair, this volume). Alternative paradigms that will not work for the present cannot work for the past either. However, prehistory gives us fleeting and disconnected glimpses of individuals and individual actions; only in a very limited way can we get at individual biographies (as with skeletal and dental markers that reflect past episodes of vaguely-defined stress), and this seems to make reasoning individuals largely invisible archaeologically. I have no problem, however, with postulating entities that we know are there, even if we cannot detect them. I reject the contrary ontology that says that if we cannot detect something it is not there, or at least we must not think about it. This belongs to the sort of extreme logical empiricism that is now rightly discarded.

Rationality is somewhat context-specific, but not totally so. Rather than leaving it vague and muddy, can we steer a nuanced and well-reasoned course between these extremes? I offer a few suggestions.

There seem to be recurrent types of context, and within a particular type of context there are recurrent situations with regard to which people often reason. There are recurrent concerns, tensions, even contradictions. Relevant dimensions include the type of house-hold/family (nuclear, extended, or something else), the difficulty or ease of dissolving marital unions, the relative status of men and women, considerations involved in forming new household units, modes of subsistence, and relations between elites and commoners. One type of context might be agrarian households composed of extended families where marriage is difficult to dissolve, women are subordinated to men and juniors to seniors, good land is in short supply, and landlords or the state extract heavy rents. Another type could be foraging households consisting primarily of a married couple and their children, with little gender-based difference in status, easy divorce, no rents or taxes, and considerable sharing among households. I emphatically do not set these up as tight packages of traits that always go together; they are simply examples, and there are all sorts of variations and different combinations of these and many other variables. My point is that at least some of the variables I have listed are archaeologically accessible. A particular configuration of these variables does not *determine* the issues about which people will recurrently reason, nor just how they will perceive their interests, but it does seem to narrow the range of what is likely. It suggests things archaeologists should look for and think about.

Suppose archaeologists had excavated a reasonable sample of the remains of a commu-nity of the society discussed by Bledsoe and Banja (1997), but had no other knowledge of it. Would they entertain the *possibility* that women might have been concerned with the issues that Bledsoe and Banja report and that women were practicing similar reproductive strategies? I hope so. Certainly anyone who reads this article should. And simply being aware that this might have been the case is important, because it broadens the range of possibilities to be taken seriously, and helps to avoid uncritically projecting modern Western assumptions into the past. Would archaeologists be able to go further, and gain evidence that women *probably* were pursuing such strategies? At present this is a sticky point; I'm not sure that we could, but once the issue is clearly framed, if we think about the matter enough perhaps we could see how to gain such evidence.

We can also ask whether it matters whether the ancient people were concerned with these issues and pursued similar practices. It does matter. It matters, for example, to any proposed explanation of why fertility and population were increasing, decreasing, or staying about the same, and causes of population change are frequently discussed issues in archaeology.

How do I use agency theory in practice?

In the space available I will not present any extended case studies; examples pertaining to the ancient city of Teotihuacan can be found elsewhere (Cowgill 1979, 1983, 1992a, 1992b, 1997). However, I will comment briefly. "Agency theory" does not give me a recipe or algo-rithm for interpreting finds, and I use many resources other than agency theory. These include ethnohistoric materials and the belief that ancient meanings of symbols are often somewhat related to their more recent meanings in Mesoamerica, even if meanings are prone to modification when contexts change and when the symbols serve different inter-ests. Nevertheless, agency theory "informs" all my thought about the past. Partly this is because it makes me highly skeptical of proposed explanations that invoke any of the assumptions I have criticized earlier (that action is highly constrained by custom, action is unconstrained, adaptation is key to explanation, selection is key, decontextualized rationality is key). For example, some assume that only the prospect of upward social mobility through prowess in war could have motivated ordinary Teotihuacanos to serve in armies. This is a narrow view of rationality that underestimates the extent to which moral sentiments, religious beliefs, *"esprit de corps,"* and other factors can motivate young men to be soldiers.

Most of all, an agency outlook affects the questions I think it most interesting to ask, and also my ideas about what is intrinsically likely, even though I hope I avoid the fallacy of assuming the truth of propositions that I'm ostensibly testing. Thus, for Teotihuacan, key questions include the means by which so many people were brought together to build such monumental civic-ceremonial complexes and to live in a rather ordered fashion. Instead of assuming universally shared norms, I am led to wonder what sorts of political negotiations and struggle went on behind what seem to be public proclamations of harmony, what led up to the eventual violent iconoclasm that marked the end of the Teotihuacan state, and how, for centuries before that time, day-to-day relations of production and distribution managed to work reasonably well. I do not have the space even to sketch tentative and complex answers here. The point is that these different questions have an effect on research priorities and strategies; on the kinds of evidence one looks for. This is the greatest merit of an agency outlook, not just that we look at old evidence and old kinds of evidence in new ways, but that our eyes are opened to new things to look for.

Acknowledgments

This chapter has benefited from comments on an earlier draft by Marcia-Anne Dobres and John E. Robb, Michelle Hegmon (who, among other things, called my attention to Jenkins' excellent book on Bourdieu), and John Kunkel. I take, of course, responsibility for the final version.

Bibliography

Barton, C. M. and G A. Clark (eds) 1997. *Rediscovering Darwin: Evolutionary Theory and Archaeological Explanation*. Archaeological Papers of the American Anthropological Association, no. 7. Arlington, Va.

Bledsoe, C. with F. Banja 1997. "Numerators and Denominators in the Study of High Fertility Populations: Past and Potential Contributions from Cultural Anthropology," in *The Continuing Demographic Transition*, ed. G. W. Jones, R. M. Douglas, J. C. Caldwell and R. M. D'Souza, pp. 246–67. Oxford University Press, Oxford.

Boone, J. L. and E. A. Smith 1998. "Is It Evolution Yet? A Critique of Evolutionary Archaeology." *Current Anthropology* 39 (supplement):S141–73.

Brumfiel, E. M. 1992. "Distinguished Lecture in Archeology: Breaking and Entering the Ecosystem – Gender, Class, and Faction Steal the Show." *American Anthropologist* 94(3): 551–67.

Caldwell, J. C., P. Caldwell, and B. Caldwell 1987. "Anthropology and Demography: the Mutual Reinforcement of Speculation and Research." *Current Anthropology* 28: 25–43.

Cowgill, G. L. 1979. "Teotihuacan, Internal Militaristic Competition, and the Fall of the Classic Maya," in *Maya Archaeology and Ethnohistory*, ed. N. Hammond and G. R. Willey, pp. 51–62. University of Texas Press, Austin.

—— 1983. "Rulership and the Ciudadela: Political Inferences from Teotihuacan Architecture," in *Civilization in the Ancient Americas*, ed. R. M. Leventhal and A. L. Kolata, pp. 313–43. Peabody Museum of Archaeology and Ethnology, Harvard University and University of New Mexico Press, Cambridge, Mass.

—— 1992a. "Toward a Political History of Teotihuacan," in *Ideology and Pre-Columbian Civilizations,* ed. A. A. Demarest and G. W. Conrad, pp. 87–114. School of American Research Press, Santa Fe.

—— 1992b. "Social Differentiation at Teotihuacan," in *Mesoamerican Elites: An Archaeological Assessment*, ed. D. Z. Chase and A. F. Chase, pp. 206–20. University of Oklahoma Press, Norman.

—— 1997. "State and Society at Teotihuacan, Mexico." *Annual Review of Anthropology* 26: 129–61.

Frank, R H. 1988. *Passions Within Reason: The Strategic Role of the Emotions*. Norton, New York.

Greenhalgh, S. 1990. "Toward a Political Economy of Fertility: Anthropological Contributions." *Population and Development Review* 16: 85–106.

—— (ed.) 1995. *Situating Fertility: Anthropology and Demographic Inquiry*. Cambridge University Press, Cambridge UK.

Hammel, E. A. 1990. "A Theory of Culture for Demography." *Population and Development Review* 16: 455–85.

Hechter, M. 1987. *Principles of Group Solidarity*. University of California Press, Berkeley.

Jenkins, R. 1992. *Pierre Bourdieu*. Routledge, London.

Johansson, S. R. 1993. "Review of Fertility Transition: The Social Dynamics of Population Change." *Population and Development Review* 19: 375–87.

Kertzer, D. I. and T. Fricke (eds) 1997. *Anthropological Demography: Toward a New Synthesis*. University of Chicago Press, Chicago.

Leacock, S. 1930. "Gertrude the Governess: or, Simple Seventeen," in *Laugh With Leacock*. Dodd, Mead, New York.

McGuire, R. H. 1992. *A Marxist Archaeology*. Academic Press, San Diego.

Mamdani, M. 1972. *The Myth of Population Control: Family, Caste, and Class in an Indian Village*. Monthly Review Press, New York.

Maschner, H. D. G. (ed.) 1996. *Darwinian Archaeologies*. Plenum, London.

Mithen, S. 1996. *The Prehistory of the Mind*. Thames and Hudson, London.

Teltser, P A. (ed.) 1995. *Evolutionary Archaeology: Methodological Issues*. University of Arizona Press, Tucson.

6 A thesis on agency

John C. Barrett

Introduction

This contribution is written as the development of a single argument (thus the title), rather than as a commentary on the work of others. It attempts both to clarify and to take forward issues that are raised in the practice of an archaeology which is engaged with the concept of agency. Such an archaeology must recognize agency as historically constituted.

The argument can be summarized in the following way. Although agency is obviously embodied and although bodies are normally regarded as singular, none the less agency cannot be analyzed in terms of isolated beings. The study of agency is not the study of individuals *per se*. Agency is always situated in the resources of time/space, a being-in-the-world whose actions carry the past into the future and which make reference to absent places in the locations of its own operations. Through those actions agency knows of itself and is known by others. Archaeology as currently practiced fails to engage ontologically with such an agency because it reduces that contextualized agency to an isolated being whose actions are represented by the archaeological record. That is to say, archaeology seeks the individual whose actions have resulted in a material trace. The epistemological problem lies in the way archaeology operates as if its main concern were with the study of the material representations of past actions, events, or processes. Such an archaeology must be replaced by an archaeology whose object of study is the range of contextual mechanisms by which different forms of agency have gained their various historical realities.

The concept of agency

Action, time, space, and agency: we must consider these together as the elements forming a single field of analysis. Action is the doing, the mobilization of resources to have an effect. Action is situated in time not only because there is a period during which this doing occurs but also because it has a past, a place from whence it comes and from whence the resources necessary for that action are drawn. It has a future which is both implied in the intentions and desires manifest in the action and is realized in the outcomes arising from action through which pre-existing resources are reproduced and transformed. Time passes thus, not as a sequence of actions but in a present which remembers a past and desires or anticipates a future. Action is also situated at the place occupied over the period of its execution, a place to which resources are drawn and from which the consequences of that action reach out. And actions are embodied; they are the work of agents whose knowledgeablity of their place in the world, and whose abilities in occupying the world, are expressed in actions which work both upon the world and upon the agent. That is to say, actions have effects which appear external to the embodied agent by being inscribed upon the world and upon others (they are objectified), but those actions also make the agent and renew that agent's understanding of their place in the world.

Schematic as these observations are, my point is to expose the ways action, time, space, and agency each interpenetrate the other. Actions are carried within, or are mapped out by time, space, and agency. Agency is constituted through knowledgeablity and action, operating in practices which occupy time/space. History is the work of binding together these conditions, a labor through which agency reproduces itself. History, the object of our study, is the actually existing conditions which include the presence of human agency. History is not the sequential passing of time, although this is how studies of history may be written, and the actually existing conditions of history involve a living through time whereby the construction of different kinds of temporality help to fix different kinds of time/space relationships.

This concept of agency will not be adequately understood if our analysis treats agency as if it were some force or object, that is if we reify it with a definition which demarcates it or abstracts it from the time/space resources which it occupies, the embodied conditions of the agent, and thus from the knowledgeable actions which it is capable of undertaking. The concept of agency must therefore be conceptualized in terms which are historically situated and which are embodied.

If we fail to understand this point, and as a consequence conceptualize agency as outside history, as something essential and timeless in its qualities which fashions the world without itself being fashioned, then we will tend to explain history as the consequence of the actions of agents (rather than agency being created within history) and our histories will be haunted by a normative and androcentric image of agency; the so called "great men" of history who act on the world to make history. We may certainly theorize about agency at an abstract and a generalizing level, but such theorization can do no more than prepare us for the competent investigation of the historically specific conditions in which agency was and is always embedded. By recognizing that agency fashions itself within materially and historically specific conditions, we refute any commitment to a transcendental and universal concept of agency. It follows that to criticize a study because it betrays a belief in agency in terms of some universal "human nature," whilst adequate in its particular refutation of an inadequate concept of agency, is not to formulate a general critique of the concept of agency *per se*.

Archaeology as representation

Archaeology currently operates as a study of representations. The validity of archaeological reasoning is taken to be grounded upon the extent to which those representations accurately display the conditions of the past. At the heart of this reasoning stands the archaeological record which is treated as the independent and material representation of certain events and processes, and it is normally asserted that archaeology can only study those aspects of the past which are capable of material representation in this record.

Archaeological analysis does three things. First, it transcribes the material record to produce an archive of representations (made up of various textual elements, images, and material samples). The accuracy of that archival representation is supposedly secured by its objectivity and by the fact that it is constructed out of a purely descriptive program that records "what is there."

Second, it establishes what the material record represents in terms of past events and processes. Simply put, such analysis attempts to identify the events in which the material originated and the processes that have transformed the material since that origination. This analysis therefore privileges the origin of the material (that is the events concerning its creation), presenting the material as primarily representing those events. Processes of transformation since that time of origination are regarded as secondary, distorting, residual and so forth to the primary meaning of the record. The reasoning by which the surviving record is linked with past dynamics is sometimes referred to as middle range theory, and most archaeologists would hope that this middle range reasoning is unambiguous so as to offer them surviving observational data which accurately represent past events.

Third, it analyzes the meaning of the events represented by the record in terms of historical processes. These processes are normally regarded as the mechanism which generated the events. In this way the events themselves now appear as representative of some general processes because they are its consequence. Thus the debris of certain activities, when regarded as the patterned residues of an activity system, come to represent a particular form of "socio-economic" or "symbolic" system which determined or structured the form which those activities took and thus the form of their material residues.

The failure of representation

If we accept the concept of agency as established earlier then such an acceptance has significant epistemological implications for the practice of archaeology as the study of representations.

First, we cannot proceed with a study of agency by assuming that the validity of such a study is grounded in the degree to which we can identify accurately its material representation, for what is being represented? Material deposits may result from actions but actions alone cannot be equated with agency. Can we capture an image of agency or, from the archaeological perspective, identify its being as recorded in the material? Agency is made in the passing of time, a making of history whose understanding cannot rest upon a static material representation. Thus, those who claim the study of agency through archaeology to be "impossible" because they are unable to "see" agency in the material can be disarmed simply because the study of agency does not adhere for its validation to such a theory of representation.

Second, any writing of history must at some point accommodate the issue of agency, not as a matter of choice, but as a matter of ontology, that is as a constituent element of the reality which we confront and which we hope to understand. Obviously it is possible to write narratives which mark the passing of time but without reference to agency. Such narratives work at a level of abstraction – economic processes operate without labor, ideologies arise without the struggle to maintain belief – and the reasons for choosing such abstractions must be explicitly understood.

Third, analysis cannot be dedicated to the representation of agency as the object of our inquiry; rather it must work on the time/space field of resources through which agency constitutes itself in its actions.

Archaeology as the study of representations cannot therefore incorporate the concept of agency. This failure is not a product of the data but arises in the intellectual failure to engage with the data in a sense that confronts real conditions of history. The logical failure of that program is set out here.

Archaeological evidence is treated as a record of the past where material things and material conditions are taken to represent the events which created them and, also, the additional events or processes which have modified their original form. Events are therefore defined in terms of their material consequences. If agency is ever allowed to occupy the historical process then it is as a facilitator. For example, flint knapping debris is regarded as the material record of a series of knapping events, the significance of which was that they produced a certain range of artifacts and knapping debris. The agency of the flint knapper is thus known to the observer through the consequence of that agency's actions. These actions are, in turn, assumed to be the direct consequence of the agents' intentions to create those artifacts. Agency thus becomes a force whose significance is defined entirely in terms of its consequences.

The past events in which such an agency appears to make itself known are then interpreted for their significance with reference beyond the intentions of the agent and with reference to more general historical processes. Events are taken to be the consequence of those processes; indeed under this light events can be regarded as representing those processes. Economic processes, for example, are represented archaeologically because the events of production, circulation and consumption might all have left a material record of certain deposits and certain distribution patterns. Further, the general processes which are represented by events are then actually defined by those events. In other words the kinds of event which occur as a consequence of the process also define that process. In this economic example, different types of economy can be defined in terms of the different ways the various events associated with those economies were organized, and the way that the different organization resulted in a different material signature.

Understanding processes in terms of their consequences defines a range of sociological, anthropological and archaeological approaches towards interpretation which come under the general headings of *functionalism* and *structuralism*. In functionalism the processes which demarcate the workings of various social institutions exist to achieve certain ends. These ends are required to maintain the overall system within which the particular institutions function. In other words they represent the needs of the system which have to be fulfilled if the system is to maintain stability. Structuralism operates by a similar logic whereby consequences betray an underlying structural logic, whether it be social structural organization, the structure of the human brain, or simply the grammatical rules of the particular cultural game which is being played out. Structures are therefore equated with generative principles which design the workings of certain forces, mechanisms or agencies, the outcomes of which betray the structural logic which ultimately determines their form. In structuralist analysis it is therefore necessary to see behind the form in which the consequences appear – be it art styles or economic activities – to the generative principles which design the workings of the system as a whole.

It is worth remembering that the adoption of both functionalism and structuralism in anthropology enabled the anthropological discipline explicitly to divert attention away from historical explanations for the institutional phenomena it had chosen to study. It seems ironic that a historical discipline, such as archaeology, should have found so much to commend the adoption of a similar strategy. It is also worth noting that in both functionalism and structuralism, systemic needs and structural determinacy can appear to operate "behind the backs" of the human agents whose roles appear merely to facilitate the operation of those underlying conditions.

A failed concept of agency is linked to an archaeology of representations. Such an archaeology involves an unwarranted reductionism. From this perspective agency is normally represented by the actions of the individual agent or the actions of the collective. Those actions are defined by their consequences as perceived by the archaeologist in terms of material representation. Those actions are also explained by those consequences in as much as the action was supposedly designed or motivated to achieve that which we perceive it as having achieved. At a higher level of analysis social structural conditions are normally regarded as determining an agent's actions. From this perspective the agent appears to be fulfilling certain structural needs necessary to maintain the stability of the system as a whole. Thus an agent's actions appear merely to achieve the conditions necessary to maintain the social structural/symbolic system.

Agency, knowledge, and structure

It is now important to distinguish between *structural conditions* and *structuring principles*. The distinction draws upon the two senses in which the word "structure" is used; first as a noun (or adjective derived from it) to describe an arrangement of things or forces (*a* structure), and second as a verb to describe the making of an arrangement (*to* structure). Considerable confusion has arisen from collapsing both these uses into the single concept of "structure."

Structural conditions can be regarded as all those conditions which agency may be able to inhabit including the various distributions of material resources, the available technologies, and the systems of symbolic order. These conditions obviously have their own histories of formation which are intimately bound up with the practices of human agency; they are the accumulated mass, the debris of history, which confronts the living. As such they can be studied in abstraction, divorced from the practices which brought them into being such as the study of signs in the discipline of semiotics, but these conditions do not in themselves *do* anything.

Structuring principles on the other hand are the means of inhabiting certain structural conditions: they are expressed in the agents' abilities to work on those conditions in the reproduction and transformation of their own identities and conditions of existence. Structuring principles are therefore created in the active maintenance of traditions of knowledgeability whereby experiences are read with reference to the opportunities and constraints within which agents operate. Structuring principles are discovered in ways of seeing and feeling, and in ways of moving and acting, and are thus the penetration of structural conditions through an embodied knowledgeability. Such a penetration of conditions is partial and is prejudiced, coming as it does from a specific history which maintains certain traditions of knowledge through discourses of social constraints, and the agents' own biographies.

Attempts to recover agency from the position of being fully determined by structure have been made by claiming that the agent is "knowledgeable." This much is certainly true. However, such knowledgeability has sometimes been taken as simply having the ability to apply most effectively the functionalist concept of *systemic requirements* as discussed earlier. It is as if agents were chess players who understand the rules of the game. Agents are not chess players, however, in the sense that game theory might imply, rather they are chess players who are situated as to recognize that the making of their own identities is partly facilitated by engaging in the game. They select and maintain a certain cultural capital for ends other than simply winning the game and are faced by consequences of their actions which lie outside their immediate desires and expectations, and beyond the game itself. The structural conditions of the game include the furniture, board, gaming pieces and the rules of the game, all the products of human action. The structuring principles of the game on the other hand are present in the ability and the decision to take up the game. They are therefore present only in the varying practices of the players and involve not simply the acts of playing (they cannot be reduced to the rules of the game), but also the dispositions of the players during the game, as well as their walk to and from the table. Structuring principles are thus created through practice, and in the game of chess they address not simply the game itself but the outer world to which the playing of the game makes reference. It is the structuring principles that continue to make the agent through enablement and knowledgeable action, and it is structuring principles set within the context of structural conditions that give the acts of that agency their historical significance. It is from this complex "situatedness," with its open chains of reference and where the consequences of action extend beyond motivations and desires, that the possibilities of change arise. These are highly complex and essentially indeterminate systems whose histories are not driven by an essential structuralist logic of needs or requirements.

Archaeology

Agents make themselves with reference to a world. They build a recognition of that world and through that recognition they make themselves known to others. They find a way of reading the significance of the world through their own bodily experiences, they find a way of locating themselves in that world, and from that location they speak of themselves to others. This making of the agent, a being-in-the-world, takes place in the passing of time as the practices of agency both recognize something of the world as it is and also formulate their desires upon it (see also Hodder, this volume). The agents are enabled according to the abilities of their bodies, the resources they can command, their knowledgeability, and the extent to which this knowledgeability penetrates the world around them. They therefore participate in a particular way of recognizing the world and of expressing their own security within it. They read the world according to certain traditional prejudices which they share with others, and become social beings by being recognized, through discourse and relationships of power.

Actions are therefore understandable in the context of knowledge, and knowledge is something which is built, sustained and re-evaluated through interpretation. It is embodied and it is also partial and variable. Thus for human agency the conditions of the inhabited world are made available or appropriated through experience and interpretation, and agencies' actions then draw upon those interpretations in various attempts to satisfy desires and to fulfill certain requirements. Action therefore expresses the social context, the identity and the capabilities of the agent, and the consequences of action range from consequences which were intended to those which were unintended.

Action is also understood minimally from a dual perspective, from the perspective of the agents who undertake the action and monitor its consequences, and from the perspective of those who observe the execution of the actions of others. This dual perspective may bring together two very different traditions by which the world is understood and an agent's position in that world is located. The social sciences therefore involve this "double hermeneutic," a relationship or dialogue between those who act within one context of knowledge and are observed by others who occupy a different context of knowledge.

An archaeology of inhabitation

The material conditions which are investigated archaeologically are the contexts in which an agency was once able to construct itself. A fundamental change in archaeological perspectives occurs when we think about archaeologically recovered material as having once ordered a world in which different kinds of human agency could find their place. This rethinking begins an inquiry into how such material might have been perceived and understood through biographically constructed knowledges. These knowledges will have varied according to experience and social position in the past and were, as a whole, very different from our own perspectives on the world. The material initially represents part of the structural conditions inhabited by that other agency. The archaeological challenge presented by the material is not to fix its moment of origin, and to assert that the purpose of the material, and thus its meaning, was also fixed at that moment of origin. Rather the challenge is, given certain material structural conditions, to consider how those came to be known and to trace the consequences which arose from a working through of those knowledges. An "archaeology of inhabitation" therefore considers the various possible structuring principles which agents practiced in their movement through time/space, given the structural conditions that were available to them. These practices will have resulted in certain modifications to existing material conditions, and they will have left some form of trace, part of which may have been incorporated into other and later readings of the world. A new age does not, therefore, rewrite the world and inscribe new meanings upon it which archaeologists should hope to recover; rather, each age confronts the debris of its history, material and traditional, as a way of finding a home for itself. Archaeology must now be interested in considering how that may have been achieved and the various political and social consequences that arose from or were maintained by those practices.

An "archaeology of inhabitation" is fundamentally concerned with the situated context of action and it may be characterized in terms of the following elements:

- the existing material structural conditions operating at any particular time, parts of which may be occupied and used by different communities of people
- the practical use of available stocks of knowledge through which those material conditions were apprehended or recognized
- the ways different communities may have been defined in terms of their practical deployment of different stocks of knowledge, the access they could gain to different sets of material conditions, and the mechanisms of interaction operating between these communities.
- the practical reworking of the structuring principles which secured these communities' identities and the various outcomes of those actions.

This is an archaeology that confronts historical processes in the detailed contexts of the material conditions being studied. History was made in the routine inhabitation of those conditions. It is, therefore, an archaeology that is concerned to tie the investigation of its empirical data directly into the writing of historical analysis.

Archaeology is an interpretive discipline. In terms of the thesis presented here, that interpretation does not set out to discover what meaning archaeological materials may have had, as if they were the authored statement of some earlier agency which it is our task to understand. Archaeologists should refute the claim that the material could ever have had a single meaning or that a privileged meaning resides in the moment of its origin. Instead, interpretation involves an engagement with the possibilities of a human agency which could occupy the material worlds we recover archaeologically. That occupation involved finding a place in that world for communities who defined themselves through principles which appeared secure in the practicalities of their daily lives; interpretation also involves tracing the moments when, and the conditions under which, those securities crumbled. It is thus our privilege as archaeologists to confront something of the diversity of the human agencies through which history has been made. The privilege is considerable as are the responsibilities.

Acknowledgments

I have avoided the usual mechanisms of bibliographical support in this contribution in an attempt to avoid deflection from the line of argument being developed. Obviously that argument does derive from the provisional understandings I have gained from various readings, from my acceptance of some of the arguments contained therein, and my rejection of others. To fully list this literature would be a naming of the usual suspects: Giddens for the theory of structuration with which this argument has attempted to engage, Bourdieu for an understanding of the "logic" of practice, Foucault for a view of an embodied agency submitting to disciplines of power/knowledge, Ricouer for the treatment of action in terms of a text, and Bauman for the characterisation of the post-modern condition and its ethical consequences (e.g., Bauman 1995; Bourdieu 1990; Foucault 1980; Giddens 1984; Ricoeur 1991). These are all complex arguments and archaeology's engagement with them has been at best erratic. I do not regard this as a problem, for we are surely engaged in a long term project in the remaking of the discipline, a point which those who demand some instantaneous demonstration of "how it all works and how it can be applied *now*" will never understand. Few of these critics seem to have heeded the initial challenges (e.g. Hodder 1982; Shanks and Tilley 1987), content instead to demand adherence to the norms of the discipline as they see them, or merely to accept some minor modifications to their archaeology because they admit to forgetting that the people whom they thought they were studying actually had ideas of their own (e.g. Yoffee and Sherratt 1993). The challenge now is to continue in the reworking of archaeological practice, a process demanding not simply theoretical debate but the participation of all those working in the discipline to create a practice of archaeology which does justice to its subject matter, the lives of others. In writing this paper I am grateful for the comments and suggestions of a number of colleagues, Jane Downes, Mark Edmonds, Kathryn Fewster, Chris Jones, and Liam Kilmurray, none of whom will wish to be held responsible for the final product. I have also benefited from the advice, support and tolerance of John E. Robb and Marcia-Anne Dobres.

Bibliography

Bauman, Z. 1995. *Life in Fragments: Essays in Postmodern Morality*. Blackwell, Oxford.

Bourdieu, P. 1990. *The Logic of Practice*. Polity Press, Cambridge UK.

Foucault, M. 1980. *Michel Foucault: Power/Knowledge. Selected Interviews and other Writings 1972–1977*, ed. C. Gordon. Harvester Wheatsheaf, London.

Giddens, A. 1984. *The Constitution of Society*. Polity Press, Cambridge. UK

Hodder, I. (ed.) 1982. *Symbolic and Structural Archaeology*. Cambridge University Press, Cambridge UK.

Ricoeur, P. 1991. *From Text to Action: Essays in Hermeneutics, II*. Athlone Press, London.

Shanks, M. and C. Tilley 1987. *Re-Constructing Archaeology: Theory and Practice*. Cambridge University Press, Cambridge UK.

Yoffee, N. and A. Sherratt (eds) 1993. *Archaeological Theory: Who Sets the Agenda?* Cambridge University Press, Cambridge UK.

Part 3
Using agency

7 The founding of Monte Albán

Sacred propositions and social practices

Arthur A. Joyce

The founding of Monte Albán at about 500 BC in the Valley of Oaxaca (Figure 7.1) was one of the most dramatic social and political developments in the history of Pre-Columbian civilization. During Monte Albán's earliest period of occupation, Period I in the Oaxaca Valley ceramic chronology (500 – 100 BC), the site grew to become one of the largest in Mesoamerica at the time (Blanton 1978: 36). Social complexity also rose dramatically and included the emergence of distinct noble and commoner classes (Joyce 1997; Kowalewski et al. 1989). The power of Monte Albán's nobility was in part built on ideological changes and the increasing control of politico-religious knowledge and institutions (Joyce and Winter 1996; Marcus and Flannery 1994). The social and political changes set in motion by the founding of Monte Albán established the general framework of urban Oaxaca Valley society that would continue until the collapse of the Monte Albán polity around AD 800.

Most current models for the founding and early development of Monte Albán focus on interpolity competition and conflict as a major causal factor in the establishment of the urban hilltop center. These models argue that Monte Albán was founded in response to threats posed by competing polities either within the Valley of Oaxaca (Marcus and Flannery 1996) or in neighboring regions (Blanton 1978: 40). The case for interpolity competition as a factor in the founding of Monte Albán is compelling. However, viewing the founding of Monte Albán as solely a society-wide response to an external threat underplays the complex changes in intrasocietal social practices that constituted this major transformation. This article elaborates on my previous work on agency, ideology, and power in the founding and early development of Monte Albán (Joyce 1997; Joyce and Winter 1996). I explore the founding of Monte Albán based on a theoretical perspective rooted in practice theory (Ortner 1984; Sewell 1992) that examines the intrasocietal dynamics of social change.

Agency, structure, power, and ideology

Practice theories argue that sociocultural change results from human agency (Archer 1996; Bourdieu 1977; Giddens 1979, 1984; Hodder 1991; Sewell 1992; Shanks and Tilley 1988). Agency refers to the actions of individual social actors embedded within a broader sociocultural and ecological setting (for other views, see Pauketat, Shackel, this volume). Individuals have motivation, purpose, and interests while entities like social groups, coalitions, and institutions do not have goals beyond those that are negotiated by their members (see Bell 1992; Giddens 1979: 94–5). Agency, however, does not imply a voluntarism in which atomistic individuals are driven solely by personal motivations. Agency cannot be considered apart from its structural context. Structure consists of principles and resources

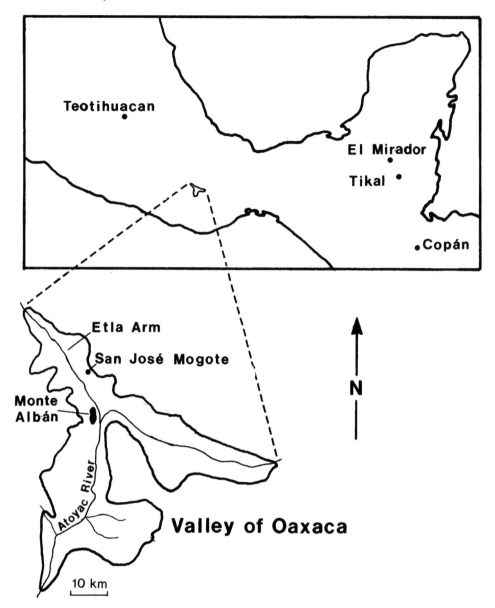

Figure 7.1 Map of Mesoamerica showing sites mentioned in the text

that both enable and constrain agency such as religious beliefs or prestige goods. Principles include symbols and meanings as well as rules for behavior that are learned, both directly and indirectly, from the people with whom one interacts. In Bourdieu's (1977) terms, struc- ture is interiorized in the dispositions of individual actors as habitus. These dispositions, however, are not simply the imprinting of structural principles on the individual mind. To fully understand agency we must also consider human psychology and how personality develops in interaction with the structural environment (Cowgill, this volume; Ortner 1984). Likewise, principles are neither rigid nor inflexible and there is constant negotiation and struggle over structures of signification, legitimation, and domination (Giddens 1979). Individual agents are, thus, decentered subjects whose identities are in part determined by their structural settings, but who are competent and knowledgeable about those settings. The interests of individual actors and their strategies for achieving those interests will be both enabled and constrained, but not entirely determined, by the structural setting, especially through various affiliations with interest groups like class, kinship, gender, faction, polity, community, and ethnicity (Cowgill, this volume; also Brumfiel 1992; Brumfiel and Fox 1994; Earle 1991; Gero and Conkey 1991; Hodder 1991; McGuire 1992).

Social systems, or patterns of social behavior within groups, are the outcome of regularized practices. In turn, regularized practices imply rules about how one should behave, although different actors may infer somewhat different rules, expectations, and proscriptions from their understandings of the structural setting (Giddens 1979). As products of unique histories, agents can distance themselves from rules and creatively strategize to alter system and structure (Hodder, this volume; Ortner 1984). Therefore, it is the structurally conditioned and situated actions of individuals that result in social systems and which in turn reproduce or change structure, thereby creating the setting for future action. Imperfect knowledge, unacknowledged conditions, and the often unpredictable outcomes of social action, however, can result in unintended consequences over which agents have no control.

In this view of the agency–structure dialectic, power is the transformative capacity of an agent to achieve an outcome which can either reproduce or change system and structure (Giddens 1979: 88–94). Power, however, is not a possession of individuals. The transformative capacity of agents is determined by the compromise struck between their creativity, skill, and awareness of the world along with structures of domination that create asymmetries in access to resources. All people have some power, even if it is in the form of passive resistance, thus the consequences of the actions of even the least powerful can affect system and structure (Walker and Lucero, Shackel, this volume). In the works of Giddens (1984) and Bourdieu (1977), structural contradictions, especially those actualized in conflict, often lead to change. Contradictions usually revolve around major social categories such as class, gender, ethnicity, and community affiliation. However, ideology as an aspect of structure, often conceals domination so that contradictions do not automatically lead to conflict. In turn, subordinates always have some degree of penetration of dominant ideologies (Shackel, this volume). In addition, as will be demonstrated in the case study to follow, dominant ideologies often provide the framework in which subordinates can resist (Scott 1990).

Power and the sacred covenant in prehispanic Oaxaca

The structures of domination that contributed to political power among the Otomanguean-speakers of Oaxaca, as well as among other prehispanic Mesoamericans, involved sacred propositions (Drennan 1976a; Marcus 1989; Monaghan 1994; Schele and Freidel 1990). Ethnographic and ethnohistorical evidence can be used to unlock the meanings of these sacred propositions for prehispanic peoples. While ritual practices and the political significance of religious belief have changed, there is considerable evidence suggesting that basic beliefs about the relationship of people to the sacred, especially the important role of sacrifice, have persisted from the Formative period (1800 BC – AD 200) to the present (Marcus and Flannery 1994; Monaghan 1994; Schele and Freidel 1990).

At the time of the Spanish Conquest, Otomanguean religion was based on the belief in a vital force that animated all living things (Marcus and Flannery 1994; Monaghan 1994,

1995). For the Oaxaca Valley Zapotec, this vital force was known as *pée*. *Pée* was manifest not only in living things but in a range of natural and supernatural forces/deities. The most powerful of Otomanguean deities, representing the two great halves of the cosmos, were associated with the earth and sky/rain/lightning. In her treatment of Otomanguean religion and ideology in the Formative period, Joyce Marcus (1989) has focused on the role of ancestor worship in the creation and legitimation of elite power. She argues that the power of nobles was legitimated because elite ancestors were closely associated with supernatural forces, especially the powerful forces associated with earth and sky. Living Zapotec elites, acting as ritual specialists, could access these supernatural forces by contacting their ancestors through various petitions and offerings.

While elite ancestors were important in Oaxacan religion, I would like to stress the ideo-logical implications of another element of Pre-Columbian religion. Building on the work of John Monaghan (1990, 1994, 1995), the central aspect of Otomanguean and other Mesoamerican religions can be understood as a covenant formed between humans and the supernatural forces/deities that control the cosmos, especially those of earth and sky. The covenant is a creation myth setting out the fundamental relationships between humans and the sacred. Versions of this creation myth are central themes in many sixteenth-century indigenous documents, including the Mixtec codices (Vienna and Nuttall), the Quiché Maya *Popol Vuh*, and in Mexica writing and oral literature (Hamann n.d.; Monaghan 1990, 1994; Taggart 1983; Tedlock 1986). Iconographic representations of portions of this creation myth have also been found on sculpture as well as painted pottery and murals that date to the Formative and Classic periods (Schele and Freidel 1990). Versions of the sacred covenant are still found among traditional Mixtec communities in Oaxaca (Monaghan 1994, 1995). Mixtec creation stories speak of the dawning of the current sun and the destruction of the *tiumi*, the immortal and uncivilized "stone people" of the previous creation. The first Mixtecs emerge from a cave or a cleft in the earth. Mixtec ancestors form a covenant with the powerful deities of earth and rain/sky allowing them to practice agri-culture. The covenant is necessary because the turning of the soil and the harvesting and consumption of maize, the daughter of the earth and rain, causes the deities great pain. In return for being allowed to practice agriculture, humans are required to sacrifice their bodies in death, going into the earth where they are assimilated by the deities. The contem-porary Nuyooteco Mixtecs studied by Monaghan (1990: 562–3) describe this covenant by saying: "we eat the earth and the earth eats us."

The covenant establishes relationships of debt and merit between humans and the sacred, with sacrifice as a fundamental condition of human existence (Monaghan in press). In prehispanic Mesoamerica there were many forms of sacrifice in addition to offering bodies to the earth in burial. People invoked the covenant through a variety of sacrificial practices, including human sacrifice and the autosacrificial letting of blood by piercing parts of the body such as the tongue or genitals (Boone 1984; Schele and Miller 1986). Many offerings of goods and labor made to the nobility also appear to have been conceived of as forms of sacrifice (Monaghan 1994: 23). By activating this covenantial relationship through sacrifice, agents actively petitioned supernaturals to bring fertility.

Mesoamerican elites occupied a special place in relation to the sacred covenant and the acts of sacrifice it required. In several versions of the covenant the ancestors who made the first sacrifice to the earth and sky were elite priests (Hamann n.d.; Monaghan 1990). Human and autosacrifice performed by and on the bodies of nobles were the most potent form of sacrifice (Boone 1984; King 1988; Schele and Miller 1986). Thus, sacrifice was a kind of social contract between commoners, elites, and supernaturals (Monaghan 1994: 23) with nobles acting as intermediaries between people and the sacred. Commoners offered sacrifices to nobles in the form of goods and labor (ibid.: 10–11) and, in return, elites enacted the most potent forms of sacrifice, thereby invoking the covenant, opening up contact with the supernatural, and providing for human and natural fertility. Noble ancestors constituted another level in this chain of interaction between humans and supernaturals in that certain rituals performed by elites contacted the sacred via their ancestors (Marcus and Flannery 1994). In terms of the theoretical principles discussed above, the relationships between commoners, elites, and the sacred, as mediated by sacrificial practices, were structural elements both constructing and allowing for the negotiation of agency.

The covenant was a key aspect of prehispanic ideologies since it established and reinforced both the hierarchical relationship between people and deities and that between commoners and nobles (Monaghan 1994). The interests of the elite were universalized by linking their ritual practices to the maintenance of fertility and the prosperity of all people. Noble status was reified by tracing the close relationship between elites and the sacred to the dawn of the current creation. Commoners, however, were not entirely dependent on elites for contact with the sacred since they could perform rituals, including certain forms of sacrifice, independent of the nobility.

Many key elements of the sacred covenant have a deep history in Mesoamerica and can be considered examples of the long-term structure of meaning (Hodder 1991: 83–94). Evidence for autosacrificial bloodletting (Flannery 1976a; Grove 1987; Joyce *et al.* 1991) and indications that elites acted as intermediaries between commoners and supernaturals (Grove and Gillespie 1992) date to the Early Formative period (1800 – 850 BC). There is possible Early Formative iconographic evidence for the division of the supernatural into realms of earth and sky (Marcus 1989; Reilly 1996). Iconographic and burial evidence for human sacrifice, however, is very limited until the end of the Middle Formative (Angulo 1987; Clark *et al.* n.d.: 17; Reilly 1989: 16; Sedat and Sharer 1984). Most Middle Formative (850 – 500 BC) iconographic representations of human sacrifice are located in settings with little available space, suggesting restricted participation in rituals associated with these images (Grove and Angulo 1987; Reilly 1989: 16).

While practices involving the sacred covenant can be traced far back in Mesoamerican prehistory, it is clear that significant changes occured in how the covenant was defined and in the power relations that it constituted (see Conrad and Demarest 1984; Grove and Gillespie 1992; Joyce and Winter 1996; Monaghan 1994; Schele and Freidel 1990). In particular, the period from the late Middle Formative through the Late Formative, between roughly 700 and 100 BC, was a time of major changes in power relations in Oaxaca and other regions of Mesoamerica that were in part driven by struggle over peoples' relations to the sacred.

System/structure in Middle Formative Oaxaca

Archaeological research in the Valley of Oaxaca has provided a detailed picture of the structural and social system setting among competing chiefdoms of the Middle Formative period (Blanton *et al.* 1993; Drennan 1976b; Feinman 1991; Flannery 1976b; Marcus 1989; Marcus and Flannery 1996; Whalen 1981). The dominant center was San José Mogote located in the northern, or Etla, arm of the valley. San José Mogote had been the largest community in the region since the beginning of the Early Formative due, in part, to its advantageous location in the most fertile area of the valley. By the Guadalupe phase (850 – 700 BC), San José Mogote had reached a size of 70 hectares (ha), making it roughly twenty times larger than any other settlement in the valley (Flannery and Marcus 1983a). A cluster of about a dozen sites in the Etla arm appear to have been communities subject to San José Mogote elites.

As in other chiefdoms, the power of Middle Formative Oaxacan elites appears to have been manifest in their ability to attract followers either directly or through alliances with subordinate elites at other sites. Marcus and Flannery (1996: 93 – 120) argue that elite generosity was an important factor in commoners' decisions to align themselves with particular elites and provide labor and resources. Elites demonstrated their generosity by providing gifts to followers, including prestige goods and food, presumably during ritual feasting. The exchanges of prestige goods and perhaps intermarriage, were used to cement alliances with other elites. There is little evidence, however, that elites had either direct economic control over land or centralized stores (Feinman 1991), and until the Rosario phase (700 – 500 BC) there is little evidence that they had significant coercive power.

Religious principles appear to have been a key to defining generosity, and therefore power, in Middle Formative chiefdoms of Oaxaca (Feinman 1991; Marcus 1989). Archaeological evidence suggests that the agency of people at all status levels involved contacting the sacred through ritual practices, including autosacrifice (Flannery 1976a; King 1997). However, ritual paraphernalia, especially exotic goods obtained from distant regions, were more abundant in excavations of high status households (Flannery 1976a; Marcus 1989). In particular, certain kinds of exotic bloodletting implements, such as stingray spines, were associated with elites (Marcus and Flannery 1994: 62). These data suggest that some elites carried out special sacrificial rituals which may have been another form of generosity used to attract followers. As delineated in the sacred covenant, Middle Formative elites may have been seen as having a closer relationship to the supernatural forces that controlled the cosmos, especially those of earth and sky (Marcus 1989).

While commoners were able to conduct various rituals, they also may have contacted the sacred indirectly, by "sacrificing" goods and labor to elites in return for special ritual services. At chiefly centers, commoners contributed their labor to construct public buildings for communal ritual performances presumably led by elite ritual specialists (Marcus and Flannery 1996). By the Guadalupe phase (850 – 700 BC), public buildings consisted of impressive wattle-and-daub temples built on pyramidal platforms measuring up to 2 m in height and 15 m wide. The rituals perfomed in these buildings probably attracted people from surrounding communities and presumably were directed by elites.

In Middle Formative Oaxaca, sacrifice in the context of the sacred covenant appears to have been a key idiom in the construction and negotiation of both elite and commoner agencies. Religious beliefs were ideological, in that they legitimated the advantages that elites had in terms of acquiring surplus goods and labor. Commoners, in turn, gained from their association with powerful elites. Elites attracted followers both by providing access to prestige goods and by conducting important rituals. Commoners had the means to express either allegiance to or distance from particular nobles through their choice of those to whom they sacrificed goods and labor. Commoners could also express resistance to elite authority by contacting the sacred without the assistance of elite ritual specialists.

In many chiefdoms, the need to attract clients without significant coercion creates intense factional competition among elites (Earle 1978, 1991: 13; Redmond 1994). Paramount chiefs have to guard against raids by competing chiefs from other polities, as well as against rebellions by subordinate elites. The fact that San José Mogote was by far the largest community in the Oaxaca Valley from the Tierras Largas phase (1450 – 1150 BC) until the end of the Rosario phase (700 – 500 BC) suggests that elites at the site were successful in coalition building in the face of interelite competition. In fact, until the Rosario phase, there is little evidence in the Valley of Oaxaca for warfare (Marcus and Flannery 1996), suggesting that interpolity conflict was limited to low-level raiding. It was advantageous for commoners to settle at San José Mogote to gain access to prestige goods, potent rituals, and perhaps defense against occasional raids. The large coalition that San José Mogote elites built, in turn, reinforced their ability to mobilize labor and resources, construct impressive public buildings, defend against raids from competing chiefs, and forge exchange relations with nobles from distant polities. Through much of the Formative period, the rulers of San José Mogote appear to have been the most powerful in the valley. Yet, by the Rosario phase evidence suggests increasing interelite and factional competition. At San José Mogote, these developments created a political crisis for elites and their followers.

A political crisis at San José Mogote

During the Rosario phase (700 – 500 BC), immediately preceding the founding of Monte Albán, the Oaxaca Valley was occupied by several competing polities, probably complex chiefdoms (Kowalewski *et al.* 1989). The dominant center in the valley continued to be San José Mogote, but evidence suggests that its rulers were struggling to maintain control of their coalition of supporters in the face of intensifying factional competition.

Survey and excavation data from the Oaxaca Valley suggest increasing competition, including warfare, among nobles and their followers (Marcus and Flannery 1996). Evidence for warfare includes a high frequency of structures destroyed by fire and a sparsely occupied buffer-zone separating the Etla arm of the valley from the two other arms which were occupied by competing polities (Kowalewski *et al.* 1989: 70–5). Status competition may explain the large increase in monumental building activities taking place at San José Mogote and other sites (Flannery and Marcus 1983a; Kowalewski *et al.* 1989: 78). At San José Mogote, public buildings were concentrated on Mound 1, a natural hill architecturally modified into a huge platform (Flannery and Marcus 1983a). Mound 1 supported a large wattle-and-daub temple built on a substructure (Building 28). During the Rosario phase, the temple on Building 28 was burned to the ground, perhaps as a result of raiding (Marcus and Flannery 1996: 129). If Marcus and Flannery are correct, then the most restricted and ritually important part of the site had been penetrated by a raiding party.

While it is not clear why factional and inter-elite competition increased during the Rosario phase, such competition would have created problems for nobles and commoners alike. As one response, San José Mogote nobles may have increased their demands for goods and labor from commoners, as suggested by the increase in the scale of monumental construction on site. In turn, commoners had a number of potential strategies for dealing with the hardships created both by conflict and by increasing elite demands for goods and labor, which would have been burdensome even if viewed in sacrificial terms. Commoners could have intensified agricultural production to provide resources to nobles. Some commoners may have withdrawn from elite sponsored ceremonies and communicated with the sacred solely through private household rituals (King 1997; Marcus and Flannery 1994), although they might have risked sanctions from elites. Archaeological data suggest, however, that many commoners in the Etla arm of the valley resisted increasing elite demands by "voting with their feet." San José Mogote declined from roughly 70 ha during the Guadalupe phase to 33.7 ha by the Rosario phase (Kowalewski *et al.* 1989: 72–7) and population in the Oaxaca Valley as a whole was more evenly distributed, suggesting that the Etla arm lost some of its demographic advantage (Blanton *et al.* 1993: 66).[1] The combined evidence for a decline in the population of commoners, along with greater monumental construction activities, suggest increased per capita labor demands at San José Mogote.

This loss of followers apparently created a crisis for nobles at San José Mogote. Immediately following the burning of the Structure 28 temple, archaeological evidence suggests major changes in the use of Mound 1 that may have been the result of an elite response to this political crisis. After the temple was destroyed, a series of high-status residences were built over the ruins (Flannery and Marcus 1983a). Ritual objects associated with these residences included an obsidian bloodletter and a ceramic effigy brazier (Marcus and Flannery 1996: 131–3). Also associated with these elite residences were two tombs, the first formal stone masonry tombs known in the Oaxaca Valley. These data represent a significant change in the use of Mound 1, from an area strictly for public ceremonial activities to a combination of public politico-religious buildings and elite residences in a distinct precinct.

Yet another possible elite response to increasing factionalism during the late Rosario phase concerns human sacrifice. The first good evidence for ritual human sacrifice in the Oaxaca Valley is found on Mound 1 at San José Mogote (Marcus and Flannery 1996: 129–30). Monument 3 (Figure 7.2) on Mound 1 depicts a naked man with eyes closed. The trilobe heart glyph is shown on his chest with blood emanating from the heart, indicating that he was a sacrificial victim. The person on Monument 3 is identified as 1-Eye, his name in the 260-day ritual calendar.[2] If Monument 3 is correctly dated to the late Rosario phase (cf. Cahn and Winter 1993), it would be the first example of a *danzante* sculpture. The *danzantes* consist of over 310 carved stones at Monte Albán that, like Monument 3, depict sacrificial victims (Figure 7.3). Given that the *danzantes* are shown naked except for head gear, most researchers agree that they were humiliated war captives (Coe 1962; Marcus 1976; Scott 1978). In addition to the iconography of Monument 3, a burial interred under a wall of one of the high-status houses on Mound 1 has been interpreted as a sacrificial victim (Flannery and Marcus 1983a: 58).

The creation of an elite-ceremonial precinct on Mound 1, coupled with the evidence for human sacrifice, suggests a change in structural principles involving the sacred covenant. Based on the available data, these developments seem to have been part of a creative, though perhaps risky, elite strategy to bolster commoner support and reinforce their coalition. The demographic decline at San José Mogote suggests that the traditional means that Etla nobles used to attract followers and mobilize resources, by appeal to the covenant, were no longer as effective as they once were. Commoners appear to have been resisting elite demands to increase sacrificial offerings of goods and, especially, labor. In response, nobles acted, still through the sacred covenant, to provide supporters with a more potent form of sacrificial offering: human sacrifice. By offering human sacrifices to the deities of earth and sky, nobles at San José Mogote were demonstrating both their ritual potency and their generosity to supporters. In terms of the sacred covenant, the innovation of human sacrifice would have been familiar to commoners and would have been an attempt to make their allegiance to nobles appear more attractive.

Elite generosity would have been especially evident if the new practice of human sacrifice was also restricted largely to captured elites (Boone 1984; Freidel 1986). While human sacrifice may have been known from other regions, the Mound 1 data at San José Mogote represent the earliest evidence for such rituals in Oaxaca. Given the physical setting of Monument 3, the audience for these sacrifices may have been restricted, much like the

Figure 7.2 San José Mogote Monument 3

Source: redrawn from Flannery and Marcus 1998a: Figure 3.10

Figure 7.3 Late Formative *danzante* portraits from Monte Albán

Source: redrawn from Scott 1978

setting of Middle Formative iconography dealing with human sacrifice in other parts of Mesoamerica (Grove and Angulo 1987; Reilly 1989: 16).

A strong indication that the changes of the late Rosario phase (ca. 600 – 500 BC) involved manipulation of ultimate sacred propositions is the change in the orientation of new buildings erected on Mound 1. The structures built on Mound 1 after the burning of the temple were all oriented 3° to 6° east of north which represents a change from the 8° west of north orientation of earlier public buildings throughout the valley. By 500 BC, 3° to 6° east of north would become the dominant orientation of public buildings at Monte Albán (Peeler and Winter 1992). In prehispanic Mesoamerican world views, there was a close association between site orientations and layouts, the movement of celestial bodies/deities, and conceptions of time (Ashmore 1991; Sugiyama 1993).

Despite the attempt of nobles to alter sacred propositions and the social practices that they implied, no major social transformation occurred at San José Mogote. In about 500 BC, monumental construction activities on Mound 1 ceased and the site may have declined still further in size (Kowalewski et al. 1989: 89–90; Marcus and Flannery 1996: 139). Other Rosario phase sites in the Etla arm also declined in size or were completely abandoned (Drennan 1976b; Flannery and Marcus 1983b; Kowalewski et al. 1989: 91; Winter 1972). At the same time, the hilltop center of Monte Albán was founded and rapidly grew into the largest community in the Valley of Oaxaca.

It is not clear why the people who were embracing this new set of beliefs and practices left San José Mogote to found Monte Albán. Factional competition and conflict may have been so intense that a more effective location for defense was sought (Blanton 1978; Marcus and Flannery 1996). The promotion of a new view of the sacred covenant may have been resisted by a significant proportion of people in the San José Mogote polity, in effect creating a legitimation crisis and necessitating a move to a new location. It may also have been difficult to construct a new discourse that would come to legitimize the power relations of the emerging Monte Albán state literally on the foundations of the earlier San José Mogote chiefdom. Nobles who were attempting to alter the principles and practices of the sacred covenant were apparently not entirely successful in consolidating power at San José Mogote. Their move to Monte Albán ultimately resulted in a structural transformation that profoundly altered systems of social relations in Oaxaca in ways that even the founders of the site did not forsee.

The founding of Monte Albán

Monte Albán was founded about 500 BC on a previously unoccupied series of hills in the center of the Valley of Oaxaca. Similarites in public architecture and elite residences between San José Mogote in the late Rosario phase (ca. 600 – 500 BC) and Monte Albán in Period Ia (500 – 300 BC) indicate that elites from the former site made the decision to establish the latter (Flannery and Marcus 1983b; Winter and Joyce 1994). Almost immediately after its founding, Monte Albán far exceeded any other site in the Oaxaca Valley in size, population, and scale of monumental architecture (Blanton 1978; Kowalewski et al. 1989; Winter and Joyce 1994). By the end of Period Ia, Monte Albán covered 320 ha with a mean estimated population of 5,250 (Blanton 1978: 36). Regional population also rose dramatically from a mean estimate of 1,835 people during the Rosario phase (700 – 500 BC) to 14,650 by Period Ia (Kowalewski et al. 1989: 90). As is argued later, a key reason for the dramatic growth in population at Monte Albán may have been the popularity of the sacred principles and practices that were a central motivating factor for the early inhabitants of the site.

Evidence from Monte Albán suggests that an important goal of the earliest inhabitants was to construct a ceremonial center that symbolized the version of the sacred covenant developed at San José Mogote during the previous century. The founders of Monte Albán initiated a program of monumental building that far exceeded anything previously seen in Oaxaca (Winter and Joyce 1994). The civic-ceremonial center of the site was the Main Plaza, a huge public plaza measuring roughly 300 m north–south by 150 m east–west. In its final form the Main Plaza was bounded on its north and south ends by high platforms supporting numerous public buildings (Figure 7.4). The eastern and western sides of the Main Plaza were defined by rows of monumental buildings; a third row of structures ran north-to-south through the center of the plaza. The Period I version of the Main Plaza consisted of only the western row of buildings along with much of the eastern half of the North Platform (ibid.). While fill was used during Period I to create a flat surface on the eastern end of the Main Plaza, no buildings appear to have been constructed there until Period II.

The pattern of architecture and iconography in and around the Main Plaza shows that the new version of the sacred covenant was a central organizing principle for the founders of Monte Albán (also see Masson *et al.* 1992: 12; Orr 1994; Winter 1994: 22). The sacred geography of Monte Albán resembles other Mesoamerican cities such as Tikal, Copán, and Teotihuacan, where the cosmos is rotated onto the surface of the site's ceremonial center so that north represents the celestial realm and south the earth or underworld (Ashmore 1991; Sugiyama 1993: 123).

The southern end of the Main Plaza contained iconographic references to earth, sacrifice, and warfare. Building L was the location of the more than 310 *danzante* portraits of sacrificial victims. The *danzantes* represent the largest single corpus of carved stones for Late Formative Mesoamerica and constitute roughly 80 percent of the total monument record from Monte Albán. The energy expended on the *danzantes* suggest the significance of this new form of ritual. Sacrificial victims would go into the earth at death. The genital mutilation apparent on many *danzantes* suggests a combination of earlier forms of auto-sacrifice with death sacrifice. The sacrifice of captives was one way for nobles to open portals to the underworld (Masson *et al.* 1992) and activate the covenant, thereby assuring fertility and prosperity for themselves and their followers. In this new version of the sacred covenant, however, warfare and human sacrifice became notable themes. The Period II (100 BC – AD 200) "conquest slabs" from Building J spell out the covenantial relationship even more overtly, with the decapitated head of a captured ruler extending down beneath the terrestrial hill glyph and vegetation sprouting from the top of the hill sign (Figure 7.5). Ballgame rituals probably also played a part in this newly configured warfare and human sacrifice-based covenant (Orr 1997), and it is during Period I that the earliest ballcourts are found in the Oaxaca Valley (Kowalewski *et al.* 1991).

The North Platform included iconographic references to sky, rain, and lightning. The earliest celestial reference is found with the stucco frieze known as the "viborón" located beneath the southeast corner of the North Platform (Acosta 1965: 816; Urcid 1994: 64–5). The frieze dates to Period Ic (300 – 100 BC) and consists of a sky band with scrolls similar to the s-scroll rain cloud motif (Reilly 1996: 36). The sky band is broken by serpentine *cociyo*-like figures that appear to be representations of the sky-dwelling rain serpent. A pair of cloud scrolls form the mouth and bifid tongue or fangs. Rain issues from the figure's mouth, and its goggle eyes resemble those of Tlaloc, the later Central Mexican rain deity.

The symbolism of the cosmos and the sacred covenant resonating in the layout of the Main Plaza clearly marked Monte Albán as a mountain of creation, a common concept in

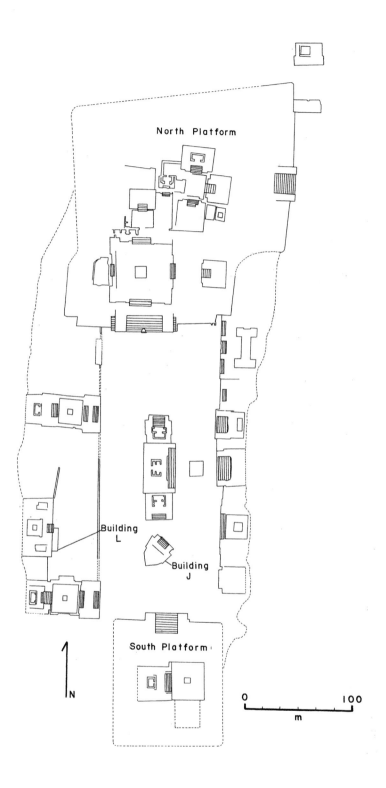

Figure 7.4 Monte Albán's main plaza

Figure 7.5 Building J conquest slab from Monte Albán

Source: redrawn from Caso 1947: Figure 41

Otomanguean world views (Monaghan 1995: 108; Parsons 1936). The Main Plaza, however, was not just an architectual symbol of the sacred covenant. It was a public arena where thousands of people participated in rituals that invoked the sacred covenant. Commoners standing on the Main Plaza would have been physically engaged in the proceedings. These rituals may have also included commoners presenting material offerings to nobles. In such a setting, simultaneously public and symbolic, the new practices involving human sacrifice would have been dramatic events graphically enacting and renewing the covenant. The effects of ritual drama and mass psychology on participants would have created powerful psychological forces (Caspary 1993; Kertzer 1988), affecting people's dispositions by binding them to the rulers, the symbols, and the new social order centered at Monte Albán.

While the actual practice of human sacrifice may have been restricted to nobles, the construction of the Main Plaza and its elaboration with symbolic imagery, as well as the sacrificial rituals perfomed there were clearly viewed and experienced in communal terms. The huge volume of monumental building activities during the early years at Monte Albán represents active and uncoerced commoner involvement that served to enroll them in the new version of the sacred covenant as embodied in the ceremonial center. Commoners were very much an active part of the political changes occuring at Monte Albán. Yet, as insightfully argued by Timothy Pauketat (this volume), the unforseen tragedy was that commoners were also inadvertently contributing to their own subordination. Monumental buildings housed politico-religious institutions that would soon come to embody and affirm dominant ideologies that constrained the agency of commoners. While these institutions may have originally been conceived at least partially in corporate terms, unifying ritual practices, labor appropriations, and centralizing beliefs were increasingly appropriated by the nobility alone.

Attempts by nobles to dominate religious ideas, institutions, and practices may first be seen with the construction of the elite residence on Mound 1 at San José Mogote discussed previously. It is with the architectural layout of Monte Albán, however, that we see elites increasingly appropriating sacred ideas, institutions, and practices to serve their political ends. For example, as early as Period Ia elite residences and tombs were concentrated in areas around the North Platform (Martínez Lopez *et al.* 1996: 236; Winter and Joyce 1994), indicating an association between the celestial realm, nobles, and noble ancestors. Tombs built in this area contained effigy vessels depicting *Cociyo*, the Zapotec lightning (sky) deity. These data suggest not only an increasing association of nobles with the celestial realm, but the deification of noble ancestors as well (Marcus and Flannery 1996: 159). This association of living nobles and their ancestors with *cociyo* suggests that some elites were "Rain people." Among the Mixtec today, the "Rain people" (or *tenuvi*) act as shamans, priests, and sacrificers who possess special ritual powers (Monaghan 1995). That nobles were gaining control over ritual practices in addition to human sacrifice is suggested by an increasing association between elite residences and religious symbols and artifacts during the Late/Terminal Formative (Joyce and Winter 1996: 36).

The interment of elites in formal masonry tombs, first seen at San José Mogote and immediately after that at Monte Albán, can be interpreted in sacrificial terms. Starting between 600 and 400 BC, nobles did not sacrifice their bodies at death in the same way as commoners. Instead, their bones remained in tombs and were not assimilated by the earth in the same way as the remains of commoners. As a result, nobles could directly consult their ancestors by reopening the tomb and performing appropriate rituals (Miller 1995). The separate and accessible resting place of elites in tombs may have helped deify noble ancestors. The Mixtec codices also show that during the Postclassic and Early Colonial periods the remains of nobles were often kept as mummy bundles in sacred caves and temples, where they acted as priestly oracles (Byland and Pohl 1994). Perhaps the earlier tomb burials were precursors to the caves of the Postclassic.

Human sacrifice, interment in stone-masonry tombs, and the close association of elite residences and public politico-religious buildings were means by which the identity of nobles came to be marked as fundamentally separate from that of commoners (Joyce and Winter 1996; Marcus 1992). By the Late/Terminal Formative period (500 BC – AD 200) a separate noble identity and set of practices were increasingly evident. Elite identities were symbolized by control of exotic artifacts such as urns and incense burners, and of knowledge including hieroglyphic writing and calendrics. Enemies also would have been redefined not just as competitors in inter-elite and factional conflict, but in sacred terms as potential sacrificial victims. As competing factions began to adopt these ideological changes they also became a threat as potential capturers and sacrificers of Monte Albán's nobility. Warfare was no longer being waged just to defeat competing elites and obtain tribute, but to capture sacrificial victims that would ultimately contribute to human fertility and the politico-religious role of elites. Since commoners were increasingly dependent on nobles for ritual communication with the sacred, the possibility of the capture and sacrifice of nobles by competing elites had dire consequences for all people. This more sacred form of warfare may have further united people of the Monte Albán polity (Joyce and Winter 1996: 38–9).

It is likely that as people increasingly associated nobles with the sacred, sacrifices of goods and labor were made directly to elites (see Monaghan 1994). Elites could then appropriate larger proportions of communal sacrifices of goods and labor for their own use, leading to rising social inequalities (Joyce 1997). However, the relative scarcity of nobles represented in monumental public art, at least until Period IIIb (AD 500 – 800), may reflect an ideology that attempted to conceal the relationship between communal sacrifice and elite interests (Joyce and Winter 1996: 37). Overall, human sacrifice and the more general appropriation of sacred principles, institutions, and practices by nobles altered the ideological aspects of the sacred covenant and increased the power of elites to attract followers, mobilize material resources, defeat competitors, and interact with the sacred.

While the power of Monte Albán's nobles increased during the Late/Terminal Formative, it is unlikely that they administered the entire valley until Period II (100 BC – AD 200) or Period IIIa (AD 200 – 500; Kowalewski *et al.* 1989). Data suggest that resistance to social and structural changes continued to be expressed by some commoners and competing elites. For example, the *danzantes* at Monte Albán probably depicted competing nobles from within the Oaxaca Valley. Moreover, the Late/Terminal Formative population expansion into the mountains north of the Oaxaca Valley (Drennan 1983) and into the Miahuatlán (Markman 1981), Ejutla (Feinman and Nicholas 1990), and Sola (Balkansky 1997) valleys may represent commoners actively resisting these ritual innovations and the greater sacrificial demands being placed on them. Period I female figurines that exhibit stylistic continuity with Middle Formative ones may even represent household-level resistance to elite appropriation of ritual activities (King 1997: 43).

Structural changes in ideological principles and social practices led to many unanticipated outcomes in Oaxaca Valley systems of social relations. It is doubtful that the founders of Monte Albán could have forseen the dramatic increase in the scale of their polity as people moved to the hilltop center. The huge population concentrating at Monte Albán created provisioning problems that forced elites to mobilize food from commoners in the valley. The provisioning problem may have encouraged nobles to conquer and incorporate independent communities in the valley to gain control of more agricultural land. Provisioning Monte Albán also led to the short-lived piedmont strategy that involved population expansion and agricultural intensification in the piedmont (Kowalewski *et al.* 1989: 123–6) but triggered landscape degradation (Joyce and Mueller 1997). Productive intensification by commoners also increased the demand for labor, making it advantageous to have larger families, but further driving the tremendous population growth of Period I. Furthermore, some people began to specialize in certain crafts, such as ceramics and stone tools, taking advantage of the fact that most commoners would have had less time to carry out the full array of productive tasks that they had previously undertaken (Feinman *et al.* 1984; Kowalewski *et al.* 1989: 149–51). Markets may have been developed to provide a central location to obtain products manufactured by these specialists (Feinman *et al.* 1984). Finally, the increasing importance of warfare probably gave elites both the ideological justification and military apparatus to use coercive force against their own subjects as well as against enemies (Joyce and Winter 1996: 38–9). While human sacrifice may have initially been seen by followers as a form of elite generosity, it probably came to act as a kind of terror tactic. These and other unanticipated problems created by the increasing scale of the Monte Albán polity probably contributed to the development of new administrative institutions, further leading to the emergence of the state (Joyce 1997; Kowalewski *et al.* 1989; Spencer 1982).

The social transformation in the Oaxaca Valley was apparently part of a broader structural transition in Mesoamerica involving the negotiation of elite and commoner power relations through the sacred covenant. Towards the end of the Formative period, human sacrifice became an important form of elite-controlled ritual practice in many regions (Freidel 1986; Joyce and Winter 1996; Sugiyama 1993). At the same time, emerging urban centers like Teotihuacan, El Mirador, and Tikal exhibited sacred programs conceptually similar to Monte Albán's. These programs involved the layout of public architecture and iconography showing the relationship between nobles and the sacred, especially as activated through the sacrifice of war captives (Ashmore 1989; Freidel 1986; Freidel and Schele 1988; Schele and Freidel 1990; Sugiyama 1993). Oaxaca Valley nobles were thus not only engaged with their own followers in a negotiated discourse on the sacred, but also with elites from many parts of Mesoamerica.

Conclusions

Practice theory with its emphasis on active, knowledgeable agents and the intrasocietal dynamics of social change provides a more sophisticated approach to understanding historical transformations such as the founding of Monte Albán than more passive/externalist accounts (see Clark, this volume). By considering the interplay of agency and structure, and by locating the agency of commoners, the model developed here – while admittedly hypothetical – provides a richer and more human-centered view of the social changes in Oaxaca between 700 and 100 BC. An important advantage of an agency perspective is that it peoples the past not just with powerful nobles, but with knowledgable commoners who also contributed to history.

The model developed here views the founding of Monte Albán as an outcome of struggle over human, material, and symbolic resources that structured power relations, especially a set of fundamental sacred propositions embodied in Mesoamerican creation myths. The outcome of this struggle included profound changes in the social construction of agency involving alterations in social categories such as commoner, elite, enemy, community, and faction. By repositioning themselves relative to the sacred, through a new set of sacrificial principles and practices, elites and commoners, first at San José Mogote and later at Monte Albán, negotiated a new body of knowledge through which agency and power were constructed.

The events leading to the founding of Monte Albán began with the development of new ritual practices to deal strategically with immediate contingencies in the lives of people. Elites struggled to develop new ways of attracting coalitions of commoner supporters, while commoners sought to resist excessive demands by the nobility and to align themselves with those elites who would provide material and ritual benefits. The nobles that began to perform human sacrifice during the Rosario phase at San José Mogote were creatively changing the cultural principles and social practices that largely constituted power relations. Yet the development of human sacrifice should not be viewed simply as a calculated response by nobles at San José Mogote to deal with a political crisis triggered by increasing commoner resistance as well as inter-elite and factional competition. Innovations in sacrificial principles and practices were developed as an accommodation to commoner resistance to elite demands for goods and labor based on pre-existing forms of sacrificial power. Human sacrifice provided a potent new means of activating *peé* on the behalf of all people. The cultural rules of the late Middle Formative that privileged elite ritual practices, as well as the relative disadvantage that commoners had with respect to social, religious, and material resources allowed elites to monopolize the practice of human sacrifice. Commoners, however, could communicate with the sacred by providing materials and labor as forms of sacrifice to the community as well as to the nobility.

Monte Albán was founded, in part, as a symbol of the altered sacred covenant as well as an arena for the performance of the new human sacrificial rituals engendered by these ideological changes. Commoners were drawn to Monte Albán because this change in the sacred covenant spoke to their interests as well as those of the elite. While nobles probably led the faction that founded Monte Albán, it was commoner labor that built the ceremonial center. Commoners, however, were contributing to their own subordination by constructing the buildings that housed the institutions and sacred practices that would come to embody a dominant ideology (see Pauketat, this volume). Human sacrifice and the more general appropriation of sacred ideas, institutions, and practices by nobles altered the ideological aspects of the sacred covenant and increased the power of elites to attract followers, mobilize material resources, defeat competitors, and interact with the sacred.

Practice theory also helps us understand the unintended consequences of small-scale actions for which no one can take credit. Unintended consequences of the actions of both elites and commoners at the end of the Formative probably included the development of the first city in the Mexican highlands, population growth, craft and military specialization, markets, the separation of noble and commoner identities, and perhaps many of the administrative changes that led to the formation of a state polity. Like many key developments in human history, the emergence of Monte Albán as a city and as a state capital could not have been forseen by the site's founders.

Acknowledgments

I would like to thank the following people for comments on earlier drafts of this chapter: John Clark, Marcia-Anne Dobres, David Freidel, Byron Hamann, Ian Hodder, Catherine Howard, Scott Hutson, John Janusek, John Monaghan, John E. Robb, and Marcus Winter. Figure 7.4 was prepared by Hugo Antonio Domínguez and Juan Cruz Pascal. I would especially like to thank Marcia-Anne Dobres and John Robb for inviting me to participate in this volume.

Notes

1　Marcus and Flannery (1996: 125) disagree with the Oaxaca Valley Settlement Pattern Project (Kowalewski *et al.* 1989: 72–7) on the size of Rosario phase settlement at San José Mogote. The former estimate that the Rosario phase community covered 60–65 ha.
2　The glyph on Monument 3 would also be the earliest example of hieroglyphic writing and the ritual calendar if it dates to the late Rosario phase. Writing and the calendar represent other innovations in ritual ideas and practices that were developed by nobles at this time (Joyce and Winter 1996: 36).

Bibliography

Acosta, J. G. 1965. "Preclassic and Classic Architecture of Oaxaca," in *Handbook of Middle American Indians, vol. 3: Archaeology of Southern Mesoamerica, Part 2*, ed. R. Wauchope and G. R. Willey, pp. 814–36. University of Texas Press, Austin.

Angulo, V., J. 1987. "The Chalcatzingo Reliefs: An Iconographic Analysis," in *Ancient Chacatzingo*, ed. D. C. Grove, pp. 132–58. University of Texas Press, Austin.

Archer, M. S. 1996. *Culture and Agency*. Cambridge University Press, Cambridge UK.

Ashmore, W. 1989. "Construction and Cosmology: Politics and Ideology in Lowland Maya Settlement Patterns," in *Word and Image in Maya Culture: Explorations in Language, Writing, and Representation*, ed. W. F. Hanks and D. S. Rice, pp. 272–86. University of Utah Press, Salt Lake City.

—— 1991. "Site-Planning Principles and Concepts of Directionality Among the Ancient Maya." *Latin American Antiquity* 2: 199–226.

Balkansky, A. K. 1997. "Archaeological Settlement Patterns of the Sola Valley, Oaxaca, Mexico." *Mexicon* 19(1): 12–18.

Bell, J. 1992. "On Capturing Agency in Theories About Prehistory," in *Representations in Archaeology*, ed. J.-C. Gardin and C. S. Peebles, pp. 30–55. Indiana University Press, Bloomington.

Blanton, R. E. 1978. *Monte Albán: Settlement Patterns at the Ancient Zapotec Capital*. Academic Press, New York.

Blanton, R. E., S. A. Kowalewski, G. Feinman, and J. Appel 1993. *Ancient Mesoamerica: A Comparison of Change in Three Regions*. 2nd edn. Cambridge University Press, Cambridge UK.

Boone, E. (ed.) 1984. *Ritual Human Sacrifice in Mesoamerica*. Dumbarton Oaks, Washington, D.C.

Bourdieu, P. 1977. *Outline of a Theory of Practice*. Cambridge University Press, Cambridge UK.

Brumfiel, E. M. 1992. "Distinguished Lecture in Archaeology: Breaking and Entering the Ecosystem – Gender, Class, and Faction Steal the Show." *American Anthropologist* 94(3): 551–67.

Brumfiel, E. M. and J. W. Fox (eds) 1994. *Factional Competition and Political Development in the New World*. Cambridge University Press, Cambridge.

Byland, B. E. and J. M. D. Pohl 1994. *In the Realm of 8 Deer*. University of Oklahoma Press, Norman.

Cahn, R. and M. Winter 1993. "The San José Mogote *Danzante*." *Indiana* 13: 39–64.

Caso, A. 1947. "Caneldario y Escritura de las Antiguas Culturas de Monte Albán." *Obras Completas de Miguel Othón de Mendizábal* 1: 116–43.

Caspary, W. R. 1993. "New Psychoanalytic Perspectives on the Causes of War." *Political Psychology* 14(3): 417–46.

Clark, J. E., R. D. Hansen, and T. Pérez n.d. *Maya Genesis: Towards an Origin Narrative of Maya Civilization*. Manuscript in possession of the author.

Coe, M. D. 1962. *Mexico*. Praeger, New York.

Conrad, G. W. and A. A. Demarest 1984. *Religion and Empire: The Dynamics of Aztec and Inca Expansionism*. Cambridge University Press, Cambridge UK.

Drennan, R. D. 1976a. "Religion and Social Evolution in Formative Mesoamerica," in *The Early Mesoamerican Village*, ed. K. V. Flannery, pp. 345–68. Academic Press, New York.

—— 1976b. *Fábrica San José and Middle Formative Society in the Valley of Oaxaca*. Prehistory and Human Ecology of the Valley of Oaxaca, vol. 4, Memoirs of the University of Michigan Museum of Anthropology no. 8, Ann Arbor.

—— 1983 "Monte Albán I and II Settlement in the Mountain Survey Zone between the Valleys of Oaxaca and Nochixtlán," in *The Cloud People: Divergent Evolution of the Zapotec and Mixtec Civilizations*, ed. K. V. Flannery and J. Marcus, pp. 110–11. Academic Press, New York.

Earle, T. K. 1978. *Economic and Social Organization of a Complex Chiefdom: The Halelea District, Kaua'i Hawaii*. Museum of Anthropology, University of Michigan Anthropological Papers No. 64, Ann Arbor.

—— 1991. "The Evolution of Chiefdoms," in *Chiefdoms: Power, Economy, and Ideology*, pp. 1–15. Cambridge University Press, Cambridge UK.

Feinman, G. 1991. "Demography, Surplus, and Inequality: Early Political Formations in Highland Mesoamerica," in *Chiefdoms: Power, Economy, and Ideology*, ed. T. K. Earle, pp. 229–62. Cambridge University Press, Cambridge UK.

Feinman, G. M. and L. M. Nicholas 1990. "At the Margins of the Monte Albán State: Settlement Patterns in the Ejutla Valley, Oaxaca, Mexico." *Latin American Antiquity* 1(3): 216–46.

Feinman, G. M., R. E. Blanton, and S. A. Kowalewski 1984. "Market System Development in the Prehispanic Valley of Oaxaca, Mexico," in *Trade and Exchange in Early Mesoamerica*, ed.K. G. Hirth, pp. 157–78. University of New Mexico Press, Albuquerque.

Flannery, K. V. 1976a. "Contextual Analysis of Ritual Paraphernalia from Formative Oaxaca," in *The Early Mesoamerican Village*, ed. K. V. Flannery, pp. 333–45. Academic Press, New York.

—— (ed.) 1976b. *The Early Mesoamerican Village*. Academic Press, New York.

Flannery, K. V. and J. Marcus 1983a. "The Growth of Site Hierarchies in the Valley of Oaxaca: Part

I," in *The Cloud People: Divergent Evolution of the Zapotec and Mixtec Civilizations*, ed. K. V. Flannery and J. Marcus, pp. 53–64. Academic Press, New York.

—— 1983b. "The Rosario Phase and the Origins of Monte Albán I," in *The Cloud People: Divergent Evolution of the Zapotec and Mixtec Civilizations*, ed. K. V. Flannery and J. Marcus, pp. 74–7. Academic Press, New York.

Freidel, D. A. 1986. "Maya Warfare: An Example of Peer–Polity Interaction," in *Peer Polity Interaction and Socio-Political Change*, ed. C. Renfrew and J. F. Cherry, pp. 93–108. Cambridge University Press, Cambridge UK.

Freidel, D. A. and L. Schele 1988. "Kingship in the Late Preclassic Maya Lowlands." *American Anthropologist* 90(3): 547–67.

Gero, J. M. and M. W. Conkey (eds) 1991. *Engendering Archaeology: Women and Prehistory*. Blackwell, Oxford.

Giddens, A. 1979. *Central Problems in Social Theory*. University of California Press, Berkeley.

—— 1984. *The Constitution of Society: Outline of the Theory of Structuration*. University of California Press, Berkeley.

Grove, D. C. 1987. "Torches, Knuckle Dusters, and the Legitimization of Formative Period Rulership." *Mexicon* 9(3): 60–6.

Grove, D. C. and J. Angulo V 1987. "A Catalog and Description of Chalcatzingo's Monuments," in *Ancient Chalcatzingo*, ed. D. C. Grove, pp. 114–31. University of Texas Press, Austin.

Grove, D. C. and S. D. Gillespie 1992. "Ideology and Evolution at the Pre–State Level: Formative Period Mesoamerica," in *Ideology and Precolumbian Civilizations*, ed. A. A. Demarest and G. W. Conrad, pp. 15–36. School of American Research Press, Sante Fe.

Hamann, B. n.d. *The Meaning of the Past and the Morality of the Present: Indigenous Mesoamerican Archaeology*. Manuscript in possession of the author.

Hodder, I. 1991. *Reading the Past*. 2nd edn. Cambridge University Press, Cambridge UK.

Joyce, A. A. 1997. "Ideology, Power, and State Formation in Oaxaca," in *Emergence and Change in Early Urban Societies*, ed. L. Manzanilla, pp. 133–68. Plenum Press, New York.

Joyce, A. A. and R. G. Mueller 1997. "Prehispanic Human Ecology of the Río Verde Drainage Basin." *World Archaeology* 29(1): 75–94.

Joyce, A. A. and M. Winter 1996. "Ideology, Power, and Urban Society in Prehispanic Oaxaca." *Current Anthropology* 37(1): 33–86.

Joyce, R. A., R. Edging, K. Lorenz, and S. D. Gillespie 1991. "Olmec Bloodletting: An Iconographic Study," in *Sixth Palenque Roundtable 1986*, ed. M. G. Robertson, pp. 143–50. University of Oklahoma Press, Norman.

Kertzer, D. 1988. *Ritual, Politics, and Power*. Yale University Press, New Haven.

King, M. B. 1988. *Mixtec Political Ideology: Historical Metaphors and the Poetics of Political Symbolism*. Unpublished Ph.D. dissertation, Department of Anthropology, University of Michigan, Ann Arbor.

King, S. M. 1997. *Early and Middle Formative Figurines from the Valley of Oaxaca*. Paper presented at the 61st annual meeting of the Society for American Archaeology, Nashville.

Kowalewski, S. A., G. Feinman, L. Finsten, and R. E. Blanton 1991. "Pre-Hispanic Ballcourts from the Valley of Oaxaca, Mexico," in *The Mesoamerican Ballgame*, ed. V. L. Scarborough and D. R. Wilcox, pp. 25–44. University of Arizona Press, Tucson.

Kowalewski, S. A., G. Feinman, L. Finsten, R. E. Blanton, and L. M. Nicholas 1989. *Monte Albán's Hinterland, Part II: Prehispanic Settlement Patterns in Tlacolula, Etla, and Ocotlán, the Valley of Oaxaca, Mexico*. Memoirs of the University of Michigan Museum of Anthropology no. 23, Ann Arbor.

Marcus, J. 1976. "The Iconography of Militarism at Monte Albán and Neighboring Sites in the Valley of Oaxaca," in *The Origins of Religious Art and Iconography in Preclassic Mesoamerica*, ed. H. B. Nicholson, pp. 123–39. University College Los Angeles, Latin American Center, Los Angeles.

—— 1989. "Zapotec Chiefdoms and the Nature of Formative Religions," in *Regional Perspectives on the Olmec*, ed. R. J. Sharer and D. C. Grove, pp. 148–97. Cambridge University Press, Cambridge UK.

—— 1992. *Mesoamerican Writing Systems: Propaganda, Myth, and History in Four Ancient Civilizations.* Princeton University Press, Princeton.

Marcus, J. and K. V. Flannery 1994. "Ancient Zapotec Ritual and Religion: An Application of the Direct Historical Approach," in *The Ancient Mind: Elements of Cognitive Archaeology*, ed. C. Renfrew and E .B. W. Zubrow, pp. 55–74. Cambridge University Press, Cambridge UK.

—— 1996. *Zapotec Civilization.* Thames and Hudson, London.

Markman, C. W. 1981. *Prehispanic Settlement Dynamics in Central Oaxaca, Mexico.* Vanderbilt University Publications in Anthropology no. 26. Nashville.

Martínez López, C., M. Winter, and P. Antonio Juárez 1996. "Entierros humanos del Proyecto Especial Monte Albán," in *Entierros Humanos de Monte Albán*, ed. M. Winter, pp. 79–247. Contribución no. 7 del Proyecto Especial Monte Albán 1992–1994, Oaxaca.

Masson, M. A., H. Orr, and J. Urcid 1992. *Building Dedication, Nagual Transformation, and Captive Sacrifice at Monte Albán: Programs of Sacred Geography.* Paper presented at the 57th annual meeting of the Society for American Archaeology, Pittsburgh.

McGuire, R. H. 1992. *A Marxist Archaeology.* Academic Press, San Diego.

Miller, A. G. 1995. *The Painted Tombs of Oaxaca, Mexico.* Cambridge University Press, Cambridge UK.

Monaghan, J. 1990. "Sacrifice, Death, and the Origins of Agriculture in the Codex Vienna." *American Antiquity* 55(3): 559–69.

—— 1994. *Sacrifice and Power in Mixtec Kingdoms.* Paper presented at the 59th annual meeting of the Society for American Archaeology, Anaheim.

—— 1995. *The Covenants with Earth and Rain.* University of Oklahoma Press, Norman.

—— in press. "Theology and History in the Study of Mesoamerican Religions," in *Handbook of Middle American Indians: Ethnology Supplement*, ed. V. Bricker and J. Monaghan. University of Texas Press, Austin.

Orr, H. S. 1994. *The Viborón Frieze and Sacred Geography at Monte Albán.* Paper presented at the 59th annual meeting of the Society for American Archaeology, Anaheim.

—— 1997 *Power Games in the Late Formative Valley of Oaxaca: The Ballplayer Sculptures at Dainzú.* Unpublished Ph.D. dissertation, Department of Art and Art History, University of Texas, Austin.

Ortner, S. B. 1984. "Theory in Anthropology since the Sixties." *Comparative Studies in Society and History* 26(1): 126–66.

Parsons, E. C. 1936. *Mitla, Town of the Souls, and other Zapotec-Speaking Pueblos of Oaxaca, Mexico.* University of Chicago Press, Chicago.

Peeler, D. E. and M. Winter 1992. "Mesoamerican Site Orientations and their Relationship to the 260-day Ritual Period." *Notas Mesoamericanas* 14: 37–62.

Redmond, E. M. 1994. "External Warfare and the Internal Politics of Northern South American Tribes and Chiefdoms," in *Factional Competition and Political Development in the New World*, ed. E. M. Brumfiel and J. W. Fox, pp. 44–54. Cambridge University Press, Cambridge UK.

Reilly, F. K., III 1989. "The Shaman in Transformation Pose: A Study of the Theme of Rulership in Olmec Art." *The Record, The Magazine of the Princeton Art Museum* 48(2): 4–21.

—— 1996. "Art, Ritual, and Rulership in the Olmec World," in *The Olmec World: Ritual and Rulership*, ed. E. P. Benson, pp. 27–45. Art Museum, Princeton University, Princeton.

Schele, L. and D. A. Freidel 1990. *A Forest of Kings: The Untold Story of the Ancient Maya.* Morrow, New York.

Schele, L. and M. E. Miller 1986. *The Blood of Kings, Dynasty and Ritual in Maya Art.* Kimbell Art Museum, Fort Worth.

Scott, J. C. 1990. *Domination and the Arts of Resistance.* Yale University Press, New Haven.

Scott, J. F. 1978. *The Danzantes of Monte Albán. Part II: Catalogue.* Dumbarton Oaks, Studies in Pre-Columbian Art and Archaeology no. 19, Washington, D.C.

Sedat, D. W. and R. J. Sharer 1984. *Archaeological Investigations in the Salama Valley, Baja Verapaz, Guatemala.* University Museum Monographs. University of Pennsylvania, Philadelphia.

Sewell, W. H., Jr. 1992. "A Theory of Structure: Duality, Agency, and Transformation." *American Journal of Sociology* 98(1): 1–29.

Shanks, M. and C. Tilley 1988. *Social Theory and Archaeology*. University of New Mexico Press, Albuquerque.

Spencer, C. S. 1982. *The Cuicatlán Cañada and Monte Albán*. Academic Press, New York.

Sugiyama, S. 1993. "Worldview Materialized in Teotihuacán, Mexico." *Latin American Antiquity* 4(2): 103–29.

Taggart, J. M. 1983. *Nahuat Myth and Social Structure*. University of Texas Press, Austin.

Tedlock, D. 1986. *Popol Vuh*. Simon and Schuster, New York.

Urcid, J. 1994. "Un Sistema de Nomenclatura para los Monolitos Grabados y los Materiales con Inscripciones de Monte Albán," in *Escritura Zapoteca Prehispánica*, ed. M. Winter, pp. 53–79. Contribución no. 4 del Proyecto Especial Monte Albán 1992–1994, Oaxaca.

Whalen, M. E. 1981 *Excavations at Santo Domingo Tomaltepec: Evolution of a Formative Community in the Valley of Oaxaca, Mexico*. Prehistory and Human Ecology of the Valley of Oaxaca, vol. 6, Memoirs of the University of Michigan Museum of Anthropology no.12, Ann Arbor.

Winter, M. 1972. *Tierras Largas: A Formative Community in the Valley of Oaxaca, Mexico*. Unpublished Ph.D. dissertation, Department of Anthropology, University of Arizona, Tucson.

—— 1994 "El Proyecto Especial Monte Albán 1992–1994: Antecedentes, Intervenciones y Perspectivas," in *Monte Albán: Estudios Recientes* ed. M. Winter, pp. 1–24. Contribución no. 2 del Proyecto Especial Monte Albán 1992–1994, Oaxaca.

Winter, M. and A. A. Joyce 1994. *Early Political Development at Monte Albán: Evidence from Recent Excavations*. Paper presented at the 93rd annual meeting of the American Anthropological Association, Atlanta.

8 Towards a better explanation of hereditary inequality

A critical assessment of natural and historic human agents

John E. Clark

My point of departure in this chapter is the optimistic belief that better explanations of phenomena are both desirable and possible. If so, it necessarily follows that some explanations are better than others, that it is possible to make such distinctions, and that we ought to do so. Here I attempt to make such a judgment between rival explanations for the origins of hereditary inequality as seen from the perspectives of evolutionary ecology and practice or action theory. The obstacles involved in comparing explanations are formidable, as different theories are incommensurate in some basic assumptions, language, methods, and specifications of critical evidence. The notion of "better" presumes an objective standard, or exterior reality, to which rival explanations may be compared and evaluated, the better explanation being the one more closely approximating the objective standard. But the "reality" of any given phenomenon is generally part of explanatory debates and is largely defined by the theory brought to bear on it.

In evaluating rival explanations, the critical decision is the choice of standard by which to measure each. I suggest a useful criterion for explanations of social phenomena is their treatment of human agency. How does each explanation conceptualize human agents? Are they believable human beings with credible powers who could have made significant decisions in their own worlds, or are they mindless marionettes manipulated by exterior forces? If they ignore real humans, explanations are deficient, regardless of any other merits. On a related matter, the standard criterion of explanatory adequacy (the "fit" between primal data and models) is of no concern here. The critical data for the test cases considered here could easily be explained in either theoretical framework. One's commitment to a certain mode of explanation precedes, and is typically independent of, any given data set. Thus, considerations of specific archaeological or ethnographic data cannot alone resolve the question of the relative merits or utilities of the different theories. To make such an assessment, it is necessary to examine the foundational assumptions of the theories in question and compare them to an independent standard of social action and agency.

I am committed to the proposition that adequate explanations of human phenomena such as the origins of hereditary inequality must include individual human agents as part of the explanation. Within the group of theories meeting this requirement, it should be possible to evaluate each according the standard just mentioned. I attempt such an evaluation here of three different explanatory models for the origins of hereditary inequality and focus on the role accorded individual agents in each. These explanations are representative of two currently popular perspectives of social change: evolutionary ecology and practice or action theory. I first outline James Boone's (1992) evolutionary ecology explanation for the origins of social hierarchies and then Herbert Maschner and John Patton's (1996) Darwinian model of the origins of hereditary social inequality among societies of the

Northwest Coast of North America. Next, I summarize a practice model I proposed with Michael Blake (Clark 1994; Clark and Blake 1994) for the origins of hereditary inequality and rank societies in southern Mexico (I use "rank society" and "hereditary inequality" interchangeably). In attempting to assess the relative merits of each as an "agency" explanation, I examine each model's basic assumptions concerning agents, actions, and social processes.

In the following discussion, I review basic postulates of the two theoretical perspectives and specific explanations of the origins of rank society and hereditary inequality derived from each. Recourse to specific explanations highlights important features of each explanatory program. Following the summaries of the three models, the remainder of the essay evaluates the relative strengths and weaknesses of each by specifically exploring how each model conceptualizes agents in the processes giving rise to hereditary inequality. I conclude that action theories include more plausible agents than do evolutionary or Darwinian explanations and thus constitute more credible and better explanations. Given my commitment to practice theory, this conclusion should come as no surprise, but perhaps some of the arguments provided will.

The case for evolutionary ecology

The recent spate of books and essays on evolutionary ecology and Darwinian archaeology demonstrates a renewed vigor for evolutionary theorizing in the social sciences as well as a wide variety of variants to choose from (for useful summaries see Barton and Clark 1997a; Boone and Smith 1998; Kuper 1994; Maschner 1996; Mithen 1990, 1996; Moran 1990; O'Brien 1996; O'Hear 1997; Ruse 1998; Smith and Winterhalder 1992a; Teltser 1995). Rather than a single evolutionary or Darwinian theory, one is confronted with a multitude of options for making comparisons between theories and for evaluating their efficacy in explaining cultural changes. After reviewing assumptions common to theories worthy of the "evolutionary" label, I concern myself with two brands of evolutionary explanation that accord individuals some active powers in the evolutionary process. In particular, I consider Boone's (1992) optimal account for the emergence of social hierarchies and Maschner and Patton's (1996) Darwinian narrative of the origins of hereditary social inequality.

Basic assumptions

Despite striking differences (see Boone and Smith 1998), the sundry brands of evolutionary and Darwinian theory share notions of, first, variable and heritable characteristics within populations, second, natural selection, third, adaptation, and fourth, fitness. In turn, these concepts presuppose others such as competition, differential survival rates, and efficiencies of somatic design. The starting point for evolutionary explanations is to acknowledge the facts of human evolution and the process of natural selection (Ruse 1998). The human body with all of its parts, passions, and propensities (i.e., human nature) is the culled product of biological evolution. This fact is especially critical in understanding human psychology (Midgley 1978) and the evolution of the human brain and its cognitive capabilities (Mithen 1990, 1996, 1997; Ruse 1998). Over the past several million years, environmental circumstances have dictated what could constitute useful features of the primate body, mind, and psyche and, consequently, what would pass as advantageous adaptations for any particular setting. Those individual creatures better equipped for particular environments were more fit than others, meaning that they had greater chances to survive, propagate, and pass on their useful phenotypic traits to subsequent generations. Biological evolution is a blind process in which certain characteristics prove to have greater survival value than others and are selected for by environmental circumstances. In contrast to Herbert Spencer's progressive and teleological notions of social evolution, Darwinian evolution does not presuppose that the evolutionary process is progressive; rather, it is contingent on environmental circumstances (Barton and Clark 1997b: 6; Ruse 1998: 20). These basic postulates prescribe clear guidelines and expectations for all evolutionary questions. For example,

> Darwinian anthropologists think that the beliefs and values that predominate in a particular culture should be the ones that maximize reproductive success in the environment at hand. Darwinian psychologists must understand what past conditions were like, then deduce what kinds of predispositions would maximize fitness under those conditions, and finally predict the effect of the atavistic predispositions in contemporary environments.
>
> (Richerson and Boyd 1992: 87)

Explanations follow a standard argument. "Evolutionary ecology analyses typically take the form of the following question: In what environmental circumstances are the costs and benefits of behavior X such that selection would favor its evolution?" (Winterhalder and Smith 1992: 23). Bluntly stated, neo-Darwinian evolution is a solution in search of a problem. The answer to all causal questions concerning the human condition is a given, leaving the investigator the task of reconstituting the particular suite of environmental circumstances and pressures which would have selected for a particular species' characteristic.

In contrast with the traditional, cultural ecological perspective of the 1960s and 1970s, neo-Darwinian theory, as currently constituted, avoids the problem of group adaptation and benefits (or group fitness); the selective forces of biological evolution work on individuals rather than groups. Adaptive advantages of human characteristics must perforce be those of individuals (Barton and Clark 1997b: 7; Ruse 1998: 17; Smith and Winterhalder 1992b: 29–34). It follows that a focus on individuals is not only possible but is a basic requirement of evolutionary theory (Maschner and Mithen 1996). Bettinger and Richerson (1996: 227) claim that "it is surely this replacement of groups/cultures by self-interested individuals as basic units of analysis that is the most revolutionary consequence of evolutionary theory." Smith and Winterhalder (1992b: 39) argue for methodological individualism (MI) in their optimization models of decision-making in evolution; as the term implies, MI is an operational move that reduces social phenomena to the level of individuals and takes individuals as the critical point of analysis. Others argue for individual agents, agency, manipulation, morality, and free-will (Midgley 1978; Mithen 1989, 1990, 1993; O'Hear 1997; Ruse 1998). Had individuals not exhibited different behaviors and preferences in different environments, natural selection would not have been able to pick and choose from among them. Individual agency is necessary for evolutionary theory (Ruse 1998: 259); and, presumably, certain tendencies to act as independent agents were themselves selected for through the evolutionary process (Midgley 1978).

An optimal model for the origins of social hierarchies

Boone (1992) provides an elegant model for the emergence of social hierarchies based upon fundamental principles of rational optimizing behavior under certain environmental and social conditions. In decision-making, "rational choice" signifies choice of appropriate means to achieve desired ends, or means–ends thinking, but lacks specific implications about what means or ends would be appropriate in any given cultural circumstance. Boone argues that the size and structure of social groups are related to costs and benefits of group formation and the mutual self-interests of participating individuals. "Under conditions of intense competition or where unoccupied territory no longer exists, the lack of alternative strategies for individuals may promote group affiliation even in the face of extreme disad-vantage to some, perhaps most, of its members" (Boone 1992: 302). He summarizes these special conditions as follows:

> If local patches are about equal in quality and in the likelihood of falling short in a given year, and all patches do not usually fall short in the same year, systems of exchange of foodstuffs and valuables would be expected to remain on a more or less reciprocal basis indefinitely. If, however, some patches are of consistently better quality, particularly in the sense that they are subject to shortfall less frequently, the flow of valuables and foodstuffs becomes asymmetrical . . . Under these conditions a series of asymmetric relations between less risk-prone and more risk-prone patches could occur, resulting in the development of patron-client relationships (O'Shea 1981). Hence, local variation in patch quality, particularly in terms of levels of susceptibility to harvest failure in areas that are already characterized by a relatively high degree of risk, should be a major factor in the formation of relations of inequality, resulting in some degree of social stratification
>
> (Boone 1992: 307)

The critical factors here are, first, the character of subsistence resource patches and their relative susceptibilities to failure, second, an implicit assumption of lack of options for mov-ing to other resource patches, and third, the ability of individuals to control and benefit from the best and most reliable patches. Control of the best resources in a patchy environ-ment translates into control over exchanged valuables and eventually over the people con-signed to the poorer and more risk-prone resources. These conditions parallel remarkably those Carneiro (1970) proposed for the origin of the state. If competition over resources is intense, and if conditions of environmental or social circumscription apply (meaning that individuals do not have the option of leaving), then group cooperation guided by principles of social hierarchy will emerge, even though it is disadvantageous to those of lower status. Given these conditions, dominant individuals are able to exploit the situation of differen-tial access to resources and to control high social statuses. These theoretical principles of resource sharing and competition are evident in the concrete case of the emergence of rank societies in the Northwest Coast.

The origins of hereditary social inequality on the Northwest Coast

The beginning date for the emergence of hereditary inequality and its institutionalized consequent, rank society, on the Northwest Coast is debatable. The earliest evidence of an "elaborate burial complex" dates to about 1000 BC, but there is no clear evidence of "large house size and house size variation" before AD 500 (Maschner 1991: 929). One can make a case that the process was a protracted one and that ascribed differences in the social rank of lineages and lineage leaders was not fully in place until about AD 500, or perhaps as early as AD 200 (Maschner and Patton 1996: 99). Before AD 200 – 500, the archaeological record demonstrates, first, the presence of small villages, second, a reliance on a range of abundant marine and terrestrial resources, third, the elaborate burial complex just mentioned, fourth, the first appearance of labrets, jade adze blades, ground stone implements, shaman mirrors, zoomorphic art, and fifth, "differential distributions of grave goods, which include copper, shell, and amber ornaments" (Maschner 1991: 927). Recovered skeletal remains of individuals at some sites also "show evidence of decapitation, depressed skull fractures and forearm parrying fractures, suggesting intense conflict and aggression" (ibid.). Evidence of large villages and large corporate group dwellings is lacking, however. With these in evidence by AD 200 – 500, Maschner argues that hereditary inequality and lineage rank were surely in place. His explanation of the causes of this development closely parallel Carneiro's (1970) conflict theory of social evolution and its links to environmental conditions of resource exploitation and circumscription.

The content of the archaeological record and reconstructions of environmental conditions provide important clues to the processes that led to the emergence of social complexity in the Northwest Coast. In his earlier study, Maschner (1991: 931) singled out the following critical factors for the process: first, "resource abundance and predictability," second, a threshold of population size and density, third, an "uneven" distribution of resources in time and space, possibly aided and abetted by some environmental circumscription, fourth, social circumscription that prevented group fissioning, and fifth, "the opportunity for resource and political control" based upon (sixth) a particular human psychology of "hierarchical striving" (an assumption taken from Sahlins 1959). Maschner (1991: 931) asserted "that in all societies some individuals strive for status and political advantage." "When all of these conditions are met, leaders will arise from the largest lineages or kin groups" (ibid.).

In their subsequent appraisal of this same archaeological case, Maschner and Patton (1996) turn to Darwinian theory to justify Maschner's initial assumption about human psychology. The human body, brain, cognitive capacities, psychological dispositions, and capacities for culture and society are viewed as products of a long evolutionary process that selected for these aggrandizing tendencies of "human nature" (for more on psychology and agency, see Cowgill, this volume). Kin selection, a concept from sociobiology, is particularly critical for the process of emerging social complexity. It predicts that individuals will show graduated altruistic behavior according to degrees of biological relation; one sacrifices first for one's siblings and children and only secondarily for more distantly related persons. "The value of investment in each offspring [is] measured by marginal change in reproductive value, that is, by marginal change in expected contribution to the future gene pool" (Frank 1998: 36).

> Kin selection provides a theoretical foundation for a study of inheritable social inequality, properly based at the level of individual status striving. A model based on kin selection would predict that kinship be the basic unit of social organization because it provides a nexus for shared interests.
>
> (Maschner and Patton 1996: 94)

The Darwinian perspective also privileges competition over reproductive opportunities or fitness. The factors of dense, circumscribed villages coupled with inter-village warfare and high levels of competition set the stage for dominant individuals from the larger lineages within villages to take women from the smaller lineages, as in the pattern known for the Yanomamo tribes of northern jungles of South America (Maschner and Patton 1996: 95). For autocratic power to emerge, it is necessary to have large, circumscribed villages, dominant lineages and leaders, and the "ability to coerce" (ibid.: 95, 100). In contrast to Boone's model, Maschner and Patton note that control over economic resources or production and redistribution is not necessary. "What is required is a means by which a number of distantly or unrelated corporate groups are forced to live in the same community" (ibid.: 91). The size of one's lineage, and the size and lineage composition of villages, are the vital variables. One's ability to coerce others is a direct function of one's access to kin and varies as a function of group size. "The formation of corporate groups is probably the fundamental organizational change that leads to hereditary social inequalities" (ibid.: 100). The whole purpose of status striving is to increase the number of persons in one's group and thus one's power over them.

> Warfare, because of competition for kinsmen and in the defense of status, is probably the ultimate explanation for the development of multi-kin-group sedentary villages. We see the development of sedentary villages as the only basic necessity for the formation of hereditary status differences. Once independent kin groups are forced to reside in the same place, the opportunity exists for the headmen of the largest lineages to put themselves in positions of authority and get away with it. This lineage-based status is a fundamental tenet of kin selection.
>
> (Maschner and Patton 1996: 101)

This model for the evolution of ascribed social statuses for the Northwest Coast is an interesting blend of conflict theory and neo-Darwinianism. Maschner and Patton mention one necessary condition (sedentism) but stress sufficient conditions: "hereditary social status will develop everywhere the social and environmental circumstances will allow it" (Maschner and Patton 1996: 101). "It must be assumed that social ranking and political complexity will arise, whenever and wherever it is adaptively possible" (ibid.: 102). If it can happen, it will happen. This last assumption does not appear necessarily implicated in Darwinian thinking about contingent evolutionary trajectories. Whatever proves to be the case, Maschner and Patton's explanation of the origins of hereditary inequality on the Northwest Coast is audacious and claims tremendous explanatory power. If institutions of rank truly emerge whenever and wherever possible, then the explanatory chore left to archaeology, wherever confronted with evidence for rank society, is to determine the special environmental conditions that provided the sufficient opportunity. This view differs markedly from expectations arising from practice theory.

The case for history

Under the rubric of "history," I consider brands of action and practice theory which conceive of human agents as historically contingent and constituted by antecedent cultural practices and events. As with evolutionary theories, there are a variety of action theories to choose from. These are sometimes called "agency" theories because action is attributed to specific individual or group agents, but "agency theory" is a misnomer. There is no theory dedicated solely to agency because, by definition, agency implicates the broader canvass of society and culture. Any theory that deals with individuals and individual choices can be considered an "agency" theory because agents are involved, but such usage is counterproductive and blurs rather than clarifies critical distinctions, as just noted with evolutionary ecology models. Agency is an inter-subjective social phenomenon mostly concerned with the conditions and possibilities of choice and action.

Basic assumptions

The model of the origins of rank society described below is based principally on Anthony Giddens' (1979, 1984) "structuration" theory and Margaret Archer's (1995, 1996) theory of "morphogenesis." These action theories ignore biological evolution and focus instead on the social construction of social structures, culture, and agency and their modifications through time. Society, culture, practices, norms, beliefs, and so on are all socially and historically contingent because they are products of cultural-historic processes, not casual factors of time and circumstances as described above. Every individual is born and socialized into a socio-cultural system. Inculcated norms and practices provide constraints and opportunities for acting in the world, but these are also modified by and through human action. Action is motivated, intentional, and based upon various degrees of knowledge concerning the cultural norms and social mores of a given system. One's abilities and desires to act in the world are partially determined (channeled by cultural constraints), but not entirely so. Action and practice theories view the continuity or change of social institutions as dependent upon numerous decisions made by individual actors. Therefore, as models of social reproduction, these theories view social continuity and social change as equally problematic because both depend on the unpredictable actions of human agents and unintended consequences of such actions. Practice theories require a model that accords equal weight to social structure, culture, and individual agency, with special attention to time (Archer 1995). In any given circumstance, each actor has agency, meaning the power to have acted in another way (as in Sinclair, this volume; but see Gero for a critique of this position). The ability "to have done otherwise" when confronted with an opportunity for choice is the measure of one's agency and free will (see Honderich 1993; Moore 1912).

Actors have various degrees of freedom, under any given circumstances, to act in ways they deem appropriate, and for whatever reasons motivate them. They are not free, however, to choose the consequences of their actions. Once one option is chosen over another, logical and material consequences follow, and these become part of the historic, antecedent conditions for subsequent action. As with evolutionary ecology, outcomes of social action are contingent and not necessarily progressive. Agents act out of perceived self-interests, which can differ radically from one agent to another, but are not necessarily successful in bringing about the goals they desire. In short, most variants of practice theory follow Karl Marx's dictum of the historic process: "Men make their own history, but they do not make it just as they please; they do not make it under circumstances chosen by themselves, but under circumstances directly found, given and transmitted from the past" (Marx 1969: 15; see Dobres and Robb, this volume). Human agents make history while at the same time they are molded by antecedent practices. This recursiveness of social reproduction has novel implications for explaining the transition from egalitarian to rank societies.

The origins of rank societies in Southern Mesoamerica

Recent archaeological information from southernmost Mexico suggests that the earliest fully sedentary villages and rank societies developed there between 1600 – 1400 BC (uncalibrated). Michael Blake and I argue that the development of hereditary rank distinctions in this region was "the outcome of competition among political actors vying for prestige and social esteem" (Clark and Blake 1994: 17). We refer to such actors as "aggrandizers": individuals motivated for various personal reasons to accumulate and deploy surpluses in building their reputations in efforts to draw followers, clients, and other sycophants into their orbits of influence. It is important to note that our aggrandizer model is necessarily an agency model, but agency does not imply aggrandizing behavior or assumptions of "extreme self-interest" (Polly Weissner, personal communication, 1999). Our model for ranking implicates in the process the following factors and circumstances:

- a suite of environmental conditions necessary for the production of surpluses
- traditional technologies and subsistence practices
- a minimal threshold of population size and density
- social interaction among peoples and groups within a small region
- antecedent cultural beliefs and perceptions of humanity, nature, and the cosmos
- multitudes of agents, including status seekers, those motivated to follow them, and wives, children, relatives, and friends of each
- logical implications of gift-giving
- luck and historical contingencies.

We view the origins of hereditary inequality and ranking as historically contingent on cultural conditions and decisions made by individual agents rather than a necessary consequence of ecological processes or an outcome of premeditated, unbridled free will. Environmental, technological, cultural, social, and psychological conditions were all critical to the process but were not deterministic, either singly or in concert. Aggrandizer activities fundamental to the emergence of rank society in Mesoamerica may have included sponsorship of feasts and drinking parties; production of special craft goods (e.g., ceramic and stone vessels, stone jewelry) used as gifts; construction of special buildings and facilities; and patronage of sports events (Clark and Blake 1994). We argue that the first ceramics in lowland, southern Mesoamerica owe their elegant appearance and form to aggrandizer sponsorship of ceramic specialists for the express purpose of making vessels for drinking rituals or parties (see Clark and Gosser 1995), and we suspect that highland cultigens such as corn and beans may have been brought into this lowland environment for making special foods or beverages to be served on such occasions (see Blake *et al.* 1992). The recent discovery of an early ball court (Hill *et al.* 1998) at the largest community in the region leads us to suspect that aggrandizers were also involved in public works projects and that they organized competitive games. It is significant that the ball court was constructed next door to a domestic structure that soon after was literally elevated and rebuilt as the community's first chiefly residence (Blake 1991; Clark 1994; see Joyce, this volume, for a possible Mayan parallel).

The mechanism that allowed aggrandizers to be successful in their competitive endeavors was the "spirit of the gift" (Mauss 1950). Aggrandizers spent their lives crafting reputations by providing gifts and favors for others, with their principal remuneration being the praise, esteem, and loyalty returned by sycophants. Much of their prestige and fame was a logical compensation of under-reciprocated gift-giving; indebted recipients of an aggrandizer's generosity became socially obligated to him. By such a simple means, the social valuations of various persons began to change. The transition from aggrandizers to hereditary chiefs was a result of changing perceptions and village attitudes that ensued from chronic and routinized differences in achieved statuses between aggrandizers and other villagers (but see Joyce, this volume, for a different scenario). Initially, this may have been simple gratitude for favors or services rendered, but it eventually reached new heights with changing notions of personhood and heritable characteristics of social worth. People eventually came to believe that some villagers were born better than others.

A comparison of explanations

Several scholars have commented on an apparent convergence of interests and concepts between evolution and action explanations (see Maschner and Mithen 1996; Mithen 1989, 1990). As is apparent in the preceding models of hereditary inequality, both theories deal with similar explanatory problems, at similar scales of analysis, and rely on concepts of rational decision-making, individual strategies, and agency. I am more impressed, however, with deep differences underlying the superficial convergence of language and concepts. Although both theories appear to share many elements and assumptions, the touted similarities are more apparent than real. In the following discussion, I consider four dimensions of the preceding explanations as they concern, first, basic concepts related to action, agents, and society, second, perceptions of the explanatory problem, third, explanatory goals, and fourth, research methods and analyses.

On basic terms and concepts

A common thread uniting the three models for the origins of hereditary inequality is their apparent commitment to individual- or agent-centered explanations. Do the individuals in these accounts share the same sorts of active powers? Asked differently, are they the same sorts of agents? The individuals in Boone's behavioral ecology narrative are MI (methodological individualism) agents particularly adept at means–ends decision-making, game-theoretic strategies, and efficient optimizing of caloric resources. In contrast, the principal individuals of Maschner and Patton's Darwinian account appear to be quite a different sort; the primary factors are psychological tendencies of lineage leaders to compete and coerce others to do their bidding. Emphasis is on personality, as biologically determined, rather than optimal decisions for maximizing fitness at the expense of weaker individuals. Brain opposes brawn in these disparate evolutionary accounts. But in each instance, requisite cognitive and physiological characteristics are seen as products of a long evolutionary process.

In our practice narrative, Blake and I describe aggrandizing individuals who appear similar to the status strivers described by Maschner and Patton. However, because of the antecedent, egalitarian social circumstances of the process, we see aggrandizers as limited in their pursuits of self interests to non-coercive options, many requiring creative social action. We essentially ignore the biology and fitness skills of the various agents and stress rational (logical means–ends thinking) and creative decision-making. We do presume certain human capacities such as rational thought and egoism but avoid the hyper-rationalism of Boone's MI natural optimizers. Both models treat rationality in a similar way, but make different assumptions about knowledge and information. Optimal models are patterned on the assumptions of market economics and perfect information in market transactions, an analytically useful construct known to differ markedly from reality. In a real situation of imperfect knowledge, aggrandizers and other historic agents implicated in the origins of hereditary inequality could not rationally choose options related to the final outcome of the social process (i.e., rank society) as none of these were knowable prior to its pristine emergence.

The agents involved in the three plots for social inequality differ significantly in their abilities, powers, and deficiencies. Their agentive powers also derive from incommensurate sources. As the best approximation of hypothetical agentive powers, consider what the agents in each narrative are supposed actually to have done. In Boone's model there is no mention of active individuals nor of any specific decisions made by them. The bulk of the discussion concerns resource patches and their susceptibilities to failure. Certain resource conditions and periodicities of resource disparities give rise to "patron–client" relationships, and these, in turn, lead to "social stratification." Supposedly, differential access to low-risk resource patches favored some individuals over others, and this translated, by some unrevealed algorithm, into actual control by the favored over the less fortunate. But connections among natural agents, subsistence resources, and social control are never explicitly made, nor is there a hint that the implicated cultural category of property is problematic. The invisibility and passivity of individuals in Boone's account are all the more remarkable as it is quintessentially a rational choice model.

Individual agents are only slightly more visible in Maschner and Patton's account. These scholars stress control of kin rather than property; control of property is a consequence of social power and not its cause (Herbert Maschner, personal communication, 1999). Differential access to persons translates, in another unspecified way, into status differences and social hierarchy. Again, specific agents or actions are not mentioned. The few generic actions implied (e.g., abducting women from minor lineages, warring, and coercing) are passively attributed to dominant lineage leaders or status strivers. One reads, for example, that external circumstances forced people "to live in the same community" and that this provided opportunities "for the headmen of the largest lineages to put themselves in positions of authority and get away with it" (Maschner and Patton 1996: 100–1). Perhaps the most extraordinary thing about this claim is that it passes for an explanation rather than a research question. What undergirds these verbs? How did these Darwinian despots "put" themselves into [more?] authoritative positions, and how did they "get away" with it? The critical actions giving rise to hereditary inequality remain vague, unconvincing assertions.

Compared to these evolution explanations, the practice explanation for Mesoamerica appears positively hyperactive. This is not a consequence of manipulating the evolutionary accounts but is a true reflection of theoretical differences. Mesoamerican aggrandizers engaged in nearly frenetic (real) activity to accumulate and deploy surpluses in an endless pursuit of personal prestige. In particular, aggrandizer activities in southern Mesoamerica may have involved frequent ritual feasting and drinking, sponsorship of a multitude of crafts (mostly of prestige goods), sponsorship and direction of community building projects, and stewardship of special activities such as inter-community sporting events, all of which are specific activities, not generic functions. Gift-giving, rendering of favors, debt management, and innovations of many kinds were pursued by these aggrandizers.

In describing the actions of the "agents" of the three models, a clear disparity emerges among them. The evolutionary agents are portrayed as passive and lethargic, like lizards on a cold day. Even when pursuing lustful plunder, individuals are mentioned as recipients of their own actions rather than their authors. This passivity, I suspect, is not simply a matter of literary tastes in scientific reporting but reveals a fundamental ontic commitment to universal causality. The stark contrast of this comparison also works in the other direction. The aggrandizing agents are probably too active to be credible. They are also too-single minded and overly prescient in the same sense as Boone's MI natural agents. They just have different motives; one pursues food and the other fame. Aggrandizers appear to do a lot of thinking, calculating, and acting, but all of their efforts concern personal prestige, and the "little people" are amorphously lumped into supporting roles as various kinds of "followers" or clients. Not all of the agents matter in our account, or matter to the same degree. The aggrandizers are nearly as uni-dimensional as their evolutionary counterparts, and they are as active as ants at a picnic. A more plausible model of agents would negotiate a workable compromise between agentive lethargy and hyper-activity.

The two evolutionary accounts agree on the basic process (biological evolution) but stress different cognitive and psychological abilities. Boone's MI agents are naturalized versions of homo economicus, one-dimensional calculating machines devoid of personality and associated human characteristics. In turn, Maschner and Patton's alpha males brim with power and singular purpose but appear deficient in their abilities to conceive of alternative social actions to war and coercion. The aggrandizers proposed for Mesoamerica better combine personality and mind, but Blake and I are somewhat at a loss to account for their personal attributes, other than to ascribe them vaguely to socio-historic and evolutionary processes. To attribute aggrandizing behaviors to "human nature" would land us squarely in the evolutionary ecology camp, or at least beg the question. Such a consequence would be ultimately unsatisfying as we consider evolutionary ecology explanations to be tautologous: organisms survive because they have useful and adaptive traits, and these are adaptive and useful traits because the organism survives. Another option is to attribute aggrandizing behaviors to the natural variability of personality types within populations of sufficient size (also an evolutionary explanation). This is the option that we followed in our original model (Clark and Blake 1994; see also Hayden 1995), but I am less comfortable with this convenient assumption than is Blake because I believe personality types are profoundly influenced by cultural practices. Their cross-cultural validity remains to be established.

In summary, the agents involved in the various explanations are all deficient in some ways, and some more so than others. Practice theory tends to ignore biology and the physical embodiment of its historic agents (Joas 1996); it smuggles innate human capacities into its explanations by attributing them to "history" rather than to "evolution." Evolutionary theory reciprocates with its own primeval bias; it attributes everything of consequence to natural selection and downplays culture and historical contingencies. One explanation fits all phenomena. An even more serious problem, however, arises from evolution's recent appropriation of methodological individualism.

Neo-Darwinian models stress natural selection at the individual rather than group level. Older brands of evolutionary ecology, based upon group adaptation, have been discredited and replaced by individualistic accounts of social process. But as a view of social process, methodological individualism creates nearly as many problems as it solves. As Archer (1995) argues, MI accounts involve conflationary thinking; they attempt to construct an account of society from the aggregate of individual behaviors. But a society is more than the sum of its individual members and their behaviors; it has a reality of its own (Archer 1995; Bhaskar 1975). If the reality of society as a structure in its own right is not part of a social model, the emergent phenomena associated with it have to be derived analytically from individuals. To make this work, however, it is first necessary to implant emergent social properties in the individuals themselves, and then to extract these same social characteristics by analytic sleight-of-hand to explain the sociology and culture of the individualist aggregate. Evolutionary accounts, and some action ones too, do this by pre-loading their agents with abilities they cannot have *sui generis*. Cognitive abilities, basic morals, language, and so forth are all attributed to individuals whereas they should more properly be seen as pertaining to society and arising as emergent properties in social interaction (Archer 1995).

Two of these cultural implants were alluded to above. Boone implanted the notion of property in his agents and passed it off as garden-variety territorial behavior. Maschner and Patton, in turn, implanted a notion of kinship. Were these authors forced to account for the implications of these assumptions they would have to vacate their current perches and venture into the realm of culture. To avoid the kinds of conflationary thinking evident in inappropriate cultural implants, one needs to consider society, culture, and agency as real entities with their own properties, and to consider the complex dialectical interrelationships among them (see Archer 1995). According to Archer (1995, 1996), this requires a "stratified" model and "analytical dualism" (minimally consisting of individual agents and culture) not possible with MI models. The difference between MI and multi-scalar accounts of social process may derive from simple systematics and analytical methods. In most accounts, however, differences appear to be ones of ontological commitment rather than of operationalization. In either case, the implications of this difference are significant for all other aspects of modeling and explanation.

On the explanatory problem

Evolutionary ecology's commitment to methodological individualism has its most immediate effect in the delimitation of the explanatory problem. Consider the three different models for the origins of hereditary inequality summarized earlier. By bringing them together, I make the explicit claim that all relate to the same type of phenomenon: the origins of hereditary inequality. But what the models portray as problematic differs significantly. In both evolutionary accounts, the primary problem is the formation of a cooperative group of a certain type (see Frank 1998). Beginning with the MI assumption of the primacy of individuals in social process, the largest question becomes why they would ever get together and cooperate. More importantly, why form a group that privileges some individuals over others?

The evolutionist answer is that group cooperation is *a fortiori* "adaptive," cost-effective, and selected for under conditions of natural duress. It is rather easy to make the case that group cooperation requires some form of leadership and centralized decision-making and that a well-organized group is more efficient at harvesting resources than the same individuals left to their own devices. Efficiencies arising from hierarchical organization represent a better adaptation (potential fitness) for a population aggregate than would its absence, and given sufficient time and circumstances, potential efficiencies have a natural way of becoming actualities by being "selected for" and "selected from" the variety of behavioral responses to certain environmental situations. It is telling that in the case of the Northwest Coast, there is a multiplicity of possible indicators for the emergence of rank that span a millennium, but Maschner and Patton place the occurrence near the end of this epoch when the first archaeological evidence of large lineage houses becomes apparent. At first glance, their choice appears to signal scholarly restraint and caution, but given their theoretic commitment, it may perhaps more appropriately be attributed to Darwinian dicta concerning kin selection and the problem of group cooperation.

The practice theory explanation of the origins of rank society in Mesoamerica conceives the problem differently. Here the principal difficulty is to explain the changing social practices and perceptions of various categories of persons. Cultural practices and inter-subjective meanings take center stage; group cooperation is a non-problem. Basic underlying assumptions of practice theory are that social groups precede any given individuals and that culture is reproduced through social interaction of one form or another. The very notions and possibilities of human agents and rational choice presuppose human society and social interaction as prior conditions, not the result (Joas 1996). From the perspective of practice theory, the Darwinian dilemma of group cooperation disappears.

However, even given the pre-existence of society, it remains an open question why an already cooperating group would reorganize itself on asymmetric, hierarchical lines as a rank society based on ascribed status differences. We stress the emergence of aggrandizing individuals and the effects they had, through regional social interaction, on social practices.

But I remain dissatisfied with an *a priori* assumption of aggrandizers because their emergence should require its own social and historic explanation. Further, the other agents involved in this process need to be fleshed out and accounted for. Why should others follow where aggrandizers lead? For evolutionary ecology the existence of egoistic status seekers is a non-question. Some people are just born that way because of natural selection's handiwork.

On cause and adequacy

The elements of social inequality that each theory highlights differ for ontological and/or methodological reasons. Criteria for adequate explanation between theories are also incommensurate. Practice theory sees group cooperation as unproblematic whereas this is the grand question for evolution. Conversely, accounting for the existence of particular personalities is difficult for practice theory but is a non-issue for most evolutionary models. The two perspectives attribute cause to different phenomena and to different scales. Practice theory focuses on proximate causes, and most evolutionary theory stresses ultimate cause at the expense of proximate ones (see Mithen 1993; Smith and Winterhalder1992: 23). In Darwinian thinking, natural selection is the principal cause of being human and of human nature. In practice theory, agency may itself be a cause. In good recursive fashion, the shape and character of agency at any given time and place is a product of historic circumstances, but these influence all subsequent practices and changes to them. Agency is both historically caused and causal, both explanans and explanandum. Biological evolution is not denied, merely ignored as irrelevant or as an obvious antecedent condition. Likewise, the inheritance of culture is also thought to be critical but, for any given explanation, cultural antecedents are the starting point of analysis. Thus, the analyst avoids the problem of infinite regress by choosing the historic starting point, with all of its cultural content, and taking this as a "given" for a particular analysis (historic antecedents necessarily entail biological evolutionary effects as well).

The commitment to historic human agency, and its potential for fomenting change, is a crucial difference between the two theories. As noted, evolutionary explanations also claim agency for their own. But the natural agency implicated is epiphenomenal, hollow, and not accorded a significant explanatory role. Rather, evolutionary agency parallels other natural random factors and is important only because it is one source of behavioral variation in cultural systems, and such variation is critical if natural selection is to have her say in the course of human events (see Boone and Smith 1998; O'Brien and Holland 1990).

Steven Mithen (1989, 1990, 1993, 1996, 1997) is perhaps the most vocal advocate of natural agency in evolutionary explanations, but his agents *qua* "individual decision-makers" are akin to Boone's rational MI agents. Judging from the two evolutionary models for the origins of hereditary inequality summarized above, human action and agency appear to be of only minor importance. The few human actions alluded to result from genetic programming and innate tendencies, selected naturally, and are akin to behavioral instincts. In contrast, the fundamental tenet of agency is intentional and active choice, meaning that an agent could have chosen otherwise. Yet Maschner and Patton explicitly assert that, given the right conditions, rank society will emerge without fail, whenever and wherever possible. Where is there any room for real choice, or even for missing an opportunity, in this deterministic scenario? Sufficient conditions include productive environments, circumscribed human populations, and minimal population density. Human action enters into the equation as a constant rather than a variable, Thus, the critical factors for the emergence of rank are environmental circumstances, and human action is predictable, constant, and irrelevant because it lacks significant novel content. The lucky individuals placed in propitious circumstances read their lines from Nature's script, do what comes naturally, and by so doing supply the necessary, constant human ingredient to the evolutionary process. The natural agents involved behave more like wind-up toys than active agents, and the account of social change is deterministic in the final instance. Human action is explained by evolution but is not itself part of the explanation for evolution. By way of contrast, practice theory maintains the valence of human action as a variable and sees it as critical to all explanations concerned with human beings and human being.

This claim raises the key issue of human nature. Of what does it consist, and how does it work? Do practice explanations also rely on notions of human nature? In practice theory, human nature represents universal capacity and is constant, but human action is not. This is a significant difference from Darwinian models which confound the two. Practice theory holds behavioral potentials apart from their actualization. As noted, a serious problem with methodological individualism is its inherent conflationary tendency to implant social and cultural traits into its over-endowed agents. In MI modeling more is ascribed to human nature than it deserves, and cultural powers are conflated with innate ones. Whatever one chooses to call human nature, by definition it represents a universal capacity constant in space and time. Viewed as constant, innate human propensities can only be one of a combination of sufficient conditions for explaining change. From an evolutionist perspective, one needs to posit that the drive for social hierarchy is innate and only requires sufficient opportunity to bring it into reality. This gives rise to cost–benefit explanations for the origins of hereditary inequality in which more prose is expended on describing resource patches than on human actions. In such explanations, rational choices follow automatically once benefits of opportunities are known to outweigh their costs.

I believe that much of what passes for "human nature" in evolutionary accounts is actually cultural. If true, this should change the face of our explanations. We should be wary of vitalistic models that see the origins of hereditary inequality as an unfolding of innate tendencies and instincts (see Binford 1983: 221), a myth central to the Western tradition. Of particular concern should be human perceptions, motives, and actions as they are culturally constituted and modified. As Midgley (1978) points out, it is one thing to have natural drives and quite another to act on them in a particular way. Additional motives are required to explain action, or resistance to it. In this regard, it is clear that evolutionary accounts are severely under-motivated. They are particularly weak in accounting for the impressive variety of human motives and self-interests, and especially for how they play out in particular cultural and historic circumstances. Although they deal with innate propensities that may serve as motives, evolutionary accounts ultimately fail to link motives to actions or to their consequences. Even if there is a natural drive to power and inequality, it remains an historic question why the drive would have been acted upon in a particular way or would have had a particular outcome. Practice theories can handle these questions by focusing on cultural beliefs, practices, and agency as historically constituted. Since consequences of actions can only have probabilistic outcomes and are never fully determined, recourse to individual agency in social theory commits one to historically contingent narratives and to the impossibility of ultimate prediction. The emergence of any social institution, such as rank society, results from numerous choices made by historic agents in particular circumstances, thus leading to practice theory's retrodictive style of explanation and argumentation. One can only argue for necessary, insufficient conditions. This represents a clear break with the Darwinian models considered here and their emphases on sufficient conditions.

On investigatory implications

Differences between evolution and practice theories have implications for every level of investigation, from framing explanatory problems to fundamental definitions of categories, evidence, and critical variables. Maschner and Patton, for example, argue that rank societies were in place on the Northwest Coast once there were large corporate groups inhabiting long houses. This particular temporal choice appears more prescribed by theoretical commitments than by the data, which can be read in multiple ways. By privileging data for individuals and their activities (i.e., unequal distributions of prestige, trade goods and burial treatments) over those for corporate groups (i.e., long houses), a practice theory perspective could make a plausible case that rank societies in the Northwest Coast were in place centuries earlier. The different explanatory options are not trivial for either local understandings of history or general concerns with cultural processes. It should be obvious that the ways in which this problem is defined, and the criteria for delimiting the data critical for its resolution, have significant implications for the planning and execution of fieldwork and lab analyses. What should be observed, and how ought it to be interpreted? Why should evidence of corporate activity be privileged over that for individual inequalities? Are not differences in individual statuses important to this question? Why is a concept of lineage rank even necessary?

It is worth noting that were one to apply Maschner and Patton's criterion for the emergence of rank in Mesoamerica, one would be hard-pressed to make a compelling case for corporate groups and kin selection prior to the advent of state societies. Given a shared emphasis on hereditary inequality, one would think that archaeologists with either theoretical inclination who investigated this issue would make similar sorts of observations in the field. This is clearly not the case; the disparate ontic commitments of the two theories drive the fieldwork and artifact analyses in different directions. Despite rhetorical emphasis on individuals and agents, all that appears really to matter in the Northwest Coast example are data for corporate groups, the presumption being that if such groups exist the essential alpha males must necessarily have been in place calling the shots. On the face of things, it appears that evolution's commitment to "kin selection" is a clever way to retain notions of group adaptation and selection; one can have one's individual selection and group fitness, too.

Evolutionary models tout individuals and individual selection but accord them scant attention in actual explanations. I suspect that this is a logical consequence of their commitment to natural selection and ultimate cause. Individual organisms and behaviors are, of course, a theoretical prerequisite for explicating changes in characteristics of any population, but individual behaviors are of little interest in the cosmic sweep of evolutionary processes. In contrast, an action theory perspective prescribes more and more detailed analyses of the archaeological record in an attempt to break it down to fine-grained chronologies and spatial scales compatible with individual life-histories and events. It is not presumed that critical events happened beyond the notice of the agents affected by them. Rather, individual actions and events are seen as critical to the basic process, so practice theory prescribes that one actually search for them. Evidence of group activity would be unacceptably gross, as this would have to be broken down to the level of individual behaviors.

Agents of change

Action theory and evolutionary ecology share many basic explanatory commitments, and recent developments appear to be moving some brands of each towards a convergence such that it is becoming increasingly difficult to differentiate them. This makes their detailed comparison, such as I have attempted here, all the more valuable. Both frameworks are committed to some form of realism (Archer 1995; Ruse 1998), soft determinism (Ruse 1998), diachronic processes, temporal narratives, and agent-centered explanations. For all the apparent similarities in concepts, however, the agents involved in each perspective appear to be fundamentally different. In the preceding comparisons I made two claims that may appear contradictory. I characterized evolutionary agents as uni-dimensional passivists, on the one hand, and as culturally top-heavy, on the other. Both problems relate to evolution's commitment to methodological individualism and rational choice. At the outset, this may seem an odd criticism because rational choice and methodological individualism represent two areas of broad agreement between the theories (Maschner and Mithen 1996). This characterization is accurate as far as it goes. Many action theories, such as Giddens' (1984) structuration theory, also share these characteristics with evolutionary thinking. To the degree that they do so, the same criticisms apply.

I did not bring these criticisms to bear on the practice theory model because Michael Blake and I were rather eclectic in putting it together, and we tried to avoid problems of particular brands of action theory in doing so. The historic agents we postulated, however, are still deficient because we failed to supercede completely the conflationism of MI thinking (by according cultural institutions a larger role in the process), and we also depicted the principal agents involved (aggrandizers) as hyper-active and too single-minded in their actions. These problems can be avoided by tempering our assumptions and adopting a more realistic or pragmatic stance. The goal will be to come up with a better model of individual agents that avoids conflationary thinking and facile assumptions concerning rationality and accords greater analytical emphasis to social phenomena. As Joas (1996) stresses, another weakness of action theories, including ours, is their failure to consider agents as embodied beings who act pragmatically and creatively when confronted with novel circumstances. Joas's "pragmatic" thesis models social action in a more realistic way and offers a viable extension to practice theory. It also downplays the hyper-intentionality of action characteristic of practice theory. Not all significant action is as intentional as Blake and I portrayed it. Much of Joas's pragmatism appears compatible with basic assumptions of evolutionary ecology, and it is especially strong in dealing with meaningful behavior. Significantly, both evolutionary ecology and practice theory are particularly weak in their approach to meaning (hermeneutics and phenomenology).

The strengths of evolutionary thinking are its emphasis on agents as biological beings and its formal modeling of decision-making. Its explanations of human capacities, however, are ultimately unsatisfying because everything is attributed to the same blind cause (selection) and by the same tautologous logic. Given certain human physical, psychological, psychic, emotional, and cognitive capacities, it still remains an open question why such capacities would be exercised in particular circumstances by specific individuals, and why they would have their unique consequences. I can accept evolutionist arguments for a "human nature" as universal capacities and propensities, but recourse to natural drives cannot carry one far enough to explain cultural and social phenomena. Evolutionary theory only accounts for the structure and innate capacity of the empty vessel that is the human organism; it must be filled with specific human content through embodied social activity.

108 John E. Clark

A more complete explanation of human agents would treat them as the products of dual evolutionary and cultural-historic processes, with emphasis on the latter. The dual-inheritance theory of evolution (see Boyd and Richerson 1985) is moving in this direction but still falls short because, among other reasons, of its commitment to MI agents to the near exclusion of society.

How do the various agents of the three explanatory models compare to common sense understandings of agency? None of them approaches the rich complexity of real lives, but Clark and Blake's (1994) practice agents appear to be more realistic and empowered. Evolutionary agents, for all their hype, are overly passive and lethargic. They are constantly acted upon but rarely act until compelled to do so. "Reaction," rather than "action," is their watchword, with most reactions deriving from long-forgotten evolutionary programming. In Giddens' (1984) language, evolutionary processes occur largely "behind their [agents'] backs." Evolutionary agents are efficient energy harvesters and processors but are deficient in their abilities to communicate, interact with others socially, live lives of meaning, or to act creatively. In many models these agents are further burdened with an oppressive load of cultural endowments that empower them to act as a given model requires. Thus, we see Boone's dominant and subordinate individuals behaving as if property rights were involved in their passive competition for resource patches. In a truly Darwinian explanation, one would expect more competition over the best resources and fewer concessions to rights of possession. Likewise, Maschner and Patton rely on kin selection to explain the structure of shared interests, as if kinship and biological relatedness were the same thing (see Frank 1998: 39 for a different view).

Concerning the related problem of agential powers, the individuals in optimal foraging models know more than real agents could know. Rational decisions require perfect knowledge of particulars and decision-making rules, which are cultural. The rational MI agent is clearly an analytical device and not meant to be taken as an accurate representation of natural agents (Smith and Winterhalder 1992b: 51), but many models blur the fundamental, critical distinction between "models of" and "models for" human institutions (see Geertz 1966). Natural selection only provides compliant organisms of tremendous potential; these are analytically accorded cognitive and behavioral powers, in many instances, by conflating social and cultural attributes, categories, values, practices, and beliefs onto them. Capacitated agents do indeed have all of these powers, but they gain them through practice rather than natural maturation. The conflationary analytical move implants social and cultural attributes into otherwise solipsistic agents, and this blurs the critical distinction between natural and cultural powers needed to sort out questions of social process. Failure to deal with society as a real structure, even analytically, forces one to pack emergent social phenomena into individual agents. This criticism applies equally to structuration theory as well as to Darwinian theory. Archer (1995, 1996) treats this particular malady in great detail.

All in all, the signal difference between the two perspectives is most apparent in the ambiguous heading of this final section. "Agents of change" evokes entirely different phenomena as viewed in the light of the competing frameworks. For evolutionary and Darwinian thinking, "agents of change" are extra-somatic forces that affect human evolution, not the humans themselves as agents. At the end of the day, evolution's individual human organisms are not treated as competent or responsible agents, especially not agents of change; that honor is reserved for natural selection. In practice theory, "agents of change" are the multitudes of agents and actors with conflicting interests, responsibilities, imperfect abilities, and empowerments. Social reproduction becomes a gigantic power game as multiplicities of players pursue separate interests, in divergent ways, with unequal powers, and with mixed results. This latter view of agents better approaches common sense understandings of what it means to be a competent adult with freedom of choice in our own society, and probably for this reason they appear inherently more credible than Darwinian ones (cf. Gero, this volume).

Both perspectives have strengths and weaknesses and could be substantively improved by recourse to more realistic assumptions about the nature and operation of society and individual agents. Of the two frameworks, practice theory provides the better account of active agents and agency as we understand them today. It follows that practice theory, once improved along the lines mentioned above, should provide better explanations for the origins of hereditary inequality than any Darwinian alternatives. This conclusion is arguable, of course, as it is based upon an undeveloped, thin premise; it deserves to be argued at greater length through other specific comparisons between models and theories. The comparison of explanatory models from different theoretical camps attempted here is only meant as a beginning. It is useful to remember that each theoretical camp boasts many banners, all of which deserve representation before final judgements on explanatory adequacy are passed. Comparisons between different variants would doubtless suggest other strengths and weaknesses than the ones discussed here. But the ontological bases of each have logical implications and consequences for modeling and explanation that should characterize most variants of a particular theory. Of central concern is the content of human nature and the role of innate drives in social processes. To what degree are we products of, or puppets to, our biological heritage? To what degree does culture kick in and override any biological programming? Can we explain cultural processes by recourse to natural agents, or is it necessary to take a broader view that includes the cultural and social background of agents as they are historically constituted? The preceding comparison suggests that natural agents are not up to the task. Credible explanations of social phenomena require real action, agency, and historic human agents.

Evolutionary ecology's organismic view of the human agent is too limited and cannot account for the historicity and contingency of human action, or for its cultural production. Evolution can account for the human capacity for agency, but not for its exercise or its consequences. Natural agents are all together too passive and under-motivated, and too receptive to external forces, to make competent actors in social reproduction. To account for institutional changes one must bridge the gap between motives and actions, and this is best done by considering embodied, historic agents with self-actualizing potential. Some forces for change come from within the agents themselves. To account for this kind of strongly motivated action and agency, one needs a bona fide theory of social action. One conclusion that can be drawn from the preliminary comparisons of explanations presented here is that all the models considered have serious deficiencies, some correctable, others not. In line with the scientific pursuit of superior explanations, we ought actively to seek better explanations (via detailed comparisons) so we can eventually replace "better" explanations with the "best" explanation.

Acknowledgments

Marcia-Anne Dobres, Herbert Maschner, John Monaghan, John E. Robb, and Polly Wiessner substantially helped to enhance the fitness of this essay. All counter-arguments and criticisms of its content, however, should be laid at my door as the agent of record.

Bibliography

Archer, M. S. 1995. *Realist Social Theory: The Morphogenetic Approach*. Cambridge University Press, Cambridge UK.

—— 1996. *Culture and Agency: The Place of Culture in Social Theory*. Revised edn. Cambridge University Press, Cambridge UK.

Barton, C. M., and G. A. Clark (eds) 1997a. *Rediscovering Darwin: Evolutionary Theory and Archeological Explanation*. Archeological Papers of the American Anthropological Association, no. 7, Arlington, Va.

—— 1997b. "Evolutionary Theory in Archeological Explanation," in *Rediscovering Darwin: Evolutionary Theory and Archeological Explanation*, ed. C. M. Barton and G. A. Clark, pp. 3–15. Archeological Papers of the American Anthropological Association, no. 7, Arlington, Va.

Bettinger, R. L., and P. J. Richerson 1996. "The State of Evolutionary Archaeology," in *Darwinian Archaeologies*, ed. H. D. G. Maschner, pp. 221–31. Plenum Press, New York.

Bhaskar, R. 1975. *A Realist Theory of Science*. Leeds Books, UK.

Binford, L. R. 1983. *In Pursuit of the Past: Decoding the Archaeological Record*. Thames and Hudson, London.

Blake, M. 1991. "An Emerging Early Formative Chiefdom at Paso de la Amada, Chiapas, Mexico," in *The Formation of Complex Society in Southeastern Mesoamerica*, ed. W. R. Fowler, pp. 27–46. CRC Press, Boca Raton.

Blake, M., J. E. Clark, B. Chisholm, and K. Mudar 1992. "Non-Agricultural Staples and Agricultural Supplements: Early Formative Subsistence in the Soconusco Region, Mexico," in *Transitions to Agriculture in Prehistory*, ed. A. B. Gebauer and T. D. Price, pp. 131–51. Prehistory Press, Madison.

Boone, J. L. 1992. "Competition, Conflict, and Development of Social Hierarchies," in *Evolutionary Ecology and Human Behavior*, ed. E. A. Smith and B. Winterhalder, pp. 301–37. Aldine de Gruyter, New York.

Boone, J. L. and E. A. Smith 1998. "Is it Evolution Yet?: A Critique of Evolutionary Archaeology." *Current Anthropology* 39: 141–73.

Boyd, R. and P. J. Richerson 1985. *Culture and Evolutionary Process*. University of Chicago Press, Chicago.

Carneiro, R. 1970. "A Theory of the Origin of the State." *Science* 169: 733–38.

Clark, J. E. 1994. *The Development of Early Formative Rank Societies in the Soconusco, Chiapas, Mexico*. Unpublished Ph.D. dissertation, Department of Anthropology, University of Michigan, Ann Arbor.

Clark, J. E., and M. Blake 1994. "The Power of Prestige: Competitive Generosity and the Emergence of Rank Societies in Lowland Mesoamerica," in *Factional Competition and Political Development in the New World*, ed. E. M. Brumfiel and J. W. Fox, pp. 17–30. Cambridge University Press, Cambridge UK.

Clark, J. E., and D. Gosser 1995. "Reinventing Mesoamerica's First Pottery," in *The Emergence of Pottery: Technology and Innovation in Ancient Societies*, ed. W. K. Barnett and J. W. Hoopes, pp. 209–21. Smithsonian Institution, Washington, D.C.

Frank, S. A. 1998. *Foundations of Social Evolution*. Princeton University Press, Princeton.

Geertz, C. 1966. "Religion as a Cultural System," in *Anthropological Approaches to the Study of Religion*, ed. M. Banton, pp.1–46. Tavistock, London.

Giddens, A. 1979. *Central Problems in Social Theory: Action, Structure and Contradiction in Social Analysis*. University of California Press, Berkeley.

—— 1984. *The Constitution of Society: Outline of the Theory of Structuration*. University of California Press, Berkeley.

Hayden, B. 1995. "Pathways to Power: Principles for Creating Socioeconomic Inequalities," in *Foundations of Social Inequality*, ed. T. D. Price and G. M. Feinman, pp. 15–86. Plenum Press, New York.

Hill, W. D., M. Blake, and J. E. Clark 1998. "Ball Court Design Dates Back 3400 Years." *Nature* 392: 878–9.

Honderich, T. 1993. *How Free Are You?: The Determinism Problem*. Oxford University Press, Oxford.

Joas, H. 1996. *The Creativity of Action*. University of Chicago Press, Chicago.

Kuper, A. 1994. *The Chosen Primate: Human Nature and Cultural Diversity*. Harvard University Press, Cambridge, Mass.

Marx, K. 1969 [orig. 1852]. *The Eighteenth Brumaire of Louis Bonaparte*. International Publishers, New York.

Maschner, H. D. G. 1991. "The Emergence of Cultural Complexity on the Northern Northwest Coast." *Antiquity* 65: 924–34.

—— (ed.) 1996. *Darwinian Archaeologies*. Plenum Press, New York.

Maschner, H. D. G., and S. Mithen 1996. "Darwinian Archaeologies: An Introductory Essay," in *Darwinian Archaeologies*, ed. H. D. G. Maschner, pp. 3–14. Plenum Press, New York.

Maschner, H. D. G. and J. Q. Patton 1996. "Kin Selection and the Origins of Hereditary Social Inequality: A Case Study from the Northern Northwest Coast," in *Darwinian Archaeologies*, ed. H. D. G. Maschner, pp. 89–107. Plenum Press, New York.

Mauss, M. 1950. *Essai sur le don*. Presses Universitaires de France, Paris.

Midgley, M. 1978. *Beast and Man: The Roots of Human Nature*. Cornell University Press, Ithaca, New York.

Mithen, S. 1989. "Evolutionary Theory and Post-Processual Archaeology." *Antiquity* 63: 483–94.

—— 1990. *Thoughtful Foragers: A Study of Prehistoric Decision Making*. Cambridge University Press, Cambridge UK.

—— 1993. "Individuals, Groups and the Palaeolithic Record: A Reply to Clark." *Proceedings of the Prehistoric Society* 59: 393–8.

—— 1996. *The Prehistory of the Mind: The Cognitive Origins of Art, Religion and Science*. Thames and Hudson, London.

—— 1997. "Cognitive Archeology, Evolutionary Psychology, and Cultural Transmission, with Particular Reference to Religious Ideas," in *Rediscovering Darwin: Evolutionary Theory and Archeological Explanation*, ed. C. M. Barton and G. A. Clark, pp. 67–74. Archeological Papers of the American Anthropological Association, no. 7, Arlington, Va.

Moore, G. E. 1912. *Ethics*. Holt, New York.

Moran, E. F. (ed.) 1990. *The Ecosystem Approach in Anthropology: From Concept to Practice*. University of Michigan Press, Ann Arbor.

O'Brien, M. J. (ed.) 1996. *Evolutionary Archaeology: Theory and Application*. University of Utah Press, Salt Lake City.

O'Brien, M. J., and T. D. Holland 1990. "Variation, Selection, and the Archaeological Record." *Archaeological Method and Theory* 2: 31–79.

O'Hear, A. 1997. *Beyond Evolution: Human Nature and the Limits of Evolutionary Explanation*. Clarendon Press, Oxford.

O'Shea, J. 1981. "Coping with Scarcity: Exchange and Social Storage," in *Economic Archaeology: Towards an Integration of Ecological and Social Approaches*, ed. A. Sheridan and G. Bailey, pp. 167–86. British Archaeological Report International Series 96, Oxford.

Richerson, P. J. and R. Boyd 1992. "Cultural Inheritance and Evolutionary Ecology," in *Evolutionary Ecology and Human Behavior*, ed. E. A. Smith and B. Winterhalder, pp. 61–92. Aldine de Gruyter, New York.

Ruse, M. 1998. *Taking Darwin Seriously: A Naturalistic Approach to Philosophy*. Prometheus Books, Amherst, New York.

Sahlins, M. D. 1959. "The Social Life of Monkeys, Apes, and Primitive Man," in *The Evolution of Man's Capacity for Culture*, ed. J. N. Spuhler, pp. 54–73. Wayne State University Press, Detroit.

Smith, E. A. and B. Winterhalder (eds) 1992a. *Evolutionary Ecology and Human Behavior*. Aldine de Gruyter, New York.

—— 1992b. "Natural Selection and Decision Making: Some Fundamental Principles," in *Evolutionary Ecology and Human Behavior*, pp. 25–60. Aldine de Gruyter, New York.

Teltser, P. A. (ed.) 1995. *Evolutionary Archaeology: Methodological Issues*. University of Arizona Press, Tucson.

Winterhalder, B. and E. A. Smith 1992. "Evolutionary Ecology and the Social Sciences," in *Evolutionary Ecology and Human Behaviour*, ed. E. A. Smith and B. Winterhalder, pp. 3–23. Aldine de Gruyter, New York.

9 The tragedy of the commoners

Timothy R. Pauketat

> [T]hey . . . conferre all their power and strength upon one Man, or upon one Assembly of men
> . . . as if every man should say to every man, *I Authorise and give up my Right of Governing my*
> *selfe, to this Man, or to this Assembly of men*. . . . This done, the Multitude so united in one
> Person, is called a COMMON-WEALTH.
>
> (Hobbes 1985: 227, emphasis in the original)

> Picture a pasture open to all. It is expected that each herdsman will try to keep as many cattle
> as possible on the commons. . . . Therein is the tragedy. Each man is locked into a system that
> compels him to increase his herd without limit – in a world that is limited. Ruin is the desti-
> nation toward which all men rush, each pursuing his own best interest in a society that
> believes in the freedom of the commons.
>
> (Hardin 1977: 20)

In contrast to many archaeologists today, the seventeenth-century English philosopher Thomas
Hobbes portrayed the emergence of civil society as a consequence of common people acting to
establish a ruling order. Archaeologists typically deny that non-elite actors did anything of such
consequence on their own, despite a recent heightened awareness of commoner resistance, accommodation, or compliance (e.g., Brumfiel 1997; Ferguson 1992; Paynter and McGuire 1991).
Certainly, the domination of people's lives by a few politicos in various present-day contexts is
not something that can be easily denied. These powerful few coordinate and control action in
ways that most individuals can not. However, the fact that domination of one sort or another is
a global empirical fact today does little to explain how "the Multitude so united" in the past.

The standard array of archaeological scenarios offered to explain the political unifica-
tions of the past range from voluntary communal association to forced acquiescence. The
former scenario typically ignores the politics of communal social formations, especially
under centralizing conditions, while the latter casts an elite in the role of antagonist.
Neither considers that all people, not just a few political movers and shakers, actively
created social orders greater than the sum total of their actions.

This is not to say that all people acted knowingly and in a goal-oriented fashion to
confer their power upon one man, as Hobbes implies. Rather, we may take a cue from
Garrett Hardin's (1977) consideration of the "commons." Hardin considered the
"commons" – lands or resources set aside for the use and benefit of all – to be subject to an
internally generated dialectical transformation. That is, because commons are shared by
and accessible to all people, they are typically subject to abuse by individuals, ultimately
eliminating their utility as shared resources. The end product, a "tragedy of the commons,"
was not necessarily a planned or desired consequence.

Like the tragedy of the commons, the social process that resulted in "commonwealths" with their "commoners" can be seen as one that involved the unintended consequences of all people's actions and representations. Those who would become commoners were probably often unaware that their coordinated actions could restrict their own ability to coordinate action in the future, a condition that I use as a definitional characteristic of what it meant to be a commoner. Using Mississippian platform mound construction as a case in point, I argue here that commoners were responsible for their own social position, at least in a historical sense. Through coordinated actions and representations, namely mound building, people of all statuses were implicated in political orders. It appears that the social relations and representations that enabled collective action of a sort inhibited doing or thinking those same things later in time.

I elaborate below by explicating the paradoxical process in which producers actively constrained their own ability to act. For illustrative purposes, I use a material aspect of practice all too visible in the archaeological record, monumental architecture. Specifically, I extend the argument that interpretations of Mississippian platform mounds in the south-eastern United States – either as expressions of authority, attempts to legitimate control, or elements of "sacred landscapes" – are incomplete and misleading. These interpretations tend to reduce many people's histories to simple linear explanations of dominant ideologies. Instead, I consider the view that monuments, and social space in general, were the means by which inclusive social movements were constructed. Such a view, as part of a reorientation based on a theory of practice, allows us to reconsider Hobbes' question anew: how did commonwealths, with their commoners, come into being?

Practice theory

The current array of political-evolutionary models are unable to encompass a dialectical process with unintended consequences of the sort that I suggest (e.g., Blanton *et al.* 1996; DeMarris *et al.* 1996; Feinman 1995; Maschner and Patton 1996). There is an alternative that can, and this alternative is a theory of "practice" (Ortner 1984; after Bourdieu 1977 (see also Clark, this volume)). What is it? Let me begin to answer that question by explaining what practice theory is not.

Practice theory is *not* agency theory, at least not as agency theory is currently practiced! Archaeologists who advocate agency in their theories cover the full gamut of theoretical approaches (see Dobres and Robb, this volume). These archaeologists include functional-ecological processualists and Neo-Darwinian "individualists" who see the charismatic or accumulating "behaviors" or the political "strategies" of certain types of people as important "factors" in human evolution (e.g., Blanton *et al.* 1996; Feinman 1995; Hayden 1995; Maschner and Patton 1996). They also include "cognitive-processualists" who study the distributions of symbols and *chaînes opératoires*, among other things, to understand the cultural and technological constraints to social change (e.g., Renfrew 1994; see also Cowgill 1993; Dobres and Hoffman 1994; Schlanger 1994; van der Leuuw 1994; also Sinclair, this volume). Finally, there are postprocessualists, feminists, Marxists, and even some Neo-Darwinists who recognize a dynamic tension between individuals and cultural structures along with the unintended consequences of people's routinized actions (e.g., Braun 1995; Brumfiel 1992, 1994, 1997; Conkey 1990; Hodder 1986; McGuire 1992; Shennan 1993).

A key distinguishing characteristic of the various approaches to human agency is whether or not "behavior" plays a role in explanation. The idea of behavior has been a cornerstone, albeit often unstated, for those who assume a rationalist, materialist theoretical position and those who reject a concern with motivation or intent in archaeology (Binford 1983: 216; Rindos 1984: 2ff.; Schiffer 1996; for further elaboration, see Cowgill, this volume). Behavior, from this vantage point, is little more than "teleological action," with predetermined courses and predictable ends analogous to other times and places (Habermas 1984: 85). Practice, as opposed to behavior, is a homologous pheno-menon, not entirely comparable to the practices of other times and places. Historical divergence and contingency are axiomatic to practice theory, engendering a very different kind of archaeology than that based on assumptions about behavior.

Practice theory is more than the recognition that individual agency is one of many "factors" in social evolution (e.g., Hayden 1995). Practice theory is theory in the broadest sense of the word. It and other approaches to human agency have been mistakenly thought to address only top-down political behavior or to provide only proximate solutions to historical particulars (not the uniformities of social evolution), and this has made "agency theory" too easily dismissed (Johnson 1989: 190; but see Gero, this volume; Kowalewski *et al.* 1992: 260; Milner 1996; Muller 1997: 11; Saitta 1994; Tainter 1988: 35). Opposed to this characterization is practice theory itself, which is neither top-down nor narrow in its focus.

So what is practice theory? It is a theory of the continuous and historically contingent enactments or embodiments of people's ethos, attitudes, agendas, and dispositions (see Bourdieu 1977; Giddens 1979). Its roots are deep and tap the Enlightenment distinctions between thought and action. But the emphasis in today's practice theory is on the continuous part of the definition. Practice is the phenomenon at the intersection of thought and action, irreducible to the sum of those thoughts and actions.

Tradition, dispositions, and domination

Especially important to practice theory is the idea of a spontaneous, second-nature, common sense or a "non-discursive," unreflective knowledge that forms the basis of dispositions and that guides people's actions. This kind of unreflective or non-ideological thought can be opposed to "political reasoning," "discursive consciousness," or "ideology" (Comaroff and Comaroff 1991: 22–7; see also Ball 1983; Giddens 1979; Rosenberg 1988). The idea of unreflective knowledge, of course, was formalized as Saussure's *langue*, as Gramsci's "hegemony," as Durkheim's "collective consciousness," and as the Boasian culture concept (see Ortner 1984; Sahlins 1981; Stocking 1982). It is, at least partly, the idea behind the contemporary application of "structure" (Giddens 1979; Sahlins 1985), "habitus," and "doxa" (Bourdieu 1977). It is embedded within many archaeologists' sense of "tradition" (see Willey and Phillips 1958: 37), and it is this sense that I use here.

Marx, too, identified something similar to tradition – practical consciousness – as motivating action (Marx 1978). In fact, he recognized the unity of consciousness and productive action (i.e., labor) as "practice" (*praxis*), and used concepts such as "ideology" and "alienation" to explain how practice reshaped social history (Marx 1978; Marx and Engels 1989; see also McGuire 1992: 134). Weber (1978), while credited with a "social action theory," did not anticipate practice in the same way as Marx. Weber (1978: 63ff.) was concerned with action and its motivations, but he also dwelled on formalist, economic rationality, leading his sociological offspring to overemphasize action, in functionalist terms, to the detriment of meaning (see Campbell 1996; Giddens 1976, 1977).

The opposite applies to much of American cultural anthropology in the twentieth century, certainly of the symbolic and structural sort, which reflects an overemphasis of

cultural, practical consciousness over social action (cf. Ortner 1984). The results were reifications of the importance of cultural rules, thematic symbols, or cognitive templates,
reducing action, if not history, to mere expressions of unchanging cultural structures (Bell
1997: 82). The political and economic anthropology of the 1960s and 1970s avoided much
of this reductionism and presaged practice theory's elevation of human action. Political
anthropology's "factions," "coalitions," and "political communities" are easily reconciled
with the tenets of practice theory (Brumfiel 1994), even though the motivations believed
to lie behind action were sometimes the same rational ones invoked by sociologists.

The emergence of post-structuralism, on one hand, and the merger of a Marxist political
economy with a symbolic and semiotic anthropology, on the other, generated the American
version of practice theory (Marcus and Fischer 1986: 85; see also Baudrillard 1981; Cohen
1974; Ohnuki-Tierny 1990; Ortner 1984; Sahlins 1981, 1985). There are a series of
concepts commonly used to encapsulate parts of practice that I will not review here (see
Bourdieu 1977, 1990, 1994; Giddens 1979). Usually, there is a recognition that individuals
conduct themselves according to sets of "dispositions [that] generate practices, perceptions
and attitudes" (Thompson 1994: 12). Each individual's dispositions (i.e., habitus) are not
rigid and unchanging cultural or structural monoliths that all people automatically share.
Yet, neither are they rational behaviors whose ends are foregone conclusions. Instead,
dispositions are closely wedded to traditions, as defined earlier.

Recently, archaeologists have recognized that dispositions are inculcated as an inextri-
cable component of social experiences, landscapes, and representations (see Hodder, this
volume; Robb 1998; Thomas 1996). Representations are always two-way "negotiations"
between contemporary people, the past and the present, or tradition and power. That is,
inculcation is the continuous interface of people and the historically constrained contexts
of action. Thus, practice, or "negotiation," is *not* best viewed as a mechanical kind of
thought–action dyad where tradition or meaning feeds back into power or agency and vice
versa. "Meaning does not reside in artifacts or in people but in the *moment of interaction*
between the two" (Robb 1998: 337, citing Thomas 1996, emphasis added).

Shennan (1993) identifies as "surface phenomena" these moments of interaction. His
surface-phenomena idea could cover any number of bodily practices (e.g., movement,
clothing, gesture, dance), routinized practices (e.g., cooking, singing, tool making), and
space (social, cosmographic) wherein meanings reside. Shennan's point is that surface
phenomena, moments of interaction or, simply, practices are themselves not completely
understood by actors. Moreover, these practices and spaces are not necessarily microcosms
of whole traditions, ideologies, or cultural structures. Instead, like the original notions of
practical consciousness, common sense, or non-discursive knowledge, people act often
without any conscious evaluation of what their actions mean.

In fact, most of the people involved in any such negotiation would be, at best, only
partially aware of the "deep structures" or cognitive models that *might* underlie their dispositions. Yet all people would be actively involved in perpetuating meanings through such
surface phenomena, making each transmission act or interactive event an alteration of the
traditions and contexts of groups, especially as the contexts and scales of action would
never be the same twice (Sahlins 1985). Individuals might only have intended to perpet-
uate their limited understanding of tradition, but the outcomes of practice, given the ever-
changing contexts of disposition formation – not to mention changing external conditions
– might have diverged profoundly from these intentions and from some usual range of
outcomes (see also Giddens 1979; following Merton 1949).

The scale of some negotiation is of paramount concern in understanding the contingent outcomes of practice. Moments of interaction that affect only two or three others, for instance, may be of little historical significance. Actions or representations that affect hundreds or thousands of people are likely to be of considerably greater significance. Having said this, it would be easy at this point to factor out the practices of anyone but aggrandizers, charismatic leaders, or "great men." This is an error, as the action of any one individual can have no historical consequences unless others participate in the moments of interaction. That is, we cannot use a type of person, such as a charismatic leader or an aggrandizer, *as an explanation* of some historical trajectory (*contra* Hayden 1995; Maschner and Patton 1996). Such an individualist explanation fails to understand that it is the agency of all the people involved in negotiation that shapes the meanings of the moment. The leader is simply a part of this group process (Scott 1990: 221–2). So, the real concern of practice theory is not an individual's actions but the practice of *many* people in social negotiations.

The collective negotiation of primary concern here is "domination." As I use it, domination is not a condition of total control over others (*contra* Muller 1997: 43). It is unlikely that this is possible even under the harshest of conditions (e.g., Ferguson 1992; Orser 1998). Domination is also not necessarily tethered to a person or a class of people, but it may define a community, a corporation, or a social movement. In the spirit of Gramsci (1971), domination was a "compromise equilibrium" of divergent interests and dispositions. Domination was the process by which control was inserted, to variable extent, into social life (see Deagan 1990; Ferguson 1992; Hastorf 1991; Johnson 1989, 1996; Kent 1990; Miller 1989; Pauketat 1998; Paynter and McGuire 1991; Scarry and McEwan 1995). Domination was not a "strategy" used knowingly by a few central figures.

Importantly, to dominate others is to control to some extent the practice of others by accommodating, if not co-opting, the surface phenomena that comprise tradition. This parallels, of course, Gramsci's (1971) definition of "hegemony," also labeled "subjective co-optation" by Reyna (1994). Unlike the overt, objective forms, subjective co-optation is the appropriation of people's dispositions so that they are accommodated, even if resistant.[1]

Monumental practice

To examine more closely the process of domination as subjective co-optation, I will consider briefly the evidence for the construction of pre-Columbian platform mounds in portions of the Mississippi valley. My point is simple and begins with Trigger's (1990) observations on the monuments of formative civilizations around the world: the formative emergence of central authorities in a number of early civilizations corresponds with the florescence of monumental construction and the production or conspicuous consumption of luxury goods.[2] In that his observations are empirically accurate, we have little cause to question the inference that consolidation and legitimization of authority underlie the construction of monumental architecture. However, the theoretical problem with any such scenario is its failure to consider the effects of non-elite practice in social change. The common masses built the monuments and, unless we assume that they were duped, were continuously coerced, or were without dispositions, then we must admit the possibility that their dispositions in some ways shaped monumental constructions. After all, producers think and act in ways that may not accord with the political interests of leaders (e.g., Sahlins 1972). Moreover, wittingly or not, people resist change that departs from traditional routinized regimens and representations (see Abercrombie *et al.* 1980; Kertzer 1988; Lears 1985).

Here is the rub. Despite much recent theorizing about resistance to dominant groups and their ideologies, the very existence of impressive monuments that supposedly legitimized elites and their political domains could be interpreted to confirm how ineffectual resistance really was or how irrelevant non-elite practices were. Looking around the world, we could conclude that domination was all-too-easy despite the ennobling of commoners via resistance. But this would be to miss the point of subjective co-optation and a theory of practice. From that vantage point, and based on the Mississippian case material, we can neither affirm that subordinates passively acquiesced to dominant ideologies, nor corroborate the old adaptationist teleology that political order was beneficial for everyone, nor reject the seemingly incontrovertible evidence of the profound political, economic, and demographic transformations of early civilizations (*à la* Trigger 1990).

Mississippian co-optation

Mississippian chiefdoms emerged in the temperate forested river valleys of the southeastern United States after AD 1000 (see Anderson 1994; Steponaitis 1986). These chiefdoms were characterized by population centralization, social hierarchization, and monumental construction (Figure 9.1). There were elites and non-elites, at least in certain phases of Mississippian development. At the same time, early Mississippian remains evince "communal" characteristics, ranging from the prominence of fertility symbolism and group-oriented mortuary complexes to the traditional subsistence practices of settlements (Emerson 1997a, 1997b; Johannessen 1993; Knight 1986; Lopinot 1997; Muller 1997). This communal–hierarchical blend is telling of the mode of social negotiation, and should give us pause in considering why Mississippian platform mounds were built.

At Cahokia, Moundville, Winterville, Lake George, and elsewhere, chiefdoms were founded via abrupt and large-scale consolidations between AD 1000 and 1200. At the various capital grounds, mound and plaza construction was most intensive in the earliest phase of each polity (Brain 1989; Knight 1997; Pauketat 1998; Pauketat and Emerson 1997; Williams and Brain 1983).[3] In the Cahokia region, the social landscape was transformed practically overnight, as is shown unambiguously in the post-AD 1050 reconfiguration of residential settlements and population densities (Emerson 1997a; Pauketat 1998; Pauketat and Lopinot 1997). The earliest stages of earthen platforms and the first plazas were built at this time (ca. AD 1050) as part of a tightly spaced series of planned construction events (e.g., Dalan 1997; Pauketat 1998: 60).

Taking this evidence at face value, we *could* interpret each regional shift as the expression of a newly emerged political elite who sought to legitimize their newfound power. As in other parts of the world, placing the buildings of a few people atop raised platforms probably signified the social distance and apical political position of those people relative to the rest of a community. The final height of the largest earthen pyramid at Cahokia, at 30 m, may then be telling of the level of political power vested in the occupants of the uppermost terrace (Collins and Chalfant 1993). However, from the vantage point of practice theory, this interpretation is incomplete and fails to capture the process by which giant Mississippian chiefdoms suddenly appeared out of what are usually described as minimally centralized precursors (see Kelly 1990; Knight 1997; Nassaney 1992; Pauketat 1994).

If we take a closer look at the construction of the earthen platforms, we see clearly that these monuments were more than just elite symbols (Knight 1986, 1989). Mississippian platform mounds across the Southeast were built in stages (see Lindauer and Blitz 1997). While some mound construction histories have been interpreted as indicating the inaugu-

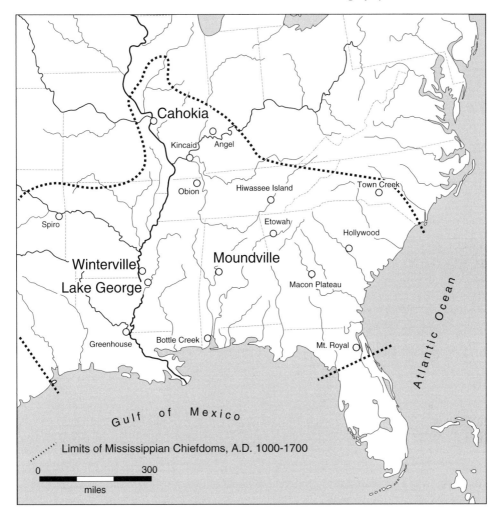

Figure 9.1 Select Mississippian centers in southeastern North America

ration of elite lineages or irregular political events, many reveal what were probably annual ritual construction cycles similar to those of the ancestors of contemporary Mississippians (Knight 1989). At and around Cahokia, there are often nearly as many individual stages – thin "blanket mantles" and "stage enlargements" – within mounds as there were years within which the mounds were built (see Pauketat 1993). This is true even of the largest and most impressive of Mississippian platforms, Monks Mound at Cahokia, with its alternating mantles and stages revealing incremental enlargements and a regular construction cycle (Figures 9.2 and 9.3). In at least one well-documented platform mound, each mantle was associated with one or more relined central hearths, replastered floors, or entirely rebuilt temples, residences, or public buildings (Pauketat 1993).

Elsewhere in the Southeast, the sequence of mound construction differs from Cahokia in its amplitude and periodicity (see Anderson 1996; Hally 1996; Knight 1989; Schnell *et al.* 1981). Although fewer construction stages seem typical, annual renewal ceremonies probably focused on other non-mound constructions, ritual purifications, and plaza

Figure 9.2 Aerial view of Monks Mound, Cahokia site

Photo courtesy of Cahokia Mounds State Historic Site

activities (see Knight 1986). The central point, however, is that no Mississippian platforms and few other central features were constructed as one-time labor projects. All appear, at present, to have been incremental constructions, with the early "stages" of some Cahokia mounds being no more than sheer mantles of silt or sand laid down to ritually sterilize the area. From this, we may infer that the central point of mound construction was not simply to construct an imposing tumulus, but was in part an effort that brought people together on a regular basis (see also Pauketat 1996).

The periodicity of such ritual labor mobilization takes on additional significance in light of the recently revised understanding of Cahokian political history (Pauketat 1994, 1998). In short, the pre-Mississippian village-level chiefdoms gave way, within a span of no more than a few decades (and perhaps considerably less), to a hypercentralized and regionally integrated Cahokian polity within the eleventh century. The political, social, and demographic changes evident in the archaeological record are so pronounced as to make unlikely anything but an abrupt and radical consolidation of the regional population under the aegis of a Cahokian capital.

In the past, under the sway of political-evolutionary models, researchers had thought Cahokia's brand of Mississippianism to be the culmination of material factors that predated AD 1050 (see Kelly 1990; Milner 1990). However, from a practice perspective, the burden of explanation shifts from the antecedent causes of some effect to the developments of AD 1050 themselves. The "moments of interaction" surrounding political consolidation, that is, were themselves the process. The ultimate outcome of the large-scale negotiations was probably unknown by any of the participants and could well have conflicted with the dispositions of many local people (see Pauketat 1997). Accordingly, we should, and do, find

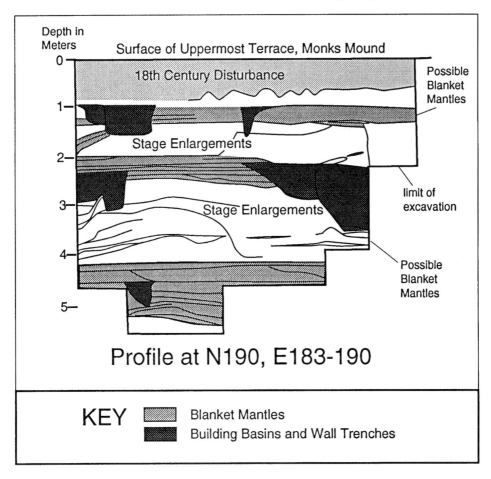

Figure 9.3 Excavation profile of the upper stages of Monks Mound

Source: adapted from Reed *et al.* 1968: Fig. 5

limited evidence of a kind of traditional resistance to region-wide Mississippian consolidation (i.e., a lack of intra-regional stylistic isomorphism). Likewise, we should, and do, have evidence of large-scale, Cahokia-centric social negotiations as subjective co-optation (Pauketat 1997, 1998).

The construction of platform mounds is one such line of evidence. Who built the mounds? The labor investment and construction history of mounds and Mississippian capital grounds is such that we can be certain that most people, non-elite farmers, labored on the tumuli. This is well documented in the historical records and ethnographic studies of southeastern natives, where such collective activities were and are conducted during annual, large-scale rituals held at central grounds (see Howard 1968; Knight 1986, 1989). This practice was also recorded in traditional stories and songs. "Behold the wonderful work of *our* hands," the Choctaw song goes, "and let *us* be glad. Look upon the great mound; its top is above the trees, and its black shadow lies on the ground, a bowshot. It is surmounted by the golden emblem of the sun; its glitter *dazzles the eyes of the multitude*" (Lincecum 1904: 532, emphasis added).

It is not novel (nor earth shaking) to recognize that the non-elite masses built Mississippian monuments. But we can go one better than this simple observation. In building the mounds, the laborers, as in the Choctaw song, identified with the mounds. As in rites at native grounds in present-day Oklahoma, rituals at pre-Columbian mound-and-plaza complexes probably created a regional "community" identity (Pauketat and Emerson 1999). The construction of mounds, that is, was also the construction of orthodox meanings (see Bradley 1990; Kus 1984). The scale of the orthodoxy and, not incidentally, the scale of a homogeneous horizon style probably correlate with the scale of the rituals of community (see also Wheatley 1975).

Discussion

In an early Mississippian context, or in any formative context, the construction of meaning, order, and identity cannot be dissociated from the social negotiation of power and tradition. I am not saying that people of all statuses spontaneously coalesced in a kind of communal utopian lovefest.[4] In the Cahokia region, and possibly in the Moundville, Lake George, Winterville, and other early Mississippian complexes, the abrupt shifts in monument building, population density, settlement organization, and material-goods production clearly signal the establishment of some new coordinated power (see Knight 1997; Pauketat 1994; Steponaitis 1991). How that authority was initially articulated is far beyond the present scope and, to large extent, beside the present point. The range of possibilities includes everything from religious movements to kin coalitions to coercive regional over-lords (see Pauketat 1994). The point is that the process was much more than any of these. The power implicated in, or the events of, consolidation did not simply cause Mississippian polities to coalesce. The process was an increase in the scale of traditional negotiations from the level of local communities to the level of regional populations constructing mounds and meanings. The laborers who invested in the central representations and the coordinators of monumental practice created the abrupt changes that instigated a new scale of negotia-tions. The mounds illustrate that these new regional chiefdoms regularly included – not excluded – large segments of the regional population (Pauketat and Emerson 1999).

Why would a population, living free of regional centralization, create the radical early Mississippian capitals and all that they entailed? Why would they participate in domination, at least to the extent that regional centralization inhibited coordinated action outside of the Mississippian capitals? The answer is three fold. First, cooperating farmers of the eleventh and twelfth centuries may not have had a clear collective sense (discursive knowledge, political ideology, etc.) of what was in the offing, even if various individuals recognized the changes that the new Mississippian capital grounds entailed. Second, the coordinators of the Mississippian constructions, the hosts of ritual gatherings, were probably acting in a traditional manner, continuing the tradition of the minimally central-ized precursors of the Mississippians (Pauketat 1994). What had changed *initially* to distinguish these Mississippians from their forebears was the scale of these practices, not necessarily their character. The burden of explanation, then, falls on explaining how coor-dinated action – at this enlarged scale – was perpetuated. This is a question about the practice of all participants, not just the coordinators.

Consequently, the third part of the answer seems to be that those people who partici-pated in "Mississippianization" recognized some benefit in doing so. I have elsewhere argued that the Cahokian evidence suggests that benefits included increased access to the produce and social valuables that defined a traditional economy (Pauketat 1994). The dramatically enlarged scale of a Cahokian economy, that is, did not necessarily violate tradition. People may have been willing to accommodate recognizable changes if those changes, via the Mississippian coordinators, were reconciled with tradition (see Lears 1985). The consequences were composite arrays of tradition and power, "compromise equilibria" and "hegemonies" created through surface phenomena.

Conceptual devices for understanding how such compromises might have been negotiated exist in political anthropology's "coalitions," "factions," "political communities," and "social movements" (see Bailey 1969; Bash 1995; Brumfiel 1994; Marger 1981; Pauketat 1994: 31; Pauketat and Emerson 1999; Salisbury and Silverman 1977). Kertzer (1988) has pointed out that social movements conjoin disparate interests through political rituals and political symbols that co-opt traditional dispositions and forge otherwise unlike interests into what Williams (1977) calls "formations." I say forge here because, from the point of view of practice, these formations were not the consequences of political evolution but were the actual structuring process of social change. All people of some particular formation may have accommodated change if it was little more than the subjective co-optation of their traditions. In monuments, we see not the consequences of political actions to legitimize centralized authority but these formations in the process of becoming.

In Mississippian times, the building of earthen platforms (along with the many other ritual creations and constructions), was a "surface phenomenon" that inculcated a co-ordinated power and an inclusive tradition. There may have been little motivation to resist this kind of domination. Once constrained by the spaces and practices of new Mississippian formations, the coordinated political actions necessary to objectively "resist" domination – with or without elite actions – would have been inhibited (Marx and Engels 1989; Wolf 1990: 587). And this would be the case despite the fact that the coordinated actions of people structured this larger-scale social formation that, after the fact, only large-scale coordinated action could have undone. Such coordination would have been lacking outside the Mississippian capitals. Compliance may have often been the only *social* option.

Conclusion

To the extent that Trigger's global observations of formative florescences are valid, there may be only one way to understand how the multitude united: those who would be dominated gave shape to the domination, this shape recapitulating "tradition" or at least those elements of tradition imperfectly reproduced through surface phenomena. How could a social movement, one that co-opted the traditions of a regional population, resist itself? We should not expect that it would, the result being subjective co-optation, a consensual mode of domination, and the multitude uniting as a commonwealth. The monuments were built but the common people did not necessarily defy, in an overt or objective sense, the large-scale social changes of formative developments. Yet neither did people passively acquiesce. They did not accept or did not understand domination for what we see it to be in the aggregate. Domination, as an historical process, could hardly have been fully anticipated by anyone, including high status movers-and-shakers who were moving and shaking in traditional ways (but with possibly unanticipated results).

We need not rationalize centralization as adaptive in the long-term development of a population in order to explain why the multitudes so united as commonwealths. Practice theory provides here not a proximate solution to some historical particular but an ultimate solution to a problem of social science. Common people actively created monumental changes, perhaps beneficial (within their historical frames of reference) in the short-run, but deleterious to their own ability to coordinate action in the long run. For in the long run, monumental practices objectified the coordination as a place if not, ultimately, as a class of aristocrats associated with that place (Eliade 1961: 41ff.; Helms 1993; Kus 1984: 106).

That the elites and commoners of any age were neither fully cognizant and rational actors nor entirely constrained automatons is in part understandable if we recognize that practice is not based solely on political ideology or higher-order "discursive" consciousness. Rather, people's dispositions are to a large degree traditional, spontaneous, and common sensical. Thus, these dispositions are subject to co-optation via surface phenomena and within the sorts of social negotiations where traditions were accommodated or appropriated via formations. My point is not that an individual commoner had as much ability to transform history as an individual king. This is patently false. Commoners do, however, share the responsibility for what, in some historical contexts, was their own subordination.

If we had attacked Hobbes' problem, how multitudes united into commonwealths, by attempting to locate the causes of a particular kind of ideology or a particular kind of organization, we would have reduced historical processes to behavioral teleology. We would have ended up with the conundrum of wanting to attribute to commoners some role in creating commonwealths, as did Hobbes, but not seeing why they would have accommodated it. Practice theory, on the other hand, accounts for domination in a novel way, as a kind of consensual co-optation where traditional practices were appropriated through coordinated constructions that subsequently disabled collective actions except as coordinated through centers. Practice theory, thus, gives meaning and historical relevance to the labor that went into monument construction.

As the potential for explaining the tragedy of the commoners exemplifies, the ultimate explanations of the social sciences still remain to be found through practice theory. These will not be the same standard solutions to the same "why" questions that have been the staple of archaeology for decades. These practice-informed solutions will be contingent on conceptual improvements, recognizing monuments, artifacts, and landscapes *as process* – as the moments of interaction – rather than as expressions or correlates *of* process. And these solutions will be contingent on tracking the scales and configurations of social negotiations – domination, collaboration, accommodation, capitulation, etc. – as combined with the collective modes of such practices, coalitions, factions, movements, and so on. We therefore need large-scale archaeological data sets with which to measure the rates and scales of relational and representational changes across time and space. These are significant contingencies that require us to alter our own archaeological practices. Only in so doing can we avoid reducing history to behavioral teleology and, thereby, perpetuating the tragedy of the commoners.

Acknowledgment

A debt of gratitude is owed to David Anderson, Thomas Emerson, John E. Robb and Marcia-Anne Dobres for their comments on an earlier version of this chapter.

Notes

1 The concept of hegemony (and subjective co-optation) does not lend itself easily to the now-common "power to" versus "power over" distinction. Some might argue that subjective co-optation would fit better within the realm of "power to," but it seems likely that "power over" was frequently based largely on subjective co-optation.
2 The opposite is not necessarily true. The mere existence of monumental architecture does not

mean that a centralized government had developed. European and North American examples abound (e.g., Bradley 1990; Gibson 1996; Mainfort 1988).

3 A Mississippian polity may be defined as a centralized population governed by an institutionalized administration, usually thought to include a simple hierarchy of chiefs, councilors, and native aristocrats.

4 I reserve the right to accuse others of making that error.

Bibliography

Abercrombie, N. S. Hill, and B. S. Turner 1980. *The Dominant Ideology Thesis*. Allen and Unwin, London.

Anderson, D. G. 1994. *The Savannah River Chiefdoms: Political Change in the Late Prehistoric Southeast*. University of Alabama Press, Tuscaloosa.

—— 1996. "Fluctuations between Simple and Complex Chiefdoms: Cycling in the Late Prehistoric Southeast," in *Political Structure and Change in the Prehistoric Southeastern United States*, ed. J. F. Scarry, pp. 231–52. University of Florida Press, Gainesville.

Bailey, F. G. 1969. *Stratagems and Spoils: A Social Anthropology of Politics*. Schocken Books, New York.

Ball, T. 1983. "On Making History in Vico and Marx," in *Vico and Marx: Affinities and Contrasts*, ed. G. Tagliacozzo, pp. 78–93. Humanities Press, Atlantic Highlands, New Jersey.

Bash, H. H. 1995. *Social Problems and Social Movements: An Exploration into the Sociological Construction of Alternative Realities*. Humanities Press, Atlantic Highlands, New Jersey.

Baudrillard, J. 1981. *For a Critique of a Political Economy of the Sign*. Telos Press, St Louis.

Bell, C. 1997. *Ritual: Perspectives and Dimensions*. Oxford University Press, Oxford.

Binford, L. R. 1983. *Working at Archaeology*. Academic Press, New York.

Blanton, R. E., G. M. Feinman, S. A. Kowalewski, and P. N. Peregrine 1996. "A Dual-Processual Theory for the Evolution of Mesoamerican Civilization." *Current Anthropology* 17: 1–14.

Bourdieu, P. 1977. *Outline of a Theory of Practice*. Cambridge University Press, Cambridge UK.

—— 1990. *The Logic of Practice*. Polity Press, Cambridge UK.

—— 1994. *Language and Symbolic Power*. 3rd edn. Harvard University Press, Cambridge, Mass.

Bradley, R. 1990. "Monuments and the Monumental." *World Archaeology* 22: 119–243.

Brain, J. P. 1989. *Winterville: Late Prehistoric Culture Contact in the Lower Mississippi Valley*. Archaeological Report no. 23, Mississippi Department of Archives and History, Jackson, Miss.

Braun, D. P. 1995. "Style, Selection, and Historicity," in *Style, Society, and Person: Archaeological and Ethnological Perspectives*, ed. C. Carr and J. E. Neitzel, pp. 124–41. Plenum Press, New York.

Brumfiel, E. M. 1992. "Distinguished Lecture in Archaeology: Breaking and Entering the Ecosystem: Gender, Class, and Faction Steal the Show." *American Anthropologist* 943.: 551–67.

—— 1994. "Factional Competition and Political Development in the New World: An Introduction," in *Factional Competition and Political Development in the New World*, ed. E. M. Brumfiel and J. W. Fox, pp. 3–13. Cambridge University Press, Cambridge UK.

—— 1997. "The Quality of Tribute Cloth: The Place of Evidence in Archaeological Argument." *American Antiquity* 61: 453–62.

Campbell, C. 1996. *The Myth of Social Action*. Cambridge University Press, Cambridge UK.

Cohen, A. 1974. *Two-Dimensional Man: An Essay on the Anthropology of Power and Symbolism in Complex Society*. Routledge and Kegan Paul, London.

Collins, J. M. and M. L. Chalfant 1993. "A Second-terrace Perspective on Monks Mound." *American Antiquity* 58: 319–32.

Comaroff, J. and J. Comaroff 1991. *Of Revelation and Revolution: Christianity, Colonialism, and Consciousness in South Africa*. University of Chicago Press, Chicago.

Conkey, M. W. 1990. "Experimenting with Style in Archaeology: Some Historical and Theoretical Issues," in *The Uses of Style in Archaeology*, ed. M. W. Conkey and C. A. Hastorf, pp. 5–17. Cambridge University Press, Cambridge UK.

Cowgill, G. L. 1993. "Distinguished Lecture in Archaeology: Beyond Criticizing New Archeology."

American Anthropologist 95: 551–73.

Dalan, R. A. 1997. "The Construction of Mississippian Cahokia," in *Cahokia: Domination and Ideology in the Mississippian World*, ed. T. R. Pauketat and T. Emerson, pp. 89–102. University of Nebraska Press, Lincoln.

Deagan, K. A. 1990. "Accommodation and Resistance: The Process and Impact of Spanish Colonization in the Southeast," in *Columbian Consequences Volume 1: Archaeological and Historical Perspectives on the Spanish Borderlands West*, ed. D. H. Thomas, pp. 297–314. Smithsonian Institution Press, Washington, D.C.

DeMarris, E., L. J. Castillo, and T. K. Earle 1996. "Ideology, Materialization, and Power Strategies." *Current Anthropology* 17: 15–31.

Dobres, M-A. and C. R. Hoffman 1994." Social Agency and the Dynamics of Prehistoric Technology." *Journal of Archaeological Method and Theory* 1: 211–58.

Eliade, M. 1961. *Images and Symbols: Studies in Religious Symbolism*. Sheed and Ward, New York.

Emerson, T. E. 1997a. *Cahokia and the Archaeology of Power*. University of Alabama Press, Tuscaloosa.

—— 1997b. "Cahokian Elite Ideology and the Mississippian Cosmos," in *Cahokia: Domination and Ideology in the Mississippian World*, ed. T. R. Pauketat and T. E. Emerson, pp. 190–228. University of Nebraska Press, Lincoln.

Feinman, G. M. 1995. "The Emergence of Inequality: A Focus on Strategies and Processes," in *Foundations of Social Inequality*, ed. T. D. Price and G. M. Feinman, pp. 255–79 Plenum Press, New York.

Ferguson, L. 1992. *Uncommon Ground: Archaeology and Early African America, 1650–1800*. Smithsonian Institution Press, Washington, D.C.

Gibson, J. L. 1996. "Poverty Point and Greater Southeastern Prehistory: The Culture that did not Fit," in *Archaeology of the Mid-Holocene Southeast*, ed. K. E. Sassaman and D. G. Anderson, pp. 288–305. University of Florida Press, Gainesville.

Giddens, A. 1976. *New Rules of Sociological Method: A Positive Critique of Interpretive Sociologies*. Basic Books, New York.

—— 1977. *Studies in Social and Political Theory*. Hutchinson, London.

—— 1979. *Central Problems in Social Theory: Action, Structure, and Contradiction in Social Analysis*. Macmillan, London.

Gramsci, A. 1971. *Selections from the Prison Notebooks of Antonio Gramsci*, trans. Q. Hoare and G. N. Smith. International Publishers, New York.

Habermas, J. 1984. *The Theory of Communicative Action*, vol. 1. Beacon Press, Boston.

Hally, D. J. 1996. "Platform-Mound Construction and the Instability of Mississippian Chiefdoms," in *Political Structure and Change in the Prehistoric Southeastern United States*, ed. J. F. Scarry, pp. 92–127. University of Florida Press, Gainesville.

Hardin, G. 1977. "The Tragedy of the Commons," in *Managing the Commons*, ed. G. Hardin and J. Baden, pp. 16–30. W.H. Freeman, San Francisco.

Hastorf, C. A. 1991. Gender, Space, and Food in Prehistory," in *Engendering Archaeology: Women and Prehistory*, ed. J. M. Gero and M. W. Conkey, pp. 132–59. Blackwell, Oxford.

Hayden, B. 1995. Pathways to Power: Principles for Creating Socioeconomic Inequalities," in *Foundations of Social Inequality*, ed. T. D. Price and G. M. Feinman, pp. 15–86. Plenum Press, New York.

Helms, M. W. 1993. *Craft and the Kingly Ideal: Art, Trade, and Power*. University of Texas Press, Austin.

Hobbes, T. 1985 [orig. 1651]. *Leviathan*, ed. C. B. MacPherson. Penguin Books, London.

Hodder, I. 1986. *Reading the Past*. Cambridge University Press, Cambridge UK.

Howard, J. H. 1968. *The Southeastern Ceremonial Complex and Its Interpretation*. Missouri Archaeological Society, Memoir 6, Columbia, Missouri.

Johannessen, S. 1993. "Food, Dishes, and Society in the Mississippi Valley," in *Foraging and Farming in the Eastern Woodlands*, ed. C. M. Scarry, pp. 182–205. University Press of Florida, Gainesville.

Johnson, M. H. 1989. "Conceptions of Agency in Archaeological Interpretation." *Journal of Anthropological Archaeology* 8: 189–211.

—— 1996. *An Archaeology of Capitalism.* Blackwell, Cambridge, Mass.

Kelly, J. E. 1990. "The Emergence of Mississippian Culture in the American Bottom Region," in *The Mississippian Emergence*, ed. B. D. Smith, pp. 113–52. Smithsonian Institution Press, Washington, D.C.

Kent, S. (ed.) 1990. *Domestic Architecture and the Use of Space: An Interdisciplinary Cross-Cultural Study.* Cambridge University Press, Cambridge UK.

Kertzer, D. 1988. *Ritual, Politics, and Power.* Yale University Press, New Haven.

Knight, V. J., Jr. 1986. "The Institutional Organization of Mississippian Religion." *American Antiquity* 51: 675–87.

—— 1989. "Symbolism of Mississippian Mounds," in *Powhatan's Mantle: Indians in the Colonial Southeast*, ed. P. H. Wood, G. A. Waselkov, and M. T. Hatley, pp. 279–91. University of Nebraska Press, Lincoln.

—— 1997. "Some Developmental Parallels between Cahokia and Moundville," in *Cahokia: Domination and Ideology in the Mississippian World*, ed. T. R. Pauketat and T. E. Emerson, pp. 229–47. University of Nebraska Press, Lincoln.

Kowalewski, S. A., G. M. Feinman, and L. Finsten 1992. "'The Elite' and Assessment of Social Stratification in Mesoamerican Archaeology," in *Mesoamerican Elites: An Archaeological Assessment*, ed. D. Z. Chase and A. F. Chase, pp. 259–77. University of Oklahoma Press, Norman.

Kus, S. 1984. "The Spirit and its Burden: Archaeology and Symbolic Activity," in *Marxist Perspectives in Archaeology*, ed. M. Spriggs, pp. 101–7. Cambridge University Press, Cambridge UK.

Lears, T. J. J. 1985. "The Concept of Cultural Hegemony: Problems and Possibilities." *American Historical Review* 90: 567–93.

Lincecum, G. 1904. "Choctaw Traditions about their Settlement in Mississippi and the Origin of their Mounds." *Publications of the Mississippi Historical Society* 8: 521–42.

Lindauer, O. and J. H. Blitz 1997. "Higher Ground: The Archaeology of North American Platform Mounds." *Journal of Archaeological Research* 5: 169–207

Lopinot, N. H. 1997. "Cahokian Food Production Reconsidered," in *Cahokia: Domination and Ideology in the Mississippian World*, ed. T. R. Pauketat and T. E. Emerson, pp. 52–68, University of Nebraska Press, Lincoln.

Mainfort, R. C., Jr. 1988. "Middle Woodland Ceremonialism at Pinson Mounds, Tennessee." *American Antiquity* 53: 158–73.

Marcus, G. E. and M. M. J. Fischer 1986. *Anthropology as Cultural Critique: An Experimental Moment in the Human Sciences.* University of Chicago Press, Chicago.

Marger, M. N. 1981. *Elites and Masses.* Van Nostrand, New York.

Marx, K. 1978. "Economic and Philosophic Manuscripts of 1844," in *The Marx-Engels Reader*, ed. R. C. Tucker, pp. 66–132. Norton, New York.

Marx, K., and F. Engels 1989. *The German Ideology*, Part I. International Publishers, New York.

Maschner, H. D. G. and J. Q. Patton 1996. "Kin Selection and the Origins of Hereditary Social Inequality: A Case Study from the Northern Northwest Coast," in *Darwinian Archaeologies*, ed. H. D. G. Maschner, pp. 89–107. Plenum Press, New York.

McGuire, R. H. 1992. *A Marxist Archaeology.* Academic Press, San Diego.

Merton, R. K. 1949. *Social Theory and Social Structure.* Free Press, Glencoe, Ill.

Miller, D. 1989. "The Limits of Dominance," in *Domination and Resistance*, ed. D. Miller, M. Rowlands, and C. Tilley, pp. 63–79. Unwin Hyman, London.

Milner, G. R. 1990. "The Late Prehistoric Cahokia Cultural System of the Mississippi River Valley: Foundations, Florescence, and Fragmentation." *Journal of World Prehistory* 4: 1–43.

—— 1996. *The Muddled Mississippian: Agendas, Analogues, and Analyses.* Paper presented at the 61st annual meeting of the Society for American Archaeology, New Orleans.

Muller, J. 1997. *Mississippian Political Economy.* Plenum Press, New York.

Nassaney, M. S. 1992. "Communal Societies and the Emergence of Elites in the Prehistoric American Southeast," in *Lords of the Southeast: Social Inequality and the Native Elites of Southeastern North America*, ed. A. W. Barker and T. R. Pauketat, pp. 111–43. Archeological Papers of the American

Anthropological Association no. 3, Washington, D.C.

Ohnuki-Tierny, E. (ed.) 1990. *Culture Through Time: Anthropological Approaches*. Stanford University Press, Stanford.

Orser, C. E., Jr. 1998. "The Archaeology of the African Diaspora." *Annual Review of Anthropology* 27: 63–82.

Ortner, S. B. 1984. "Theory in Anthropology Since the Sixties." *Comparative Studies in Society and History* 26: 126–66.

Pauketat, T. R. 1993. *Temples for Cahokia Lords: Preston Holder's 1955–1956 Excavations of Kunnemann Mound*. University of Michigan, Museum of Anthropology Memoir no. 26, Ann Arbor.

—— 1994. *The Ascent of Chiefs: Cahokia and Mississippian Politics in Native North America*. University of Alabama Press, Tuscaloosa.

—— 1996. "The Place of Post-circle Monuments in Cahokian Political History." *Wisconsin Archeologist* 77: 73–83.

—— 1997. "Cahokian Political Economy," in *Cahokia: Domination and Ideology in the Mississippian World*, ed. T. R. Pauketat and T. E. Emerson, pp. 30–51. University of Nebraska Press, Lincoln.

—— 1998. "Refiguring the Archaeology of Greater Cahokia." *Journal of Archaeological Research* 6: 45–89.

Pauketat, T. R., and T. E. Emerson (eds) 1997. *Cahokia: Domination and Ideology in the Mississippian World*. University of Nebraska Press, Lincoln.

—— 1999. "Representations of Hegemony as Community at Cahokia," in *Material Symbols: Culture and Economy in Prehistory*, ed. J. E. Robb, pp. 302–17. Center for Archaeological Investigations, Southern Illinois University, Carbondale.

Pauketat, T. R., and N. H. Lopinot 1997. "Cahokian Population Dynamics," in *Cahokia: Domination and Ideology in the Mississippian World*, ed. T. R. Pauketat and T. E. Emerson, pp. 103–23. University of Nebraska Press, Lincoln.

Paynter, R., and R. H. McGuire 1991. "The Archaeology of Inequality: Material Culture, Domination, and Resistance," in *The Archaeology of Inequality*, ed. R. H. McGuire and R. Paynter, pp. 1–27. Blackwell, Oxford.

Reed, N. A., J. W. Bennett, and J. W. Porter 1968. "Solid Core Drilling of Monks Mound: Technique and Findings." *American Antiquity* 33: 137–48.

Renfrew, C. 1994. "Towards a Cognitive Archaeology," in *The Ancient Mind: Elements of Cognitive Archaeology*, ed. C. Renfrew and E. Zubrow, pp. 3–12. Cambridge University Press, Cambridge UK.

Reyna, S. P. 1994. "A Mode of Domination Approach to Organized Violence," in *Studying War: Anthropological Perspectives*, ed. S. P. Reyna and R. E. Downs, pp. 29–65. Gordon and Breach, USA.

Rindos, D. 1984. *The Origins of Agriculture*. Academic Press, New York.

Robb, J. E. 1998. "The Archaeology of Symbols." *Annual Review of Anthropology* 27: 329–46.

Rosenberg, S. W. 1988. *Reason, Ideology, and Politics*. Princeton University Press, Princeton.

Sahlins, M. 1972. *Stone Age Economics*. Aldine, Chicago.

—— 1981. *Historical Metaphors and Mythical Realities: Structure in the Early History of the Sandwich Islands Kingdom*. University of Michigan Press, Ann Arbor.

—— 1985. *Islands of History*. University of Chicago Press, Chicago.

Saitta, D. J. 1994. "Agency, Class, and Archaeological Interpretation." *Journal of Anthropological Archaeology* 13: 201–27.

Salisbury, R. F. and M. Silverman 1977. "An Introduction: Factions and the Dialectic," in *A House Divided? Anthropological Studies of Factionalism*, ed. M. Silverman and R. F. Salisbury, pp. 1–20. Social and Economic Papers no. 9, Memorial University of Newfoundland.

Scarry, J. and B. G. McEwan 1995. "Domestic Architecture in Apalachee Province: Apalachee and Spanish Residential Styles in the Late Prehistoric and Early Historic Period Southeast." *American Antiquity* 60: 482–95.

Schiffer, M. B. 1996. "Some Relationships between Behavioral and Evolutionary Archaeologies." *American Antiquity* 61: 643–62.

Schlanger, N. 1994. "Mindful Technology: Unleashing the *Chaîne Opératoire* for an Archaeology of Mind," in *The Ancient Mind: Elements of Cognitive Archaeology*, ed. C. Renfrew and E. Zubrow, pp. 143–51. Cambridge University Press, Cambridge UK.

Schnell, F. T., V. J. Knight, Jr., and G. S. Schnell 1981. *Cemochechobee: Archaeology of a Mississippian Ceremonial Center on the Chattahoochee River*. University Press of Florida, Gainesville.

Scott, J. C. 1990. *Domination and the Arts of Resistance*. Yale University Press, New Haven.

Shennan, S. 1993. "After Social Evolution: A New Archaeological Agenda?" in *Archaeological Theory: Who Sets the Agenda?*, ed. N. Yoffee and A. Sherratt, pp. 53–9. Cambridge University Press, Cambridge UK.

Steponaitis, V. P. 1986. "Prehistoric Archaeology in the Southeastern United States, 1970–1985." *Annual Review of Anthropology* 15: 363–404.

—— 1991. "Contrasting Patterns of Mississippian Development," in *Chiefdoms: Power, Economy, and Ideology*, ed. T. K. Earle, pp. 193–228. Cambridge University Press, Cambridge UK.

Stocking, G. W., Jr. 1982. *Race, Culture, and Evolution: Essays in the History of Anthropology*. University of Chicago Press, Chicago.

Tainter, J. 1988. *The Collapse of Complex Societies*. Cambridge University Press, Cambridge UK.

Thomas, J. 1996. *Time, Culture and Identity*. Routledge, London.

Thompson, J. B. 1994. "Editor's Introduction," in *Language and Symbolic Power*. 3rd edn ed. P. Bourdieu, pp. 1–31. Harvard University Press, Cambridge, Mass.

Trigger, B. G. 1990. "Monumental Architecture: A Thermodynamic Explanation of Symbolic Behaviour." *World Archaeology* 22: 119–32.

van der Leeuw, S. E. 1994. "Cognitive Aspects of 'Technique,'" in *The Ancient Mind: Elements of Cognitive Archaeology*, ed. C. Renfrew and E. Zubrow, pp. 135–42. Cambridge University Press, Cambridge UK.

Weber, M. 1978. *Economy and Society: An Outline of Interpretive Sociology*. University of California Press, Berkeley.

Wheatley, P. 1975. "Satyanrta in Suvarnadvipa: From Reciprocity to Redistribution in Ancient Southeast Asia," in *Ancient Civilization and Trade*, ed. J. A. Sabloff and C. C. Lamberg-Karlovsky, pp. 227–83. University of New Mexico Press, Albuquerque.

Willey, G. R. and P. Phillips 1958. *Method and Theory in American Archaeology*. University of Chicago Press, Chicago.

Williams, R. 1977. *Marxism and Literature*. Oxford University Press, Oxford.

Williams, S., and J. P. Brain 1983. *Excavations at the Lake George Site, Yazoo County, Mississippi, 1958–1960*. Papers of the Peabody Museum of Archaeology and Ethnology, no. 74, Harvard University, Cambridge, Mass.

Wolf, E. 1990. "Facing Power – Old Insights, New Questions." *American Anthropologist* 92: 586–96.

10 The depositional history of ritual and power

William H. Walker and Lisa J. Lucero

The premise that human agents shaped past social and natural environments and were also constrained by those environments prompts the question: How can we, as archaeologists, glean the variable results of such activity from the archaeological record? It is tempting to assume that we must develop methods and theories to infer something of the thoughts and intentions of prehistoric actors (e.g., Hodder 1986; also Hodder, Cowgill, this volume), but as Giddens (1979: 44) has stated, the "recovery of the subject," in this case the actor, does not necessarily entail "lapsing into subjectivism," nor embracing "social phenomenology." (Bourdieu 1990: 135–40). After all, the dialectical interplay between actors and their environment leads to both intended and unintended consequences (Giddens 1979: 232, 244; 1984: 282, 344–6). In this chapter, we focus on how agents shape the flow of material objects (people, artifacts, and architecture) from and through cultural systems to the archaeological record. Our goal is to use a stratigraphic method to identify agential behavior and the ritual strategies behind it. We illustrate this method by assessing how emerging leaders in the American Southwest and the southern Maya lowlands of Central America appropriated traditional domestic rituals to promote their particular interests.

As archaeologists import concepts such as agency into their explanations of archaeological deposits (e.g., DeMarrais *et al.* 1996; Dobres and Hoffman 1994; Nielsen 1995; Roscoe 1993), it is important to consider how we can operationalize such ideas, especially those proposed by Bourdieu (1977, 1990) and Giddens (1979, 1984). To achieve this goal, we highlight how agents organize material culture in pursuing various activities including raw materials acquisition, manufacture, use, and discard (Schiffer 1976, 1995). By examining how agents create the life histories of artifacts we can link their final discard activities (the archaeological record) to earlier practices (systemic context). In this chapter, we explore the depositional history of ritual and power in the Southwest and the Maya Lowlands. These regions possess detailed ethnographic and archaeological data that allow us to examine the relationship between the activities of ritual agents and the formation of the archaeological record. In the northern American Southwest between AD 500 and 1400, Anasazi peoples of the Colorado Plateau established pit houses in farming villages, later constructing above-ground stone pueblos. At different times in this sequence their settlement patterns alternated from aggregated villages and towns to dispersed homesteads and hamlets. Periods of aggregation were often associated with the emergence of ritual traditions, created in part by the intentional acts of ritual leaders.

The ancient Maya differ from the Pueblo Southwest in that they had a more complex political organization headed by several rulers throughout the lowlands. However, in the use of ritual the history of the development of Maya rulers is similar to that in the Southwest. Prehistoric Maya settlement from about 700 BC to AD 900 was relatively dispersed, mirroring the distribution of arable land. However, after 250 BC, ritual leaders emerged as the rulers of this dispersed populace (see also Joyce, this volume). Their power, while greater than that known in the Pueblo Southwest, was similar because both had origins in earlier household rituals: ancestor veneration, dedication, and termination rituals. Emerging Maya rulers appropriated these rituals to acquire and maintain their growing power. Large Maya temples became ancestral shrines writ large, highlighting ties between the ruler's lineage and the divine realm. These processes resulted in sequences of deposits, or depositional histories, in ancient Pueblo and Maya settlements that document the successes of past ritual agents.

Agential behavior

Bourdieu and Giddens recognize that individual agents have more autonomy than they were accorded in classic structural–functional (Radcliffe-Brown 1952) and social evolutionary models (Steward 1955; White 1949); yet this freedom is not complete. To understand the interaction between actors and their social and natural environments, Giddens and Bourdieu attempt to model the actual practices and goals of the actors involved. These environments provide the arena within which agents not only act, but also participate as members of a social group. Giddens developed his theory of structuration in part to account for the internal and external forces (or constraints) that characterize the interaction between agents and these environments. Tradition, the routine of daily life, and individual motivation result in a duality, where there are both rules (a constraint) and actual practices (agential behaviors), and where the relationship between individuals and society can be reconceptualized as a dialectic between agency and structure. Even the least powerful actors, whose goals frequently go unrealized, have some power, and in the process of acting can restructure social constraints. In the process of social restructuring, agents contribute to the variability within society and the material remains it leaves behind.

The dynamic relationship between structure and the actual practice of agents leads to a state of continuous feedback. Here, structure is defined as social relations that are created, reproduced, and transformed by members of a society because "structures should be understood as enabling as well as constraining" (Hays 1994: 61). Consequently, actual practices, though governed by "cultural rules," do not always result in exact reproductions of previous or traditional practices. An outcome of such dialectical relationships is variability at a number of scales across space and time, including variation between individuals (e.g., warrior societies, religious sodalities, clans) and entire social systems such as bands, tribes, chiefdoms, and states (cf. Fried 1967; Service 1962, 1975). From day-to-day events to the rise of agrarian states, social change can be identified by this variability. Archaeologists can identify this variability in the archaeological record, both synchronically and diachronically, by understanding the organizational properties of relationships at each scale.

A brief discussion of exchange practices illustrates this variability at multiple scales. Individuals involved in balanced reciprocity can manipulate exchange to create obligations with those who cannot afford to return a gift, since "giving is also a way of possessing" (Bourdieu 1977: 195). Along with economic stratification, labor specialization, and political inequality (Brumfiel and Earle 1987), the variety of exchange types (generalized, balanced, redistributive) change in tandem in increasingly complex societies. Agential redistribution, for instance, redefines the nature of traditional gift-giving and accompanying social obligations (Bourdieu 1977: 191–5, 1990: 123–9) through the creation of unequal political and economic relationships. For example, peoples of the Pueblo

Southwest practiced a religion focused on crop fertility and moisture which comprised a series of cult institutions such as the *katsina* cult. In this cult, masked dancers impersonated ancestral spirits (*katsinas*) that danced for rain and social harmony. During public performances, *katsinas* also redistributed food brought to the ceremony by those who could afford it. Ethnohistorically, leaders of the Hopi *katsina* cult facilitated the redistribution of food to those in need, often farmers with less productive land (Eggan 1950; Levy 1992).

The origins of this cult derive from a period of aggregation in the fourteenth-century American Southwest, when competition for arable land around nucleated settlements increased (Adams 1991). Although the rise of this new religious cult grew from earlier traditions, its particular form or structure was not inevitable. Are not the material remains of this phenomenon the result, in part, of the agential behaviors of prehistoric Pueblo leaders? Leaders often mask inequities by appropriating familiar cultural "traditions." For example, prophecy, an integral part of decision making in the Pueblo world, has just this quality of transforming everyday events into evidence that legitimizes the decisions of ritual leaders (Whiteley 1988).

In larger scale societies, feasts, ceremonies, and celebrations display wealth and power and continue to serve as avenues of giving in order to possess even more (*sensu* Bourdieu 1977: 195). This "social alchemy" (Bourdieu 1977: 190–2, 1990: 128–9) allows leaders to legitimize existing structures (which are their sources of power) and to promote a sense of solidarity, inclusiveness, and equality (e.g., DeMarrais *et al.* 1996; Earle 1997; Hayden 1990; Hayden and Gargett 1990). Bourdieu (1990: 195) labels this phenomenon "collective misrecognition." The emergence of inequality and concomitant leadership thus leaves a material record of this structural change, where the social reproduction of tradition resembles an ideal never completely realized. It is no surprise, therefore, that Bourdieu and Giddens illustrate their concepts of agency by focusing on political or ritual agents and how they acquire the skill to manipulate the choices of others in order to justify and legitimize their own political goals (see also Joyce, Pauketat, this volume).

Often, public events are successful because leaders incorporate familiar ritual practices into them, which is why household rituals are embedded in the ancestral rites of lineages (Friedman and Rowlands 1978: 218; Helms 1993: 192; McAnany 1995). This pattern becomes evident in stratified societies such as the ancient Maya, where natural kinship ties incorporate supernatural relations between rulers and deities, or by non-kin ties in state-level societies where pretense is no longer required (Johnson and Earle 1987: 319–20). The significant issue here is that agents employ existing "principles of legitimation" (Earle 1989), euphemizing their acquired authority and power to mobilize the agency of others, as well as to control resources, surplus, and wealth. Thus, actions instituted by these agents have social repercussions that can result in social change.

The importance of utilizing existing principles of legitimation cannot be emphasized enough, and can best be illustrated by a few case studies where existing traditions were not so used. There have been instances where new strategies fail because leaders did not appropriate traditional practices. Webster (1976) notes, for example, that the first emperor (unifier) of China, Ch'in Shih Hwang Ti:

> made an abrupt attempt to replace the prevailing Confucianist political philosophy, which emphasized moral precepts as the basis for social tranquillity of the state, with a strongly pragmatic legalist doctrine backed by centrally administered, coercive force.... This attempt was an abject failure and resulted in the destruction of the emperors' administration and dynasty after only 15 years.
>
> (Webster 1976: 824)

In a similar vein, Hill (1944) explains that proselytizers of the Ghost Dance (a nineteenth-century revitalization movement incorporating the resurrection of the dead) failed to convert many Navajos because of their traditional fear of ghosts. These brief examples suggest that change is often more successful when built upon processes that begin with the familiar (cf. Kertzer 1988: 10).

The activities of political/ritual agents can be gleaned from the archaeological record by specifically focusing on how their activities create archaeological deposits. For example, in the American Southwest between AD 500 and 1400, we see a change in ritual abandonment practices. Before the advent of pueblos, pit houses – places of household ritual – were often ritually abandoned through burning; later, this burning shifts to the more specialized underground ceremonial rooms (*kivas*) associated with sodalities and clans. Similarly, in the Maya lowlands between 700 BC and AD 900, household ritual dedication and termination activities were first replicated in elite compounds by lineage heads (ca. 700 BC), and later in temple rituals by rulers (ca. 250 BC). In both cases, these changes in ritual activities proved relatively successful because domestic rituals familiar to all members of society were the basis of larger scale ceremonies. In the Pueblo Southwest, ritual activities still take place in kivas, while in the Maya area, post-collapse ritual only persists where it began, in the households of local communities (Thompson 1970: 163).

Evidence of ritual agents

Every time an agent interacted with an artifact, it was propelled along a pathway that began when it was fashioned from raw materials and ended in an archaeological deposit. Artifacts and architecture start as raw materials and pass through a series of activities including manufacture, use, reuse, recycling and eventually abandonment or discard. Actors literally created and changed the life histories of these objects in their dialectical struggle within the social and natural structures that constrained them. They used and reused artifacts as well as created new ones, and in the process left traces of these behaviors in the archaeological record (Deal 1988; Deal and Hagstrum 1995).

Not surprisingly, the functions of objects are not static; for example, cooking pots, while seemingly utilitarian or domestic, can become ritual artifacts if an actor takes them out of a pueblo kitchen and uses them in a kiva ceremony, or in the case of the ancient Maya, a serving plate is taken from a house, rendered useless ("killed"), and then offered in a dedicatory cache (Walker 1998; Walker and LaMotta 1995). The functions of objects do not ultimately reside in their forms, but rather in their variable pathways created by ritual and political agents.

Simplistic utilitarian/nonutilitarian functional classifications lead to equally simplistic inferences of prehistoric activities from archaeological contexts. Obvious interpretations based on the assumed functions of artifacts can be deceptive when detailed contextual clues are not considered. For example, when archaeologists in the Southwest encounter a burned pit house (a utilitarian structure) that contains whole cooking vessels and stored food (utilitarian objects), they may presume its abandonment resulted from an accident or catastrophe rather than a ritual activity, especially if human remains are mixed in with the deposits (Walker 1998). Ethnographic evidence, however, suggests a number of alternative explanations for such burning.

In the Southwest, virtually all peoples who lived in mud-and-brush structures, (similar to prehistoric pit-house dwellers of the past), practiced life-crisis religions (Underhill 1948) that involved the funerary burning of a deceased's house. In California, the Desert, Pass and

Mountain Cahuilla burned their houses (Strong 1929: 84, 121, 180–1) as did the Cocopa (Kelly 1977: 87), Halchidhoma and Maricopa (Spier 1933: 303, 309), Hsupai (Iliff 1954; Spier 1928: 234, 292), Mojave (Allen 1891: 615–6; Drucker 1941: 146–7), Navajo (Mindeleff 1898; Kent 1984: 139–41), Pima (Drucker 1941; Grossman 1873: 415), Papago (Drucker 1941; Beals 1934: 7), Quechean (Bee 1983: 89), Shoshone (Steward 1933: 62), Southern Yavapai (Gifford 1932: 185), as well as Western Apache (Bushkirk 1986: 108; Gifford 1940: 68; Goodwin 1942) living in Arizona and New Mexico. In addition to homes, other utilitarian objects owned by the deceased were also often destroyed, including tools, keepsakes, granaries full of food, and even crops in the field.

There are also compelling ethnographic and epigraphic examples of burning and the ritual deposition of both utilitarian and nonutilitarian artifacts among the Maya. Many Maya groups today conduct dedication rituals at the completion of a house. For example, among the Zinacantan Maya of highland Chiapas, builders bury the heads of sacrificed chickens in the floor with other offerings (Vogt 1993: 52–5). Afterwards, a shaman performs rites to compensate the Earth Lord for the materials he has provided, as well as to "summon the ancestral gods to provide the house with an innate soul" (ibid.: 52). Again, more offerings are buried in the floor of the new house (see also Vogt 1970: 78, 98). A similar ritual is noted among the Maya of the towns of Tizimin (Wauchope 1938: 143) and Chan Kom (Redfield and Villa Rojas 1934: 146) in the Yucatán. Epigraphic accounts carved on stelae, temples, and palaces at Palenque, Yaxchilan, Naranjo, Tikal, Copan, and other Maya centers (Freidel and Schele 1989; Schele 1990; Schele and Freidel 1990) record similar dedication and termination rituals.

Maya renewal ceremonies show a similar pattern through space and time. For example, among the Zinacantecos, yearly renewal ceremonies involve the all-important ancestral gods (Vogt 1970: 99). Among the Lacandon Maya of Chiapas, a feature of the renewal ceremony is the manufacture of new incense-burners (*incensarios*), the lighting of new fires, and the use of new utilitarian goods such as cooking vessels (Tozzer 1907: 106). During the last rite of the renewal ceremony, old *incensarios*, jars, and other items are taken out of habitation areas to a nearby cliff and deposited in a specific ritual dump (ibid.: 146–7). These rites are identical with those described by Landa for Colonial Yucatán (Tozzer 1941: 151–2; see also Thompson 1970: 173–5). Epigraphic accounts also tell of large-scale *katun* (twenty 360-day years) period-ending rites and renewal ceremonies that included the construction of twin pyramid complexes at a number of Maya centers, notably Tikal (e.g., Jones 1991; also Schele and Freidel 1990).

Ancestor veneration rites also display continuity from the past to the present (cf. McAnany 1995). Among the Zinacantecos, ancestral gods are the most important deities, even more important than the Earth Lord (Vogt 1970: 6). "The powers whose influence on human affairs is continuous and unremitting are the ancestors, who represent the great moral force" (cf. Deal 1988; also Bunzel 1952: 269; Tozzer 1907: 45). Although the ancestral gods live in sacred places such as caves or mountains, their physical remains are kept close to home, literally buried in the floors of houses. Again, Landa describes similar practices for Colonial Yucatán (Tozzer 1941: 130), where the skulls of ancestors were kept in sacred huts or house altars (ibid.: 131). Epigraphic accounts leave little doubt that Maya rulers linked themselves and their lineages to ancestral founders and deities, and that these linkages were continually displayed in ceremonies that took place on top of temples (Freidel and Schele 1988; Houston and Stuart 1996; McAnany 1995; Schele and Freidel 1990).

These examples from the American Southwest and the Maya region dramatically illustrate the central role ritual agents played in the creation of archaeological deposits. To develop more complex behavioral inferences that take into account the ritual manipulation of objects by agents during dedication, termination, ancestral veneration, and abandonment rituals requires models that take into consideration the contextual clues found in specific sequences of archaeological deposits. The processing of architecture during episodes of construction, remodeling, or abandonment often leaves traces of ritual pathways that can be inferred from the depositional histories of these buildings. Although this approach was developed as a method to discriminate different abandonment processes in the Pueblo Southwest (Walker 1998), we show here that it is widely applicable. Although agency studies typically discourage general methods, a depositional history approach is flexible enough to highlight behavioral variability within and among cultures as diverse as the prehistoric Anasazi and the ancient Maya.

A life history approach to houses, kivas, and temples

When a Maya temple was closed during a termination ceremony, caches and layers of formal fill were laid down and a new temple constructed over them (see Freidel and Schele 1989: 237–8; Schele and Freidel 1990: 104–8). These construction activities result in sequences of causally related deposits, depositional sequences or histories that document the ritual life of the temple. Although one can consider these as separate events, perhaps simply construction activities, they are evidence of ritual activities. This ritual layering (Freidel and Schele 1989), as well as the traces of ritual activities that took place on the temple top (such as bloodlettings, human sacrifices, and accession ceremonies), can be considered part of a larger unit of analysis: the temple's life history. Thus, the stratigraphic relations, or more specifically, the depositional histories of temples, provide important clues for understanding the activities of past ritual agents. For example, obsidian debitage and other utilitarian objects, when found cached in temple construction layers, may actually record evidence of past ritual activities (Deal 1988; Freidel and Schele 1989; Garber 1986, 1989).

Even the fill and floor layers of houses, if considered causally related, can provide important evidence of prehistoric ritual agency. Houses, like temples, are complex artifacts that possess life histories comprised of a number of stages (e.g., manufacture, use, reuse, abandonment, and post-abandonment). They begin their lives as raw materials and pass through one or more stages before entering the archaeological record.

Sub-stages of a structure's life history can themselves be subdivided into analytical units that correspond to the feature's stratigraphy. Events in the life histories of structures result in the creation of several interconnected deposits, including fill of floor features, artifacts on floors, the lower fill and upper fill of a structure. Such deposits often have one ritual process that connects them. In some cases, the entire stratigraphic sequence can be employed as a unit of analysis. For example, a series of variables describing their deposits can be used to define the rebuilding of a structure. If considered independently of its relationship to the rest of the structure's stratigraphy (e.g., broken *incensarios* resting on a burned floor, whole plates in the fill, obsidian cached in construction rubble), any one variable could be used to argue for several interpretations. But a life history approach forces interpretations to consider relations between multiple variables in a sequence of deposits. For example, a burned Maya house floor could be the result of warfare, accident, funerary ritual, or any number of hypothetical causes. The addition of more stratigraphic information, however, begins to differentiate strong from weak inferences, by revealing in a probabilistic sense more or less likely sequences of events.

To distinguish between warfare and ritual abandonment, for example, one could consider a series of linked deposits in a structure such as whether whole, fragmentary, or no artifacts were present on the floor; whether it was burned or not; and finally, whether or not there were whole artifacts, fragmentary artifacts, or no artifacts in the fill between floors. Differences between deposits would distinguish one structure's life history from another's. When considered alone, roof burning or the presence of utilitarian floor artifacts could not help conclusively distinguish a ritual abandonment from a fiery catastrophe. But when these floor artifacts occur in a sequence of burned floors intruded upon by caches, a depositional history is revealed that suggests the structure has been ritually remodeled.

Such ritually created sequences of deposits can be identified at Maya and Anasazi sites. Differences in these deposits can be quantified through a series of variables that describe each stratum in a structure. For example, in the Southwest, four variable strata – floor feature deposits, floor artifacts, lower fill, upper fill – can be used to describe a structure's stratigraphy (Figure 10. 1). A structure (A) with unsealed floor features, fragmentary artifacts on its floor, unburned weight-bearing (primary) roofing beams in its lower fill, and without artifacts in its upper fill, would exhibit a different pathway from another (B) with sealed floor features, whole artifacts on its floor, burned roofing material in its lower fill, and whole artifacts deposited in its upper fill. These would be two possible pathways of the many potential ones that could exist, given these four variable depositional events.

The ancient Pueblos

The large fourteenth-century ancestral Hopi pueblo of Homol'ovi II located near Winslow, Arizona (Figure 10.2), contains 1,200 surface and subsurface rooms (Figure 10.3). This is one of several late prehistoric ruins relating to the rise of the Pueblo *katsina* cult (Adams 1991). Between 1984 and 1996, the Homol'ovi Research Program (see Adams 1989, 1996; Adams and Hays 1991) excavated seven kivas and twenty-six surface structures, in part to assess variation in domestic and ceremonial architecture during the *katsina* period (Walker 1995; Walker *et al.* in press).

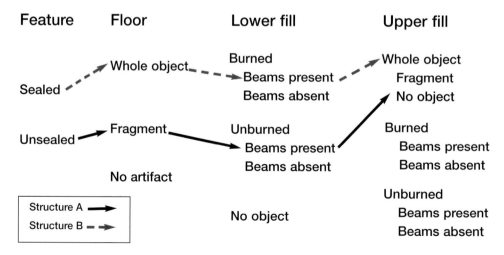

Figure 10.1 Schematic of depositional histories (pathways)

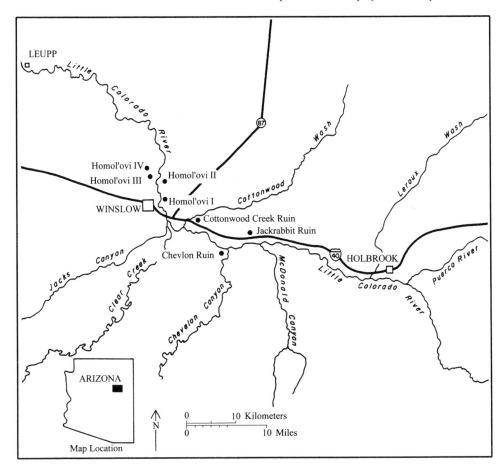

Figure 10.2 Homol'ovi Pueblos

Six of the seven kivas excavated were burned, but only one of the twenty-six surface structures. In all but one kiva, the large weight-bearing beams had been purposefully removed. In four of the seven kivas, objects (such as dog skulls, stone balls, and crystals) had been placed in the structures' internal features including hearths, ventilation tunnels, and *sipapus* (a small hole in the floor symbolically representing a door to the underworld). Several of these features had been sealed prior to burning. Whole pottery vessels were also left on the floors of several of these structures prior to burning. Afterwards, other whole artifacts found their way into the layers above the burned roofing materials. When these stratigraphic relationships are considered in aggregate, it is clear that one catastrophic event could not explain them all. Why would features have been sealed and only kivas burned? Why would victorious warriors remove primary beams and then bury whole useable artifacts in the upper fill? What appears to have happened is not a battle or series of accidents, but a carefully planned ritualized burning and burial of Homol'ovi II ceremonial structures. If the structures had burned because of accidents, kivas as well as non-kivas should have burned. If a structure had been burned in warfare, we would not expect the sealing of features, removal of roofing beams, or deposition of whole artifacts in the fill above the burned roofing strata.

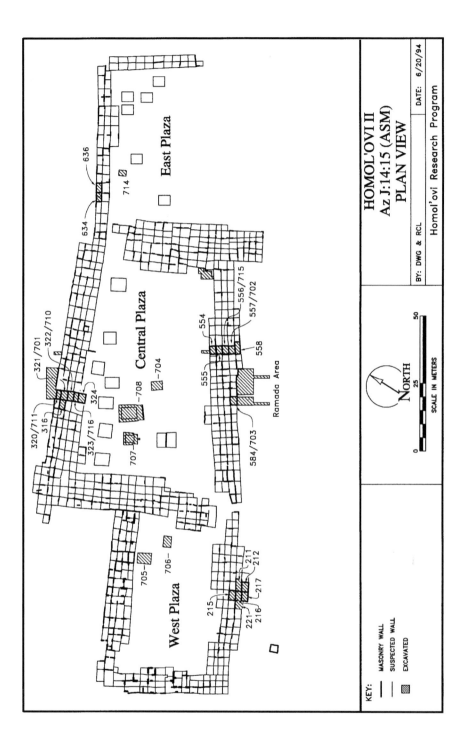

Figure 10.3 Homol'ovi II

At Homol'ovi II, there are hundreds of possible pathways if one considers all the combinations of variables. However, only a few pathways were actually found in the kivas, and these only partially overlapped with the sequences found in the non-kiva structures. Non-kiva sequences had unsealed features, no artifacts or only fragmentary objects on their floors, unburned roofs with beams, and fragmentary objects in their upper fills (sherds, lithics, bone). These pathways reflect abandoned rooms reused as trash dumps. Other possible pathways, such as sealed features, no floor artifacts, unburned roofs without primary beams, whole artifacts in the upper fill, simply did not occur.

These data suggest that the order of strata is behaviorally meaningful and can be used to identify ritual structures and to model deliberate ritual acts. Structures involved in ritual activities earlier in their life histories (e.g., construction rituals, rain making ceremonies, or tribal initiations) appear to have been propelled along pathways that culminated in their ritual abandonment. The specific abandonment procedures in the Homol'ovi case directly implicate the agency of ritual leaders associated with the early *katsina* cult. Ethnohistorically, religious fraternities such as the *katsina* society constructed and used kivas under the direction of fraternity leaders. The introduction of Spanish colonial rule and subsequent US Indian reservations altered the relatively frequent prehistoric abandonment of pueblo villages, and therefore ethnohistorical data do not describe similarly purposeful kiva abandonments. Instead, once constructed, kivas tend to outlive the group that built and used them. If the fraternity does not replace its membership nor transfer a kiva to another group, the structure has no one to abandon it. The prehistoric abandonment of kivas was more common and reflected the mobility of Pueblo peoples. Presumably, leaders guided the abandonment of kivas as well as their use and construction. Understanding depositional histories is crucial to revealing past activities, ritual and otherwise; this issue is further explored through a discussion of Maya house and temple architecture.

The ancient Maya

When people think of Maya architecture, they often envision temples, palaces, and ball-courts. However, the majority of Maya lived in pole and thatch structures dispersed throughout densely settled hinterland areas, mirroring the patchy distribution of agricultural land (Fedick 1994, 1995, 1996; Fedick and Ford 1990; Ford 1990; Lucero 1994, 1997). While there is extreme diversity in structure configuration, size, and function, current evidence indicates that they have similar depositional histories. These depositional sequences, or pathways, are similar in form to other archaeological contexts found throughout the Maya lowlands that have been attributed to dedication and termination rituals, renewal ceremonies, or ancestor veneration rites (see Freidel 1998; Mock 1998). For example, termination caches are found in the construction fill of numerous prehistoric houses as well as temples (summarized by Garber 1989: 50) including Tikal's North Acropolis (Coe 1965a, 1965b) and San Jose, Belize (Thompson 1939: Fig. 20, 184–92). These caches often include broken jade pieces (e.g., ear spools, pendants, beads), stone disks, and smashed ceramic vessels (Garber 1986, 1989: 98). In contrast, dedication rituals involve the caching of similar objects, but whole rather than broken. Further stratigraphic evidence of ceremonies in houses and temples is indicated by the continual replastering of floors and walls (renewal) or complete destruction (termination) and rebuilding (dedication) over earlier structures, with offerings sandwiched in the fill between construction phases (e.g., Haviland 1981, 1988; McAnany 1995: 97; Willey *et al.* 1965). Numerous burials also occur in these domestic and monumental archaeological contexts throughout the Maya lowlands, documenting the expansion of the household ritual practice of ancestor veneration at larger more integrative scales (summarized in Deal 1988; see also Coe 1965a, 1965b; Haviland 1981; McAnany 1995: 55–7; Thompson 1939: 193–220; Willey *et al.* 1965).

To illustrate explicitly our point about continuity and repetitive sequencing, we discuss two examples: first, a large housemound at Barton Ramie and, second, the temple complex of the North Acropolis at Tikal (Figure 10.4). Barton Ramie, a large river center located in west-central Belize, was mapped and excavated in the 1950s by Gordon Willey and others (Willey *et al.* 1965). Tikal, located in the Petén district, Guatemala, is one of the largest and most well known Maya centers, and has been extensively studied by the University of Pennsylvania research team (e.g., Coe 1965a, 1965b).

Willey and others excavated a number of mounds at Barton Ramie to assess their

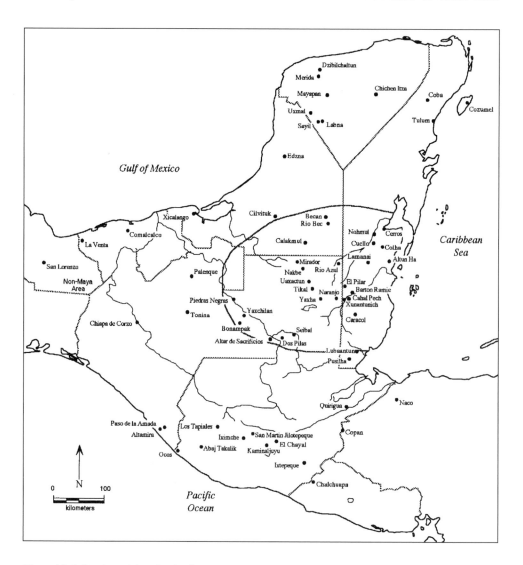

Figure 10.4 Southern Maya lowlands

function and to devise a regional ceramic chronology (Gifford *et al.* 1976; Willey *et al.* 1965). For purposes of this study, we focus on the most extensively excavated mound, BR-1, which measured 28 m in diameter and approximately 2 m high. "It was typical of the small to medium-sized mounds of the site" (Willey *et al.* 1965: 36). The depositional sequence of BR-1 consists of twelve strata, dating from about AD 0 to 1200. These strata represent a number of rebuilding phases (Figure 10.5). Twenty-four burials were recovered spanning the entire sequence. Unfortunately, not all of the burial locations were precisely described, although their numbers clearly increased through time. The earliest evidence of occupation consists of three superimposed pits with ash, probably signifying hearths. The first obvious structure (F) has a burial under its floor, as well as under its terrace (porch). A ramp was added to this structure, within which is a circular pit with rocks; in addition, sometime after the ramp was constructed a burial was placed within the fill. After a series of plaster floors (with pebble ballasts and another burial), there appears to have been a burning episode of some kind, which Willey and others suggest might have been the result of a burned thatch structure. Above the burned layer are several smashed vessels and six burials, capped by another floor. The next activity represented is a large pit dug in the structure that was subsequently filled with rocks. This pit was then covered over by another floor of thick plaster, along the edge of which a pottery vessel was cached.

Similar site formation processes shaped the temple mounds of Tikal. This center has one of the longest sequences of monumental architecture in the Maya lowlands. More than a thousand years of temple construction, destruction, and rebuilding occur in the site's North Acropolis, leaving at the time of abandonment a complex measuring approximately 100 m by 80 m, and 40 m high (Figure 10.6). Pits, tombs, caches, and ceremonial inclusions of sculpted facade fragments document ritual activities in most strata encountered. For example, the earliest architecture (300 – 200 BC) includes three superimposed temples (comparable in size to large thatched houses) on stone platforms, approximately 6 m square. Describing the last of these three temples, Coe notes:

> The roof was probably of thatch with poles at the corners. . . . This building burned, then was refloored, then charred again, as if its roof had caught fire. . . . Beneath its floors were three burials, an infant and two adults. Pits in bedrock in front of these platforms yielded other insights. One contained a young adult. . . . The other pit contained the incomplete disarticulated remains of an adult accompanied by fragments of one or more stingray spines.
> (Coe 1965a: 12–13)

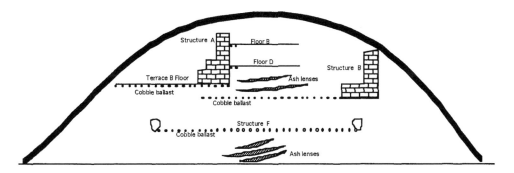

Figure 10.5 Schematic of Barton Ramie housemound depositional history

Source: based on Willey *et al.* 1965: Fig. 11

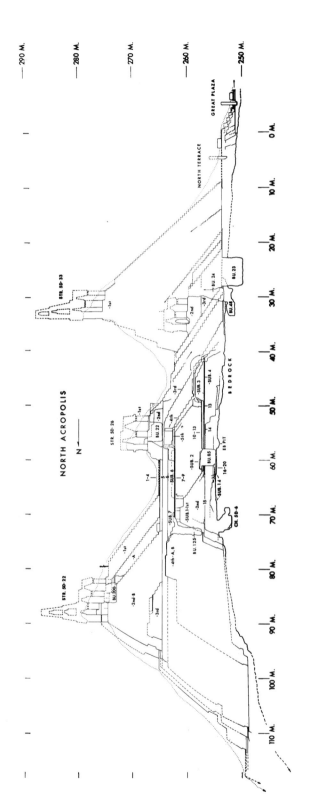

Figure 10.6 Profile of North Acropolis, Tikal (dawing by William Coe)

Source: reproduced courtesy of the University of Pennsylvania Museum, Philadelphia.

"In . . . almost constant renovation, razing, and renewed construction" (Coe 1965a: 13), ever larger temple complexes were built over these earlier deposits. This process clearly resembles household rituals, albeit on a grander scale. The depositional histories of temples even led to the purposeful reinterment of fragments of older temple facades as offerings in younger structures. For example, Miscellaneous Stone 54, originally a Preclassic sculptural decoration, was refit with another facade fragment from Late Classic temple fill, 800 years later. In such sequences, the houses of ancestors, and eventually the temples of deified royal ancestors, form one continuous familiar history.

As was the case in the American Southwest, the depositional histories of different types of Maya architecture are behaviorally meaningful. They demonstrate ritual acts that transcend the domestic realm. Every construction sequence had accompanying rituals. At the household level, the local religious leader performed these rites. At the larger and more grand scale, rulers led the dedication, termination, renewal, and ancestor veneration ceremonies that incorporated their numerous subjects. Assessing these rituals dynamically, it is possible to envision how Maya leaders appropriated traditional rituals to practice "social alchemy" and promote "collective misrecognition" (see also Joyce, this volume).

Discussion

In both the Maya and Pueblo case studies, variability in depositional histories can be considered the material results of actors manipulating social contexts associated with traditional rituals. Such social alchemy in the prehistoric pueblos of the Southwest contributed to the removal of ritual activities from the household sphere into religious sodalities under the control of ritual specialists. From an agency perspective, it is not surprising that kivas developed out of pit houses and exhibit similar depositional histories. For example, more than 50 percent of all Anasazi pit houses were burned and often contained whole objects on their floors and in their fill (e.g., Cameron 1990; Wilshusen 1986). The creation and use of kivas had dramatic religious and political consequences, yet their development was possible only because sodality leaders co-opted the daily habitus of household ritual.

In the case of the Maya, rituals never left the home, but were appropriated by elites for political purposes. Incipient leaders replicated Maya household rituals, to acquire power and mask increasing economic differentiation through large-scale ceremonies that involved numerous households. These replicated pathways were first conducted at specialized elite structures, and later at temples, through the continued use (and manipulation) of dedication and termination rituals, renewal ceremonies, and ancestor veneration rites.

Although Maya and Southwest Pueblo political histories are obviously different, political agents in both societies used common ritual forms to gain specific ends. Archaeologists can glean this appropriation through life history studies. In our comparative examples, we have outlined an analytic method for the study of depositional histories – pathways – that allow us to identify the variable religious means agents employed not only to gain, but to justify and maintain, their power. In doing so, we have also illustrated the general utility of using the stratigraphic record to operationalize the study of agential behavior.

Acknowledgments

We would like to thank the editors for inviting us to participate. We would also like to thank Cynthia Robin, Scott Rushforth, and Kirsten Olson for their useful comments.

Bibliography

Adams, E. C. 1989. "The Homol'ovi Research Program: Investigations into the Prehistory of the Middle Little Colorado River Valley." *Kiva* 54: 175–94.

—— 1991. *The Origin and Development of the Pueblo Katsina Cult*. University of Arizona Press, Tucson.

—— 1996. "Understanding Aggregation in the Homol'ovi Pueblos: Scalar Stress and Social Power," in *River of Change: Prehistory of the Middle Little Colorado River Valley, Arizona*, ed. E. C. Adams, pp. 1–14. Archaeological Series no. 185. Arizona State Museum, University of Arizona, Tucson.

Adams, E. C. and K. A. Hayes (eds.) 1991. *Excavation and Surface Collection of Homol'ovi II Ruin*. Anthropological Papers no. 55. University of Arizona, Tucson.

Allen, C. A. 1891. "Manners and Customs of the Mohaves," in *Smithsonian Annual Report for 1890*, pp. 615–16. Smithsonian Institution, Washington, D.C.

Beals, R. L. 1934. *Material Culture of the Pima, Papago, and Western Apache*. US Department of the Interior. University of California Press, Berkeley.

Bee, R. L. 1983. "Quechan," in *Southwest*, Handbook of North American Archaeology, vol. 10, ed. A. Ortiz, pp. 86–98. Smithsonian Institution, Washington, D.C.

Bourdieu, P. 1977. *Outline of a Theory of Practice*, trans. R. Nice. Cambridge University Press, Cambridge UK.

—— 1990. *The Logic of Practice*, trans. R. Nice. University of Stanford Press, Stanford.

Brumfiel, E. M. and T. K. Earle 1987. "Specialization, Exchange, and Complex Societies: An Introduction," in *Specialization, Exchange, and Complex Societies*, ed. E. M. Brumfiel and T. K. Earle, pp. 1–9. Cambridge University Press, Cambridge UK.

Bunzel, R. 1952. *Chichicastenango: A Guatemalan Village*. Publications of the American Ethnological Society, no. XXII. J. J. Augustin, Locust Valley, New York.

Bushkirk, W. 1986. *The Western Apache: Living with the Land Before 1950*. University of Oklahoma Press, Norman.

Cameron, C. M. 1990. "Pit Structure Abandonment in the Four Corners Region of the American Southwest: Late Basketmaker III and Pueblo I Periods." *Journal of Field Archaeology* 17: 27–37.

Coe, W. R. 1965a. "Tikal: Ten Years of Study of a Maya Ruin in the Lowlands of Guatemala." *Expedition* 8, 9: 5–56.

—— 1965b. "Tikal, Guatemala, and Emergent Maya Civilization." *Science* 147: 1401–19.

Deal, M. 1988. "Recognition of Ritual Pottery in Residential Units: An Ethnoarchaeological Model of the Maya Family Altar Tradition," in *Ethnoarchaeology Among the Maya Highlands of Chiapas, Mexico*, ed. T. A. Lee, Jr. and B. Hayden, pp. 61–89. Papers of the New World Archaeological Foundation no. 56. Brigham Young University, Provo.

Deal, M. and M. B. Hagstrum 1995. "Ceramic Reuse Behavior Among the Maya and Wanka: Implications for Archaeology," in *Expanding Archaeology*, ed. J. M. Skibo, W. H. Walker, and A. Neilsen, pp. 111–25. University of Utah Press, Salt Lake City.

DeMarrais, E., L. J. Castillo, and T. K. Earle 1996. "Ideology, Materialization, and Power Strategies." *Current Anthropology* 37: 15–31.

Dobres, M-A. and C. R. Hoffman 1994. "Social Agency and the Dynamics of Prehistoric Technology." *Journal of Archaeological Method and Theory* 13: 211–58.

Drucker, P. 1941. "Culture Element Distributions: XVI Yuman-Piman." *Anthropological Records* vol. 6, no. 3, University of California Press, Berkeley.

Earle, T. K. 1989. "The Evolution of Chiefdoms." *Current Anthropology* 30: 84–8.

—— 1997. *How Chiefs Come to Power: The Political Economy in Prehistory*. Stanford University Press, Stanford.

Eggan, F. 1950. *Social Organization of the Western Pueblos*. University of Chicago Press, Chicago.

Fedick, S. L. 1994. "Ancient Maya Agricultural Terracing in the Upper Belize River Area: Computer-Aided Modeling and the Results of Initial Field Investigations." *Ancient Mesoamerica* 5: 107–27.

—— 1995. "Land Evaluation and Ancient Maya Land Use in the Upper Belize River Area, Belize, Central America." *Latin American Antiquity* 6: 16–34.

—— 1996. "An Interpretive Kaleidoscope: Alternative Perspectives on Ancient Agricultural Landscapes of the Maya Lowlands," in *The Managed Mosaic: Ancient Maya Agriculture and Resource Use*, ed. S. L. Fedick, pp. 107–31. University of Utah Press, Salt Lake City.

Fedick, S. L. and A. Ford 1990. "The Prehistoric Agricultural Landscape of the Central Maya Lowlands: An Examination of Local Variability in a Regional Context." *World Archaeology* 22: 18–33.

Ford, A. 1990. "Settlement and Environment in the Upper Belize River Area and Variability in Household Organization," in *Prehistoric Population History in the Maya Lowlands*, ed. T. P. Culbert and D. S. Rice, pp. 167–82. University of New Mexico Press, Albuquerque.

Freidel, D. 1998. "Sacred Work: Dedication and Termination in Mesoamerica," in *The Sowing and the Dawning: Termination, Dedication, and Transformation in the Archaeological and Ethnographic Record of Mesoamerica*, ed. S. B. Mock, pp. 189–93. University of New Mexico Press, Albuquerque.

Freidel, D. and L. Schele 1988. "Kingship in the Late Preclassic Maya Lowlands: The Instruments and Places of Ritual Power." *American Anthropologist* 90: 547–67.

—— 1989. "Dead Kings and Living Temples: Dedication and Termination Rituals among the Ancient Maya," in *Word and Image in Maya Culture: Explorations in Language, Writing, and Representation*, ed. W. F. Hanks and D. S. Rice, pp. 233–43. University of Utah Press, Salt Lake City.

Fried, M. H. 1967. *The Evolution of Political Society: An Essay in Political Economy*. Random House, New York.

Friedman, J. and M. J. Rowlands 1978. "Notes Toward an Epigenetic Model of the Evolution of 'Civilization'," in *The Evolution of Social Systems*, ed. J. Friedman and M. J. Rowlands, pp. 201–67. Duckworth, London.

Garber, J. F. 1986. "The Artifacts," in *Archaeology at Cerros, Belize, Central America*, vol. I. ed. R. A. Robertson and D. A. Freidel, pp. 117–26. Southern Methodist University Press, Dallas.

—— 1989. *The Artifacts: Archaeology at Cerros, Belize, Central America*, vol. II. Southern Methodist University Press, Dallas.

Giddens, A. 1979. *Central Problems in Social Theory: Action, Structure and Contradiction in Social Analysis*. University of California Press, Berkeley.

—— 1984. *The Constitution of Society: Outline of a Theory of Structuration*. University of California Press, Berkeley.

Gifford, E. W. 1932. *Southern Yavapai*. University of California Publications in American Archaeology and Ethnology, Vol. 29, No. 3. University of California Press, Berkeley.

—— 1940. Culture Element Distributions XII Apache Pueblo. *Anthropological Records* 4: 1, University of California Press, Berkeley.

Gifford, J. C., R. J. Sharer, J. W. Ball, A. F. Chase, C. A. Gifford, M. Kirkpatrick, and G. H. Myer 1976. *Prehistoric Pottery Analysis and the Ceramics of Barton Ramie in the Belize Valley*. Peabody Museum of Archaeology and Ethnology Memoirs, vol. 18. Harvard University, Cambridge, Mass.

Goodwin, G. 1942. *The Social Organization of the Western Apache*. University of Chicago Press, Chicago.

Grossman, F. E. 1873. "The Pima Indians of Arizona," in *Smithsonian Annual Report* for 1871, pp. 407–19. Smithsonian Institution, Washington, D.C.

Haviland, W. A. 1981. "Dower Houses and Minor Centers at Tikal, Guatemala: An Investigation into the Identification of Valid Units in Settlement Hierarchies," in *Lowland Maya Settlement Patterns*, ed. W. Ashmore, pp. 89–117. University of New Mexico Press, Albuquerque.

—— 1988. "Musical Hammock at Tikal: Problems with Reconstructing Household Composition," in *Household and Community in the Mesoamerican Past*, ed. R. R. Wilk and W. Ashmore, pp. 121–34. University of New Mexico Press, Albuquerque.

Hayden, B. 1990. "Nimrods, Piscators, Pluckers, and Planters: The Emergence of Food Production." *Journal of Anthropological Archaeology* 9: 31–69.

Hayden, B. and R. Gargett 1990. "Big Man, Big Heart?: A Mesoamerican View of the Emergence of Complex Society." *Ancient Mesoamerica* 1: 3–20.

Hays, S. 1994. "Structure and Agency and the Sticky Problem of Culture." *Sociological Theory* 12: 57–72.

Helms, M. W. 1993. *Craft and the Kingly Ideal: Art, Trade, and Power.* University of Texas Press, Austin.

Hill, W. W. 1944. "The Navaho Indians and The Ghost Dance of 1890." *American Anthropologist* 46: 523–7.

Hodder, I. 1986. *Reading the Past.* Cambridge University Press, Cambridge UK.

Houston, S. and D. Stuart 1996. "Of Gods, Glyphs and Kings: Divinity and Rulership Among the Classic Maya." *Antiquity* 70: 289–312.

Illif, F. G. 1954 [orig. 1901]. *People of the Blue Water: My Adventures Among the Walapai and Havasupai Indians.* Harper, New York.

Johnson, A. W. and T. K. Earle 1987. *The Evolution of Human Societies: From Foraging Group to Agrarian State.* Stanford University Press, Stanford.

Jones, C. 1991. "Cycles of Growth at Tikal," in *Classic Maya Political History: Hieroglyphic and Archaeological Evidence*, ed. T. P. Culbert, pp. 102–24. Cambridge University Press, Cambridge UK.

Kelly, W. H. 1977. *Cocopa Ethnography.* Anthropological Papers no. 29, University of Arizona, Tucson.

Kent, S. 1984. *Analyzing Activity Areas: An Ethnoarchaeological Study of the Use of Space.* University of New Mexico Press, Albuquerque.

Kertzer, D. I. 1988. *Ritual, Politics, and Power.* Yale University Press, New Haven.

Levy, J. E. 1992. *Orayvi Revisited: Social Stratification in an Egalitarian Society.* School of American Research Press, Santa Fe.

Lucero, L. J. 1994. *Household and Community Integration among Hinterland Elites and Commoners: Maya Residential Ceramic Assemblages of the Belize River Area.* Ph.D. dissertation, Archaeology Program, University of California, Los Angeles. University Microfilms, Ann Arbor.

—— 1997. *Self-Sufficient Communities in Complex Society: The Ancient Maya.* Paper presented at the 62nd annual meeting for the Society for American Archaeology, Nashville.

McAnany, P. A. 1995. *Living with the Ancestors: Kinship and Kingship in Ancient Maya Society.* University of Texas Press, Austin.

Mindeleff, C. 1898. "Navaho Houses," in *17th Annual Report of the Bureau of American Ethnology*, pp. 469–517. Smithsonian Institution, Washington D.C.

Mock, S. B. 1998. "Prelude," in *The Sowing and the Dawning: Termination, Dedication, and Transformation in the Archaeological and Ethnographic Record of Mesoamerica*, pp. 3–18. University of New Mexico Press, Albuquerque.

Nielsen, A. E. 1995. "Architectural Performance and the Reproduction of Social Power," in *Expanding Archaeology*, ed. J. M. Skibo, W. H. Walker, and A. Neilsen, pp. 47–66. University of Utah Press, Salt Lake City.

Radcliff-Brown, A. R. 1952. *Structure and Function in Primitive Society.* Oxford University Press, London.

Redfield, R. and A. Villa Rojas 1934. *Chan Kom: A Maya Village.* University of Chicago Press, Chicago.

Roscoe, P. B. 1993. "Practice and Political Centralisation: A New Approach to Political Evolution." *Current Anthropology* 34: 111–40.

Schele, L. 1990. "House Names and Dedication Rituals at Palenque," in *Vision and Revision in Maya Studies*, ed. F. S. Clancy and P. D. Harrison, pp. 143–57. University of New Mexico Press, Albuquerque.

Schele, L. and D. Freidel 1990. *A Forest of Kings: The Untold Story of the Ancient Maya.* Morrow, New York.

Schiffer, M. B. 1976. *Behavioral Archeology.* Academic Press, New York.

—— 1995. *Behavioral Archaeology: First Principles.* University of Utah Press, Salt Lake City.

Service, E. R. 1962. *Primitive Social Organization: An Evolutionary Perspective.* Random House, New York.

—— 1975. *Origins of the State and Civilization: The Process of Cultural Evolution.* W. W. Norton, New York.

Sharer, R. J. 1994. *The Ancient Maya.* 5th edn. Stanford University Press, Stanford.

Spier, L. 1928. *Havasupai Ethnography.* Anthropology Paper no. 3. American Museum of Natural

History, New York.

—— 1933. *Yuman Tribes of the Gila River*. University of Chicago Press, Chicago.

Steward, J. H. 1933. *Archaeological Problems of the Northern Periphery of the Southwest*. Bulletin no. 5. Museum of Northern Arizona, Flagstaff.

—— 1955. *Theory of Culture Change: The Methodology of Multilinear Evolution*. University of Illinois Press, Urbana.

Strong, W. D. 1929. *Aboriginal Society in Southern California*. University of California Publications in American Archaeology and Ethnology, vol. 26. University of California Press, Berkeley.

Thompson, J. E. S. 1939. *Excavations at San Jose, British Honduras*. Carnegie Institute of Washington, Publication no. 506, Washington, D.C.

—— 1970. *Maya History and Religion*. University of Oklahoma Press, Norman.

Tozzer, A. M. 1907. *A Comparative Study of the Mayas and the Lacandones*. Macmillan, New York.

—— 1941. *Landa's Relación de Los Cosas de Yucatán*. Papers of the Peabody Museum American Archaeology and Ethnology, no. 28. Harvard University, Cambridge, Mass.

Underhill, R. M. 1948. *Ceremonial Patterns in the Greater Southwest*. Monograph XIII, American Ethnological Society. J. J. Augstin, New York.

Vogt, E. Z. 1970. *The Zinacantecos of Mexico: A Modern Maya Way of Life*. Holt, Rinehart and Winston, New York.

—— 1993 [orig. 1975]. *Tortillas for the Gods: A Symbolic Analysis of Zinacanteco Rituals*. University of Oklahoma Press, Norman.

Walker, W. H. 1995. "Ceremonial Trash?" in *Expanding Archaeology*, ed. M. Skibo, W. H. Walker, and A. Neilsen, pp. 67–79. University of Utah Press, Salt Lake City.

—— 1998. "Where Are the Witches of Prehistory?" *Journal of Archaeological Method and Theory* 5: 245–308.

Walker, W. H. and V. LaMotta 1995. *Life Histories as Units of Analysis*. Paper presented at the 60th annual meeting of the Society for American Archaeology, Minneapolis.

Walker, W. H., V. M. LaMotta, and A. C. Adams, in press. "Katsinas and Kiva Abandonment at Homol'ovi: A Deposit-Oriented Perspective on Religion in Southwest Prehistory," in *The Archaeology of Regional Interaction in the Prehistoric Southwest*, ed. M. Hegmon. University of Colorado Press, Boulder.

Wauchope, R. 1938. *Modern Maya Houses: A Study of their Archaeological Significance*. Publication Carnegie Institution of Washington, Publication no. 502, Washington, D.C.

Webster, D. L. 1976. "On Theocracies." *American Anthropologist* 78: 812–28.

White, L. 1949. *The Science of Culture: A Study of Man and Civilization*. Noonday Press, New York.

Wilshusen, R. H. 1986. "The Relationship Between Abandonment Mode and Ritual Use in Pueblo I Anasazi Protokivas." *Journal of Field Archaeology* 13: 245–54.

Willey, G. R., W. R. Bullard, J. B. Glass, and J. C. Gifford 1965. *Prehistoric Maya Settlements in the Belize Valley*. Peabody Museum of Archaeology and Ethnology Papers, vol. 54. Harvard University, Cambridge, Mass.

Whiteley, P. M. 1988. *Deliberate Acts: Changing Hopi Culture through the Oraibi Split*. University of Arizona Press, Tucson.

11 Agents of change in hunter-gatherer technology

Kenneth E. Sassaman

Hunter-gatherer prehistory has a disturbing anonymity about it. Not only are its subjects unknown to us, their authorship or agency is thoroughly subjugated by the very methods archaeologists use to construct prehistories. Artifact typologies downplay idiosyncratic variation in favor of "normative" properties. Stratigraphic interpretations presuppose unilineal sequencing of events. Cross-dating reduces temporal variability by synchronizing form. Functional analyses of form overlook variations in use. And, finally, inadequate chronology ensures that none of these shortcomings come to the fore, preserving, as it does, the quiet, faceless account of an ancient past without subplots, contrary characters, or unpredictable endings.

Method is, of course, informed by theory, no matter how implicit it may be, and therein lies the root of the problem. Despite recent advances in the recognition of hunter-gatherer diversity (Kelly 1995), mobile, small-scale formations lacking food production continue to be promoted as the antecedents or antitheses of complex societies (Kehoe 1990). Viewed as lacking the social and political institutions that reproduce inequality, hunter-gatherers are without differentiation. Only the biological imperatives of age and sex get in the way, although their cultural manifestations, such as adulthood or gender, are usually treated as essentialist categories, as if all men, or all women, think and act alike (Gero, this volume). To the extent people really do exist, theories ranging from selectionism to structural marxism regard individuals as consequences of emergent properties (adaptation) or institutions (communalism) that are greater than the sum of their constituent parts. Such "methodological individuals" are thus timeless, having values and motives that transcend personal experience (Bell 1992; Halperin 1994: 36).

Theory which situates individual thought, intent, or will at the forefront of explanation has the potential to revolutionize studies of prehistoric hunter-gatherers. This potential is hardly self-evident, however, for theories of agency and practice offer little guidance on applications to nonstratified societies, particularly those of the ancient past. At least two theoretical hurdles confront us. Building on established principles of agency theory, students of hunter-gatherer prehistory must first decouple individual intent and action from the societal structures which are presumed to reproduce egalitarianism among constituent members and thus preclude material manifestations of differential power. Having done this, prehistorians need to think differently about the creation and expression of social identity, particularly as regards the material disjunctures in time and space usually equated with collective identities or adaptations.

Important as they are, these theoretical challenges are but a secondary concern to the purpose of this chapter, which is to show how an agency perspective improves our understanding of variation in hunter-gatherer technology. My case study comes from the Stallings

Culture of the middle Savannah River valley of the southeastern United States (ca. 4500–3000 BP). As makers and users of the oldest pottery in North America, bearers of Stallings Culture left a distinct and indelible mark in the archaeological record of hunter-gatherer prehistory. Contrary to the typological and evolutionary precepts that have shaped archaeological recognition of Stallings pottery, the timing, contexts, and consequences of its use evince multiple, often contradictory social identities. After reviewing the many new observations that are undermining systems-level perceptions on Stallings vessel technology, I consider how the collective structures of gender, kinship, and ethnicity were reproduced and transformed by the incompatible actions of individuals, actions whose unintended consequences contributed to the dissolution of Stallings society within a few centuries of its genesis.

Agency and hunter-gatherer prehistory

If we define agency in the minimal sense that the self is an authorized social being, then the question ought to be: Why not agency sooner? As Ortner (1996: 10) flatly states, agency is "simply part of being human, and thus its absence or denial is as much a problem as its construction." Theory, however, emphasizes emergent properties or abstractions over particular human experiences. Examples of such abstractions include Durheim's superorganic, Darwin's adaptation, and Marx's class (Bloch 1983; Giddens 1984: 171; Levins and Lewontin 1985). Each constitutes an emergent property which is greater than the sum of its parts, but whose very existence cannot be taken for granted. At best, such abstractions exist, but at scales that individual actors neither perceive nor anticipate (Bell 1992); at worst, they exist merely in the minds of modern observers, whose categories and methods of observation presuppose the outcome. Far from being politically neutral, research programs which deny the agency and intentionality of its subjects "must be seen very critically as effects of power" (Ortner 1996: 10). It follows that agent-free prehistory serves well the goals of dominant structures (i.e. states) for it subjugates human will to the invisible hand of adaptation, or the economy, and thus deflects attention away from the social contradictions of the modern world (Leone 1986; Trigger 1984).

Agency theory recognizes emergent properties (e.g. structure, habitus), too, but these are viewed as derivative of individual action, and therefore have no life of their own beyond the agents who create and live in structures via habitus. By the same token, individual actions and the motives that guide them do not exist independent of structure. The mutual dependence of structure and agency, what Giddens (1984: 25) calls the duality of structure, is thus a property of all human experience.

All individuals in all societies are agents of culture insofar as they have the power to recursively create and alter structure or tradition through action. Some of the contributors to this volume maintain the contrasting view that agency is the power to act differently from "the norm" (cf. Bell 1992: 42). Intentionality and agency are the same in this view, because action contrary to the norm presupposes conscious perception of what is socially acceptable. I propose that actions to build consensus or norms are likewise agential in that they derive ultimately from efforts to create rules or traditions in opposition to other structures. At this level of "collective action," intentionality gives way to habitual, learned actions that are done without conscious thought. In other words, normative structures are long-term derivatives of agency.

In relating collectivism to agency, I do not intend to suggest that collectivities consist solely of like-minded actors. Rather, agency theory allows that individuals with varied, even contradictory motives or goals converge in collective formations in relation to similarly constituted formations. Importantly, the variety of goals or motives subsumed under such collectivities provides the basis for social change (Bell 1992: 39).

Agency is intrinsically bound up with the notion of power, specifically social power. Broadly defined, social power is the ability of human actors to pursue goals within the parameters of structural properties of interaction. This ability is dependent on the actor's position in social interactions, as this determines access to the resources which are the basis for action. Giddens (1981) makes a distinction between two types or resources of power: dominion of humans over the material world, or allocative resources; and dominion over the social world, authoritative resources. How these two types of resources relate to one another varies among societies, but Giddens considers authoritative resources to be the primary media of social power in noncapitalist societies. He downplays the significance of allocative resources in band-level societies, for instance, because they generally lack the capacity for material storage and resource ownership. Instead, power is manipulated through authoritative resources, wherein storage potential lies not in material resources, but in the retention and control of information. Lacking material means of storing or encoding information (e.g., writing), "knowledge is stored through its incorporation in traditional practices, including myth-telling: the only storage 'container' in such circumstances is the human memory" (ibid.: 95).

Giddens' discussion of authoritative resources in band-level societies is somewhat misleading for it was designed to draw a distinction between classless and class-divided social formations and, as such, does not fully explore the potential for social power in resources other than the human memory. Herein lies the challenge for archaeologists interested in adapting agency concepts to the study of mute, lifeless records of human experience. How do we connect the intentions and goals of self-interested agents to the material consequences of their actions? Judging from the results to date, the answer would seem to lie in analyses of ritual objects or the built environment (e.g., Nielsen 1995; Pauketat and Emerson 1991; Smith 1992). However, as these studies generally refer to structures of domination and the reproduction of elite control, they provide little guidance to the materiality of agency in nonstratified societies. In remedying the situation, we must be careful not to reify Giddens' dichotomy for resources of power, or the rhetorical uses of "primitive" which served so well the political agenda of classical marxism (Bloch 1983). Agency approaches to hunter-gatherer prehistory will do well to cultivate more generalized perspectives on social reproduction, not simply those embedded in institutional structures of domination (e.g., Saitta 1994).

In this regard, the structures of gender and kinship are potentially fruitful points of departure. Gender and kinship are universal means of constituting and integrating social roles in nonstratified, hunter-gatherer society. The extent to which these categories embody the potential for inequality and domination is a matter of some debate. Societies organized by unilineal descent, for instance, provide ample opportunity for manipulating the productive and reproductive capacities of others for political gain, often at the expense of women's status (Chevillard and Leconte 1986; Collier 1988; Goodale 1971; Kelly 1995: 270–91; Meillassoux 1972; Sacks 1979). Such cases are often portrayed as problematic in that the ideal model for hunter-gatherers (e.g. southern African Bushmen) is a society based on principles of inclusion and egalitarianism, such as bilateral descent and flexible postmarital residence. Still, aside from the fact that one out of four ethnographic hunter-gatherer societies was in fact organized by unilineal descent (Kelly 1995: 271), the egalitarian ideal cannot be understood apart from structures of domination. Recent studies have documented the historical depth of connections between ethnographic hunter-gatherers and nation states (e.g., Denbow 1984; Gordon 1984; Headland and Reid 1989; Schrire 1984; Trigger 1990; Wilmsen 1983, 1989). These histories provide compelling proof that egalitarian structures which ensure equality within hunter-gatherer bands arose from resistance to domination from without (Grinker 1994; Trigger 1990; Woodburn 1988). It follows that societies lacking institutional inequalities exist only in opposition to hegemonic forces.

Referring hunter-gatherer social organization to the level of intergroup relations places gender and kinship squarely in the purview of ethnicity. Following Comaroff (1987) and Grinker (1994), I regard ethnicity primarily as the symbolic classification of social inequality. In institutional terms, ethnic process involves the ways in which groups define themselves in opposition to each other. Thus, whereas a focus on gender and kinship may hide the relationships between people who are not otherwise part of the same corporate or descent group, a focus on ethnicity emphasizes the relations among cultures "as constituting variables in social organization" (Grinker 1994: 13).

But how do cultural relations of inequality form and how do they contribute to the boundaries we draw archaeologically between one culture and another or one ethnic group and another? The answers are not readily apparent in the collectivity of social groups. This seems counter-intuitive, but makes sense if we decouple the emergent properties of collectivities from the actions of human agents. For instance, in his study of the ethnic relations between the Lese and their Efe partners of the Congo, Grinker (1994) identifies two distinct structures. The lineage or clan – the traditional subject of anthropological observation – is a model of equality, serving to mobilize individuals as collectives for actions involving others, as in warfare and marriage alliances, and thus muting inequality among households, or families. It is within the household that we find the model and actions of inequality, predicated on the fundamental differences between the two major genders – men and women – and metaphorically extended outward to discriminate insiders (men) from outsiders (women) in their system of patrilocal residence. As mates for Lese men, Efe women often become incorporated into the patrilocal village, but Efe men (metaphorical women/outsiders) are forbidden from taking a Lese wife, even though they are valued trading partners to Lese men and thus integrated into Lese households. All told, the household is not simply a component of a larger social collective, but a model of the conceptual organization of ethnic and gender relations.

This example is but one illustration of the relationship between agency and collectivity emanating from an action as common as marriage. It is valuable, too, in illustrating the potentially contentious mix of social identities (age, gender, kinship, affinity, ethnicity) in the union between two individuals, families, and lineages. These potential inequalities exist at multiple scales, from household, to lineage, to ethnic group. Any such perceived boundary can be viewed as a manifestation of inequality inasmuch as we refer such boundaries to the intent of individuals to include some and exclude others through alliances such as marriage.

The archaeological utility of the foregoing concepts depends in large measure on fundamental rethinking of the very data archaeologists assert to divide prehistory into analytical units. Archaeological systematics involving cultural boundaries of time and space consist generally of technological traits. In this sense, technology is regarded as a series of passive, normative traits whose variations in time and space are often cited to serve the goals of culture history. Agency theory requires a vastly different perspective on technology, one in which technologies or technical acts are expected to vary at the microscalar level of daily interactions among people in different contexts of social power. A rich theoretical foundation for this perspective exists in the work of Lechtman, Heidegger, and Lemmonier, among others, synthesized recently for archaeological purposes by Dobres and Hoffman (1994) and

Dobres (in press). I review here only briefly those aspects of an "anthropology of technology" that inform my reading of Stallings container technology.

Following Lemonnier (1992: 1–2), I define technology as all aspects of the process of action upon matter. Included in this process are not only the objects and means for altering physical phenomena, but also the social circumstances influencing the choice of one action over another. The social content of technology is determined by the interplay of action and tradition, a duality similar to Giddens' theory of structuration. In this regard, all technology is shaped by structure or tradition, but is simultaneously mediated by intentions and meanings that vary with an individual's social position, social context, and access to social power.

Because technology is socially constituted, technical choices are sometimes "arbitrary," to use Lemonnier's term (1992: 79–80), in the sense that they are not restricted or predetermined by physical constraints alone. In the process Lemonnier calls "social representation," arbitrariness refers to the ascription of meaning to an object or technical act which itself is not the source of the meaning. The power underlying the meaning of specific social representations can be understood only in the context of social interactions; that is, technical choices are made in reference to what others are or are not doing. Lemonnier's ethnographic study of Anga technology provides ample illustration of differential social representation. For instance, the techniques for making bark skirts and capes embody variations of form that represent ethnic differences, whereas variations in raw material represent gender divisions (ibid.). Within a set of traditional representations, individuals manipulate combinations of form and raw material to either reproduce or alter social distinctions.

Methods for discovering socially meaningful variation in technology are woefully underdeveloped. Even Lemonnier's methods are at odds with agent-centered theory. His is a process of elimination in which social and symbolic factors are considered only after physical factors fail to explain variation. This is reminiscent of Dunnell's (1978) distinction between function and style, or Gould's (1980) treatment of anomalous patterning. Explanatory prioritization such as this is inadequate if we accept that all human action creates and reproduces culture, not just those that appear anomalous to emergent properties.

Promising methodological directions for an agency of technology are explored in research by Dobres (1995, in press). In her analysis of Magdalenian bone and antler technologies, Dobres (1995) develops a "microscalar" approach for seeking variation in the contexts of material culture production. Arguing that different social contexts of intimate interaction structured technical acts in different ways, Dobres attributes intersite variation in the making and remaking of organic tools to the non-discursive negotiation of gender roles. Multiscalar comparisons of production steps (*chaînes opératoires*) exposed potentially meaningful technical variation relative to social representations such as gender, while site-specific technical variation provided intimate details of the process of representation.

The approach taken by Dobres situates agency and social power at the forefront of explanation without ignoring the material constraints of particular technologies. Her approach is less satisfying in its specific explication of social meaning for lack of detailed cultural and historical context. Granted, archaeologists may never have adequate means to unlock the symbolic content of material production. Still, if we are to have any success in linking material culture variation to social representation, we have to have intimate knowledge of the details of social interaction and group formation. Necessary to bridging the material social aspects of technological variation are many of the usual pursuits of culture reconstruction: community size, household organization, rules of descent and post-marital residence, patterns of exchange, and the like. Agent-centered approaches may be convincing only with rich, ethnographic-like detail, or what Sinclair (this volume) refers to as the "amplification of context" (also Walker and Lucero, this volume). This is not to suggest that archaeologists must await the development of better reconstructions before considering agency. Rather, we can begin by deconstructing the archaeological constructs that regard material culture, however implicitly, as the *de facto* signifiers of passive bearers of culture. Agency theory provides the basis for reexamining old data in new light, for actively seeking social variation long-hidden by the normative strictures of culture history and certain processual approaches. My work with Stallings prehistory is a modest attempt to develop such new insight.

Agent-free Stallings prehistory

Stallings is the name given to a set of material and behavioral traits that are believed to signify a discrete Late Archaic culture of the southeastern United States. In its broadest terms, Stallings Culture occupies a temporal span of some 1,500 radiocarbon years, beginning at about 4500 BP, when ceramic vessel technology first appeared on the scene. Shellfishing also became prevalent at this time, and the accumulated by-products of this created conspicuous markers of Stallings sites. The geographic distribution of these traits encompasses much of coastal South Carolina and Georgia, as well as the Savannah River valley, which divides these states, and the adjacent Ogeechee River of Coastal Plain Georgia (Figure 11.1). This broad expanse is usually subdivided into lesser units based on differences in pottery technology and style, although as a whole, the greater Stallings area represents a series of cultural expressions whose collective differences from other traditions of early pottery in the Southeast far outweigh any internal differentiation (Sassaman 1993).

Pottery is indeed the hallmark of Stallings Culture. Not only is it among the oldest, if not the oldest, ceramic vessel technology in North America, Stallings pottery is "a distinct and separate ware readily definable from all other types of Southeastern pottery" (Claflin 1931: 17). In its classic expression (3700–3500 BP), Stallings pottery is a fiber-tempered ware decorated with a variety of linear punctations, particularly the so-called "drag and jab" punctations prevalent at the type site, Stallings Island, in the middle Savannah River near Augusta, Georgia.

Other aspects of Stallings Culture have mythical qualities. In the 1850s, C. C. Jones was awestruck by the number of human interments uncovered in his digging at Stallings Island. He regarded the site as "a huge necropolis," whose accumulation of shell was intended "to impart a permanency to the graves of the dead" (Jones 1861: 16–17). Subsequent excavations sponsored by Harvard's Peabody Museum documented evidence for habitation functions, as well as additional burials. In his report of this work, Claflin downplayed Jones's fanciful interpretation, but agreed that the large accumulation of shell and refuse signified long-term, permanent settlement by one "tribe," which he called the "Stalling's [sic] Island people" (Claflin 1931: 7). Although Claflin and his contemporaries had little to offer on the economic foundation for this presumed permanency, it was reasonable for them to conclude that the Stallings Island people were farmers who took advantage of the annual bounty of anadromous fish runs. In keeping with Childe's notion of the neolithic revolution, Stallings Culture, particularly its conspicuous pottery, was generally viewed as the expected outcome of progressive evolutionary development.

Modern investigations at Stallings Culture sites in the region have undermined most of these ill-supported conclusions. Chronometric dating shows that Stallings pottery and its people predate the local advent of food production by over three millennia. Evidence for anadromous fish harvesting has never materialized. Stallings groups appear to have

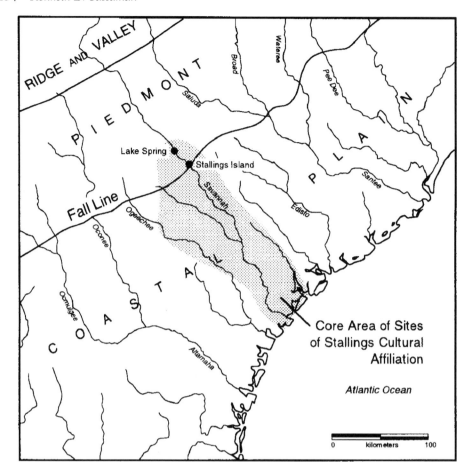

Figure 11.1 Physiographic map of portion of the South Atlantic Slope showing regional distribution of sites of Stallings cultural affiliation, ca. 4400 – 3500 BP

maintained some degree of seasonal mobility throughout much of their history. And finally, Stallings Culture was an "experiment" that began to fail after about 3500 BP, succeeded by social formations of diminished integration and complexity.

Advances in knowledge about Stallings Culture have sprung from an interplay of new data and conceptual innovation. Especially beneficial has been the application of theory which privileges social variation and human agency over emergent, systemwide properties such as adaptation (e.g., Sassaman 1993, 1998a; Wilson 1997). Specifically, its application to analyses of Stallings technology has exposed variation long shrouded in the cloak of typology, crossdating, and stratigraphic interpretation. In the subsections below I summarize three of the more significant breaks from an agent-free reconstruction of Stallings prehistory, and then follow with the prospects for agent-centered alternatives.

Unilineal sequences and multi-ethnic neighborhoods

Early investigations of Stallings prehistory targeted large sites with deep, stratified deposits. Those of the middle Savannah River valley, notably Stallings Island (Claflin 1931) and

Lake Spring (Miller 1951), contained extensive shell strata with abundant Stallings artifacts underlain by shell-free layers lacking pottery. The flaked stone artifacts in these deeper strata differed from those of Stallings affiliation in both raw material and style (Bullen and Greene 1970). Together, the contrasts in assemblage content and context provided undeniable proof of a marked cultural change involving the introduction of pottery, among other things. Investigators speculated on whether preceramic populations evolved in situ, simply adopted innovations from neighbors, or were displaced by interlopers from the coast (cf. Claflin 1931; Crusoe and DePratter 1976; Waring 1968).

The stratigraphy of middle Savannah River shell middens was unambiguous as regards the temporal sequence of preceramic and ceramic components. Coastal shell middens, on the other hand, offered no supporting evidence. Absent from the basal strata of early pottery shell middens was definitive proof of preceramic occupations (e.g., Waring 1968; Waring and Larson 1968). In fact, sites with preceramic components were notably lacking throughout the coastal zone. Whereas sea-level rise no doubt destroyed or buried many such sites (DePratter and Howard 1980; Russo 1996), the complete absence of preceramic components at the base of ceramic-bearing shell middens influenced perceptions of culture history in significant, albeit subtle ways. Chiefly, it suggested that pottery originated on the coast and diffused rapidly and thoroughly among its constituent populations. Further, stratigraphic correlations with middle Savannah sites seemed to indicate that pottery traditions completely supplanted local preceramic traditions. None of the large sites investigated through 1960 produced stratigraphic evidence to the contrary.

By the late 1960s, applications of radiocarbon dating would begin to undermine the simplicity of a unilineal model for early pottery (Figure 11.2). Investigations in the lower Savannah valley pushed back the origins of Stallings pottery to the mid-fifth millennium BP (Stoltman 1966, 1974). A few years later, large-scale excavations in the upper Savannah valley yielded abundant evidence for preceramic components dating throughout the fifth millennium (Anderson and Joseph 1988). Thus, evidence for the prolonged coexistence of at least two distinct cultural traditions began to take form. Additional dating showed that the regional spread of pottery was incredibly slow. Nearly two millennia elapsed before pottery was widely utilized throughout the region. The slow and uneven rate of diffusion for an innovation often portrayed as revolutionary had become a problem with which to reckon (Sassaman 1993).

Its protracted history notwithstanding, the coexistence of two distinct cultural traditions was hardly startling news. After all, these traditions appeared to be separated by space, if not time, and so the process of change simply mimicked a wave advance model of innovation diffusion. However, at the head of this wave, in the middle Savannah area, the histories of these respective traditions proved more intertwined than ever imagined. For at least 200 radiocarbon years after pottery was introduced in the area, factions of the local population persisted in traditional lifeways without pottery (Sassaman 1998b). Known to us now as the Mill Branch phase (Elliott *et al.* 1994; Ledbetter 1995), bearers of this culture abandoned locations of intensive settlement along the river, and established more permanent residence in the adjacent hillcountry. The riverine sites they abandoned were subsequently occupied by bearers of Stallings Culture, who left behind shell refuse, pot sherds, and human interments as testimony to their territorial imposition. The stratified deposits of predecessors and successors would remain silent on their coexistence, leaving instead a record that would mislead generations of archaeologists. What appeared to be a unilineal sequence is now acknowledged to be a multi-ethnic neighborhood.

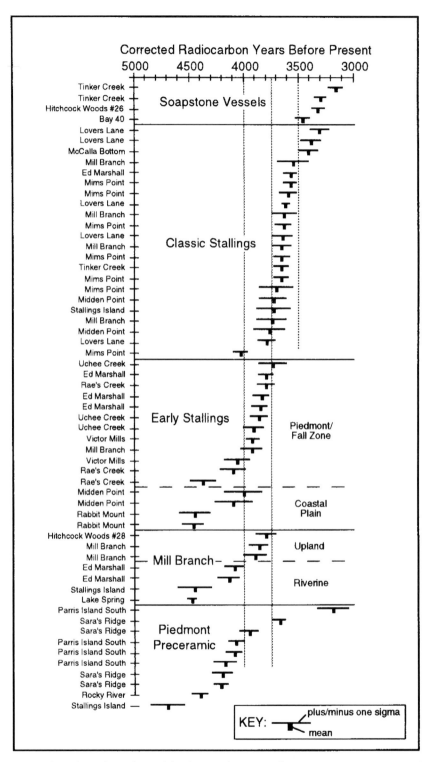

Figure 11.2 Radiocarbon chronology of the Savannah River valley region, 5000 – 3000 BP, divided by cultural-historical phase and physiography

Technological antecedents and cultural antitheses

A similar change in perception has accompanied modern analysis of nonceramic vessel technology. Throughout much of the Eastern Woodlands a talc-rich rock known as soap-stone or steatite was quarried to manufacture a variety of items, including cooking vessels (Figure 11.3). Investigations into the quarrying and manufacture of soapstone vessels began in the nineteenth century, but remarkably few data exist on the timing of this technology. Because soapstone vessel sherds are often found in contexts lacking pottery, they have long been considered the technological precursors to pottery. Some limited stratigraphic

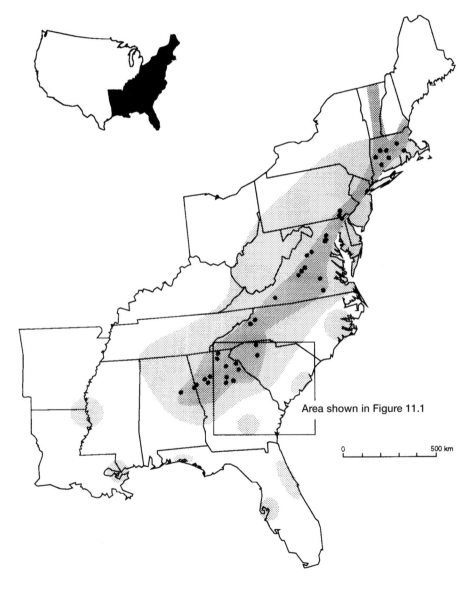

Figure 11.3 Generalized distribution of geological formations containing talc-rich deposits (dark shading) quarried for soapstone (dots), and archaeological occurences of soapstone vessels outside source areas (light shading)

evidence seemingly supported this proposition (e.g., Coe 1964), as did comparative analyses of form. Particularly influential in this regard was the presumed evolution of vessel technology in the Middle Atlantic region, where early pottery not only mimicked soap-stone vessels in form, but included the use of crushed soapstone for temper (Manson 1948). The sequence is often interpreted as a response to demand for greater efficiency in cooking technology brought on by an increasingly sedentary lifestyle. Given their outstanding thermal properties, soapstone vessels were highly effective cooking devices, but they were costly to obtain, manufacture, and transport. Following Brown (1989), we may surmise that pottery was an improvement over soapstone because its production could be expanded under sedentary conditions with proportionately less investments in labor.

Hence, in locales with good access to soapstone, pottery would not be favored as an alternative vessel technology until sedentary conditions made possible an economy of scale. Is this why pottery was so slow to spread in the Savannah River valley? Were mobile groups with direct access to soapstone, such as those of Mill Branch affiliation, perfectly satisfied with stone vessel alternatives?

This could hardly be the case because bearers of Mill Branch culture did not make and use soapstone vessels, let alone pottery. None of the large stratified sites with Mill Branch components below Stallings strata have produced soapstone vessel sherds, nor have any of the upland Mill Branch sites yielded such items. Soapstone vessels were indeed used throughout the area, but they tend to occur with pottery of the post-Stallings era, generally at small upland sites with poor organic preservation.

Although soapstone vessel sherds are rarely recovered from contexts with datable organic remains, their exterior surfaces frequently hold traces of soot, the tell-tale evidence of use over fire. In 1995, I began to collect soot samples from upland sites for dating by accelerator mass spectrometer (Sassaman 1997a). Results to date confirm that soapstone vessels were not made or used locally until after 3500 BP, the time of Stallings dissolution and a full millennium after pottery appeared. In other words, rather than soapstone vessels as practical predecessors to the pottery vessels of sedentary, classic Stallings people, these data show non-practical, nonlinear patterns of presence and absence.

Soot from samples across the lower Southeast pushes the origins of soapstone vessel technology back only a century or two, still well after the regional inception of ceramic vessel technology. Remarkably, some of the more spectacular occurrences of soapstone vessels occur in locations far removed from geological sources (Figure 11.3). Both coastal South Carolina and peninsular Florida were recipients of imported soapstone vessels from sources at least 250 km distant (Sassaman 1996). Pottery traditions in both locales predate soapstone vessel trade by at least 500 years. Eclipsing both of these cases is the huge volume of soapstone transported some 400 km to the Poverty Point area of northeast Louisiana. Once believed to be completely preceramic, and thus in need of stone vessels for cooking, Poverty Point groups in fact had a long tradition of ceramic technology, including knowledge of vessel technology (Gibson 1996).

In sum, long-standing knowledge about the evolution of vessel technology is flawed. In vast portions of the Southeast, soapstone vessel technology was the cultural antithesis, not the technological precursor, of pottery. As I have discussed elsewhere (Sassaman 1997a, 1997b), and below, soapstone vessel technology first appeared on the cultural fringes of pottery-using communities, and was adopted more widely only after these communities fissioned, relocated, and reconstituted themselves. Untested assumptions about the evolu-tion of vessel technology have masked the variety of social identities and power relations underlying this process of ethnogenesis.

Form to function to dysfunction

A third and final shortcoming of an agent-free account of Stallings prehistory is seen in the functional analysis of technological form. In broad outline, the history of Stallings pottery records the transition from indirect-heat to direct-heat cooking methods (Sassaman 1993, 1998b). Indirect-heat cooking, or "stone boiling," is a moist cooking technique that predates the beginnings of pottery making by many millennia. Archaeological evidence for stone boiling is often ubiquitous. Clastic materials like granite, quartz, or limestone are poor at resisting the thermal shock of rapid temperature changes, so their use in stone boiling resulted in abundant waste (i.e., fire-cracked rock). From about 5500 BP, inhabitants of the middle Savannah valley began to apply locally available soapstone to their stone boiling needs. Because it absorbs and dissipates heats very slowly, and is therefore resistant to thermal shock, soapstone makes an excellent medium for indirect-heat cooking. The oldest soapstone cooking stones were crudely modified nodules. By 4800 BP, nodules were routinely ground to a flat profile, then perforated so that they could be transferred from fire to container with a stick or antler tine. Clay-lined pits, baskets, and perhaps wooden containers were used with soapstone slabs for indirect-heat moist cooking. Again, soapstone vessels would not be employed locally for another 1,400 years.

By the time pottery began to be made by Coastal Plain and coastal populations, around 4500 BP, middle Savannah valley residents had a well-established soapstone slab industry. Their lowcountry counterparts likewise utilized soapstone slabs, acquiring them either directly, during seasonal rounds to the lower Piedmont, or through exchange with partners near Piedmont sources. The earliest pottery was well suited to indirect-heat cooking functions (see Reid 1989; Schiffer and Skibo 1987 for mechanical performance criteria of indirect-heat vessels). Designed to retain internal heat, early vessels were shallow basins with insulating, porous pastes provided by fiber temper, thick vessel walls to retard heat loss, and flat, thick bottoms for radiating an internal source of heat. Although the high orifice to volume ratio of this form allowed heat to escape, its wide-mouthed, shallow design was necessary for the manipulation of vessel content, particularly the cooking stones that were cycled through for continuous heating. In essence, these ceramic basins were portable versions of the cooking pits used by generations of predecessors.

Shortly after flat-bottomed basins were introduced, coastal residents began to experiment with forms and manufacturing techniques to develop vessels for direct-heat cooking. This change was probably stimulated by the high procurement costs of soapstone and lack of a local substitute, accentuated, perhaps, by growing ethnic divisions between riverine and coastal groups. Thereafter, the technological trajectories of early pottery diverged, with innovations enabling direct-heat cooking appearing on the coast while indirect-heat cooking techniques persisted for centuries in the middle Savannah valley.

A series of technological changes on the coast reflect refinements in direct-heat cooking. Vessel forms diversified to include bowl and jar forms with lower orifice to volume ratios than basins, hence lower rates of heat loss. Slightly incurvate rim profiles enhanced thermal efficiency by reducing orifice size without loss of volume. Rounded bases permitted greater air flow to the heat source for better combustion (Hally 1986: 280). Thermal conductivity was increased as pastes were made progressively sandier and less porous. Further improvements in conductivity were provided by thin vessel walls although, initially, walls became thicker on average to accommodate taller forms. The innovation of coiling, appearing later in the coastal sequence (Trinkley 1980), alleviated the limitations on thinner walls. Shell-scraped interiors attest to efforts not only to thin walls for maximum conductivity, but also to achieve uniform thickness for greater thermal shock resistance (Sassaman 1993: 179).

Many of these same innovations for direct-heat cooking had parallel expressions in the classic Stallings pottery of middle Savannah valley, yet such vessels were not routinely used over fire. Independent evidence for use alteration illustrates the functional distinction. Whereas over 42 percent of coastal Stallings vessels bear traces of soot on exterior surfaces, only five percent of riverine vessels are sooted, a proportion even lower than that seen among flat-bottomed basins of the early Stallings period (Sassaman 1993: 158–9).

Thus, middle Savannah potters designed pots for effective direct-heat cooking, in the fashion of their coastal neighbors, but they used them simply as containers for stone boiling with soapstone slabs. What is so remarkable about this is that the innovations they adopted diminished the functional efficiency of indirect-heat cooking. In essence, traditional forms were replaced by innovative forms that were rendered inconsequential, if not dysfunctional, by the persistence of traditional cooking practices. Clearly, factors other than energetic efficiency were at play.

Agents, structure, and power in Stallings prehistory

The foregoing examples illustrate the fundamental shortcomings of an agent-free view of Stallings prehistory. To reiterate, unilineal sequences have precluded recognition of ethnic diversity; models of technological progress are at odds with historical and cultural contexts; and inferences about vessel function have wrongly assumed conformity within form. In each of the agent-free versions of Stallings prehistory, change has a life of its own, with rationality, pragmatics, and practicality being the agent, not the people. My deliberate use of the passive voice to recount some of details of technological change is a classic symptom of agent-free prehistory.

The foregoing examples also demonstrate how a strong empirical foundation is essential to advancing Stallings prehistory beyond the misleading abstractions of extant interpretations. However, the data do not speak for themselves. Accordingly, in the balance of this chapter, I aim to illustrate how agency theory lends itself to the interpretation of time–space variation in Stallings container technology. My emphasis here, as in the preceding sections, is on the structures of gender, kinship, and ethnicity, and the social power enacted by individuals of diverse identity to reproduce or to alter these structures in relation to one another.

Because the relationships between structure and action in a given cultural context is contingent upon prior conditions, I am obliged to begin with a brief account of the historical context for the actions that created Stallings Culture. Historical developments on two distinct fronts are relevant in this regard. First, in the Coastal Plain province of the Savannah River valley we find the precedent for Stallings Culture in a poorly defined archaeological complex I refer to here as the Allendale phase. This is a preceramic complex dating from about 5000 to 4500 BP and best known from its distinctive stemmed lanceolate bifaces, application of thermal alteration to Allendale chert, and intensified tool production (Sassaman 1994). These material signatures are truly intrusive in the local sequence, indicative of a probable influx of people from outside the Savannah River region. In fact, the Coastal Plain province of the Savannah valley was largely abandoned over the previous few millennia, due, in part, to the early and pervasive expansion of southern pine forests (Watts *et al.* 1996), which reduced carrying capacity for key game species (deer, turkey) compared to the hardwood dominated forests of the early Holocene. After 6000 BP, when the rate of sea level rise slowed to promote aggrading floodplains (Brooks *et al.* 1986), riverine habitats became more productive and stable for human exploitation. In the ensuing millennium groups bearing the material signature of the Allendale phase begin to settle along the lower Savannah, and on the coast. Intensive use of riverine locales is signified by the inception of shellfishing by 4500 BP; Allendale phase artifacts typically occur at the base of these freshwater shell middens.

Over this same period, from 6000 to 4500 BP, the lower Piedmont and Fall Zone of the middle Savannah River valley was the venue for mobile hunter-gatherers with seemingly deep historical roots in the region. The local phase of the Morrow Mountain tradition (Coe 1964) reaches back to at least 7500 BP, and persisted well into the sixth millennium BP in a relatively stable pose of high residential mobility, expedient technology, and generalized land use. I have argued elsewhere that the Morrow Mountain tradition arose from the efforts of individuals to assert egalitarian relations among themselves in response to trends toward intensive riverine settlement elsewhere in the region, conditions which nurtured interpersonal strife and intolerable demands on social surplus (Sassaman 1995). Frequent residential moves, flexible co-resident and marriage arrangements, and generalized reciprocity were among the actions individuals took to reproduce egalitarian relations in this "culture of resistance."

At about the time that expressions of the Allendale phase appeared in the Coastal Plain, middle Savannah residents began to alter patterns of settlement and material culture. Few emergent patterns are evident for several centuries as individuals and small groups experimented with a variety of arrangements and cultural forms. But by about 4800 BP, material and behavioral aspects of their varied expressions converged on some repetitive schemes. One scheme known today as the Paris Island phase is characterized by seasonal transhumance between the Savannah River and adjacent uplands sites in the lower Piedmont, along with distinctive stemmed bifaces and the production of winged bannerstones or atlatl weights (Elliott *et al.* 1994). This phase represents the cultural foundation for the subsequent Mill Branch phase (4200 – 3800 BP) mentioned in my discussion of unilineal sequences above. Bearers of Mill Branch culture elaborated on many of the material and behavioral traits of their forebears, notably in their more intensive seasonal occupation of riverine sites, selection for specific raw materials for bifaces, and production of hypertrophic forms of bannerstones (Sassaman 1998a). Paris Island and especially Mill Branch culture appear to have been created and reproduced through deliberate actions to differentiate among varied ethnic identities.

These two successive cultural complexes existed in the middle Savannah valley at the very time Coastal Plain residents began experimenting with pottery. This technological innovation is perhaps the most conspicuous element of emergent Stallings Culture, but not the only one. Rather, coastal and Coastal Plain groups experienced much greater residential permanency than their upcountry counterparts, and they began to incorporate shellfish into their diet, both saltwater and freshwater. This widening distinction between upcountry and lowcountry groups would seem to suggest that the two were virtually isolated from each other, explaining, among other things, the slow rate of innovation diffusion.

However, individuals in both locales had at least one thing in common, namely soapstone. Quarried from Piedmont sources for bannerstones, as well as the perforated cooking slabs described earlier, soapstone was one medium of interaction or integration between individuals of neighboring groups. Elsewhere I argued that individuals who had invested in the soapstone trade were likely to be resistant to the adoption of pottery, particularly its innovations for direct-heat cooking, for it may have undermined the utilitarian value of soapstone and thus potentially eroded any symbolic value given to it by participants in exchange (Sassaman 1993). I regarded these circumstances as a basis for tension between genders, as I asserted that women were the primary innovators in pottery, while men, through their long history of bannerstone production and exchange, also controlled the extraction, production, and exchange of perforated cooking slabs.

Regardless of the accuracy of my gender ascriptions, it is quite obvious that cultural distinctions were accentuated as Stallings groups moved from the lower to the middle Savannah valley after 4200 BP, influencing members of the indigenous population to assert cultural forms we recognize today as Mill Branch. Among the potential factors contributing to increased ethnic differentiation in the middle Savannah were the rules of postmarital residence in Stallings Culture. With data on the handedness of Stallings potters, along with independent evidence from ceramic technology, I have been able to infer that members of Stallings Culture practiced matrilocal postmarital residence (Sassaman and Rudolphi 1995).[1] Rules for recruiting men into the relatively permanent riverine communities of the middle Savannah elude us, but it seems certain that Stallings women did not routinely relocate to their spouses' communities upon marriage. As the stable residential elements of the middle Savannah, women were the chief agents of Stallings Culture. Their pottery became highly elaborated, and shellfishing, another probable female task, assumed larger proportions. Neither of these features extended beyond the geographical boundaries of Stallings Culture. Matrilocality no doubt contributed to this closure of gender-specific traits, but more important perhaps was the asymmetry of exogamy. That is, men of Mill Branch affiliation may have occasionally joined Stallings communities through marriage, but nothing in the assemblages of Mill Branch sites suggests that Mill Branch men were permitted to take Stallings women away from their natal communities.

Although rules of descent cannot be inferred from the evidence for postmarital residence alone, it is likely that Stallings Culture was organized by unilineal descent. If so, every marriage imposed upon women a duality in social identity that had enormous potential for contradiction, as well as manipulation. For instance, women's productive responsibilities to cognates, as sisters and daughters, may at times have been incompatible with those to affines, as wives and daughters-in-law (Sacks 1979). The effects on household economy are not yet clear, but if biological health is any indication, the products of women's labor may have been appropriated for nonsubsistence purposes. Modern skeletal analysis reveals high levels of iron-deficiency anemia, systemic infection, and trauma among Stallings women (Wilson 1997). Rates for these insults exceed appreciably those among Stallings men, as well as Mill Branch men and women combined. Even if demands on women's labor did not directly affect the quality and quantity of subsistence, resistance to technological innovations indirectly impacted on household budgets by impeding changes that would have freed time and energy for nonsubsistence pursuits.

How resistance to change was manifested in individual actions is difficult to say. Individuals (men?) who had invested in soapstone exchange had sufficient cause to resist innovations likely to undermine a major source of social power. In so far as soapstone exchange was embedded in or helped to underwrite marriage alliances, actions of technological resistance (by men) would at least indirectly affect women's actions. Even if I cannot specify the particular actions of resistance or compliance, they were probably situational given the potential for diverse, often contradictory social identities of unilineal social systems. For instance, outside the context of large co-resident groups, namely those of the riverine shell middens, we find some evidence that some Stallings women acted differently. At the small upland sites located to date, Stallings pottery sherds occasionally bear the tell-tale traces of direct-heat cooking. Were some Stallings women asserting autonomy to adopt and use innovations as they saw fit, outside the context of aggregations of members of different lineages? This seems likely, especially considering that only two centuries after coalescing into its archaeologically recognizable form, Stallings Culture was transformed as groups fissioned and relocated permanently into the adjacent uplands of the middle Savannah valley. Exercising their social power as sisters, as opposed to wives, Stallings women may have actively rewritten the rules of kinship and ethnicity to make them more inclusive and egalitarian.

Before Stallings Culture dissolved, a similar process of ethnogenesis was under way among bearers of Mill Branch culture in the uplands surrounding Stallings territory. The apparent asymmetry in exogamy noted earlier probably left some Mill Branch men without prospective wives. The inequity of this relationship may have motivated Mill Branch individuals into social action. Occupying as they did the upland margins of the middle Savannah, Mill Branch groups used mobility, deer hunting, and portable technology to assert an ethnicity of outsiders, an ethnicity of (metaphorical) men. Alliances with individuals and groups farther afield began to increase. Over the course of the two centuries during which Stallings Culture flourished, Mill Branch people and culture became increasingly remote, smaller in number and less conspicuous in the archaeological record. I suggest that their dwindling presence in the area was spurred by the dwindling opportunities for marriage and alliance with their Stallings neighbors.

In this milieu of shifting personnel and alliances appear the first soapstone vessels in the region. Individuals of Mill Branch descent were clearly involved in this innovation, as were perhaps other Piedmont enclaves with lineal connections to land surrounding the major outcrops of Soapstone Ridge near present-day Atlanta, Georgia. Given the cultural and historical circumstances summarized in the preceding paragraphs, it is significant that soapstone vessels embody something of a compromise or mediation of the two technologies of gender and ethnicity. That is, soapstone vessels combined the form of (metaphorical) women/Stallings (pottery) with the raw material of (metaphorical) men/Mill Branch (soapstone). As such, this new technology may have been manipulated to assert more inclusive relations among regional populations, predicated, perhaps, on bilateral-bilocal social organization. Evidence for this will depend on detailed historical reconstructions elsewhere. For now, I can suggest that the record of soapstone vessel exchange to non-source areas includes examples of alliance-building initiated by Piedmont suppliers (descendants of Mill Branch communities among them). Flows of material culture and probably personnel appear to be more bidirectional than before. For instance, ceramic vessel technology begins to be incorporated into assemblages of Piedmont communities after about 3600 BP, even as soapstone vessel production and exchange flourished. In the next century, Stallings Culture was itself transformed as large riverine settlements were abandoned permanently and local populations distributed themselves widely across the interior uplands. Under these circumstances soapstone vessels were finally incorporated into local inventories, and they were routinely used over fire for direct-heat cooking. A marked reduction in the decorative elaboration of pottery coincides with these events, signifying, it would appear, an end to the gender-based ethnicity of Stallings Culture.

Conclusion

Variation in the timing, form, and function of alternative vessel technologies in the Savannah River valley cannot be understood apart from the motives and actions that residents took to assert identities of gender, kinship, and ethnicity in relation to one another. Is this case study unique in its cultural and historical details? Perhaps, but not to the extent that it cannot enlighten us about the circumstances of technological variation elsewhere and at other times. Agency theory forces us to confront the fact that people actively create and recreate the structures that influence or impede technological change. Certainly the circumstances or structures each individual inherits as a cultural being are beyond their control, just as the outcomes of their actions are sometimes unpredictable. However, each individual contributes to the production and reproduction of structure with every action taken, irrespective of consciousness or purpose. Inasmuch as individuals vary in their access to social power, the effects of their actions on social reproduction will vary. Tensions and contradictions are expected qualities and powerful forces in a social world comprised of self-interested agents.

Hunter-gatherers are not exempt from an existence shaped by agents. Recent ethnography has taught us that the very qualities attributed to "classical" hunter-gatherer societies (e.g., mobility, sharing, flexible residence) are a product of encapsulation and marginalization. It follows that so-called egalitarian behavior is a form of resistance to the imposition of will. Viewed as autonomy for all, egalitarianism is the purest form of agency. Importantly, however, the structures of egalitarianism are asserted, not inevitable. They are created and recreated each time food is shared, a group moves freely, and a marriage unites families in equality. In my case study, at least two instances of asserting egalitarian relations are observed: the formation of Mill Branch Culture, and the dissolution of Stallings Culture. Both processes were predicated on relations of inequality with others, as individuals enacted choices of settlement and technology to circumvent or undermine oppressive conditions.

Only archaeology can teach us what hunter-gatherers were like in a world of hunter-gatherers. To do so, archaeologists need to abandon many of their long-held notions about social complexity and technological determinism. Many such simplistic ideas, some borrowed from old ethnography, others from natural science, condition us to read archaeological patterning in set ways. I have reviewed here the shortcomings with stratigraphic interpretation, analysis of form, and technological models as they apply to Stallings prehistory. Overcoming these shortcomings depended on detailed cultural reconstructions from excavations at a wide variety of site types, refined chronology, and new functional analyses, among other advances. I trust my case study goes to show just how vital solid, empirical data are to an agent-centered prehistory. Agency is not anti-science, nor is it postprocessual in any postmodern sense of the term.

Ultimately, archaeologists must aim to reconstruct detailed histories, or long-term palaeoethnographies of their prehistoric subjects in order to apply the full potential of agency theory to archaeological data. This is not a call to revive traditional culture history. Rather, agency theory requires that we seek out and explain variation that has long been shrouded by the normative and essentialist aspects of culture history. This is not a call to locate and study particular individuals in the archaeological record. Agency is about the process of making culture, a process that is participated in differentially, to paraphrase Binford (1965), because it is experienced and perceived by individuals of diverse and multiple, cross-cutting identities, and with unequal access to social power. The archaeological record holds enormous potential to build comparative studies of processes of culture building, and to link these in the fashion of modern historical anthropology (e.g., Wolf 1982). In cultivating this potential, archaeologists will do well to reunite with colleagues in ethnography who confront action in their fieldwork in order to realize the full potential of agent-centered prehistories.

Acknowledgments

My thanks to Marcia-Anne Dobres and John E. Robb for inviting me to contribute to this volume and for their thoughtful, detailed comments on an earlier draft of this chapter. Institutional support for this research was provided by the Savannah River Archaeological Research Program, South Carolina Institute of Archaeology and Anthropology, US Department of Energy – Savannah River, and Department of Anthropology, University of Florida.

Notes

1   The orientation of punctations on Stallings "drag-and-jab" pottery is a proposed measure of the handedness of potters, that is, whether a potter was right-handed, left-handed, or ambidextrous. To date, rim sherds from over 600 vessels from twenty-seven sites in the Stallings area have been coded for orientation. Just over 10 percent of the entire assemblage has left-oriented puncta-tions. Inasmuch as this figure matches the proportion of left-handed people worldwide (Coren and Porac 1977), the orientation data appear to be a good measure of handedness. The inferen-tial basis for postmarital residence comes from distributional patterns in the incidence of pots made by left-handed potters. The three major sub-areas of Stallings occupation in the middle Savannah region show distinctive proportions of left-handedness. Sites on the Ogeechee River contain assemblages with about 10 percent left-handed pots, while those along Brier Creek have only 2 to 3 percent, and those on the middle Savannah proper have about 20 percent. The proportions of left-handed pots are consistent within each of these sub-areas and all pairwise comparisons are statistically significant. Because the samples span at least two centuries, these consistent patterns would seem to suggest conditions that ensured generational continuity among potters within each of the subareas. Much of the literature on handedness dwells on the relative contributions of genetics and learning environment in transmitting hand preference. Regardless of the relative influences, handedness frequencies in any population are affected by family arrangements and residential patterns. Offspring with at least one left-handed parent are as much as nine times more likely to be left-handed than offspring with no left-handed parents (Chamberlain 1928; Porac *et al.* 1986). Maternal influence appears to be a particularly strong factor (Ashton 1982; Carter-Saltzman 1980; Porac *et al.* 1986). It follows that residential prac-tices which keep related females together through multiple generations would have the conse-quence of maximizing the incidence of left-handedness in the local population. If we allow that Stallings pots were indeed made and decorated by women – a reasonable assertion given ethno-graphic regularities (Arnold 1985: 101; Skibo and Schiffer 1995) – then the handedness data are indicative of matrilocal postmarital residence patterns.

Bibliography

Anderson, D. G. and J. W. Joseph 1988. *Prehistory and History Along the Upper Savannah River: Technical Synthesis of Cultural Resource Investigations, Richard B. Russell Multiple Resource Area.* Russell Papers, Interagency Archeological Services Division, National Park Service Atlanta.

Arnold, D. 1985. *Ceramic Theory and Culture Process.* Cambridge University Press, Cambridge UK.

Ashton, G. C. 1982. "Handedness: An Alternative Hypothesis." *Behavior Genetics* 12: 125–47.

Bell, J. 1992. "On Capturing Agency in Theories about Prehistory," in *Representations in Archaeology*, edited by J-C. Gardin and C. Peebles, pp. 30–55. Indiana University Press, Bloomington.

Binford, L. R. 1965. "Archaeological Systematics and the Study of Culture Process." *American Antiquity* 31: 203–10.

Bloch, M. 1983. *Marxism and Anthropology.* Oxford University Press, Oxford.

Brooks, M. J., P. A. Stone, D. J. Colquhoun, J. G. Brown, and K. B. Steele 1986. "Geoarchaeological Research in the Coastal Plain Portion of the Savannah River Valley." *Geoarchaeology* 1: 293–307.

Brown, J. A. 1989. "The Beginnings of Pottery as an Economic Process," in *What's New? A Closer Look at the Process of Innovation*, ed. S. E. van der Leeuw and R. Torrence, pp. 203–24. Unwin Hyman, London.

Bullen, R. P. and H. B. Greene 1970. "Stratigraphic Tests at Stallings Island, Georgia." *Florida Anthropologist* 23: 8–23.

Carter-Saltzman, P. 1980. "Biological and Structural Effects on Handedness: Comparison between Biological and Adoptive Families." *Science* 209: 1263–5.

Chamberlain, H. D. 1928. "The Inheritance of Left-handedness." *Journal of Heredity* 19: 557–9.

Chevillard, N and S. Leconte 1986. "The Dawn of Lineage Societies: The Origins of Women's Oppression," in *Women's Work, Men's Property: The Origins of Gender and Class*, ed. S. Coontz and P. Henderson, pp. 76–107. Verso, London.

Claflin, W. H., Jr. 1931. *The Stalling's Island Mound, Columbia County, Georgia*. Peabody Museum of American Archaeology and Ethnology Papers 141, Cambridge, Mass.

Coe, J. L. 1964. *The Formative Cultures of the Carolina Piedmont*. Transactions of the American Philosophical Society, no. 54. Philadelphia.

Collier, J. F. 1988. *Marriage and Inequality in Classless Societies*. Stanford University Press, Stanford.

Comaroff, J. L. 1987. "Of Totemism and Ethnicity: Consciousness, Practice, and the Signs of Inequality." *Ethnos* 52: 301–23.

Coren, S. and C. Porac 1977. "Fifty Centuries of Right-Handedness: The Historical Record." *Science* 198: 631–2.

Crusoe, D. L. and C. B. DePratter 1976. "A New Look at the Georgia Coastal Shellmound Archaic." *Florida Anthropologist* 291: 1–23.

Denbow, J. R. 1984. "Prehistoric Herders and Foragers of the Kalahari: The Evidence for 1500 Years of Interaction," in *Past and Present in Hunter-Gatherer Studies*, ed. C. Schrire, pp. 175–93. Academic Press, Orlando.

DePratter, C. B. and J. D. Howard 1980. "Indian Occupation and Geologic History of the Georgia Coast: A 5000 Year Summary," in *Excursions in Southeastern Geology: The Archaeology-Geology of the Georgia Coast*, ed. J. D. Howard, C. B. DePratter, and R. W. Frey, pp. 1–65. Georgia Geological Society Guidebook 20.

Dobres, M.-A. 1995. "Gender and Prehistoric Technology: On the Social Agency of Technical Strategies." *World Archaeology* 27: 25–49.

—— in press. *Technology and Social Agency: Outlining a Practice Framework for Archaeology*. Blackwell, Oxford.

Dobres, M-A. and C. R. Hoffman 1994. "Social Agency and the Dynamics of Prehistoric Technology." *Journal of Archaeological Method and Theory* 13: 211–58.

Dunnell, R. C. 1978. "Style and Function: A Fundamental Dichotomy." *American Antiquity* 43: 192–202.

Elliott, D. T., R. J. Ledbetter, and E. A. Gordon 1994. *Data Recovery at Lovers Lane, Phinizy Swamp and the Old Dike Sites Bobby Jones Expressway Extension Corridor Augusta, Georgia*. Occasional Papers in Cultural Resource Management, no. 7. Georgia Department of Transportation, Atlanta.

Gibson, J. L. 1996. "Poverty Point and Greater Southeastern Prehistory: The Culture That Did Not Fit," in *Archaeology of the Mid-Holocene Southeast*, ed. K. E. Sassaman and D. G. Anderson, pp. 288–305. University Press of Florida, Gainesville.

Giddens, A. 1981. *A Contemporary Critique of Historical Materialism, vol. 1: Power, Property and the State*. Macmillan, London.

—— 1984. *The Constitution of Society: Outline of a Theory of Structuration*. University of California Press, Berkeley.

Goodale, J. 1971. *Tiwi Wives*. University of Washington Press, Seattle.

Gould, R. A. 1980. *Living Archaeology*. Cambridge University Press, Cambridge UK.

Gordon, R. J. 1984. "The !Kung in the Kalahari Exchange: An Ethnohistorical Perspective," in *Past and Present in Hunter-Gatherer Studies*, ed. C. Schrire, pp. 195–224. Academic Press, Orlando.

Grinker, R. R. 1994. *Houses in the Rainforest: Ethnicity and Inequality among Farmers and Foragers in Central Africa*. University of California Press, Berkeley.

Hally, D. J. 1986. "The Identification of Vessel Function: A Case Study from Northwest Georgia." *American Antiquity* 51: 267–95.

Halperin, R. H. 1994. *Cultural Economies: Past and Present.* University of Texas Press, Austin.

Headland, T. and L. Reid 1989. "Hunter-Gatherers and Their Neighbors from Prehistory to the Present." *Current Anthropology* 30: 43–66.

Jones, C. C., Jr. 1861. *Monumental Remains of Georgia.* James M. Copper, Savannah.

Kehoe, A. B. 1990. "Points and Lines," in *Powers of Observation: Alternative Views in Archeology,* ed. S. M. Nelson and A. B. Kehoe, pp. 23–37. Archeological Papers of the American Anthropological Association, no. 2. Arlington, Va.

Kelly, R. L. 1995. *The Foraging Spectrum: Diversity in Hunter-Gatherer Lifeways.* Smithsonian Institution Press, Washington, D.C.

Ledbetter, R. J. 1995. *Archaeological Investigations at Mill Branch Sites 9WR4 and 9WR11, Warren County, Georgia.* Technical Report no. 3, Interagency Archeological Services Division, National Park Service, Atlanta.

Lemonnier, P. 1992. *Elements for an Anthropology of Technology.* Anthropological Papers no. 88, Museum of Anthropology, University of Michigan, Ann Arbor.

Leone, M. P. 1986. "Symbolic, Structural, and Critical Archaeology," in *American Archaeology: Past and Future,* ed. D. J. Meltzer, D. D. Fowler, and J. A. Sabloff, pp. 415–33. Smithsonian Institution Press, Washington, D.C.

Levins, R. and R. Lewontin 1985. *The Dialectical Biologist.* Harvard University Press, Cambridge, Mass.

Manson, C. 1948. "Marcey Creek Site: An Early Manifestation in the Potomac Valley." *American Antiquity* 13: 223–26.

Meillassoux, C. 1972. "From Reproduction to Production." *Economy and Society* 1: 83–105.

Miller, C. F. 1951. "The Lake Spring Site, Columbia County, Georgia." *American Antiquity* 15: 254–8.

Nielsen, A. E. 1995. "Architectural Performance and the Reproduction of Social Power," in *Expanding Archaeology,* ed. J. M. Skibo, W. H. Walker, and A. E. Nielsen, pp. 47–66. University of Utah Press, Salt Lake City.

Ortner, S. B. 1996. *Making Gender: The Politics and Erotics of Culture.* Beacon Press, Boston.

Pauketat, T. R. and T. E. Emerson 1991. "The Ideology of Authority and the Power of the Pot." *American Anthropologist* 93: 919–41.

Porac, C., S. Coren and A. Searlemen 1986. "Environmental Factors in Hand Preference Formation: Evidence from Attempts to Switch the Preferred Hand." *Behavior Genetics* 16: 251–61.

Reid, K. C. 1989. "A Materials Science Perspective on Hunter-Gatherer Pottery," in *Pottery Technology: Ideas and Approaches,* ed. G. Bronitsky, pp. 167–80. Westview, Boulder.

Russo, M. 1996. "Southeastern Mid-Holocene Coastal Settlements," in *Archaeology of the Mid-Holocene Southeast,* ed. K. E. Sassaman and D. G. Anderson, pp. 177–99. University Press of Florida, Gainesville.

Sacks, K. 1979. *Sisters and Wives: The Past and Future of Sexual Equality.* Greenwood, Westport, Conn.

Saitta, D. J. 1994. "Agency, Class, and Archaeological Interpretation." *Journal of Anthropological Archaeology* 13: 201–27.

Sassaman, K. E. 1993. *Early Pottery in the Southeast: Tradition and Innovation in Cooking Technology.* University of Alabama Press, Tuscaloosa.

—— 1994. "Production for Exchange in the Mid-Holocene Southeast: A Savannah River Valley Example." *Lithic Technology* 19: 42–51.

—— 1995. "The Cultural Diversity of Interactions among Mid-Holocene Societies of the American Southeast," in *Native American Interaction: Multiscalar Analyses and Interpretations in the Eastern Woodlands,* ed. M. S. Nassaney and K. E. Sassaman, pp. 174–204. University of Tennessee Press, Knoxville.

—— 1996. "Technological Innovations in Economic and Social Contexts," in *Archaeology of the Mid-Holocene Southeast,* ed. K. E. Sassaman and D. G. Anderson, pp. 57–74. University Press of Florida, Gainesville.

—— 1997a. "Refining Soapstone Vessel Chronology in the Southeast." *Early Georgia* 25: 1–20.

—— 1997b. *Acquiring Stone, Acquiring Power.* Paper presented at the 62nd annual meeting of the

Society for American Archaeology, Nashville.

—— 1998a. "Crafting Cultural Identity in Hunter-Gatherer Economy," in *Craft and Cultural Identity*, ed. C. Costin and R. Wright, pp. 93–107. Archeological Papers of the American Anthropological Association, no. 8. Arlington, Va.

—— 1998b. "Distribution, Timing, and Technology of Early Pottery in the Southeastern United States." *Revista de Arquelolgia Americana* 14: 101–33.

Sassaman, K. E. and W. Rudolphi 1995. *The Handedness of Stallings Potters and Its Implication for Social Organization*. Paper presented at the 52nd annual meeting of the Southeastern Archaeological Conference, Knoxville.

Schiffer, M. B. and J. M. Skibo 1987. "Theory and Experiment in the Study of Technological Change." *Current Anthropology* 28: 595–622.

Schrire, C. 1984. "Wild Surmises on Savage Thoughts," in *Past and Present in Hunter-Gatherer Studies*, ed. C. Schrire, pp. 1–25. Academic Press, Orlando.

Skibo, J. M. and M. B. Schiffer 1995. "The Clay Cooking Pot: An Exploration of Women's Technology," in *Expanding Archaeology*, ed. J. M. Skibo, W. H. Walker, and A. E. Nielsen, pp. 80–91. University of Utah Press, Salt Lake City.

Smith, B. D. 1992. "Mississippian Elites and Solar Alignments – Reflection of Managerial Necessity, or Levers of Social Inequality?" in *Lords of the Southeast: Social Inequality and the Native Elites of Southeastern North America*, ed. A. W. Barker and T. R. Pauketat, pp. 31–51. Archeological Papers of the American Anthropological Association, no. 3. Arlington, Va.

Stoltman, J. B. 1966. "New Radiocarbon Dates for Southeastern Fiber-Tempered Pottery." *American Antiquity* 31: 872–4.

—— 1974. *Groton Plantation: An Archaeological Study of a South Carolina Locality*. Monograph of the Peabody Museum of Archaeology and Ethnology, no. 1. Harvard University, Cambridge, Mass.

Trigger, B. G. 1984. "Alternative Archaeologies: Nationalist, Colonialist, Imperialist." *Man* 19: 355–70.

—— 1990. "Maintaining Economic Equality in Opposition to Complexity: An Iroquoian Case Study," in *The Evolution of Political Systems: Sociopolitics in Small-Scale Sedentary Societies*, ed. S. Upham, pp. 119–45. Cambridge University Press, Cambridge UK.

Trinkley, M. B. 1980. "A Typology of Thom's Creek Pottery for the South Carolina Coast." *South Carolina Antiquities* 12: 1–35.

Waring, A. J., Jr. 1968. "The Bilbo Site, Chatham County, Georgia," in *The Waring Papers: The Collected Works of Antonio J. Waring, Jr.*, ed. S. Williams, pp. 152–97. Papers of the Peabody Museum of Archaeology and Ethnology, Harvard University, Cambridge, Mass.

Waring, A. J., Jr. and L. H. Larson, Jr. 1968. "The Shell Ring on Sapelo Island," in *The Waring Papers: The Collected Works of Antonio J. Waring, Jr.*, ed. S. Williams, pp. 263–78. Papers of the Peabody Museum of Archaeology and Ethnology, Harvard University, Cambridge, Mass.

Watts, W. A., E. C. Grimm, and T. C. Hussey 1996. "Mid-Holocene Forest History of Florida and the Coastal Plain of Georgia and South Carolina," in *Archaeology of the Mid-Holocene Southeast*, ed. K. E. Sassaman and D. G. Anderson, pp. 28–38. University Press of Florida, Gainesville.

Wilmsen, E. 1983. "The Ecology of Illusion: Anthropological Foraging in the Kalahari." *Reviews in Anthropology* 10: 9–20.

—— 1989. *Land Filled with Flies: A Political Economy of the Kalahari*. University of Chicago Press, Chicago.

Wilson, K. J. 1997. *Biocultural Investigation of Late Archaic Stallings Culture*. Unpublished M.A. thesis, Department of Anthropology, University of South Carolina, Columbia.

Wolf, E. R. 1982. *Europe and the People Without History*. University of California Press, Berkeley.

Woodburn, J. 1988. "African Hunter-Gatherer Social Organization: Is it Best Understood as a Product of Encapsulation?" in *Hunters and Gatherers: vol. 1, History, Evolution and Social Change*, ed. T. Ingold, D. Riches, and J. Woodburn, pp. 31–64. Berg, New York.

12 Tension at funerals

Social practices and the subversion of community structure in later Hungarian prehistory

John Chapman

Introduction

The principal objects of archaeological study are the remains of past material culture, people and places. In the last decade, many theorists have identified a more active contribution to the creation of culture from objects, bodies, and sites. Lubar has claimed that objects are not passive intermediaries but agents, always creating the world anew (Lubar 1993: 197). Meskell (1996: 7) proposes that lived and corporeal bodies are vital to the construction of individual identities and criticizes Barrett, Shanks, Tilley and Thomas for treating archaeological bodies as passive reflectors of large-scale processes, as mere scenes of display, whether in posture, gesture, costume or sexuality. Barrett (1988: 6) argues that locales (his term for 'places') play an important role in structuring action as well as being structured by action. All of these views share the same concern with the active role, with social action and therefore with agency (see also Barrett, this volume).

This outlook has much in common with what philosophers refer to as "pragmatism," whose most general insight was summarized by Rorty (1989: 3): "About two hundred years ago, the idea that truth was made rather than found began to take hold of the imagination of Europe." The denial of "an external reality" is common to most pragmatists, who hold the social construction of reality to be essential to understanding the human condition (Goodman 1995). This view is also found in recent gender studies, both in anthropology (Connell 1987; Moore 1993) and in archaeology (Dobres 1995; Robb 1994; Sofaer Derevenski 1998). Such writers are quick to reject a homogenized, unified picture of culture or society which renders social relations invisible (Sofaer Derevenski 1998), arguing instead that culture is contested rather than shared and that social practice is an argument rather than a conversation (Ledermann 1990). In this view, the continuous construction of society is an object of strategy and, if it happens, is itself an achievement rather than a presupposed postulate of structuration theory (Connell 1987: 44). This view privileges the gendered individuals and corporate groups who make and re-make their own history on a daily basis, struggling to create their own representations of themselves and find standpoints from which to promote their interests (Arsenault 1991).

However, the difficulty for social pragmatists is the reification of the dichotomy between structure and agency, which they seek to abolish. Barrett (1994: 5, 36) attempts to collapse this dichotomy by linking "agency," as the means of knowledgeable action, to structure recast as "tradition" (see also Barrett, this volume). Here, "tradition becomes a necessary condition of agency, where such traditions are the structural conditions reproduced, monitored and re-evaluated in actions and speech" (Barrett 1994: 5, 36). In Barrett's (ibid.: 95) archaeology of memory and practice, "traditions are the dispositions towards understanding which people routinely display by their actions." People know the world they inhabit and they re-work that knowledge through active engagement with that world. However, action and structure (as tradition) in this account still stubbornly refuse to dissolve into a unity of process and a framework of knowledge. Are there alternative ways of deconstructing the recursive agency/structure opposition that would provide a means of relating the creative potential of things, places, and people to each other and to explanations of prehistoric social change?

In this chapter, I discuss two theoretical accounts which seek such a stance, and work through their implications for gendered archaeological research with a mortuary data set from later Hungarian prehistory. The first account combines Danny Miller's (1987) presentation of a theory of culture with his earlier (1985) discussion of the categorization of artifacts. The second concerns Emma Blake's (1999) treatment of dynamic nominalism and its application to archaeological problems of structure, agency and self-categorization. Although categorization lies at the heart of both accounts, it must also be remembered that gender is as much about performance and about process as it is about categorization.

Danny Miller and objectification

Miller defines "objectification" as the foundation for a theory of culture. For Miller (1987: 18), objectification is a process of development in which neither social nor cultural form is prior but in which both are mutually constitutive. Basing himself on Hegel, Miller (ibid.: 28) characterizes objectification as a dual process whereby human subjects externalize themselves in a creative act of differentiation and in turn re-appropriate this externalization through sublation. If objectification is the very essence of the development of the human subject, externalization amounts to the creation of particular cultural forms, while sublation is necessary for externalization not to be experienced by people as rupture or loss. This view of culture – where culture is the externalization of society in history – can have no independent subjects, since they are reflexively constituted; it is also, by the same token, an assertion of the non-reductionist nature of culture as process. Objectification implies that the process of culture must always include an element of self-alienation as a stage in its accomplishment, meaning that the process of culture is inherently contradictory! Miller (ibid.: 33) emphasizes that materiality plays a role in the constitution of this contradiction.

Miller takes examples from social anthropologist Nancy Munn to provide concrete examples of objectification. In her earlier work on the Walbiri hunter-gatherers of Central Australia, Munn (1973) identifies externalization as the projection of individuals in iconographic representations, which leads to an understanding of personal experience in relation to a set of landscape-based media which contrast people as social beings and certain overarching social relations. These projections are then internalized, which creates the individual's "being" in relation to age, gender and social group. For the Walbiri, the particular medium of objectification is the landscape; the moral and social order is mapped on to a cultural landscape, which is "naturalized" by being mapped in turn on to natural features of the geographical landscape. The properties of the mapped landscape in turn provide permanence, authority and massivity, which can legitimize the social world. There is an interdependence between people and landscape in the creation of Walbiri culture.

In her later work on the Gawa islanders near Papua New Guinea, Munn (1986) examines the problem of constructing the self-image of a society in relation to outside groups. Here, objectification is a process of externalization and sublation, which depends upon inter-societal relations. The exchange relations between islands objectify the social relations between traders and others, based upon the way the Gawans "invest" themselves in the act of creating an object for exchange. In this way, objects are creative of social relations, through a process whereby people self-alienate as an externalization (the giving of a gift), only to have this aspect of themselves returned in a new form which accretes to itself the substance of the exchange (sublation as the receiving of a counter-gift). There is a similar interdependence between people and objects in the creation of Gawan culture.

In a similar way to Munn, I have previously examined the personalization of artifacts in relation to the cultural creation of individual actors by enchainment and accumulation (Chapman 1996, in press). Enchainment relies upon the direct relationship between person and object, in which inalienable objects were created out of persons and the exchange of these objects carried part of the previous owner with it to the next person, leading to a chain of social relations defined by material culture. In contrast, accumulation led to the strengthening of a new type of relationship between persons and objects which was in tension with traditional, enchained relationships. This was constituted by the loss of the direct relationship between person and object in favor of a representation of an abstract value, such as wealth, by the object now devoid of its most intimate personal connotations. In both ways of relating, artifact production, as one form of externalization, and consumption, as one type of sublation, are deeply constitutive of emergent social orders.

Miller (1987: 105) reinforces the importance of things when he states that "artifacts are simultaneously a form of natural materials whose nature we experience through practice and the form through which we continually experience the very particular nature of our cultural order." Indeed, for Miller (1985: 205) material forms are part of the central order of cultural construction. But the material world, as an established environment for social action, always tends towards naturalization, not because of reification but because of its very materiality; the way in which the material world acts to objectify a particular representation of society tends to favor that representation which reflects the interests of particular social groups as they pursue their social strategies (ibid.: 184, 192). Miller distinguishes between artifact "categorization" and "classification"; while the latter refers to the secondary level of evidence, the very varied division of artifacts into groups by the producers themselves, the former represents the order imposed upon the world by the creation of a cultural order and may be used to study social and material relations. Thus categorization enables the objects to integrate the individual within the normative order of the wider social group, where it serves as a medium of inter-subjective order inculcated as generative practice in some version of "habitus" (Miller 1987: 129–30). However, while antecedent material culture may be normative, norms are but tools for fulfilling strategies and effecting change (Johnson 1989). Thus, the introduction of history into cultural creation allows for the possibility of cultural or social change.

This extended summary and discussion of Miller's ideas prompts the proposal of a linkage between objectification and agency. The forms of externalization are produced against the background of a constraining yet enabling tradition (as structure), in which the naturalization of the material world is drawn upon by powerful groups against competing traditions. But exactly because objectification is the essence of an individual's development, it is also constantly the source of individual action. Thus, for each individual, externalization consists of actions taken by knowledgeable actors in a process of cultural creation. In this way, objectification as agency may be characterized as the main process by which individual self-identities are created through externalization and sublation. One example of the specific means by which objectification works in practice is the process of development captured by dynamic nominalism.

Dynamic nominalism

The approach termed "dynamic nominalism" is, broadly speaking, a form of agency theory, developed in the writings of Foucault (1973, 1979). The aim is to reconcile structure and agency within a single mechanism through the attribution of a more active role to identity. Hacking (1995: 247–8) defines the core notion: categories of people come into existence at the same time as kinds of people come into being to fit these categories in a two-way interaction. An example which Hacking draws from Foucault (1973) is the way that, owing to the development of new institutional forms of discipline and uniforms, soldiers in the Early Modern period "became" different kinds of people from Medieval soldiers. If social change "generates new kinds of people" (Hacking 1995: 248), this underlines the essential role of history in nominalism. This approach has recently been used in a study of Sardinian *nuraghi* by Emma Blake, who maintains that the generative power of self-categorization means that it is not only a type of agency but also a structuring device; it is a process in which individuals engage as well as a framework for other practices (Blake 1999: 36). This means that agency and structure come together in the formation of identities, which may be described as the practice of self-description through categorization. Identity, then, cannot simply be reduced to a function of habitus but is rather a way of coming to terms with the world and the Other. As Beaudry *et al.* (1991: 154) note, cultural identity is a public act of mediation between self and others, through any sign or object that allows a person to "make his self manifest."

At the level of the group, identities become a selection of defining characteristics, insofar as to define a group is to map its limits and define it in terms of what it is not. A key cultural resource to which selection is applied is the material world and the places where this is displayed; these storehouses of cultural resources (Barrett 1988) provide material for the re-writing of group origins, a process of locating the Other in the past (Blake 1999: 50). The self-definition of a group is a selection from one's own history and origins, a narrative of inclusions and exclusions.

This approach differs in two main ways from the agency theories of Giddens, Bourdieu, and Barrett. First, in agency theory agency and structure are distinct, while, in dynamic nominalism, self-categorization can work only if structure and agency are coterminous. Here, structures are constituted by ingrained practices, which define self and group in quotidian action but are open to change. This position is consistent with Connell's (1987: 94) criticism of Giddens' ahistorical agency, namely that, where the link between structure and agency is a logical one, the form of the link cannot change through history. Second, whereas theorists such as Barrett see human subjects defining themselves through a continuous process of rediscovery of practical knowledge, Blake argues that self-definition channels the process of knowledge acquisition, providing actions with a description which is already part of the process of self-definition. Thus, people and groups are constituted by a reflexive historical process, the creation of categories of people which leads to the emergence of people who fit the new categories. This approach leads to the question of the creation of categories of gendered people.

Gender and representation

In their discussions of cultural identity, neither Miller nor Blake comment explicitly upon gender relations but, since cultural discourses are the primary means whereby gender is created and structured, it is useful to extend their approaches to this field. At the outset, it is important to avoid the essentialist trap of treating all females (or indeed all males, hermaphrodites, gays and lesbians) as a single, unified group with identical goals, strategies, and social power resources (see also Gero, this volume). Since these vectors vary with all other forms of identity, whether age, ethnic affiliation or kin group, agency theory is in no way predicated upon essentialism. Rather, each individual and each gender group would have drawn upon the cultural resources available to them for objectification and self-categorization (Swidler 1986; Johnson 1989).

These resources clearly include their own bodies and the material and social worlds which encapsulate those bodies. Connell (1987: 81) has observed that the construction of the categories of "female," "male," "hermaphrodite," and "queer" requires a negation of their natural biological similarities, not least at birth and throughout childhood. The size variation amongst these groups is far greater within the genders than between them. Furthermore, humans of any gender are much more similar to each other than to any other biological species. There is a common-sense assumption, widespread in archaeology and anthropology, that the physically discrete nature of the body is evidence for the unity of the person. A central paradox of the human life-cycle, however, is the contrast between the physical identity and social, including gender, changes which occur and the "fact" that they occur to/in the "same" person. While babies are born into a social and cultural context (as members of a clan, a lineage, a household, etc.), they are minimally differentiated one from another, inherent personality traits apart. Such babies' bodies take meaning rather than conferring it and continue so to do through socialization. If bodies become human through the incorporation of the symbolic order, bodies can change insofar as the symbolic order changes. The very fact that identity is a social creation means that identities can and do change. But such incorporation takes time and experience – a process of active creation of personhood which is part of a set of discursive practices – material, practical and linguistic (Moore 1993).

Hence, the self-categorization of gender would have been constructed on the basis of cultural discourses, which may have emphasized gender similarity, ambiguity, multiplicity or binary opposition. Those individuals whose externalization included the making of human representations contributed in a specific way to the construction of the normative order of the wider social group; the manner in which they gendered the representations is an indication of the importance of current gender similarities or differences. In this way, gendered artifact categories integrated individuals into a normative social order, just as new cultural forms may have challenged or resisted those norms. Sofaer Derevenski (1998) maintains that, just as repeated group adherence to a repertoire of material forms and social practices lends gendered structure to society, so gender identity is the cumulative identification of elements from this repertoire. This is similar to Lesick's (1996) view that gender embodies the nature of experience of each person's "material environment," which is constituted by tangible material forms; in this way, engendering becomes associated with a particular set of material forms. This view can be extended by the notion of object inalienability through the personalization of objects; the result is the recursive creation of material and personal identities through externalization.

Returning to cultural representation, image-making is a fundamental social practice and the body is frequently the object of such representation. The constitution of the body as an "analogical operator" for the production of social divisions implies the existence of schemes whereby the body is itself perceived in terms of social divisions. These schemes of perception of the body are what separate the body itself from the representation of the body, schemes which are doubly grounded in the sexual and social divisions of labor (Bourdieu

1990: 72–3). Re-presenting posits a difference between the original and the re-presented, often seen in terms of partial images or images related to carefully selected categories of other information. Sanday (1990) observes that representations stressing the disparagement of women or a rigid separation between the sexes do not necessarily imply male domination but, rather, a social strategy for the control of gendered relations. Similarly, Schlegel (1990) stresses that ritual representations do not necessarily inform the whole cultural picture but can often relate to specific facets of social relations. Schlegel (ibid.: 38) further relates the interpretation of a gendered representation to whether gender *per se* is being represented, or whether a particular aspect of gender is on display (see also Joyce 1992; March 1983; Whitehouse 1992).

The reasons for re-presenting the human body in myriad forms is by now clear: the body is a crucial social arena for arguments over political claims and personal strategies. With its extra skin (that is, clothing) and its own potential for taking on meaning, the body remains the *locus classicus* for re-presentation of the cultural, social and gender claims made on behalf of a wider audience through an inherently powerful medium. However, the interpretation of the wider cultural picture from the biased and incomplete re-presentations common in image-making requires, at best, a multi-media set of images and, at the least, a clearly defined context for the display itself. The tactical and strategic use of such representations and the different spatial contexts of their use may be contrasted with the uses of the body itself and the spatial contexts of its use to build up a relational nexus of how social practice is at variance with perceptual schemes. One such context which is particularly valuable for an archaeological approach to bodily representation and gender research is the mortuary domain.

To summarize, the perceptual schemes used in cultural representations are a vital part of the community's categorizations of the material world and their place in it. The actualization of the gendered potential for making statements is as important a part of agency as any other cultural act, providing the framework for self-description and the ongoing creation of personal and cultural identities. Because the selection of the medium of objectification is central to social power struggles, this can lead to a great variety of material strategies through which self-identity is constructed and proclaimed. Representation, then, is a key part of externalization, and hence central to human agency. The mortuary domain is used here to explore the implications of this approach.

The mortuary domain in later Hungarian prehistory

Most archaeologists take the basic unit of analysis in the mortuary domain to be the single body. The situation in Central and Eastern Europe is no different (Chapman 1983, 1994). The buried remains of individuals in the Balkan Neolithic and Copper Age (henceforth NCA) may initially be categorized by three cross-cutting divisions: incomplete or complete; single or grouped; and intramural (within the settlement) or extramural (in a separate cemetery). The great majority of mortuary evidence from most periods of the NCA concerns the burial of complete bodies. Here the socio-spatial scale changes from the relationship between different bones from the same body, including dispersed burial of body parts, to different members of family or corporate groups. With human bone deposits, personhood is related to group membership as expressed by those who care for the relics of the ancestors or the place of their burial. The enchainment of artifacts is mirrored in the distribution of human body parts, which are deposited with(in) vessels, houses, pits and hoards (see Chapman, in press). At the broader spatial scale of whole body burial, the formation of personhood is related to group membership, expressed spatially in the burial location and socially as those with whom a person is buried. The real significance of the change to burial of complete articulated bodies is the shift in emphasis from fragments: complete objects to complete objects: sets. This shift is related to the change in scale of several different kinds of cultured material, among them human bodies (Figure 12.1).

Five socio-spatial groupings have been identified in the mortuary practices of the NCA (Chapman 1983). These are:

- the burial of an individual under or in a house
- the burial of a group of people near a house, the so-called "Household Cluster" (Winter 1976)
- the burial of kinship members in one or more small groups on unoccupied parts of a settlement
- the burial of corporate group members in small cemeteries (tens of graves)
- the burial of members of a large corporate group in large cemeteries (hundreds of graves).

From the perspective of personhood, the more complete the buried corpse, the more complete the statement about the deceased's social persona and the greater the potential it provides for the communication of social and cultural messages. Equally, the larger and more-encompassing the corporate group, the more rule-bound the mortuary domain. Thus the expectation is that mortuary practices within larger entities offered more opportunities both to make statements about individual personalities and to differentiate individuals, especially along lines of age and gender, as well as defining group membership. It is a truism that the discovery of cemeteries – a rare site category in the NCA – is an indication of successful group formation and maintenance; dead lineages tell no tales!

Since Binford, Saxe, and Painter, the archaeological study of larger burial entities – cemeteries or large groups of intramural burials – is predicated upon the selection of a decently large sample of graves and the analysis of the variability of the complete set of buried individuals. Analysis of this pooled sample often results in the identification of the global range of mortuary practices at a particular site and a set of "rules" by which archaeologists may categorize the community in question. This type of analysis is based upon an amalgam of individual social acts: a palimpsest of all the burials that have survived in material form. This is indeed the "standard" practice for archaeological analysis of mortuary data sets (this author included; see Chapman 1983, 1996; for numerous other examples, see chapters in Beck 1995); it is the equivalent of the approach to multi-phase monuments criticized by Barrett (1994). In the case study, I use smaller groupings within the complete cemetery or intramural grouping and any existing directionality, as exhibited in lines of burials, to break down a 'global' approach to the mortuary palimpsest.

In this approach, I recognize the limitations of temporal control on the formation of the different burial groups, in contrast to the more secure spatial understandings. What we often know about the burial groups comprising a cemetery is the number of burials they contain, the age–gender categories of the deceased members together with associated objects, and the distance of the farthest burial from the center of any nearby structure (e.g. a house). What we *do not* know about the burial groups is their chronology relative to each other and the time interval between the successive burials, whether within the group or between groups (days, weeks, months, years). We are usually also unaware of the proportion of the whole community given full burial (for an exception, see the excellent physical

HOARDING AND SETS

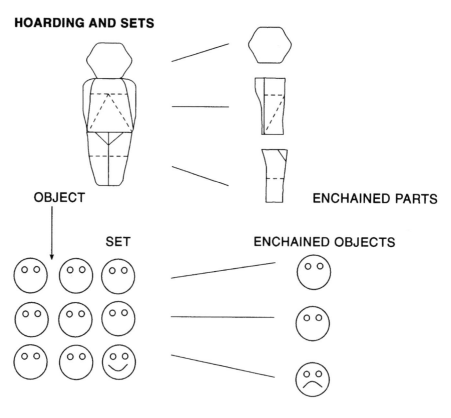

OBJECT

ENCHAINED PARTS

SET

ENCHAINED OBJECTS

BODY PARTS, WHOLES AND SETS

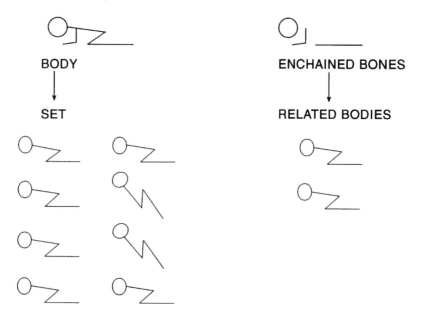

BODY

ENCHAINED BONES

SET

RELATED BODIES

Figure 12.1 Individuals and sets (drawn by Yvonne Beadnell)

anthropological study of Mokrin, in Rega 1996). The assumption is made that each burial was deliberately placed where it was in substantial knowledge, through oral tradition and/or personal witness, of previous burials in the same group and in general awareness of the evolving range of mortuary variability practiced by the community as a whole.

Mizoguchi (1993) has explored this issue in connection with the sequence of Late Neolithic/Early Bronze Age burials in Britain. He observes that, because all human social practices are situated in unique time/space contexts, people are never free from the consequences of what they did prior to their current action (Mizoguchi 1993: 223). In becoming "routinized, this repeated action constrains social freedom for new action. What separates past action from present decisions is social memory traces, which become an authoritative resource capable of manipulation by leaders who, in some sense, control the community's past" (ibid.: 233). The mapping of the newly-dead onto the places inhabited by the ancestors is thus a deliberate social strategy for expressing a kinship calculus, a socio-spatial categorization of persons with their complex cultural identities (for discussion of the location of barrows, see Barrett 1990). It thus becomes possible to take each burial group within the total site mortuary sample as a micro-tradition to investigate, first, the ways in which the micro-tradition is supported or challenged with each successive interment and second, the relationship between the "global" or community tradition and the "local," burial group micro-tradition. The assumption is made that, in a linear grouping of burials, the burials are indeed made in the sequence that can be inferred from the final order and that no burials are inserted into the order at the "wrong" time. It is also assumed that placing the newly-dead in a particular group indicates close kinship links.

In this case study, I wish to examine the micro-traditions of the Late Neolithic open settlement of Kisköre-Damm on the middle Tisza (Korek 1989) (Figure 12.2). This site is selected because of its excellent publication and moderate sample size. The method I use to attempt to demonstrate this more complex pattern of gender relations relies on the notion of artifacts as categories, as discussed above.

Kisköre-Damm and the Late Neolithic

The first flowering of the tell tradition in Hungary dates to the Late Neolithic, ca. 4500-3900 BC (cal.). Even then, fewer than twenty tells and tell-like sites are known from eastern Hungary, their number being exceeded by usually larger flat sites (Kalicz and Raczky 1987). The height of the tells at 3–4 m indicates intensive building and re-building, with rubble from earlier houses flattened and re-incorporated into new houses, a material strategy for the incorporation of ancestors into the world of the living (Chapman 1997). The houses are well-built, comfortable, full of life, fertility, furniture and fittings and possessions, including pottery, figurines, and other ritual paraphernalia. There is little doubt that the domestic arena of social power is salient on Hungarian tells. Because of their small numbers in the Alföld, each Late Neolithic tell assumed a greater place-value, in a wider social setting, than in tell-dominated Bulgaria (Chapman 1991).

The principal single burial mode in the Late Neolithic is intramural inhumation, found on tells and within flat settlements.[1] All the recently excavated Late Neolithic tells boast numerous partial or complete inhumations, usually of articulated skeletons, on unoccupied parts of the tell but, without exception, outside the houses (Chapman 1994; Kalicz and Raczky 1987). Tell burials indicate ancestral continuity in the realm of the living, as is demonstrated by the frequent positioning of houses directly on top of earlier structures (Bailey 1996). The first signs of gender differentiation occur with tell burial, with females lying on their left side

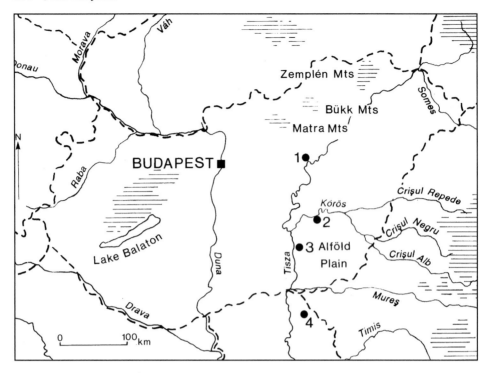

Figure 12.2 Location map of Hungary, with sites mentioned in the text (drawn by Yvonne Beadnell)
    1 – Kisköre-Damm   2 – Öcsod
    3 – Gorzsa   4 – Čoka

and males on their right, both with predominant body orientation of SE–NW (Raczky 1987), just like the preferred Middle Neolithic burial orientation and the orientation of many tell houses. However, this depositional polarization is rarely reinforced by gendered grave-good differentiation. It is also in this period that the earliest hermaphrodite figurines occur (e.g. the famous throned figure from Szegvár-Tüzköves (Korek 1987: Fig. 70), replete with breasts and penis), in the same occupation horizon as the gender-neutral "sickle-god" (Csalog 1959).

The best-published example of intramural burial on a Late Neolithic settlement is Kisköre-Damm (Korek 1989: 23–45, 74–124). Area excavation exposed part of a Middle Neolithic (AVK: ca. 5200 – 4500 BC (cal.)) settlement, a flat, unenclosed Tisza settlement with intramural burials and an Early Copper Age occupation (ca. 4500 – 4100 BC (cal.)). Four, possibly five, AVK burials were identified through the contracted inhumation rite that typifies all of the known Middle Neolithic burials on the Hungarian Plain (Chapman 1983, 1994; Kalicz and Makkay 1977). Only one of these burials contained grave goods: Grave 12, with a grey rounded bowl characteristic of the AVK (Korek 1989: 41). By contrast, thirty-one Tisza burials were documented on the basis of the extended inhumation rite, which is typical for that period on the Plain; in addition, many of the graves contained Late Neolithic Tisza pottery. Despite the small sample size, Korek's excellent recording of the mortuary features permits a wide-ranging analysis of the structure of the intramural burials. Skeletons were aged and sexed by I. Lengyel on the basis of both morphological and serological data. The two identification methods produced a high degree of consistency, enabling a differentiation into children (aged 1 to 16), young adults (aged

17 to 35) and mature adults (aged 36 and over). Other sex/gender categories were not sought or discussed in the physical anthropological report. The rich cultural data sets include the depth and orientation of graves, the cranial orientation, the costumes and grave goods found with the burials and the elemental materials used in costumes and grave goods.

There are two cultural antecedents with spatial meanings relevant to the Kisköre burials. The first is the line of earlier burials, made in the earlier AVK period (ca. 5200 – 4500 BC (cal.)), which bisects the area of the Tisza community excavated in 1964–6 (Figure 12.3). An important issue is whether these four graves (nos. 10 to 13), with a single outlier (no. 22), represented "distant ancestors" for the earliest Tisza occupants or whether the location of the graves remained unknown in the Tisza period (ca. 4500 – 3900 BC (cal.)). One cultural and two spatial points are germane here. Spatially, the greatest concentration of Late Neolithic burials lies close to the AVK graves, which are nevertheless not disturbed by any later burial. Culturally, the only Tisza burials with the typical AVK orientation – quite different from the typical Tisza direction – lie close to the AVK burial line. It therefore seems probable that knowledge of the earlier burials was transmitted in oral tradition, much in the manner that Küchler (1993) has outlined the mental mapping of previous land use in the decision-making of New Ireland groups for the establishment of new house-sites. The focus of Tisza burials close to the earlier

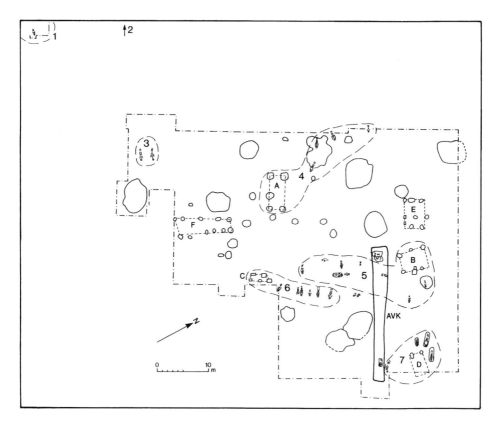

Figure 12.3 Site plan, Kisköre-Damm (drawn by Yvonne Beadnell)
  Numbers refer to Grave Groups (all Late Neolithic except no. 5). No. 5, in hard line, refers to the earliest, Middle Neolithic, burials on site. Letters refer to Late Neolithic houses. Irregular outlines refer to pits

ancestors betokened a series of acts of reverence towards the long-dead and the cultiva-
tion of roots within the ancestral soil.

The second antecedent feature at Kisköre was the six Tisza houses that can be identified
at Kisköre. The assumption is made here that each burial group found near a house (Figure
12.4) post-dated the building of that house, as part of a household cluster.[2] Since Late
Neolithic houses tended to be more spacious and permanent than earlier Neolithic houses,
it is assumed that the Kisköre houses formed a major structuring element in the settlement,
a counterpoint to the "permanence" of the buried ancestors, a group of features in which
the materialization of the domestic ideology was powerfully expressed and which, in turn,
provided a range of material culture to be drawn on in the mortuary domain. A further
three burial clusters were not associated with a house, a negative relationship that remains
problematic. Are these groups any less "domesticated" than the groups near houses?
Equally, there is an unexplained absence of burials close to two large houses, E and F.

Before we examine each individual burial group, it is important to understand the
"global" range of community mortuary practices. These can be summarized in eight points
(for more details of the original analyses, see Chapman, in press):

1   the importance of fluid, cross-cutting categorizations rather than opposed, ranked or
    binary categories

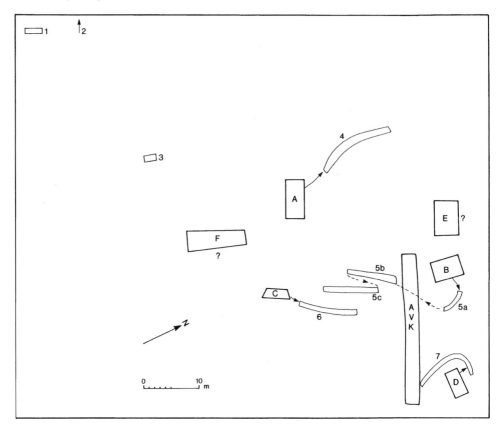

Figure 12.4 Simplified site plan, Kisköre-Damm (drawn by Yvonne Beadnell)
          Numbers refer to grave groups. Letters refer to Late Neolithic houses

2   great variation in body orientation and skull direction, relating to subtle and cross-cutting age and gender differences rather than major identity differentiation
3   the differentiation of mortuary rites through the introduction of costume, the deposition of individual objects, and the scattering of red ocher
4   a tendency for male costume to become increasingly elaborate with age of the deceased
5   a tendency for younger females to have more elaborate costume than children or mature females
6   a tendency for more and more varied grave goods to occur with mature females as compared to younger females and female children
7   an emphasis on the exclusive use of costume elements by adult females or males, counterbalanced by the overlapping use of whole-body costumes for all categories of deceased
8   a tendency for more grave goods categories to co-occur with costumed rather than un-costumed corpses.

The analyses of the Kisköre mortuary domain indicates several cross-cutting trends in the formation of "personhood." While most deceased are buried along a specified orientation, the combination of skull and grave orientation produces great variety in all age–gender categories. This is also true for the elements and raw materials comprising mortuary costume, those items in which the body was dressed up. The older the age of death, the more diverse the grave goods accompanying both females and males and the more elaborate the male costume (unlike female costume, which is most elaborate for younger adults). Variations in grave goods and costumes emphasize categorical differences between males and females far more than the differences between adults and children, but these differences are expressed not through binary opposition but through the selection of different combinations of elements common to all age–gender classes. It is in this sense that, at the global level, the development of personhood at Kisköre can be described as relational rather than oppositional, based as it is on categories re-stated time and again in the mortuary domain but part of the habitus of the living.

The membership of each burial group by age and gender, together with that of the two isolated burials, is shown in Table 12.1 and Table 12.2.

The Kisköre burial groups consist of between two and six burials, each group with a different set of age-gender categories and with an absence of double burials. The distance of the farthest burial from the center of the nearest house varies from 7 m to 24 m. With

Table 12.1 Membership of burial groupings by age and gender, Kisköre-Damm

Cluster	Females	Males	Children	Unknown	Total
1	23–40/23–25		2–3	one	4
2	12–14/	46–50/25–27/			3
3	41–50/36–45/				2
4	23–30/23–27/	41–50/41–50/			4
5	23–35		9–15/10–12/9–12 /2–5/2–3		6
6	36–45/23–30/23–45/	23–30/?one/	one		6
7	50/	58–62/48–52/	12/		4
Isolates		25–35	2–4		2
Total	11	9	10	1	31

Table 12.2 Mortuary treatment of individual burials by order within group

Group/burial	Grave	Deposited in grave
3/5	74cm deep rectangular grave	shroud; sherds; 2 red ocher lumps
3/6	99cm deep rectangular grave	shroud + red ocher; necklace, skin cloak, cattle vertebrae, pot, shell
2/36	65cm deep irregular pit	shroud; necklace; shell bracelets; armlet; pot; flint blade; shell bead
2/37	106cm deep grave	bone polisher
2/35	70cm deep rectangular grave	ocher; 2 shell bead armlets;
1/ 4	45-50cm deep pit	necklace; armlet; shell bracelet; head-braid; pot; bead necklace
1/1	85cm deep pit	2 shell bracelets; necklace; pot
1/ 2	90cm deep pit	2 necklaces; sherds
1/3	50cm deep pit	none
7/34	sloping rectangular grave (75–97cm)	2 necklaces; 2 pots; pig femur
7/32	trapezoidal sloping grave (85–130cm)	red ocher; head-braid
7/28	85cm deep pit	necklace
7/14	26cm deep pit (disturbed skeleton)	none
4/7	119cm deep pit	belt
4/8	Top fill of pit	red ocher
4/9	127cm deep pit	bracelet; necklace; shell bracelet; bead belt
4/21	158cm deep pit	necklace; head-braid; 2 shell bracelets; chest-braid
6/15	43cm deep pit	none
6/16	56cm deep pit (skeleton disturbed)	pottery
6/17	69cm deep pit	red ocher
6/18	85cm deep pit	red ocher; shroud + ocher; shells; shell belt
6/19	93cm deep rectangular grave	red ocher
6/20	115cm deep rectangular grave	none
5/33	96cm deep pit	none
5/25	93cm deep rectangular grave with rounded corners	none
5/31	depth ?? of partial skeleton	none
5/26	depth ??	none
5/24	78cm deep rectangular grave	head-dress; necklace
5/29	60cm deep pit, damaged skeleton	red ocher
5/30	85cm deep rectangular grave	none
5/27	85cm deep pit	none

one exception, each group is unambiguously closer to a single house than to any other structure. However, the equidistance of the complex Group 5 between Houses B and C, both of which have their "own" burial group, suggests a deliberate ambiguity or special status for this line of mainly children's burials.

Burials not related to houses

The analysis of the micro-traditions in the Kisköre burial groups emphasizes the dialectics of current norms versus new principles. We shall start with groups without houses. Group 3 is the smallest: a dyadic pair comprising two mature females. Their shared age/gender identity is emphasized by the standard orientation at Kisköre (SE–NW), a rectangular grave pit, and the use of red ocher. However, personal and/or social differences are indicated by a different depth of grave and by variations in costume, grave goods, and location of ocher. The earlier burial provided the second burial with a set of cultural resources for reinforcement or contradiction.

In the case of the three burials in Group 2, temporal priority is also unknown but the same result is produced: a strong contrast between the (similar) outer burials – two adult males – and the middle burial, a young female. These age–gender differences are marked by similarities between the outer burials, and difference from the middle, in the form of the grave (irregular grave/pit/rectangular grave), its orientation (standard on left side/alternative/standard on left side), its depth (shallow/deep/shallow), the use of ocher (absent/ present/absent), and the use of costume (elaborate/absent/minimal). However, the differences between the outer graves, perhaps relating to age – mature adult *versus* young adult – are also significant: a more varied costume and set of grave goods occurs with the older male, who is nonetheless buried in an irregular grave. This is the only series of burials where the maximum number of contrasts – six – is used. The differences continue to a more detailed level, as in the different armlet forms used: limestone beads for the SW burial, shell beads for the NW burial. Here, age–gender principles acting between three closely related persons are used to differentiate each successive burial from the previous one, while a secondary age principle is used for further differentiation. The choice of one of the several alternative body orientations for the female child would appear to relate her burial to the AVK ancestral tradition.

Four burials in Group 1, placed in a line from SW to NE, form the third group without a house: child/young adult female/unknown/young adult male. This group exhibits two important decisions: group features shared among all burials, and a directionality in one or more mortuary dimensions. Two negative group features are found: the absence of rectangular graves and the absence of red ocher. If the burial line began at the SW end, there was a fall-off in the variety of costume and grave goods (or the converse if the NE burial was the first) (Table 12.3).

The necklaces with three of the burials share the same limestone beads, while the first and third burials share perforated red deer teeth in contrast to the fired clay of the second burial. A summary of differences between successive burials shows low-level differentiation, masked by the missing data on ageing and sexing in the third burial: differences between burials 4 and 1 in grave depth, costume and grave goods; between 1 and 2 in costume and grave goods and between 2 and 3 in grave depth and orientation, costume and grave goods. These variations in burial 3 are combined with the choice of alternative orientation to produce a startlingly different mortuary representation. Is this representation partly prefigured in the directional trends in offerings and costumes or is this the first of the group? In an attempt to reduce the temporal ambiguities, I now turn to burial groups associated with houses.

Table 12.3 Grave good and costume contrasts in Group 1, Kiskőre-Damm

Grave 4	Grave 1	Grave 2	Grave 3
whole pot	whole pot	sherd	—
headscarf	—	—	—
2 necklaces	necklace	2 necklaces	—
bracelet	2 bracelets	—	—
—	—	—	—

Burials related to houses

Group 7 – a set of four burials grouped around House D – is a classic example of a house-hold cluster. However, in the absence of evidence for a house door, it is not clear which burial has priority. One potential temporal clue is the proximity of burial 14 to the AVK burial line but this burial is, in turn, farthest from House D. The initial hypothesis is that the burial nearest to the house is the first interment, leading to the sequence: mature female (burial 34)/mature male (32)/female child (28)/mature male (14). However, since there are no directional trends in burials in this group, this order may perhaps be reversed. In either case, the main differences in this group are between the first two and the last two burials.

The group is defined by a special body position: the standard SE–NW orientation, with head facing up. Since only two bodies are placed in this way on the rest of the site, this position is a strong sign of this group and, by extension, the members of House D. Grave offerings and ocher are deposited sparingly, but the main variations in the group are, in particular, in the pit depth but also in burial pit form and body costume (Table 12.4).

The unusual sloping graves with their extreme depth (97 cm and 130 cm at the deeper ends) do more to link the mature female and male buried there than to reinforce their gender difference; perhaps a marriage or brother–sister link is documented here? In any case, the other two burials are differentiated from the first pair by burial in shallower pits, a difference only partly transcended by the similarity in the form of necklaces (limestone beads and perforated red deer teeth) found in the first and third burials. But plotting of successive differences shows that variations decline with distance from the house: between burials 34 and 32, grave depth and form, costume, red ocher, and grave goods; between 32 and 28, grave depth and form, costume, and red ocher; and between 28 and 14, grave depth and costume. Thus, Group 7 is distinguished both by its body position and by its sloping graves, the latter not found elsewhere at Kisköre. The sloping graves are used to mark within-group difference as well as between-group differences, while other mortuary dimensions more frequently used in other groups (costume, ocher, offerings) are less actively used here.

Taking the principle that the burial nearest the house is the earliest interment, there is an unambiguous sequence near House A, with its four burials constituting Group 4, with a sequence moving further from the house: young adult female (burial 7)/mature male (8)/mature male (9)/young adult female (21). Two directional trends appear to override the two gender pairs in this group: an increase in burial pit depth and greater elaboration of costume with distance from the house (Table 12.5).

Although the costume elements appear to overlap, the raw materials differ in subtle ways (belts of limestone *versus* limestone and fired clay; bracelets of limestone bead *versus* *Spondylus* shell; necklaces of limestone bead and deer teeth necklaces *versus* those elements and perforated *Spondylus* shell). The gendered identity of the pairs is also overridden by the group's two negative common features – a lack of regular graves and an absence of grave goods – and still further by the variation in body position: standard on the right/standard on the right/alternative on the left/standard? It is intriguing that, despite the age–gender

Table 12.4 Grave form and costume contrasts in Group 7, Kisköre-Damm

Grave 34	Grave 32	Grave 28	Grave 14
sloping rectangular grave	sloping trapezoidal grave	—	—
2 necklaces	head ornament + ocher	necklace	—

Table 12.5 Grave form and costume contrasts in Group 4, Kisköre-Damm

Grave 7	Grave 8	Grave 9	Grave 21
—	ocher near head	—	head-dress
—	—	necklace	necklace
—	—	bracelet	bracelets
—	—	—	chest-decoration
belt	—	belt	—

differences of the two pairs in Group 4, not a single burial or mortuary trait refers back to age/gendered identity. Rather, this group exemplifies the significance of material culture in creating difference from the community norm as well as intragroup difference from burial to burial through directional variations: differences between burials 7 and 8, grave depth and form, costume and red ocher; between 8 and 9, grave depth, form and orientation, costume and red ocher; and between 9 and 21, grave depth and orientation and costume.

Perhaps the most regular, and convincing, line of burials is Group 6, which extends 12m NE from House C, stopping 6m short of the AVK ancestral burial line. This line includes six burials, in a sequence moving further from the house: young adult male (burial 15)/young adult female (16)/young adult female (17)/child (18)/adult male (19)/mature female (20). The group is defined negatively by the near-complete absence of body costume except for one ocher-strewn shroud on the child's burial and, positively, by the near-complete dominance of standard body orientation, once the first burial had been completed. There is no age–gender criterion for the exclusion of costume as a multifaceted, colorful and impressive part of the funeral rites; perhaps the material circumstances of household C did not allow for the deposition of such finery. As with Group 4, the main directional feature in Group 6 is the increasing depth of burial pits with distance from the house; it appears that bodily depth is cross-referenced to kinship distance from the ancestral house-builders. The sporadic use of grave offerings and ocher is another means of differentiating successive burials: none/pot/ocher/ocher and shell/ocher/none. The final within-group difference is the appearance of rectangular graves for the last two burials, which also have the deepest graves in the line. This group exhibits little age- or gender-linked material differentiation; rather, the absence of differentiation in costume and the overriding directional increase in burial depth indicates overall homogeneity, with a generally low level of successive burial differentiation: differences between burials 15 and 16, grave depth and orientation and grave goods; between 16 and 17, grave depth, red ocher and grave goods; between 17 and 18, grave depth, costume and grave goods; between 18 and 19, grave depth and form, costume, red ocher and grave goods; and between 19 and 20, grave depth and red ocher.

The final group exhibits by far the most complex spatial structure. Group 5 may in fact be an amalgam of three sub-groups: 5A, two burials to the northeast of the AVK ancestral burial line; 5B, a line of three burials southwest of the AVK line; and 5C, a line of three burials parallel to 5B. But there are four important group features that may mean that these eight burials once formed a coherent group. This group contains the highest proportion of children's burials (six out of eight) in the whole settlement, none of the burials uses grave offerings, and costume and ocher appear very rarely (only once each). If this coherence is genuine, there is a claim that Group 5 would have been the key group in the whole intramural burial layout, since its structure is based upon uniting the two settlement zones on either side of the AVK ancestral line by laying out a line of burials at right angles to the

AVK burials (for arguments relating the Tisza group to their AVK ancestors, see above). However, the possibility remains that sub-group 5A is closely connected to House B, while sub-groups 5B and 5C, on the other side of the AVK line, are more closely related to House C, if not so closely related to it as Group 6. In this analysis, it is assumed that Group 5 forms a coherent group consisting of three sub-groups. Since sub-group 5A is closest to House B, this is taken to be the earliest group of burials. The female child (burial 33) and young adult male (burial 25) were both buried without grave goods, in irregular pits dug to similar depth and according to the standard orientation, although the skulls faced different ways. In sub-group 5B, the three burials – young adult female (burial 31)/female child (26)/female youth (24) – were poorly preserved, but with variable orientation: standard?/standard?/alternative on the left. Burial 24 was adorned with a limestone-bead head-dress and necklace. A similar variety in orientation is found in sub-group 5C, with its three female burials: child (burial 29)/youth (30)/youth (27): alternative?/alternative on the left/standard UP. Almost all the "alternative" orientations in Group 5 are closely related to the norms of the AVK burial line, the SW–NE direction. The exception is burial 30, with her head to the NE and feet to the SW, a unique occurrence in the Tisza burials at Kisköre but found in AVK burial 11. Thus, in two ways Tisza-period practice takes a key aspect of the ancestral past and transforms it into the rite of extended inhumation that was in the process of becoming the new Tisza norm. The three instances of the head facing upwards parallel the UP body position characteristic of burials in nearby Group 7. Hence, materialized references to the past (the AVK line) and coeval neighbors (Group 7) typify the Group 5 burials and support that group's internal differentiation. The paucity of grave offerings, costume, and ocher leave few other means for the differentiation of successive burials: differences between burials 33 and 25, grave form; between 25 and 31, grave form; between 31 and 26, none; between 26 and 24, grave form, orientation, and costume; between 24 and 29, grave depth and form, costume, and red ocher; between 29 and 30, grave depth, form and orientation, and red ocher; and between 30 and 27, grave form and orientation. This group includes the only pair of successive burials on site (nos. 31 and 26) which are essentially identical.

Personhood and group identities

This detailed examination of a small number of intramural burials at Kisköre-Damm yields a pattern of cross-cutting principles of variability in which we can begin to see the effects of group identity, age, gender, and group trajectory on the material remains. The first question relates to the manner in which group identities were materialized. In Table 12.6, the features common to all, or all but one, of the members of the group are defined together with any directional traits that define the group trajectory irrespective of age and gender identities. In the Group Features column of this table, a trait listed as "rare" means that it occurs only once.

The striking observation about the group features is that all of the six main dimensions of variability are used to proclaim group identity, whether they are used positively or negatively. If the group features and group directional traits are compared with the amalgamated community trends in mortuary practices, the intriguing thing is that so few of the "local" characteristics are related to the "global" patterning. An example is the global tendency for increasingly elaborate costumes to be associated with older males and young adult females. In the two groups where costume elaboration changes directionally, no gendered relationship is found. Again, while the global pattern suggests a direct relationship between increased frequency of grave goods and more costumed corpses, the group patterns offer no "local" support for this proposition.

Table 12.6 Group features and directional traits, Kisköre-Damm

No.	Group features	Group directional traits
3	age–gender identity	n/a
2	differentiation by (1) age-gender and (2) age principles	n/a
1	no graves; no ocher	decreasing elaboration of costume and ceramic grave goods
7	body position; sloping grave form; grave goods rare; ocher rare	—
4	no graves; no grave goods; ocher rare	increasing pit depth; increasing elaboration of costume
6	costume rare; mostly standard orientation	increasing pit depth
5	many children's burials; no grave goods; costume rare; ocher rare	—

These findings suggest that the local is not a mere "reflection" of the global, the communal writ small. Instead, the micro-traditions established over unknown temporal durations in the seven groups at Kisköre indicate considerable variability in their mortuary practices. The internal site chronology is, unfortunately, quite unknown. We cannot be sure whether we are talking about intervals between burials of a month, a year, a decade or a century, though the latter would seem improbable for the given community size. Nonetheless, what we see here is a series of different households, each dependent upon varied inter-community and some extra-community relations, making strategic use of material/symbolic resources to construct their own social order. Although there are instances of local deviation from the constructed norm (e.g. the only burial in Group 7 where ocher was scattered), often every burial in the group conformed to the emergent choice of group traits. This shows how individual cumulative actions become the structure which establishes a further cultural context for action. How does this finding relate to the negotiation of each successive interment against the micro-tradition of earlier burials?

It is clear from the summary of the group differences in successive burials that the full range of material culture and grave form options was utilized in the pursuit of difference (Table 12.7).

Table 12.7 Contrasts in each successive pair of burials by group, Kisköre-Damm

Group no.	1st–2nd pairs	2nd–3rd pairs	3rd–4th pairs	4th–5th pairs	5th–6th pairs	6th–7th pairs	7th–8th pairs
3	--:DCG						
2	AS:DFOC RG	AS:DFOCR G					
1	A-:D<u>C</u>G	??:<u>C</u>G	??:DOCG				
7	-S:DFCRG	AS:DFCR	AS:DC				
4	AS:D<u>FC</u>R	--:<u>DFO</u>CR	AS:<u>DO</u>C				
6	AS:<u>DO</u>G	--:<u>DR</u>G	A-:<u>D</u>CG	A-:<u>D</u>FCRG	-S:<u>D</u>R		
5	AS:F	-S:F	A-:none	--:FOC	--:DFCR	--:DFOR	--:FO

Key:
Before the colon: AS: difference in age and sex between burial pair   A-: age difference but sex same
                    -S: difference in sex but same age
After the colon: only differences stated: D – grave depth   F – grave form   O – grave orientation
                                                 C – costume   R – red ocher   G – grave goods

The extremes of differentiation are relatively rare, with only one burial identical to an adjoining one (Group 5) and only two pairs using the full range of six dimensions to express maximal difference (both in Group 2). Instances of directional trends are underlined in Table 12.7 because they represent the development of structure in the micro-traditions of these burial groups. They define the co-emergence of group structure through the directionality of the trends, and personal identity through the contrasts with the previous burial. The remaining dimensions in groups with such directional trends are statements more concerned with age, gender, and individual identities.

In groups with no discernible directional trends, the structure of the micro-tradition emerges in the positive or negative selection of group features (Table 12.2). Deviation from these traits marks an emphasis on individual identity rather than group orientation, as in the use of grave goods and red ocher each in a single burial in Group 7. Other aspects of identity are also at work. The oppositions represented in the three burials of Group 2 show the strongest age–gender differentiation in the community, underlining age–gender tensions latent in the community or a strategic emphasis on difference. The variations in grave form, costume and red ocher in the last five burials in sub-groups 5B and 5C – burials of the same age, gender, and presumably household group – suggest that individual differentiation between the newly-dead and the most recent burial was often important.

Working through the Kiskőre materials enables an understanding of how small-scale actions can form the beginning of a micro-tradition, just as placing two burials side by side can start a burial line. The Kiskőre community was so small – probably not more than fifty people at any one time – that it can be assumed that all of the living could have attended the funeral of a newly-dead, even if not all of them did attend. These open and public events were the setting for the crystallization of action and structure and the material objects were as much part of that setting as the spatial location of the burial. How does the body of ideas about objectification as agency relate to the Kiskőre study?

Tension at funerals

Although processualists from Saxe (1970) and Binford (1971) onwards recognized that funerals were a vital moment for community self-reflection and statements about cultural order, they rarely used this insight to deal with small-scale, "local" processes, preferring to amalgamate data to make "global" community-wide statements. Agency theory rejects neither the one nor the other approach, but seeks to integrate the global and the local by means of an understanding of the material environment in which engendering takes its place.

The final journey of the corpse of each of the newly-dead is, on the one hand, a representation of what the living wish to say about that person, their community and their views of the world: a cultural externalization. On the other hand, the journey is a movement through and towards sites of consumption, where a final sublation takes place for both the deceased and the living. In this sense, mortuary rites are but one form of social practice rooted in the wider principles of objectification through which individuals and culture are interwoven in the fabric of the quotidian. But what does this mean for the community of mourners who have just lost a two year-old girl or have to come to terms with the loss of the oldest and (perhaps) most respected member of their community, a sexagenarian female? We begin with the reflexive relationship between people and things.

At burial 29 (sub-group 5C), the two year-old is interred next to a 10–12 year-old, in a shallower pit (not a grave), in the same SW–NE orientation (not standard for the site), similarly without grave goods, but with red ocher powdered on the skull (unlike the 10–12 year-old, who had limestone-bead costume elements on head and neck). Here is a formal burial of a very young member of a community, whose journey of self-definition had hardly begun. Yet the household defined that child's persona in a formal way, using material presences and absences to make references to wider cultural themes (the presence of ocher; the absence of grave goods) and linking the girl's death to the AVK ancestral line through body orientation. It is not known whether burial 29 was the first child to be buried at Kiskőre, but the formal burial itself shows that the category of "two year-old girl" was socially recognized as emergent at the time of the child's funeral. The funeral, as a public act of mediation between the mourners and a wider society, provided the elements of cultural identity for the newly-dead. The precise form of burial that we see is a snapshot of the social processes of categorization, the practice of description of a particular individual who, at the same time, is a member of a wider category of people. If we do not know the ages and genders of the people who made the representation, we are nonetheless aware of the wider mortuary discourse used for gender categorization.

In contrast to the oldest member of the community, few material objects were laid to rest with the two-year-old at burial 29. If, as we suppose, the mature female of burial 34 is likely to have been the first burial made in Group 7, her funeral set the direction of the group's mortuary practices. Her sloping rectangular grave form was unique to the site, being imitated in a variant form only once, in the immediately following burial. Her body position (SE–NW, UP) initiated what became a defining group feature but was rare outside the group. Her costume was cross-referenced to other burials and social categories in two ways. The use of necklaces without other costume elements is found with other women and with children. The precise form of necklace – made of a combination of limestone beads and perforated red deer teeth – is the commonest form of necklace, found in all age-gender categories on the site and in burials in four groups; both elements of the necklace make reference to wider social networks (see below). In terms of grave goods, the only objects deposited in Group 7 burials were those in burial 34. The deposition of fragments of two hemispherical Tisza bowls on the right side of her body and a pig's femur near her left knee creates an opposition between nature/left and culture/right that is rarely replicated at Kiskőre; both of the bowls were large enough and ornate enough to have been used as serving dishes for the joint of pork, an offering unique at Kiskőre. Hemispherical bowls were placed in only two other burials, both mature individuals, one female (burial 6) and one male (burial 36), and in both instances on the right side of the body. Through the categorization of people and things, objects such as the necklaces, pottery, and pork joint of burial 34 integrate the person within the normative order of the social group, not only at household level, but also in the wider community and beyond. Whoever made the decisions leading to the particular cultural form of burial 34, they were adhering to a repertoire of material forms and social practices whose repetition, with variations, created long-term structure. Their choice to associate the female in her sixties with specific costume elements and objects came out of past engendered practices and led to their persistence.

The second structuring relationship concerns the relationship between people and places, as betokened in the spatial relations of the site. Kiskőre shows, in microcosm, the closeness of household life and death, the familiarity of nearby places, and the tight nexus of domestic and mortuary arenas, not to be transcended until the succeeding Copper Age (Chapman 1995, 1996).

A primary factor is the location of the AVK ancestral line bisecting the site. The burial groups are as strongly attracted by the magnet of the AVK line as are the houses, all of whose nearest walls lie within 30 m of a point on the AVK line. This line grounds the Late

Neolithic settlement in a past, timeless tradition, while at the same time providing cultural material on which to draw for similarities, contrasts, and oppositions. After the burial group is located in relation to the ancestral line, the choice of direction of the burial line is important. It is perhaps significant that burial lines 4–7 all expand in the direction of the AVK ancestral line or its extension; in the case of Group 5, the AVK line is crossed while, in the case of Group 4, the line stops short of an extension of the AVK line. This double influence of the ancestral line, on the origin and the end-point of several lines, says much for the overall spatial structure of the site in relation to temporal principles.

It is also clear by now that the location of successive burials in a straight or curved line increasing in distance from a house is another form of self-structuring social practice. A linear arrangement of burials provides a kinship calculus defined by both inclusion in the line (or exclusion from it) and relative position, including distance from the house and from the ancestral line. Because most burials lie between their households and the ancestral line, there is movement along the burial line between the living and the ancestors, with the earliest burials closest to the living. The implications of this interesting principle remain to be fully elucidated.

Another general spatial structuring principle concerns house and burial orientation, since the latter could have drawn upon the cultural resources of the former. This in fact happens relatively rarely. Only two out of the six houses (Houses A and E) were oriented in the standard SE–NW burial line, and one of these (House E) had no associated burials. In three cases, all the burials in a group were placed on different orientations from that of their associated house (Group 7 and House D; Group 6 and House C; Group 5 and House B). The other house with no associated burials, House F, is oriented SW–NE, as is House C and the several burials from Group 5B–C. At this site, the avoidance of house orientation is an important structuring principle of burials, as if to emphasize the difference between the living and the dead. This is not the case in other parts of Europe, for instance the Neolithic of the north European plain, where long mounds often mimic the orientation of long houses (Hodder 1984).

A third aspect of structuring in the Kisköre burials is the manner in which the community related its social practices to other Tisza settlements and their social practices. In the most recent general summary of Tisza and other Late Neolithic mortuary practices in the Alföld Plain, Kalicz and Raczky (1987) outline the salient practices of tell burial: small groups of pit burials, occasionally in coffins, common orientation of adult males, often in contrast to the orientation of adult females, frequent use of red ocher, and restrained use of grave goods as a form of differentiation (see also other chapters in Raczky 1987). This summary indicates that the main forms of variability were common throughout the Late Neolithic of eastern Hungary, but that different communities drew differently upon these traditions to tell often similar stories about their community's newly-dead. An example is the use of the predominant NW–SE orientation – rather than the SE–NW orientation at Kisköre – of the burials at the low tell of Öcsöd, with adult males lying on the right side and adult females lying on the left side (ibid.). This picture is remarkably similar to the different ways in which three Bulgarian Late Copper Age communities made different, village-specific use of broadly similar material culture to send rather similar messages about age and gender categorization in eastern Bulgaria (Chapman 1996). We may suppose that, had a Tisza-group family from another settlement been present at a burial in Kisköre village, they would have been familiar with the overall practices but perhaps mystified at the differences in detail from their own traditions, prompting them to wonder why "those Kisköre people" were a little bit strange!

A fourth structured way of situating the Kisköre community is in relation to the sources of the objects incorporated into burials. Here, we can distinguish three categories of objects: local objects and materials, remote objects (originating within the Carpathian ring) and exotic objects (coming from outside the Carpathian chain). The categories of material found in the Kisköre burials are listed according to provenance (Table 12.8).

Each of these local materials would have carried with them a pre-existing range of symbolic associations as well as particular biographies of their acquisition, manufacture and distribution, which gave them their personal value for members of a community such as Kisköre. Objects such as *Dentalium* shells may appear to have little to distinguish them, but it is well to recall that they were probably collected from the oxbows and meanders of the palaeo-Tisza and their occurrence in burials presenced those age/gendered collecting activities and fed back onto them in the future. The perforated red deer canines used in jewellery held quite different associations. In view of the limitation of canines in each animal to two, these canines are simultaneously a symbol of power, with reference to the *agrios* and male hunting, and a means of mortuary differentiation (for discussion, see Chapman in press). Hence, the inclusion of twenty-three canines in the necklace in burial 21 (Korek 1989: Fig. 37) implies control over twelve dead cervids, while in burial 34, each necklace included only two canines.

The remote and exotic materials told wider biographical narratives. While the flint source is not known, the limestone probably derived from across the Alföld plain, either from the Bükk or Matra Mountains to the north or from the west Carpathians to the southeast. By contrast, the *Spondylus* shells, common in Late Neolithic hoards and burials (Chapman in press), derive from a long-distance exchange network connecting the Alföld plain to the Black Sea coast via the Lower Danube valley. The dense concentration of *Spondylus* shells in coeval Vinča sites in northeast Serbia indicates the likely point of entry into the Middle Danube basin, followed by regional exchange networks into the middle Tisza valley (Chapman 1981). The enchainment of objects and persons, as a primary means of establishing social relations in the Neolithic, leads to a continuous space–time structuring with recursive implications for travellers and those negotiating with strangers compared to those who stay at home (Helms 1988). Those mourners deciding to place a *Spondylus* bracelet in one of their kinsfolk's graves associated not only the specific item's biographical reputation with the newly-dead, but also the fame of those who traded for the bracelet and wore it in past ceremonies. The age/gendered nexus of associations thus produced established the cultural framework for the next burial, and so on, in relation to the potential of objects as grave goods. The creation of costume sets, comprising several different costume elements, markedly increased the biographical reputation and diversity thereby associated with the newly-dead.

Table 12.8 Provenance of materials found in the Kisköre-Damm burials

Local	Remote	Exotic
fired clay	flint	*Spondylus* shell
pottery	limestone	
red ocher		
pig femur		
cattle vertebra		
red deer teeth		
Dentalium shell		
plant material		

In short, there were four ways in which structuring was built into the Kisköre burials: the accumulated set of associations between persons and objects; the spatial relations that developed with the slowly growing number of burials; the embedding of this particular community's mortuary practices in a wider nexus of regional trends; and the presencing of the extensive set of exchange relationships betokened by the material culture of the Kisköre grave goods. At any time, the people gathered around the burial site of a newly-deceased member of the community had many choices for the exact form of burial. Two choices in particular weighed on those mourners: the choice of how to bury their kith and kin differently from the last burial in their burial group, and the choice of how to relate the ceremony to other burials within the village. The tension between the household's micro-tradition and the potential inherent in the new statement shortly to be made about the newly-dead encapsulates the dialectic of structure and agency within an enfolding debate about self-identity at both individual and community levels.

Conclusions

In this chapter, I have defined the tension at funerals as a microcosm of the structure/agency dialectic. This dialectic is encompassed within a broader process of cultural constitution: the objectification of people through their externalization in things and places, and the subsequent sublation of the values and identities created through materialization. I propose that the process of objectification is the principal form of structuring through which people create their own material environments, but that people always oppose past traditions – the naturalization of material forms – through cultural resistance. As far as agency theory is concerned, the key feature of objectification is that it is an individual process through which group norms and past traditions are constraining but not determining. The representation of humans as cultural categories is the central material form of individual externalization, and its medium is a very political choice. Gendered identities are created through the process termed "dynamic nominalism," in which new categories of people come into existence at the same time as the people who fill those categories. This works as much in the mortuary domain as in any other cultural context, through the form of the burial rituals selected for any given individual.

It is the sequence of burials and their spatial locations within a place already heavy with the past that lends salience to the set of intramural burials from the Hungarian Late Neolithic site of Kisköre-Damm. Most of the thirty-one burials are grouped into seven burial sets, including arcs and lines. Most of the burial lines are associated with a specific house, although some lines have no house and two houses are far from the nearest burial line. Each burial line is treated as a distinct micro-tradition within the totality of community burials and, where it is possible to establish the probable sequence of burials, an analysis is made of the differentiation of each successive burial from the previous one. In this way, it is possible to define "global" or community traditions, "local" or micro-traditions and the resistances that individuals make to micro-traditions and that local traditions make to the community level.

Four ways of structuring the mortuary domain at Kisköre are defined: associations between persons and grave goods; gradually enfolding spatial relations; the embedding of community mortuary practices in the regional patterns; and the presencing of exchange partners through grave good deposition. This leads to a further tension between each village and the regional totality of mortuary practices. The negotiation of such tensions at a multiplicity of levels constitutes the framework for the creation of both personal and group identities.

Acknowledgments

Although the research on the Kiskőre case study was completed far later, the approaches used in this chapter derive from research leave in 1996/97. I should like to thank the University of Durham for this leave and the Department of Anthropology, University College London, and the Head of Department, Mike Rowlands, for hosting me for a year. I appreciate discussions on agency with Matthew Johnson and Koji Mizoguchi. Emma Blake was kind enough to allow me to quote from what was, at time of writing, unpublished work. I am grateful to Jo Sofaer Derevenski for granting me access to her unpublished Ph.D. thesis. Yvonne Beadnell produced the illustrations with her usual skill, for which many thanks are offered. Finally, I appreciated the light but firm hand of the editors, Marcia-Anne Dobres and John E. Robb, in urging me to complete the work and, of course, for inviting me to participate in the first place. Any errors and misunderstandings remain my problem.

Notes

1 Kalicz and Raczky (1987) hint at the discovery of extramural cemeteries near Late Neolithic tells.
2 In the open-area rescue excavations, no longitudinal sections were made to indicate the precise stratigraphic relations of the houses to adjacent burial lines. However, the absolute depths of the upper part of the burials and the top of the house post-holes are consistent with a close temporal relationship.

Bibliography

Arsenault, D. 1991. "The Representation of Women in Moche Iconography," in *The Archaeology of Gender*, ed. D. Walde and N. D. Willows, pp. 313–26. University of Calgary Archaeological Association, Calgary.

Bailey, D. W. 1996. "The Life and Times of House 59, Tell Ovcharovo," in *Neolithic Houses of NW Europe and Beyond*, ed. T. Darvill and J. Thomas, pp. 143–56. Oxbow, Oxford.

Barrett, J. 1988. "Fields of Discourse. Reconstituting a Social Archaeology." *Critique of Anthropology* 7(3): 5–16.

—— 1990. "The Monumentality of Death." *World Archaeology* 22(2): 179–89.

—— 1994. *Fragments from Antiquity. An Archaeology of Social Life in Britain, 2900–1200* BC. Blackwell, Oxford.

Beaudry, M. C., L. J. Cook, and S. A. Mrozowski 1991. "Artifacts and Active Voices: Material Culture as Social Discourse," in *The Archaeology of Inequality*, ed. R. H. McGuire and R. Paynter, pp. 150–91. Blackwell, Oxford.

Beck, L. A. (ed.) 1995. *Regional Approaches to Mortuary Analysis*. Plenum Press, London.

Binford, L. R. 1971. "Mortuary Practices: Their Study and Potential," in *Approaches to the Social Dimensions of Mortuary Practices*, ed. J. A. Brown, pp. 6–29. Society for American Archaeology Memoirs no. 25. SAA, Washington, D.C.

Blake, E. 1999. "Identity Mapping in the Sardinian Bronze Age." *European Journal of Archaeology* 2(1): 35–55.

Bourdieu, P. 1990. "La Domination Masculine." *Actes de la Recherche en Sciences Sociales* 84: 2–31.

Chapman, J. C. 1981. *The Vinča Culture of South East Europe. Studies in Chronology, Economy and Society*, 2 vols. British Archaeological Report I–119, Oxford.

—— 1983. "Meaning and Illusion in the Study of Burial in Balkan Prehistory," in *Ancient Bulgaria* vol. 1, ed. A. Poulter, pp. 1–45. University of Nottingham Press, Nottingham.

—— 1991. "The Creation of Social Arenas in the Neolithic and Copper Age of South East Europe: The Case of Varna," in *Sacred and Profane*, ed. P. Garwood, P. Jennings, R. Skeates and J. Toms, pp. 152–71. Oxford Committee for Archaeology Monograph no. 32. Oxbow, Oxford.

—— 1994. "The Living, the Dead, and the Ancestors: Time, Life Cycles and the Mortuary Domain in Later European Prehistory," in *Ritual and Remembrance. Responses to Death in Human Societies,* ed. J. Davies, pp. 40–85. Sheffield Academic Press, Sheffield.

—— 1995. "Social Power in the Early Farming Communities of Eastern Hungary — Perspectives from the Upper Tisza Region." *A Jósa András Múzeum Évkönyve* 36: 79–99.

—— 1996. "Enchainment, Commodification and Gender in the Balkan Neolithic and Copper Age." *Journal of European Archaeology* 4: 203–42.

—— 1997. "The Origins of Tells in Eastern Hungary," in *Neolithic Landscapes*, ed. P. Topping, pp. 139–64. Oxbow, Oxford.

—— 1999. "Where are the Missing Parts? A Study of Artifact Fragmentation." *Parmátky Archeologické* 90: 5–22.

—— in press. *Fragmentation in Archaeology: People, Places and Broken Objects in the Prehistory of South Eastern Europe.* Routledge, London.

Connell, R. W. 1987. *Gender and Power. Society, the Person and Sexual Politics.* Polity Press, Cambridge UK.

Csalog, J. 1959. "Die Anthropomorphen Gefässe und Idolplastiken von Szegvár–Tüzköves." *Acta Archaeologica Hungarica* 11: 7–38.

Dobres, M.-A. 1995. "Gender and Prehistoric Technology: On the Social Agency of Technical Strategies." *World Archaeology* 27(1): 25–49.

Foucault, M. 1973. *Madness and Civilisation: A History of Insanity in the Age of Reason.* Random House, New York.

—— 1979. *Discipline and Punish: the Birth of the Prison.* Vintage Books, New York.

Goodman, R. B. 1995. "Introduction," in *Pragmatism: A Contemporary Reader*, pp. 1–20. Routledge, London.

Hacking, I. 1995. "Three Parables," in *Pragmatism: A Contemporary Reader*, ed. R. B. Goodman, pp. 237–49. Routledge, London.

Helms, M. W. 1988. *Ulysses' Sail. An Ethnographic Odyssey of Power, Knowledge and Geographical Distance.* Princeton University Press, Princeton.

Hodder, I. 1984. "Burials, Houses, Women and Men in the European Neolithic," in *Ideology, Power and Prehistory*, ed. D. Miller and C. Tilley, pp. 51–68. Cambridge University Press, Cambridge UK.

Johnson, M. 1989. "Conceptions of Agency in Archaeological Interpretation." *Journal of Anthropological Archaeology* 8: 189–211.

Joyce, R. A. 1992. "Images of Gender and Labor Organisation in Classic Maya Society," in *Exploring Gender through Archaeology*, ed. C. Claasen, pp. 63–70. Monographs in World Archaeology no. 11. Prehistory Press, Madison, Wisconsin.

Kalicz, N. and J. Makkay 1977. *Die Linienbandkeramik in der Grossen Ungarischen Tiefebene.* Akadémiai Kiadó, Budapest.

Kalicz, N. and P. Raczky 1987. "The Late Neolithic of the Tisza Region. A Survey of Recent Archaeological Research," in *The Late Neolithic of the Tisza Region*, ed. P. Raczky, pp. 11–30. Szolnok County Museums, Budapest-Szolnok.

Korek, J. 1987. "Szegvár–Tüzköves," in *Alltag und Religion. Jungsteinzeit in Ost-Ungarn*, ed. P. Raczky, pp. 53–70. Szolnok County Museums, Budapest-Szolnok.

—— 1989 *Die Theiss-Kultur in der Mittleren und Nördlichen Theissgegend.* Inventaria Praehistorica Hungariae 3. Magyar Némzeti Múzeum, Budapest.

Küchler, S. 1993. "Landscape as Memory," in *Landscape: Politics and Perspectives*, ed. B. Bender, pp. 85–106. Berg, Oxford.

Ledermann, R. 1990. "Contested Order: Gender and Society in the Southern New Guinea Highlands," in *Beyond the Second Sex: New Directions in the Analysis of Gender*, ed. P. R. Sanday and R. G. Goodenough, pp. 45–73. University of Philadelphia Press, Philadelphia.

Lesick, K. S. 1996. "Re-engendering Gender: Some Theoretical and Methodological Concerns on a Burgeoning Archaeological Pursuit," in *Invisible People and Processes. Writing Gender and Children into European Archaeology*, ed. J. Moore and E. Scott, pp. 31–41. Leicester University Press, Leicester.

Lubar, S. 1993. "Machine Politics: The Political Construction of Technological Facts," in *History from*

Things: Essays on Material Culture, ed. S. Lubar and W. D. Kingery, pp. 197–214. Smithsonian Institution Press, Washington, D.C.

March, K. 1983. "Weaving, Writing and Gender." *Man* 18: 729–44.

Meskell, L. 1996. "The Somatization of Archaeology: Institutions, Discourses, Corporeality." *Norwegian Archaeological Review* 29(1): 1–16.

Miller, D. 1985. *Artefacts as Categories. A study of Ceramic Variability in Central India.* Cambridge University Press, Cambridge UK.

—— 1987 *Material Culture and Mass Consumption.* Blackwell, Oxford.

Mizoguchi, K. 1993. "Time in the Reproduction of Mortuary Practices." *World Archaeology* 25(2): 223–35.

Moore, H. 1993. "The Differences Within and the Differences Between," in *Gendered Anthropology*, ed. T. del Valle, pp. 193–204. Routledge, London.

Munn, N. 1973. *Walbiri Iconography: Graphic Representation and Cultural Symbolism in a Central Australian Society.* Cornell University Press, Ithaca, New York.

—— 1986. *The Fame of Gawa. A Symbolic Study of Value Transformation in a Massim (Papua New Guinea) Society.* Duke University Press, London.

Raczky, P. 1987. "Öcsöd-Kovashalom. A Settlement of the Tisza Culture," in *The Late Neolithic in the Tisza Region*, ed. P. Raczky, pp. 61–83. Szolnok County Museum, Budapest-Szolnok.

Rega, E. 1996. "Age, Gender and Biological Reality in the Early Bronze Age Cemetery at Mokrin," in *Invisible People and Processes. Writing Gender and Children Into European Archaeology*, ed. J. Moore and E. Scott, pp. 229–47. Leicester University Press, Leicester.

Robb, J. E. 1994. "Burial and Social Reproduction in the Peninsular Italian Neolithic." *Journal of Mediterranean Archaeology* 7(1): 27–71.

Rorty, R. 1989. *Contingency, Irony and Solidarity.* Cambridge University Press, Cambridge UK.

Sanday, P. 1990. "Introduction," in *Beyond the Second Sex: New Directions in the Analysis of Gender*, ed. P. R. Sanday and R. G. Goodenough, pp. 1–19. University of Philadelphia Press, Philadelphia.

Saxe, A. A. 1970. *Social Dimensions of Mortuary Practices.* Ph.D. dissertation, Department of Anthropology, University of Michigan, Ann Arbor.

Schlegel, A. 1990. "Gender Meanings: General and Specific," in *Beyond the Second Sex: New Directions in the Analysis of Gender*, ed. P. R. Sanday and R. G. Goodenough, pp. 23–41. University of Philadelphia Press, Philadelphia.

Sofaer Derevenski, J. 1998. *Gender Archaeology as Contextual Archaeology.* Unpublished Ph.D. Dissertation, Department of Archaeology, Cambridge University.

Swidler, A. 1986. "Culture in Action: Symbols and Strategies." *American Sociological Review* 51: 273–86.

Whitehouse, R. 1992. "Tools the Manmaker: the Cultural Construction of Gender in Italian Prehistory." *Journal of the Accordia Research Centre* 3: 41–53.

Winter, M. 1976. "The Archaeological Household Cluster," in *The Early Mesoamerican Village*, ed. K. V. Flannery, pp. 25–31. Academic Press, New York.

13 Constellations of knowledge

Human agency and material affordance in lithic technology

Anthony Sinclair

Introduction

In recent years the conceptual and real link between technology and social action has been coherently drawn. Many authors have already noted that technology is not simply a body of explicitly formulated and objectively described knowledge (Dobres 1995; Dobres and Hoffman 1994; Edmonds 1995; Ingold 1990; Pfaffenberger 1988; Schmidt 1997; Sigaut 1994; Spector 1991, among many others). It is a suite of technical gestures and knowledge that is learned and expressed by individuals in the course of social practices. Technology is one of the social processes by which individuals negotiate and define their identities, in terms of gender, age, belief, class, and so on. Sometimes these actions may be explicitly formulated; more often than not they are habitual and tacit. In its very essence, therefore, technical action parallels social action, and should be understood as social agency.

In what follows I do not wish to make the case again for the need to enmesh technical practice and social action, even though there is possibly greater need for this in Palaeolithic studies than for the archaeology of any other time or place (see also Wobst, this volume). Rather, I shall attempt to show that technological studies provide an ideal medium for prehistoric archaeologists to describe and interpret aspects of real human agency through the material record itself. This avoids some of the apparent problems of the "absent" individual as the locus of explanation in prehistory; that has been raised by some commentators (Johnson 1989, see also Hodder, this volume), and countered by others on the grounds that an agency-centered interpretation does not require physically present agents (Barrett 1989). One reason why technology is so amenable to the analysis of past social agency is that the material record itself supports an identification of action. The specificity of materials used and the techniques employed to create particular tool forms provide a range of factors that bring the agency of individuals to life, exposing their decisions and their reflections. Perhaps nowhere is this more visible than in the analysis of lithic technology where the scars of individual, momentary actions remain visible for later identification and interpretation. Another, rarely mentioned, factor is that the conceptual framework of description and analysis and, to a certain extent, even the vocabulary which technologists have already developed, be they of the French school or the Anglo-Saxon, easily lends itself to translation into the language of agency. Even if the explanations offered by prehistoric technologists have often been framed in terms of practical or adaptive expedience rather than social agency, the knowledge structures that they employ and the relationship between technical strategies and the actions that they facilitate are uncannily similar to the relationship between structure and action that is the central focus of agency theories.

Although it is clear that social agency fleshes out interpretations of technical practice, I shall also argue that agency theorists might themselves learn from studies of technology and of the performance and acquisition of skills. In simple terms, the concept of action may be easy to define, but structure is not. Studies of craft skills, their learning, and performance have begun to define the complexities of knowledge structures that lie behind even the simplest actions. Structure can no longer be left as simply "structure." It must be defined and hence made sense of if it is to be more than a joker in a theoretical card game.

A repertoire of tools and techniques

Since the beginning of research into the European Palaeolithic record, the "Solutrean" has been both recognized and classified as a discrete "cultural" phenomenon (e.g. Avebury 1913; de Mortillet and de Mortillet 1903; Girod 1906; Sollas 1911). Like most prehistoric cultures in the archaeological record, the "Solutrean" was recognized and classified on the basis of a series of specific, distinct and recurring material forms. These include a series of leaf-shaped points – laurel leaf and willow leaf points (types 68 to 70 in the typology of de Sonneville-Bordes and Perrot, 1954) – as well as particular forms of shouldered points (type 71). Since there are other artifact types of leaf-shaped points and shouldered points (for example Jermanovizcian points and Font-Robert points), the definition of Solutrean implements also includes particular attributes of shape and manner of retouch. Specifically, leaf-shaped points are retouched on both dorsal and ventral surfaces in such a manner that the retouch flakes removed during the retouching process thin the implement, leaving negative flake scars across much of the upper and lower surfaces, and result in a lenticular cross section. Shouldered points, however, may vary in their degree of retouch from copious and covering retouch, as might be recorded for the leaf-shaped points, to simple retouch concentrated along the outer edges that determines the plan shape of these points but leaves most of surfaces clear of any secondary retouch scars (Figure 13.1).

[14]Carbon dates from Solutrean sites have shown that "Solutrean" tools were produced during stage 2 of the oxygen isotope curve, corresponding to the peak of the last glacial maximum. Specifically, these dates indicate that these tools were manufactured between approximately 22,000 BP and 16,500 BP in radiocarbon years (which may correspond to the period 24,000 BP and 18,000 BP in calendar years; van Andel 1998). Geographically, Solutrean assemblages have been identified throughout Iberia, all across southern France and northwards to the Loire valley (Figure 13.2). There are, however, gross differences in the presence of classic Solutrean tool types between these different regions. The large bifacially-retouched, leaf-shaped points so often illustrated in studies of the Solutrean are present in France but absent in Spain. In Cantabrian Spain, there are large, shouldered bifacial points and concave-based bifacial points; in Levantine Spain, the bifacial leaf points are small in size, and there are tanged, bifacially-retouched points, often thought to be similar and hence related to the Aterian industries of northern Africa (Figure 13.1).

These are, of course, not the only tool forms made at this time. Solutrean lithic assemblages included other types of stone tool such as varieties of end-scrapers and burins, notches, denticulates, small backed bladelets, and so on. These tool forms are common in lithic assemblages of the Upper Palaeolithic in western Europe and the Near East from approximately 40,000 BP to 11,000 BP. Indeed these other tools, whilst made at the same time (and perhaps by the very same craftspeople) as the more elaborately retouched pieces, could easily be "lost" in most other assemblages from this time range: they are not distinctively "Solutrean" in the same way that the classic pieces are. Furthermore, the material repertoire of the time was not limited to stone. Implements in bone, antler, and ivory have

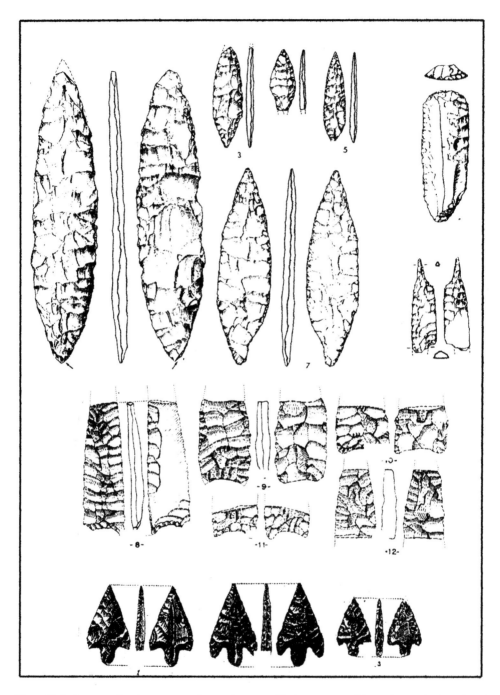

Figure 13.1 A range of tool types manufactured as part of Solutrean assemblages during the last glacial maximum

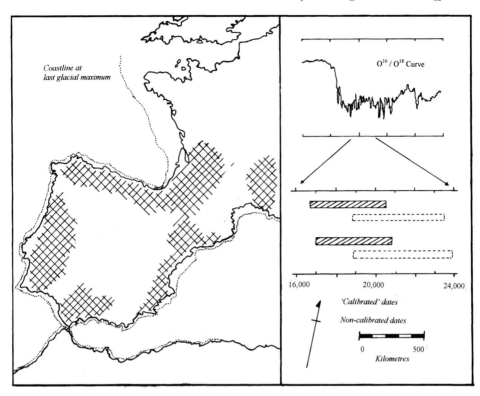

Figure 13.2 The chronological and geographic spread of Solutrean industries in France and Iberia

also survived, including points (both projectile and awl-like forms), eyed and non-eyed needles, spear throwers, soft hammers, and even musical instruments (flute forms). Despite their archaeological absence, it is also unthinkable to suggest that there was not also a broad array of tool forms made from wood, plant fibers, animal skin, and other biodegradable materials. Recent finds from Pavlov I, in the Czech Republic, cast some light on the potential array of plant-fiber based tools that may have existed (Adovasio *et al.* 1996), while well-weighted wooden "javelins" found at the site of Schoningen in Germany (Thieme 1997) attest to the skillful use of wood from at least the Middle Pleistocene (approximately 400,000 years ago).

It is, however, the classic lithic pieces that caught the eye of typologically minded prehistorians so early on, and upon these the temporal and cultural construct known as the "Solutrean" was created. Archaeologists also argued that it was possible to see chronological developments in classic Solutrean pieces. Essentially, the leaf-shaped points were progressively more extensively retouched (from unifacial to bifacial to finer bifacial), whilst the shouldered points were themselves a later development in the "Solutreanization" of the classic implements of their lithic technology. With the help of a database centered on southwestern France, such logic was applied to Solutrean implements discovered in Vasco-Cantabrian Spain and, later, Levantine Spain, although with less success (Straus 1976, 1983). There are also specific regional sub-types of leaf and shouldered point that have been recognized within the French material (Smith 1973), whilst there have always been gross differences in Solutrean tools between France and Iberia.

It is, however, fair to say that these classic Solutrean tool types are identical in the same way that mass-produced implements necessarily are. While the recognized attributes of these artifacts are common to all the pieces, there is however, considerable variability observable in the size and specific shape of individual artifacts as well as in the degree and "quality" of retouching between artifacts which, typologically speaking, are identical. It might be better to describe the making of each piece as an interpretation of the artifact type embodying a particular individual's relationship(s) between the intended form, the raw materials employed, the tools available for use in the manufacturing process, and the manufacturing techniques at that particular maker's disposal. These interpretations can be said to differ at a broader scale both regionally and temporally.

Constellations of knowledge

The anthropologist Tim Ingold (1990) has drawn attention to the fact that our common understanding of the term "technology" refers solely to implements themselves and their standardized modes of use. Technology is equated to the machine. The development of mass manufacture and machinery has resulted in a removal of the personal so that procedures for tool manufacture or use have become standardized and objectified, related to the tools and not their users. The operating knowledge for machines is now separable from the individual skills of craft workers. Machines, and now tools, come with manuals of instructions providing objective information on how they should be handled. Ingold has argued that technology more properly embodies a relationship between tools themselves and the personally acquired techniques for their use. But we may go further than this. The making or the use of artifacts involves not only a variety of particular techniques or processes, and certain implements to be used in these processes, but also particular raw materials and an idea of what the artifact might look like when "finished": its desired end-point.

Together, these component parts form what has been called a constellation of knowledge (Dougherty and Keller 1982; Keller and Keller 1991), a conjunction of the different elements involved in tool use, and in this case artifact manufacture (Figure 13.3). It is properly a constellation of *knowledge* because the materials used, the implements and techniques that might be employed, and the desired end-points of use or manufacture, depend upon the knowledge that an individual has acquired of them. The constellation of knowledge is specific to a particular form of tool use. The knowledge of the techniques that may be employed is appropriate to knowledge of the raw material's properties; the implements used are those known to be effective in the application of particular techniques, and so on. A constellation of knowledge is also reflexive: the specific relationships between the component parts of the constellation may change as the tool user or manufacturer monitors the way action is proceeding in light of the visualized end-point of the process (Wynn 1994: 396ff). This monitoring process does not necessarily or primarily have to do with efficiency or effectiveness as might be inferred from some studies of lithic technology (see Torrence 1989), but may take into account aesthetic, stylistic, procedural, and functional considerations. Over time, common episodes of tool use, or common constellations of knowledge, may lead to a situation in which the apparent reflexivity of the action may disappear as the composition and co-ordination of the components becomes routine and habitual. In this sense, tool use and manufacture and the constellation of knowledge approximate what social theorists have called agency, reflexive and potentially variable, but often habitual and routine action.

To understand the manufacture and use of technology at the last glacial maximum, therefore, we need to reconstruct constellations of knowledge. And for this, we need to

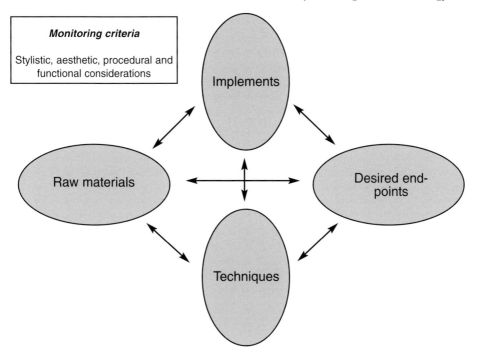

Figure 13.3 The components of a constellation of knowledge

identify the potential range of materials used, the techniques or processes employed, the implements used in manufacture, and the desired end-points of the manufacturing process (Table 13.1). Our understanding of artifact manufacture at this time is, to some extent, clearly hampered by the relative absence of preserved organic materials in the archaeological record, whilst the specific elements identified as materials, techniques, end-points, and implements are limited by the current state of our archaeological knowledge. Thus, while it is possible to argue that many lithic tools would have been fixed in hafts of organic materials, their exact form and the specific techniques of their manufacture are impossible to determine. Experimental work suggests that organic materials were shaped by techniques of cutting, smoothing, scraping, and shaping, using implements such as knife forms, endscrapers, notches, and denticulates. Such work also reveals, for example, that antler is easier to work when softened by soaking in water. Likewise, in this table, our archaeological knowledge means that the end-points of technical procedures overlap with the implements employed in those same procedures. Despite these limitations, it is clear that any constellation may contain a considerable number and diversity of elements, each of which represents some element of acquired knowledge.

From these elements, however, we might begin to frame the elements of specific constellations of knowledge for the technology of the last glacial maximum. The distinction between the classic Solutrean tool forms and other simply made tool forms suggests that we start with framing two constellations of knowledge, one for each group. Given the problems noted above, we might begin by considering the production of the lithic component of these tool forms.

In the simplest of terms, in making tools individual artisans will have first manufactured blanks appropriate in their size, shape and raw material, and then retouched these blanks

Table 13.1 Potential elements for the reconstruction of constellations of knowledge during the last glacial maximum

Materials	Processes	Implements	End-points
flint	flaking	hard hammer	piercer
chert	bifacial flaking	soft hammer	chisel (burin)
quartzite	alternate flaking	pressure flaker	scraper
chalcedony	pressure flaking	piercer	saw (denticulate)
	heat treatment	chisel (burin)	knife
bone	cutting	scraper	points
antler	smoothing	saw (denticulate)	needles
wood	polishing	knife	"crochet hook"
ivory	weaving	points	anvil
plant fibres	binding	needles	pads
skin	knotting	"crochet hook"	
sinew	scraping	anvil	
meat	softening (water)	pads	
resins	hardening (fire)		
feathers	mixing		
down	gluing		
water			

into their final forms. While variation occurred in the choice of blanks, the greatest area of choice was in the retouching of the blank; that is, in the techniques employed and in the extent of retouching. From the perspective of the constellations of knowledge employed, each stone-working technique would have involved a separate constellation, though numerous constellations might be bound together in a single strategy of lithic reduction.

In the production of the non-bifacial forms (Figure 13.4), blank types chosen include flakes of various shapes and sizes and prismatic blades of various lengths, whilst retouching was simple and either direct (from ventral to dorsal surfaces) or indirect (dorsal to ventral). This retouching resembles the simplest form of flaking, in which attention is paid to the angle of the platform and the flaking surface, with repetition of the process leading to a continuous sequence of retouch flaking along an edge. Hard and soft hammers may be used. Retouching is more complex in the manufacture of burins, in which a platform must be created or found on the piece, enabling the positioning of a retouch blow to remove a small matchstick-like sliver of material, leaving an edge comparable to that on a modern chisel, albeit usually smaller. Observation of such tools from assemblages in France (Laugerie-Haute, La Combe Saunière) and Spain (La Riera, Las Caldas, Altamira, Ermittia, Aitzbitarte, Parpallo, Les Mallaetes) indicates that monitoring of the retouching process worked towards an end-point in which the potential working edge (and just the working edge) was finished. A range of raw material types might be used including flints, cherts, chalcedonies, and even quartzites.

In the manufacture of the classic Solutrean tools (Figure 13.5), including bifacial leaf points and shouldered points, the most easily visible differences are in the degree to which the blanks have been retouched and in the techniques employed in the retouching process. Whether the tools take the form of leaf points or concave base points, bifacial retouching removes "excess" material, successively thinning the blank till it is lenticular in cross-section. On many examples, this bifacial thinning leaves negative retouch scars that reveal

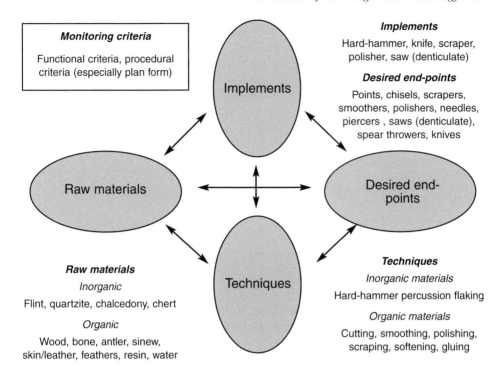

Monitoring criteria

Functional criteria, procedural criteria (especially plan form)

Implements

Implements
Hard-hammer, knife, scraper, polisher, saw (denticulate)

Desired end-points
Points, chisels, scrapers, smoothers, polishers, needles, piercers , saws (denticulate), spear throwers, knives

Raw materials

Desired end-points

Techniques

Raw materials
Inorganic
Flint, quartzite, chalcedony, chert
Organic
Wood, bone, antler, sinew, skin/leather, feathers, resin, water

Techniques
Inorganic materials
Hard-hammer percussion flaking
Organic materials
Cutting, smoothing, polishing, scraping, softening, gluing

Figure 13.4 A possible constellation of knowledge for the manufacture of non-Solutrean lithic tools

that the maker was able to remove excess material across the whole of the upper and lower surfaces. Such retouching requires precise weighting of the retouch blow and careful preparation of the platform in order to achieve the desired end-point. This knowledge only comes with considerable practice (John Lord, personal communication, 1998). We can see from incomplete examples (often a result of accidental breakage) that this retouching was a long, structured process in which the blank was successively thinned all over its surface. To those unfamiliar with stone tool working techniques, this thinning process might be best described as the successive unwrapping of layers from an object. Preparation for each retouch blow becomes progressively more critical, with less allowance for error and possible corrections and a greater chance of accidental breakage.

Examples of bifacial leaf-shaped implements from southwestern French sites such as Jean-Blancs and Pech-de-le-Boissière reveal that the final retouching of the ends of leaf points was often accomplished not solely through percussion but also by means of pressure flaking (Figure 13.6). In this technique, the precision of the aim for the retouch blow is taken care of by direct placement of the pressure flaker on the piece. Attention must, however, still be paid to the preparation of the platform used and to the degree and consistency of pressure applied to remove the retouch flake from the surface. The archaeological examples that we can observe indicate that in the process of monitoring this particular constellation, attention was paid to consistency in the careful spacing of the pressure flake to be removed, resulting in regularly spaced and sized retouch flake scars. The selection of appropriate blanks is also more critical. Some of the finished bifacial pieces may be more than 20 cm in length, requiring the production of considerably larger blanks than those required for other tool forms.

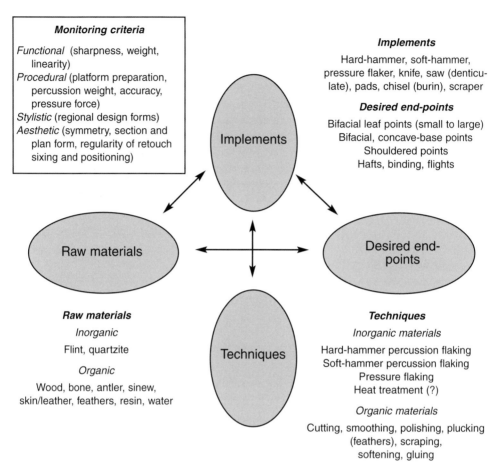

Figure 13.5 A possible constellation of knowledge for the manufacture of Solutrean lithic tools (bifacially-retouched, leaf-shaped points and shouldered points)

There is also clear evidence for the selection of appropriate raw materials. In southwestern France many bifacially retouched pieces are made on locally available black or honey-brown Senonian-age flints, while in Cantabrian Spain, fine grained, silver-grey or black-blue quartzites are often used, as at the site of Las Caldas. The reasoning behind the choice of raw materials most probably had to do with the internal qualities of these particular material types, allowing them to withstand repeated percussion blows without serious breakage. There has even been some discussion as to whether "Solutrean" flintknappers were able directly to manipulate the qualities of their raw materials at this time by means of heat treatment (Bordes 1969). The number of incomplete and broken pieces in assemblages attests to the high incidence of failure to achieve the desired end-point in the manufacture of these bifacial pieces even with the right materials. It is important to note that the bifacially retouched points from Cantabria and other areas of Iberia are smaller than their French contemporaries. They also take the form of concave base points.

In contrast to bifacial points, shouldered points from both France and Cantabrian Spain show greater variability in the nature of the blanks chosen, the retouching techniques employed (percussion and pressure flaking), and in the degree of retouch as well. According

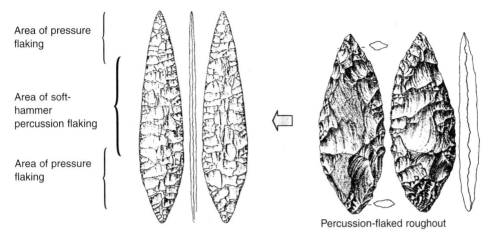

Area of pressure flaking

Area of soft-hammer percussion flaking

Area of pressure flaking

Percussion-flaked roughout

Figure 13.6 The use of percussion and pressure flaking in the production of bifacially-retouched leaf-shaped points

to some analysts (Geneste and Plisson 1990; Plisson and Geneste 1989), this variation falls into three groups, revealing a close relationship between the type of blank used and the degree of retouching employed, at least in French assemblages. The first group includes pieces where the lateral shape of the point is created by percussion flaking, direct and/or indirect, leaving the original negative flake scars from the blank still largely visible; for this the blank used was a predominantly parallel-sided blade flat in cross-section. The second group includes pieces unifacially retouched on the dorsal surface with minor retouch at the proximal and distal ends on the ventral side; and blanks with less parallel sides and more curvature in cross-section were used. The third group includes pieces that are fully bifacially-retouched, made on blanks still more irregular in plan and curved in cross-section. In short, when the blank was more irregular and its curvature greater, more retouching was employed to achieve the desired end-point: a shouldered-point shape in plan form, and a piece flat in cross-section (Figure 13.7).

Saliency of knowledge in the "Solutrean" repertoire

Still to be explained is the preferential use of particular techniques for certain tool forms. In terms of agency, what would have been the value of these techniques for the expression of personal identities at the last glacial maximum? A clear argument can be made for the link between particular techniques of tool manufacture and the (re)creation of particularly valued characteristics of individual identity at the last glacial maximum. We might refer to this as the presence of salient links between different constellations of knowledge.

Saliency between different actions has been noted previously in technology studies in general (Schmidt 1997), and in hunter-gatherer craft activity in particular. Graburn (1976) has shown how Inuit men, when carving soapstone, attempt to embody boldness, perseverance, and exactitude in their carvings. They express boldness by their choice of a complicated design; exactitude in the details of the design they carve; and perseverance through the difficulties of carving the hard soapstone itself. Graburn argues that these are the qualities considered most important for a successful Inuit hunter. In the process of carving soapstone, therefore, Inuit hunters are both expressing and recreating their own personal identities as hunters of renown, and reinforcing these qualities as those of value to hunters. Rosaldo (1986) provides a similar example

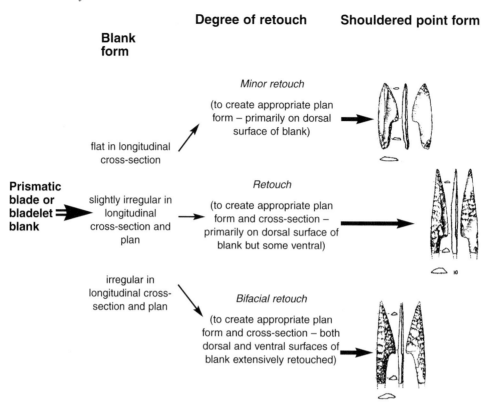

Blank form

Degree of retouch

Shouldered point form

Minor retouch

(to create appropriate plan form – primarily on dorsal surface of blank)

flat in longitudinal cross-section

Prismatic blade or bladelet blank

slightly irregular in longitudinal cross-section and plan

Retouch

(to create appropriate plan form and cross-section – primarily on dorsal surface of blank but some ventral)

irregular in longitudinal cross-section and plan

Bifacial retouch

(to create appropriate plan form and cross-section – both dorsal and ventral surfaces of blank extensively retouched)

Figure 13.7 Technological choices and their relationship to blank form in the manufacture of Solutrean shouldered points

when describing how the manner of Ilongot story-telling about hunting exploits emphasizes exactly those same qualities considered to be important in the hunt itself. A well-told Ilongot hunting story, like a successful Ilongot hunt, reveals the adaptability and quick-witted nature of the hunter (or storyteller) when faced with difficult situations. In both these cases there is clear correspondence and salience between skilled activities of seemingly quite different sorts.

When comparing the classic "Solutrean" lithic tools with their contemporaries, it is clear that Solutrean tools are not simply more retouched. They are an altogether more complex creation, requiring a better knowledge of retouch techniques and raw material qualities, together with the ability to co-ordinate a variety of techniques and to monitor a number of changing variables, including plan form, section profile, shape symmetry, consistency, and regularity of spacing. Following the lead of Graburn and Rosaldo, and using knowledge derived from replicating the manufacture of Solutrean tools, we might suggest that other salient qualities included perseverance, boldness, and adaptability. Perseverance can be inferred from the time that it takes to manufacture the bifacial leaf points: anything up to eleven hours for the largest leaf points, three or four hours for pieces above 20 cm in length (Jacques Pelegrin, personal communication, 1990), and up to thirty minutes for the retouching of the more elaborate shouldered points. This is in comparison with just five minutes to make the simplest laterally retouched pieces. Boldness can be seen in the making of these larger more retouched pieces that are liable to greater accidental failure in manufacture. Adaptability appears in dealing with the unforeseen problems that may result from errors in manufacture. In making Solutrean pieces, perseverance, boldness and adaptability go inseparably hand in hand. Similar arguments have been made for the expression of boldness in the painting of Greek archaic period ceramics (Shanks 1993).

Following Graburn and Rosaldo once more, it is tempting to suggest that the qualities expressed in the making of "Solutrean" tools are those qualities that were salient to the identities of Solutrean hunters. There can be little doubt that during the last glacial maximum meat contributed the major portion of the diet and derived from the hunting of reindeer and other large herbivores, such as horse, red deer, and mountain goats (Boyle 1990; Delpech 1983; Straus 1983). Reindeer are easier to hunt as they migrate (Burch 1972), and this is further evidenced by the positioning of major sites by river fords (White 1985) and the overwhelming abundance of reindeer in certain faunal collections at sites such as Les Combarelles (Boyle 1990; Delpech 1983). Such hunting required great knowledge, careful planning and preparation. Likewise, the encounter hunting of non-herd animals, such as the mountain goats, required planning, boldness in the pursuit of individual animals, adaptability when the animal did not behave as expected and perseverance to try again when unsuccessful. Many other potentially salient skills might be mentioned as well as these few.

The simple equation of skills between lithic technology and hunting does not account for all the contexts of evidence at a technological and regional level. It also presupposes a separation between hunting and other non-hunting activities, as appears to be the case among most modern hunting and gathering societies, where the hunting of large animals is strictly the activity of adult men. In southwestern France, however, salient skills involved in the production of bifacially retouched tools do not just strike a metaphorical relationship with the salient skills of hunters. There is also a direct metonymic relationship drawn, through the very same use of bifacial retouch, in the making of tools that were used throughout the process of acquisition, preparation, and distribution of animal parts, as well as other currently indecipherable activities. Shouldered points and many bifacial implements were indeed projectiles – they reveal the fracture patterns typical of experimentally used projectile points (see Bradley 1982 for a concrete study) – but the larger, elaborate bifacial implements are much more likely to have been butchery knives. The completeness of the largest and most elaborate pieces, such as those found at the site of Volgu, suggests that these implements may perhaps never have been intended for "practical" use. Therefore, in looking for salient knowledge and skills we must also look beyond hunting to the complexities of butchery (the preparation of different cuts and perhaps their symmetries, left to right), not to mention food preparation and consumption. In modern hunter-gatherer societies, debt relations (and hence social relations) are created in the dismembering and sharing of cuts of meat, and the "ownership" and distribution of a kill is a very important procedure for the creation of social identities (Dowling 1965). In the Solutrean of southwestern France, socially meaningful technical action extends from procurement, through distribution, to consumption, as is the case for many societies (see Goody 1982). By way of a contrast, in Cantabrian Spain bifacially retouched tools are all essentially hunting implements. An approach that focuses on the saliency of agents as hunters, and the process of production over consumption, makes sense of the evidence more effectively (Figure 13.8).

Agency and affordance in technology

In numerous Palaeolithic studies, emphasis is given to the limitations imposed upon technical behavior by the raw materials – their quality and availability. An advantage of considering technical action as agency is that from the case above we can see that raw materials

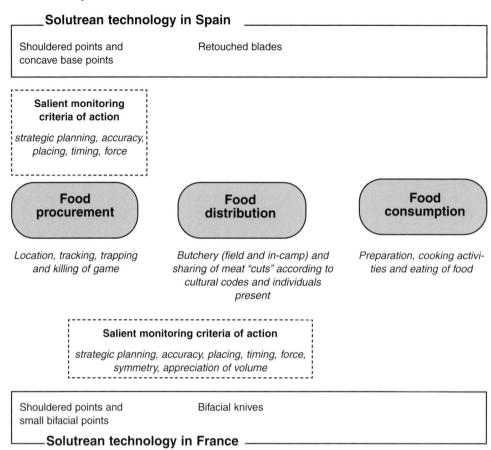

Shouldered points and concave base points | Retouched blades

Solutrean technology in Spain

Salient monitoring criteria of action

strategic planning, accuracy, placing, timing, force

Food procurement

Location, tracking, trapping and killing of game

Food distribution

Butchery (field and in-camp) and sharing of meat "cuts" according to cultural codes and individuals present

Food consumption

Preparation, cooking activities and eating of food

Salient monitoring criteria of action

strategic planning, accuracy, placing, timing, force, symmetry, appreciation of volume

Shouldered points and small bifacial points | Bifacial knives

Solutrean technology in France

Figure 13.8 Aspects of saliency between tool manufacture, food procurement and consumption during the last glacial maximum in France and Spain

do not simply constrain choice. As in the use of soapstone by Inuit sculptors, raw materials offer opportunities that may be exploited for expression, when considered within the framework of a constellation of knowledge. To use another terminology, the perception of raw material qualities affords opportunities for the use of particular techniques and expressions of skills and knowledge salient in the creation and maintenance of individual identities.

The concept of affordance derives from ecological approaches to perception (Gibson 1969; Kugler *et al.* 1982; other references cited in Colley 1989; Colley and Beech 1988). This approach proposes that certain actions are not mediated by high-level, cognitive processes, but are the outcome of direct perceptual clues afforded by the environment. While this may indeed account for certain actions, such as the pulling in of the wings of a bird diving for prey or into water, most cognitive psychologists now favor a hybrid approach that combines both higher level cognitive "plans" as well as low level perceptual clues derived from the physical nature of the environment (Colley and Beech 1988: 3).

In the case of the manufacture of Solutrean tools, we can suggest that within the context of specific constellations of knowledge, the presence of Senonian-age flints in France or fine-grained quartzites in Cantabrian Spain offered perceptual clues that afforded the expression of these salient skills. We might also suggest that the relationship between blank form and degree of retouch in the manufacture of Solutrean shouldered points is also a relationship of affordance in the production of tool forms whose functional requirements of plan and cross-section form and weight were more exacting. The irregularities of blank form afforded opportunities for knappers to express salient knowledge through the employment of percussion or pressure flaking techniques.

And back to agency

Despite the age and apparent paucity of evidence from Palaeolithic times, the study of lithic technology is enriched beyond measure by a concern for the agency of its makers. What is perhaps surprising, however, is that it has taken so long for lithic technologists to consider agency, since both the material for study and the methods already developed for describing lithic manufacture lend themselves to agency approaches. Actions, even if not by discernible discrete individuals, are readily identifiable from the physical evidence itself. Moreover, habitual but learned actions are a key element in the identification of the strategy of manufacture, whether of the Levallois technique, prismatic blade production, or pressure flaking. The existence of pre-existing structure, interpreted through action, lies at the heart of traditional approaches to lithic technology and also modern replication experiments, even among those who see lithic technology as essentially practical rather than social (e.g. Bradley 1975). More anthropologically informed technologists, such as Leroi-Gourhan (1965), have always seen techniques as essentially social in the sense coined by Mauss (1979; see Schlanger 1990 for discussion). Of equal importance, and perhaps worthy of further study, are the similarities between the structures of knowledge and memory posited by different approaches to understanding technical action and those proposed by leading agency theorists, such as Giddens (1984). The process of learning and practice moves technical knowledge from a discursive domain back to an habitual or practical domain, itself underlain by more basic psychological or technical knowledge (Figure 13.9). These similarities make the "translation" from technical action to agency almost seamless. Technologists, therefore, have nothing to fear in agency theory. Indeed, like the bourgeois gentleman in Molière's

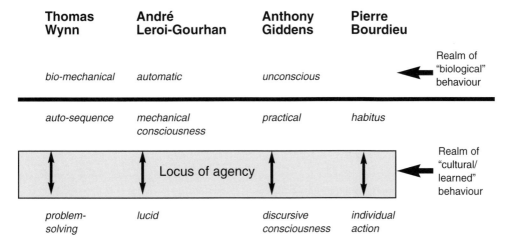

Figure 13.9 Agency and technology: some similarities in the structure of language and thought between Bourdieu, Giddens, Leroi-Gourhan and Wynn

play who discovers the true meaning of prose, technologists might find that for more than forty years they have been speaking of agency without knowing it.

There is, however, a sense in which the study of agency might learn from studies of skilled behavior. Commentators have noted that the agency approaches of Bourdieu (1977) and especially Giddens' notion of structuration (1984: 16–28) provide better understandings of action than of other elements of agency such as structure and individuality. In the work of Giddens, for example, the term "structure" must account not just for the mechanism by which the actions performed by individuals are "determined," but also for much higher levels of behavioral regularity such as the "structure" of the capitalist system (see Craib 1992). It is very hard to imagine the form that such a structure might take (but see Pauketat, this volume, for a possible exception). Indeed, Craib (ibid.) has gone so far as to suggest that the agency theory of Giddens is really a theory of action in disguise and cannot account for the broader sense of structure that Giddens assumes it can.

The work of cognitive psychologists, however, has revealed the depth of structure as learned knowledge called into play in even the simplest examples of skilled behavior. Stringed sequences of skilled action (see Dougherty and Keller 1982 for an example), constellations of knowledge, saliency, affordance, hierarchical knowledge structures, and salient classifications, all point to the complexities of structure and the specificity of the way in which structure interacts with action and especially memory. Agency theorists might benefit from taking a look at some more of the apparently basic skills of life, such as technical action, when they start to flesh out their conception of structure and their understandings of the nature of individuality and personal identity.

Acknowledgments

I would like to thank John Lord and Jacques Pelegrin for conveying to me some of the complexities of their constellations of knowledge in the manufacture of Solutrean bifacial points. I would also like to thank Chris Duke for bringing to my attention some of the literature on the cognitive psychology of skilled action. Finally I would like to thank Marcia-Anne Dobres and John E. Robb and other reviewers for their cogent criticism of the first draft of this chapter.

Bibliography

Adovasio, J. M., O. Soffer, and B. Klima 1996. "Upper Palaeolithic Fibre Technology from Pavlov I, Czech Republic, c. 26,000 years ago." *Antiquity* 70: 526–34.
Avebury, Lord 1913. *Prehistoric Times Illustrated by Ancient Remains and the Manners and Customs of Modern Savages.* 7th edn. Williams and Norgate, London.
Barrett, J. C. 1988. "Field of Discourse: Reconstructing a Social Archaeology." *Contextual Archaeology* 7: 5–16.
Bordes, F. 1969. "Traitement Thermique du Silex au Solutréen." *Bulletin de la Societé Préhistorique Française* 66: 197.
Bourdieu, P. 1977. *Outline of a Theory of Practice*, trans. R. Nice. Cambridge University Press, Cambridge UK.
Boyle, K. V. 1990. *Upper Palaeolithic Faunas of South-West France: A Zoogeographic Perspective.* British Archaeological Reports, International Series no. 557, Oxford.
Bradley, B. A. 1975. "Lithic Reduction Sequences: A Glossary and Discussion," in *Lithic Technology: Making and Using Stone Tools*, ed. E. Swanson, pp. 5–14. Houghton Mifflin, The Hague.
—— 1982. "Lithic Technology," in *The Agate Basin Site. A Record of the Palaeoindian Occupation of the North-Western High Plains*, ed. G. C. Frison and D. J. Stanford, pp. 175–96. Academic Press, New York.

Burch, E. S. 1972. "The Caribou/Wild Reindeer as a Human Resource." *American Antiquity* 37: 339–68.

Colley, A. M. 1989. "Learning Motor Skills: Integrating Cognition and Action," in *Acquisition and Performance of Cognitive Skills*, ed. A. M. Colley and J. R. Beech, pp. 173–89. Wiley, Chichester.

Colley, A. M., and J. R. Beech 1988. "Grounds for Reconciliation: Some Preliminary Thoughts on Cognition and Action," in *Cognition and Action in Skilled Behaviour*, pp. 1–11. Elsevier Science, North–Holland.

Craib, I. 1992. *Anthony Giddens*. Routledge, London.

Delpech, F. 1983. *Les Faunes du Paléolithique Supérieur dans le Sud-Ouest de la France*. Cahiers du Quaternaire no.6. Centre National de Recherche Scientifique, Paris.

de Mortillet, G., and G de Mortillet 1903. *Musée Préhistorique*. Schleicher Frères, Paris

de Sonneville-Bordes, D., and J. Perrot 1954. "Lexique Typologique du Paléolithique Supérieur. Outilage Lithique. I) Grattoirs. II) Outils Solutréens." *Bulletin de la Société Préhistorique Française* 51: 327–35.

Dobres, M.-A. 1995. "Gender and Prehistoric Technology: On the Social Agency of Prehistoric Technologies." *World Archaeology* 27(1): 25–49.

Dobres, M.-A., and C. R. Hoffman 1994. "Social Agency and the Dynamics of Prehistoric Technology." *Journal of Archaeological Method and Theory* 1(3): 211–58.

Dougherty, J., and C. M. Keller 1982. "Taskonomy: A Practical Approach to Knowledge Structures." *American Ethnologist* 5: 763–74.

Dowling, J. 1965. "Individual Ownership and the Sharing of Game in Hunting Societies." *American Anthropologist* 70: 502–7.

Edmonds, M. 1995. *Stone Tools and Society*. Batsford, London.

Geneste, J.-M., and H. Plisson 1990. "Technologie Fonctionelle des Points à Cran Solutréens: l'Apport des Nouvelles Données de la Grotte de La Combe Saunière," in *Feuilles de Pierre*, ed. J. Kozlowski, pp. 293–320. Etudes et Récherches Archéologiques de l'Université de Liège no. 42, Liège.

Gibson, J. J. 1969. *The Ecological Approach to Visual Perception*. Houghton Mifflin, Boston.

Giddens, A. 1984. *The Constitution of Society*. Polity Press, Cambridge UK.

Girod, A. 1906. *Les Stations de l'Age du Renne dans les Vallées de la Corrèze*. Bailliare, Paris.

Goody, J. 1982. *Cooking, Cuisine and Class*. Cambridge University Press, Cambridge UK.

Graburn, N. 1976. "Eskimo Art," in *Ethnic and Tourist Arts*, ed. N. Graburn, pp. 7–35. University of California Press, Berkeley.

Ingold, T. 1990. "Society, Nature and the Concept of Technology." *Archaeological Review from Cambridge* 9: 5–17.

Johnson, M. 1989. "Conceptions of Agency in Archaeological Interpretation." *Journal of Anthropological Archaeology* 8: 189–211.

Keller, J. D., and C. M. Keller 1991. *Thinking and Acting with Iron*. Beckman Institute Cognitive Science Technical Reports, University of Illinois, Urbana.

Kugler, P. N., J. A. S. Kelso, and M. T. Turvey 1982. "On the Control of Naturally Developing Systems," in *The Development of Movement and Control*, ed. J. A. S. Kelso and J. E. Clark, pp. 27–56. Wiley, New York.

Leroi-Gourhan, A. 1965. *Le Geste et La Parole II. La Mémoire et ses Rythmes*. Albin Michel, Paris.

Mauss, M. 1979 [orig. 1935]. "Body Techniques," in *Sociology and Psychology: Essays of Marcel Mauss*, trans. B. Brewster, pp. 97–123. Routledge and Kegan Paul, London.

Pfaffenberger, B. 1988. "Fetishised Objects and Humanised Nature: Towards an Anthropology of Technology." *Man* 23: 236–52.

Plisson, H. and J.-M. Geneste 1989. "Analyse Technologique des Pointes à Cran Solutréens du Placard (Charente), du Fourneau du Diable, du Pech de la Boissière et de Combe Saunière (Dordogne)." *Paléo* 1: 65–106.

Rosaldo, R. 1986. "Ilongot Hunting as Story and Experience," in *The Anthropology of Experience*, ed. V. Turner and E. Bruner, pp. 137–65. University of Illinois Press, Urbana.

Schlanger, N. 1990. "Techniques as Human Action: Two Perspectives." *Archaeological Review from Cambridge* 9(1): 18–26.

Schmidt, P. 1997. *Iron Technology in East Africa*. Indiana University Press, Bloomington, Indianapolis.

Shanks, M. 1993. "Style and Design of a Perfume Jar from an Archaic Greek City State." *Journal of European Archaeology* 1: 77–106.

Sigaut, F. 1994. "Technology," in *Companion Encyclopaedia of Anthropology: Humanity, Culture and Social Life*, ed. T. Ingold, pp. 420–59. Routledge, London.

Smith, P. E. L. 1966. *Le Solutréen en France*. Mémoires de l'Institut de Préhistoire de l'Université de Bordeaux no.5. Delmas, Bordeaux.

—— 1973. "Some Thoughts on Variations Among Certain Solutrean Artefacts," in *Estudios Dedicados al Prof. Dr Luis Pericot*, ed. E. Ripoll, pp. 67–75. Disputacion Provincial, Barcelona.

Sollas, W. J. 1911. *Ancient Hunters and their Modern Representatives*. Macmillan, London.

Spector, J. D. 1991. "What this Awl Means: Towards a Feminist Archaeology," in *Engendering Archaeology: Women and Prehistory*, ed. J. M. Gero and M. W. Conkey, pp. 388–406. Blackwell, Oxford.

Straus, L. G. 1976. "A New Interpretation of the Cantabrian Solutrean." *Current Anthropology* 17: 342–3.

—— 1983. *El Solutrense Vasco-Cantabrico: Una Nueva Perspectiva*. Centro de Investigacíon y Museo de Altamiral Monografia no. 10., Madrid.

Thieme, H. 1997. "Lower Palaeolithic Hunting Spears from Germany." *Nature* 385: 807–10.

Torrence, R. 1989. "Re-Tooling: Towards a Behavioural Theory of Stone Tools," in *Time, Energy and Stone Tools*, pp. 57–66. Cambridge University Press, Cambridge UK.

van Andel, T. J. 1998. "Middle and Upper Palaeolithic Environments and ^{14}C Dates Beyond 10,000 B.P." *Antiquity* 72: 26–33.

White, R. 1985. *Upper Palaeolithic Land Use in the Perigord: A Topographic Approach to Subsistence and Settlement*. British Archaeological Reports, International Series no. 253, Oxford.

Wynn, T. 1994. "Three Levels of Thinking in Technology," in *Tools, Language and Communication*, ed. T. Ingold and K. Gibson, pp. 393–402. Cambridge University Press, Cambridge UK.

14 Self-made men and the staging of agency

Matthew Johnson

This chapter argues for the central importance of agency to archaeological interpretation. It underscores an important but neglected point in recent studies: that agency itself only exists in a dialectical relationship to structure. In other words, different social structures produce, and are reproduced or transformed by, different forms of agency. Forms of agency, then, must be seen as historically particular, specific and changing: what constitutes "agency" will vary from society to society, and from historical context to context.

To clarify this point: we cannot talk about the individual social agent without at the same time talking about the cultural background from which that agent came and against which that agent operates. Pots are made by people, but the people are created by society, and re-create society in their turn. The *way* people make pots and the way the form and decoration of those pots express their knowledge of the world about them and their interests will vary as much as the form and decoration of the pots themselves. Cross-cultural models of agency (such as that implied by much of my own earlier work, cf. Johnson 1989) are therefore problematic.

I first elaborate on the theoretical underpinnings of this argument, then explore it empirically by looking at an historical period that is generally supposed to be a critical moment in the definition of the self and the individual: the Renaissance.

Theories of agency

Agency is without doubt one of the central concepts in modern archaeological interpretation and in social theory generally. I came to appreciate the importance of agency in the human sciences as a whole through reading the sociologist Erving Goffman (1959, 1971), but concrete, empirically rich discussions of humans making their own history that I encountered in the work of British Marxist historians, particularly Christopher Hill (1964) and E.P. Thompson (1963), were especially influential. More recently, I have found the work of Henrietta Moore (1985) and anti-essentialist feminist texts such as Lois McNay (1992; see also Gero, this volume) to be central. All these works, in different ways, stress how understanding patterns of historical change depend on understanding the identities of social agents; and how those identities were themselves changing, either were historically transient and shifting (Hill 1964; Thompson 1963) or could not be said to have a concrete, essential basis outside history (McNay 1992).

I am suspicious of cross-cultural interpretations of agency as a rational process (or indeed cross-cultural views of human consciousness and volition as fundamentally "irrational," as in the thought of Freud and Jung where agents are driven by forces beyond their conscious control), as they tend to rely on a lurking essentialism in which all human beings are seen as possessing the same fundamental traits. Many of the other chapters in this volume argue for such a position, but I feel its underlying assumptions have been undermined by anti-essentialist arguments that by now should be very familiar to a theoretically informed audience (McNay 1992: 11–48). A very common criticism of the Giddens/Bourdieu view of agency, and in particular its application to archaeological interpretation, runs as follows: the main aim of Giddens and Bourdieu is to put together a theoretical apparatus that helps us to describe and understand the study of contemporary societies. Their social theories may therefore be useful and even of central importance in the practice of modern sociology, but cannot be applied in an *a priori* fashion to past societies regardless of area or period. If they are, they run the risk of being criticized as essentially cross-cultural in nature. Such a criticism runs in parallel to Joan Gero's point (this volume) that agency is not a concept that can be applied regardless of gender; most existing models of agency center on what men, rather than women, "have." In other words, forms of agency are not just particular to a historic period; they are particular to gender also. If there cannot be models of agency outside social structure, there also cannot be gender-neutral models of agency.

The theoretical relationship between the individual, the social collective, and agency will vary according to context. Consequently, it follows that different methods will be appropriate for identifying agencies and developing convincing interpretations in different contexts. I suggest in this chapter an *historicity of agency*: that is, we will find it difficult to develop models of agency that are cross-cultural, but we can develop models of agency for particular historical epochs or periods (as I suggest for late medieval and Renaissance England below).

This does not mean that we are doomed to an endless historical particularism, in which nothing general can ever be said about agency or indeed about any other feature of human behavior. It does, however, mean that such general statements need to be prefaced with a careful construction of the specific context.

In practice, agency, like archaeology as a whole, remains massively undertheorized. Archaeologists, particularly traditional or "atheoretical" scholars working in historic periods, link the individual social agent with the larger scale rhetorically, through narrative and the conscious or unconscious use of anecdote. Thus for Hugh Tait (1997), a brief description of the career and works of one late sixteenth-century art critic, Richard Haydocke, "represents the fundamental change that had taken place in English cultural life [between 1400 and 1600]." Tait, as is typical in discussions of this genre, gives no evidence to suggest one way or another if this biography is "typical" or how we might situate Haydocke within changing social structures (ibid.: 6–7). As such, Lewis Binford (1983: 31) is quite accurate in his protest that much of this type of archaeology simply ends up telling stories with little way to judge the relative accuracy of competing narratives.

One way we might move beyond just telling stories is to theorize agency more adequately, take it more seriously. Broadly, I suggest that if we are to avoid agency becoming no more than a "new buzzword," we must avoid "recipe-book" approaches to agency (or any other aspect of archaeological interpretation for that matter) in which we apply a single pre-determined set of methods regardless of area or period. I mean by a "recipe-book" approach the way in which a new theoretical concept, after a period of initial enthusiastic proselytizing within the archaeological community, is applied blindly to any set of data from any period or area in an identical manner regardless of context; the interpretations such a concept produces then often come to look naive and insensitive to the nuances and particularities of the evidence. Of course we all use general concepts and guidelines, but these should be a source of inspiration, never a substitute for thinking self-critically and imaginatively about the archaeological material we are working with.

Creating the subject

How do we construct a more subtle approach than that of a recipe-book? One first step might be to avoid "airless theory" for the time being, and to examine the very period when, according to some accounts, there was a very fundamental transformation in the way women and men thought about themselves and their own agency: the Renaissance.

That the Renaissance involved a new sense of the individual and the self is not a new point; the notion that a new spirit of "the individual" was the *zeitgeist* of the Renaissance goes back to Burckhardt's nineteenth-century studies of Italian Renaissance art and architecture, if not beyond. What has been new in Renaissance scholarship of the last two decades, and what offers new opportunities for a theoretically informed archaeology of the Renaissance, is a stress on three areas.

The first is the need for interdisciplinary work: in particular the literary and artistic achievements of Renaissance "high culture" must be put in their social and historical context. Conversely, the material culture with which Renaissance elites chose to surround themselves has to be understood in more complex ways than by regarding them simply as artifacts of "conspicuous consumption." The studies of literature, of cultural history, and of material culture have therefore converged in their themes and preoccupations (for typical studies see Bermingham and Brewer 1995; Hunt 1989; Jardine 1995).

Second is an awareness that the new values of the Renaissance were gendered at a very basic level, that the "humanism" that Burckhardt posited at the very center of Renaissance values was inevitably an androcentric construction. Therefore, it is increasingly acknowledged that if we want to understand the changing sense of the individual and of the self at the Renaissance, we need to see this changing understanding of the self as existing in a problematic, even difficult and anxious, relationship to the patriarchal values and structures of the period. Mark Breitenberg (1996: 7) writes:

> Older accounts of the emergence of a distinctly modern identity in the Renaissance have been decidedly masculine without saying so, as if to ask questions about identity were by definition to ask them about men. It is not surprising to find such an assumption in Jacob Burckhardt's celebration of the "perfecting of the individual" in Renaissance Italy, nor in Tillyard's pronouncement that in Elizabethan England "Not only did Man, as man, live with uncommon intensity at that time, but he was never removed from his cosmic setting."
>
> (Breitenberg 1996: 7)

Of course, this new sense of the individual was not only gendered, it was also constructed with reference to new structures of capitalism, nation state, and colonial Other. Renaissance studies have therefore become transformed from a rather dull humanistic backwater into a key battleground of current theoretical trends, including New Historicism, literary Cultural Materialism, postcolonial studies, feminism, and queer theory (see for example studies in Dollimore and Sinfield 1991; Goldberg 1994; Jardine 1983, 1996).

The third point is that, however constructed, the new sense of the individual was created and transformed *actively*, in particular through changing notions of the body. How can we see this active creation? Many studies have concentrated on language and literature; in the field of literature, these include studies of "Renaissance self-fashioning," most obviously in the work of Stephen Greenblatt (1980). However, an increasing number of studies have focused on the presentation of the self through material culture: dress, architecture, art.

Most of these studies have been concerned with "polite" or elite culture though there is an increasing emphasis on how everyday objects were consumed by non-elite groups, and how such actions changed identities at a more vernacular level (cf. Williams 1990). Indeed, James Deetz's (1977) famous model of the "Georgian Order" as originally formulated can be seen as an exploration of how what Deetz implicitly sees as a system of thought born in Renaissance Italy was eventually diffused to the ordinary folk of the Chesapeake and New England.

It should be stressed that the majority of archaeological scholarship in this area remains largely traditional and atheoretical in scope (see Gaimster and Stamper 1997 for a representative cross-section of current activity). As a result, most of the theoretically innovative work on architecture, landscape, and material culture discussed above has, paradoxically, been carried out not by archaeologists but rather within the spheres of literature and cultural history.

The case study below will look at two buildings from fifteenth- and sixteenth-century England and see how each is implicated in particular social and cultural structures, particular contexts, particular agencies. In many ways, these monuments and their builders are very similar. Both are medieval castles that had existed for centuries before the period of study; both were altered by elite men whose social position was at or near the apex of the social structure. These two men shared similar interests and outlooks in many ways (they were involved in the mechanics of estate management; they schemed to set up and extend dynastic and marriage interests; they were peripatetic in their lifestyle, spending the year moving from great house to great house). As such, they were implicated in the construction and reconstruction of elite masculinities; both would see themselves in terms of being at the top of a stratified, patriarchal social ladder. Both men however can be seen in many ways as being insecure (both in terms of their position as individuals locked into the chance fortunes of a structure dependent on competition and factional conflict and at another level: in terms of overt and implicit anxiety about the possibility of collapse of the patriarchal social structure (cf. Breitenberg 1996)).

Lord Cromwell rebuilds a medieval castle

Tattershall Castle stands on the edge of the Lincolnshire Fens, on the eastern side of Midland England (Figures 14.1 and 14.2). Today, the most striking surviving piece of its fabric is the monstrous brick tower, that rises from this flat land as a visible marker of the wealth, power, and agency of its fifteenth-century builder and owner, Ralph, Lord Cromwell.

Cromwell (a very distant relation of the two more infamous Cromwells) was a "new" or "self-made man," from a minor Lincolnshire family, who rose to be one of the most wealthy and powerful men in England. He was born in 1393 and, as was not unusual, spent his youth in the service of the duke of Clarence and of Henry V in the wars with France. According to traditional historical accounts, he owed his rapid rise to administrative ability and to marriage. From 1433 he was Treasurer of England but resigned in 1443, probably as a result of factional politics. Cromwell's income was substantially increased by the financial opportunities that came with the post of Treasurer and by his 1423 marriage to the heiress Margaret Deincourt. This marriage brought him properties worth over £500 a year, a sizeable sum at that time.

Cromwell qualifies explicitly as a knowledgeable social agent in Giddens' (1979) terms. In 1433 he was responsible for writing a statement on the condition of the English economy

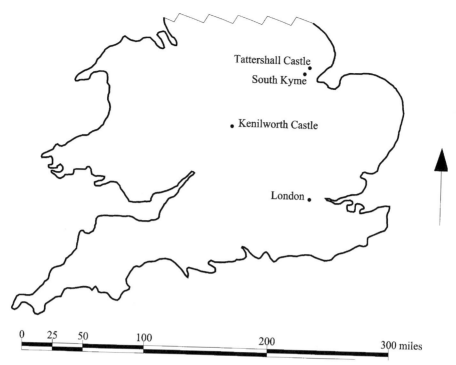

Figure 14.1 Location map of places mentioned in the text (Kenilworth, South Kyme, Tattershall)

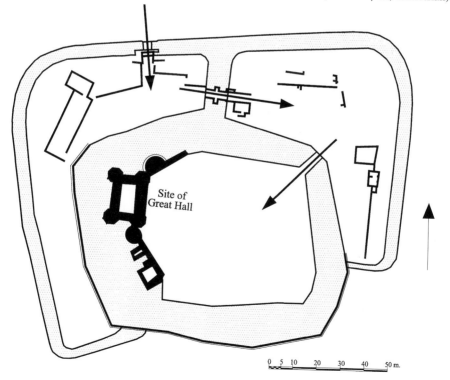

Figure 14.2 Plan of Tattershall

that in the view of twentieth-century historians was reasonably balanced, forthright, and carefully prepared. His strategies included creating political alliances and consolidating estates through his own marriage and those of his relations; he made marriages for his niece and heir with members of the Yorkist faction at court. Cromwell was involved in constant legal battles, for example over the ownership of manors, but also over the symbolic culture and etiquette of social precedence. As one would expect of an elite male of the fifteenth century, "he was extremely touchy on matters affecting his honour . . . pointing out that as he had always followed the correct procedures, he must necessarily be in the right" (Emery 1985: 218–2), an attitude that was thoroughly in tune with a late medieval mentality of the importance of form and precedent to concepts of masculine honor. Goods worth over £16,000 were stolen from his estate after his death (ibid.; see Rosenthal 1996: 44–53 for the readiness of men to go to court over such questions).

Cromwell's building program was an important arena for the negotiation of his social position. As was usual for elite households at the time, he moved seasonally between several residences, each in a different part of his scattered estates, and in addition owned a large house in London; it was clearly important to Cromwell not just to own a series of large residences of a grand form, but to be *seen* to be building and rebuilding, just as he had to be seen always to follow the correct feudal procedures. For many years the yearly costs of building projects at his estates of Collyweston, Wingfield and Tattershall amounted to between a third and a half of his annual income (Emery 1985: 330).

In contrast to many later Renaissance structures, Tattershall castle reveals itself gradually to the visitor. The tower is visible for many miles across the fens and acts as a landmark. As one approaches, however, one sees that this is merely the largest of a series of towers; as new work in brick, it is sharply differentiated from an older inner court studded with towers in much lighter-colored stone. A fifteenth-century visitor might note this difference in building material and conclude that here was a great man who wished not simply to be seen following the correct procedures, but also to be seen in a constant program of building and rebuilding. One gains access to the inner court circuitously, through three separate gatehouses and across two separate moats (Figure 14.2). Elite visitors arriving on horseback would enter the first gate, then leave their horse at the stables in the outer court, it being disrespectful to approach the core of the castle directly on horseback. Within the inner court, the castle changes character, with the hall as the central dominating feature; the great tower rises behind the hall and is secondary to it, more "private" and restricted in access, in terms of circulation pattern. Status, then, is communicated at Tattershall partly through movement through the building, twists and turns, gates, passageways, and sudden openings into courtyards.

Cromwell's tower appears to be a relatively late addition to the scheme, possibly an afterthought to the reconstruction of the rest of the castle (Figure 14.3). A combination of evidence from below- and above-ground archaeology and from building accounts suggests that Cromwell took over an old site, consisting of ranges of buildings in a rough courtyard plan all built up against the stone curtain wall and facing inwards, not dissimilar to the thirteenth-century castle of Bolingbroke a few miles away. His first act was to rebuild large parts of the internal ranges behind the curtain wall of Tattershall, though the thirteenth-century stone towers were retained and continued to be an important part of the ensemble.

As for Cromwell's great tower, we find that its meanings are complex and only to be understood with reference to its context, in particular to comparable structures of the period. One dimension is rivalry with the late medieval house at South Kyme a few miles

Figure 14.3 Tattershall tower

to the southeast: the two sites are intervisible across the flat lands, at least on the rare occasion of a day clear of the prevailing Fenland mist. South Kyme now survives only as an isolated system of moats, within which stands a stone tower of the mid-fourteenth century. The tower is now isolated, a desolate sight, with its grotesque medieval heads grinning from the parapets over a deserted field. Joist holes and other features in the tower, however, indicate that as at Tattershall the tower was connected to a now vanished hall block, though the tower, hall block and whole ensemble of South Kyme were rather smaller in scale.

In 1437, South Kyme was inherited by Walter Tailboys, an old friend from a Lincolnshire gentry family of long association with the Cromwells. Walter died in 1444 and his eponymous son Walter became Cromwell's arch-enemy. According to legal records, the younger Tailboys':

seething animosity against Cromwell knew no bounds . . . [and Tailboys] decided to kill him. In 1449 he sent spies to Tattershall to see if he could be kidnapped, and when that proved impossible, Tailboys sent men to Collyweston and Wingfield manors in 1450 to murder Cromwell whilst walking with his chaplain. As that proved abortive because he was too well protected by his household staff, Tailboys laid plans to blow up the house adjacent to Cromwell's London residence. Tailboys was arrested and imprisoned.

(Emery 1985: 329)

According to the recent re-analysis by Anthony Emery (1985), the tower at Tattershall was a late addition to Cromwell's building program, a relative afterthought in his rebuilding of the site. The Tattershall building accounts seem to suggest that Cromwell first rebuilt the court-yard and main domestic apartments, and refashioned the moats around the dwelling, and only then turned his attention to the tower. If so, the tower dates from immediately after the first Tailboys' death. The younger Tailboys, at long last succeeding to a family home which, if smaller than Cromwell's Tattershall residence, at least had a tower which could be seen for farther around, can hardly have viewed the almost immediate start of construction of a tower that dwarfed his with equanimity, particularly in an age when "honor" was a central compo-nent of elite male identity. (Indeed, one might speculate whether Cromwell refrained from building the tower till after his friend's death in deference to his friend's own sense of honor, but was freed from such inhibitions once his hated and disreputable son inherited the site).

The internal plan of the Tattershall tower is superficially very simple but actually of critical importance. It consists of a series of rooms stacked one on top of the other. However, the first three – the basement, ground floor, and first floor – are accessed inde-pendently. In other words, the tower is not self-contained; one cannot move from one floor to another without leaving the tower and re-entering via another building, which has now disappeared but whose position is indicated by joist holes. To gain access to the lord at second-floor level, one first mounts a circular stone stair before turning into a long corridor that is treated with rich decoration. The corridor takes one along the longer side of the tower to a small waiting chamber, equipped with fireplace and latrine, where one would wait to be admitted to the lord's presence. (Making visitors cool their heels before allowing them to enter is, of course, an important element in the impression of elite identity; at other castles, such chambers often have no fireplace at all, leaving the visitor to get thoroughly cold and shivering before being ushered into the presence of the great man.)

Cromwell's building of Tattershall tower has to be placed in two contexts to be understood in terms of agency. First, the building of a tower to mark a certain form of lordship is a recurrent motif of the period, part of an established symbolic vocabulary. A "lodging tower" was apparently added as a very late addition to one of Cromwell's other building projects at South Wingfield, as one of the last of a series of changes of mind; it consists of a series of lodging rooms for guests, stacked one on top of the other, and has its own elaborately organized latrine.

Second, the rebuilding of Tattershall castle took place in conjunction with a whole series of additions to its surrounding landscape, including an outer moat, a "Pleasaunce" or garden surrounded by water, a cross placed in the market place, and most notably the establishment of a college of priests a few hundred yards away. If Tattershall tower relates to Cromwell's concern to assert his position during his lifetime, the college on one reading is an attempt in part to assert his status after his death; one of the duties of the priests as specified in his will was to pray for his soul. So Cromwell's identity is marked through a pairing of secular and religious institutions.

Both castle and college work, in part, through *repetition*. Motifs, emblems, and "devices" appear over and over again around the fireplaces of the tower and in the stained glass of the college church (Marks 1984). Cromwell's insignia as Lord Treasurer (money bags), which by the rules of heraldry he could continue to use after leaving office, are surmounted with his motto "Ney je droit" or "Have I not the right?"; other repetitive heraldry includes his personal arms and those of his wife and family. This heraldry works in a very distinctive way: it links together monuments of very different form and function such as church and castle, and stamps them all in the same repetitive manner as the lord's own, despite their origins in very different architectural genres. The market cross itself, which the ordinary men and women of Tattershall village passed on their daily routines and which was the focus of community ceremonial in most village communities of this period (Hutton 1994), was inscribed with Cromwell's arms. This pattern of heraldry also links together Cromwell's "personal" identity (his own arms) with those of his office (Lord Treasurer). Similar emblems and motifs would be inscribed even on the bodies of the lord's followers, through their "livery" or uniform. Evetts (1994) has discussed this pattern of repetition in material form and symbolism as having direct analogies with the construction of both musical and literary forms of the period.

The Tattershall gatehouses are now destroyed, but one would expect this heraldic marking of Cromwell's identity there also. With this qualification, most of this marking of identity is internal to the structure. We have already noted how the pattern of circulation at Tattershall leads visitors to be granted access to its meanings gradually, as they move farther inside the building. The courtyard plan is essentially one to be understood from the inside out; from the outside, one sees only narrow windows in curtain walls. It is only when one stands within the inner courtyard, observing Cromwell's servants and retainers in livery standing to attention or bustling about taking food to and from the Great Hall, that one understands the nature of this great household and thus the nature of the man who is lord over it.

Cromwell was apparently unconcerned about one thing: the lack of architectural conformity. The brick tower with ashlar plinth and limestone dressings would have contrasted markedly with its smaller circular counterparts built of light-colored stone. There is apparently no attempt to mask the fact that the castle is of several phases. There is intense concern with how one moves on a winding path through the building, and with how rooms relate one to another, but little overt sense of formal architectural composition; the tower is at one end of the whole, jutting out into the moat.

The Earl of Leicester creates a Renaissance palace at Kenilworth

Kenilworth stands in the middle of England, eighty miles southwest of Tattershall (Figure 14.1). An oversimplified account of the archaeological sequence is as follows. First, there is a twelfth-century creation of an elite landscape, unusually large in scale but otherwise quite typical of the period in its layout. This landscape consists of a castle with a particularly large stone keep, an associated monastery, and a small town along the street between the two. This landscape was extended in the thirteenth century with the creation of a huge system of artificial lakes retained by dams, intended in part to defend the castle walls, and the extension of the castle fortifications in turn to protect this hydraulic system. The end result (and possibly the unintended consequence) of this defensive elaboration was to create a complex route across the lakes that was punctuated by gateways. This route was, as we shall see, utilized in ceremonial ways by later generations.

In the fourteenth and fifteenth centuries, the castle was transformed into a vast palace on a scale not seen elsewhere in England outside royal contexts; the new Great Hall alone was unrivalled in its scale except by the great halls of the King himself. Beyond the Great Hall was a grand and sumptuously appointed suite of "private" rooms, and beyond the lake was a quadrangular moated "Pleasaunce" or pleasure garden; this garden was explicitly symbolic in nature, being oriented to the four points of the compass. It had a harbor enabling access from the Water Gate of the castle.

So by the sixteenth century we have a huge stone castle, already ancient, embedded in histories, in the elite habitus (Figure 14.4). I want to focus on the transformation that happens in the latter half of the sixteenth century. This period saw the castle transformed by a new owner, Robert Dudley, Earl of Leicester. The timber buildings of the pleasure garden were dismantled and re-erected within the castle walls. Perhaps more importantly, the abbey had been dissolved and was in ruins by the end of the century. So we have an immediate contrast with Tattershall: though religion continued to be an important sphere in which identity was expressed, there is no immediate religious referent or pairing for Kenilworth's owner. There is also a changed set of bodily referents. Livery or the wearing of the emblem or badge of one's lord had been prohibited earlier in the sixteenth century as part of a Royal move to cut down feudal power. Leicester's staff did wear livery, but only by virtue of a special licence he was legally obliged to obtain through appeal to the monarch's

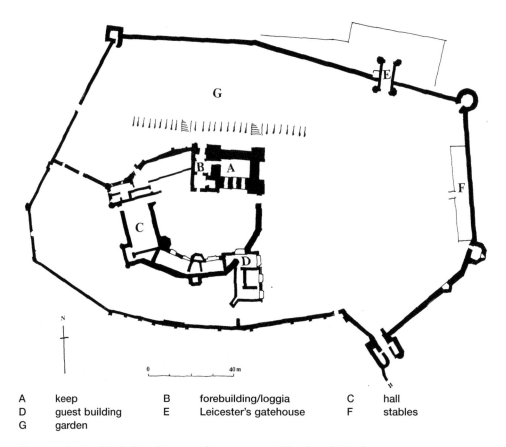

A	keep	B	forebuilding/loggia	C	hall
D	guest building	E	Leicester's gatehouse	F	stables
G	garden				

Figure 14.4 Simplified plan of inner and outer courts of Kenilworth Castle

grace and favor, a favor that could be withdrawn at a moment's notice. So one important means of displaying affiliations on the body was still there at Kenilworth, but had changed its meaning; its meanings were now associated as much with royal favor as feudal power.

Leicester effected a whole series of changes to the old pile of Kenilworth; to analyze them all would take a much longer account (see Johnson forthcoming a and forthcoming b). I now look at three buildings only from this period, all ranged around the outer court, and all, it should be noted, intervisible.

The first is a new gatehouse on the north side of the castle (Figure 14.5). In terms of circulation pattern, this gatehouse facilitates access both to the local parish church and to the deer parks for hunting to the west. It is the form of the gatehouse, a rectangular block flanked with four towers and the whole capped with battlements, which is striking. Had it been built a century earlier, a few years after Cromwell's death, its form would have been perfectly standard for the period (similar, for example, to Kirby Muxloe only twenty miles away and started in the 1480s). But such a form would be considered "out of date" by the 1570s, at least outside the colleges of Oxford and Cambridge.

Kenilworth's builder cannot simply be dismissively understood as a hidebound conservative; other buildings at the castle are of the very latest architectural style, including a formal garden in the Italian fashion, featuring a newly fashionable menagerie, and a series of Renaissance architectural details. These include a *loggia*, or covered walkway, in Italian Renaissance style and a Classical gateway from another part of the castle, later moved to the side of the gatehouse. In particular, the interior of the gatehouse itself is covered with oak panelling in the very latest fashion. The gatehouse is, I suggest, making a deliberate statement: its towers and battlements signify very definite meanings.

To whom are these meanings meant to be communicated? It is striking that the gatehouse is more easily viewed from the inside of the castle, that is from a position within the lower court looking north, than it is from the higher ground outside the castle to the south.

Figure 14.5 Kenilworth: the gatehouse

In particular, it can be seen from the second of our new buildings, a new range forming guest accommodation adjacent to the Inner Court (Figure 14.6). This new range is in the very latest Elizabethan style; it proclaims Leicester's familiarity with architectural fashion. It has huge rectangular windows echoing slightly later sixteenth-century work by Bess of Hardwick at Hardwick Hall, windows that look out over the artificial lake to the extensive system of deer parks beyond.

The gatehouse is also visible from the third new building, the stable range (Figure 14.7). The stables are also unusual, but for a different reason. Here, amidst a mighty stone castle refitted in a lavish Renaissance manner and quite obviously designed to impress, Leicester chose to use a "vernacular" style of half-timbering for the upper floor of the stables. It has been suggested that the half-timbered style is in part a reference to contemporary rural and rustic ideals (Morley *et al.* 1995: 114).

Now consider, as we have done at Tattershall, the processional route taken by a hypothetical elite visitor to Kenilworth: through the vast system of deer parks in their Arcadian splendor, and past the teeming fishponds, through the ancient outer gatehouse, turning to cross the lake, yet more vast deer parks to the left, pausing to admire the castle

Figure 14.6 Kenilworth: the visitors' block

spread out before him or her, the redness of its sandstone lit up by the setting sun. Our visitor would then enter the outer court and immediately be struck by three elements. First, a view of the rear of the gatehouse, though from this angle, the gatehouse would appear to be oriented towards the visitor; second, the sight of our visitor's horses led off to the wittily rustic half-timbered stables to the right; third, a huge blue-and-gilt clock mounted on the ancient keep farther to the left; this accommodation block for the visitor was in the very latest architectural style.

Of course, I have a specific visitor in mind. Robert Dudley, Earl of Leicester, was a man of high but precarious social status, whose father was executed in disgrace but who was raised to his present position by a female king. His visitor was that female king, Elizabeth, who in her person embodied both changing and unstable attitudes to gender and patriarchy and through her actions consciously manipulated and exploited those attitudes.

Documented accounts of Elizabeth's visit give a clearer hint of Elizabeth's view on her own gender and agency. She arrived in the early evening and was welcomed at the gate by a guard of giants, a race of men extinct, both Elizabeth and contemporary observers would note, since the days of Arthur. As Elizabeth crossed the causeway the Lady of the Lake emerged from the Mere, giving a potted history of the Castle and emphasizing its ancient origins in the process of declaring that this was the first time since the days of Arthur that she had chosen to emerge from the lake. (In one account the Lady started by describing

Figure 14.7 Kenilworth: the stables

herself as the mistress of the lake; Elizabeth remarked dryly that as Queen she was actually the mistress of the lake, whereupon the Lady, probably being played by a boy or young man, retreated in some confusion.) As Elizabeth entered the Castle, the blue and gilt clock that stood on the keep – suggestively named Caesar's Tower at that period – was stopped: during her visit time was to stand still. During the rest of her visit, Elizabeth stayed indoors till five in the afternoon; an account given by a male author remarks that this was due to her frail nature and the extreme heat of the summer, but goes on to mention that she was strong enough to get through enough administrative business to necessitate the arrival and departure of twenty horses a day carrying paperwork bound for the royal offices.

We also perceive Leicester's fashioning of himself and his ancient castle in more detail through the documents. Leicester's gatehouse, in its conscious archaism and use of battlements, alluded in part to elite male self-images of Protestant chivalry in which Elizabeth assumed the symbolic position of the Catholic image of the Virgin Mary. At the same time, Elizabeth also took the position of another medieval and chivalric image: the female, passive, unattainable object of courtly love, desired yet never attained by the male knight. Contemporary fashions in literature suggest that the vernacular style of the stable block was a deliberate play on these values through a parallel construction of "the rustic."

Conclusion: constructing agencies

What lessons can be drawn from a comparison of these two cases?

It is very tempting to look for agency in individual intention and biography. To an extent this is a useful rhetorical tool; it highlights very specific goals and strategies on the part of individual agents, as I have done here, and throws into sharp relief the things they use to work towards those goals. Unfortunately, in an age of the "death of the author" and consequently the questioning of individual biography, such an analysis is not so much wrong as shallow.

To suggest why, we should go back and consider how a traditional typology regards these structures. A narrative is normally told about castles and courtyard houses which goes as follows: castles are primarily military structures, and castle design reaches military "perfection" not just in England but in France and the Crusader states in the years preceding 1300. Thereafter, a combination of changing military tactics and patterns of lordship results in a lessening of the defense factor; castles become ranges of buildings around a courtyard, the perimeter of the ranges being a curtain wall studded with towers and often provided with an impressive gatehouse. These later medieval castles, it is suggested, are fortified not so much against a full-blown siege as against "casual violence." The courtyard house, essentially inward-looking, characteristic of northwest Europe, then succumbs to wave after wave of "Renaissance influence" from Italy in the sixteenth and seventeenth centuries.

Such an analysis is patently agency-blind; it is also, of course, gender-blind. Put very crudely, though this was a patriarchal age, the builders of many elite structures were women. Such builders, as one might predict, took a wide range of different attitudes and strategies towards the prevailing values of the time, from simple replication of the patriarchal structure to very different reorderings of it. Friedman (1997) makes some interesting points on the gendering of agency in the late sixteenth and early seventeenth centuries. She contrasts the buildings of two elite women in a generally elite age. Both Bess of Hardwick and Lady Ann Clifford were widows who controlled large estates, but there the similarity ends. Bess of Hardwick engaged in a bold and innovative building program, including the massive Hardwick Hall, with its huge expanses of glass and her initials displayed prominently on the building (Figure 14.8; the Hardwick windows and general style are very similar to Leicester's guest block at Kenilworth, and the two buildings are roughly contemporary). By contrast, Lady Ann Clifford engaged in a reconstruction of traditional buildings, at the very time when those on neighboring estates were in decay. These included the castles of Brougham, Brough and Appleby. Her own tomb erases all trace of her own body; there is no funeral effigy as was customary, but instead present only an elaborate delineation of her ancestry and lineage (Figure 14.9).

So the first shallow implication is that traditional typologies and the normative approach are pretty useless here. But is my account parasitic upon it on a deeper analysis? At a practical level, it is only the hard work of traditional scholars in archives and in the field not to mention the conservation activities of the proprietors of Tattershall and

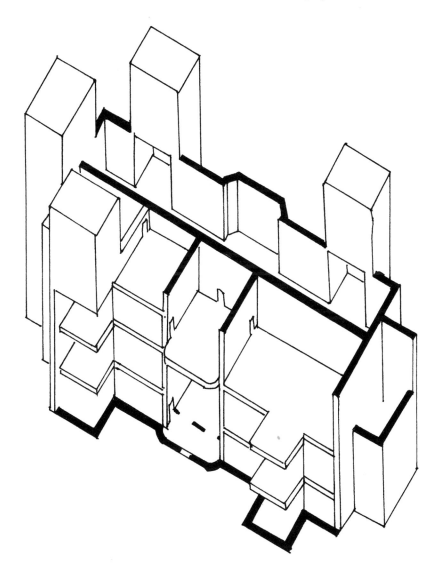

Figure 14.8 Symmetrical cutaway of Hardwick Hall, Derbyshire

Figure 14.9 The tomb of Lady Anne Clifford, Appleby-in-Westmorland

Kenilworth – the National Trust and English Heritage respectively – which have created the material I have used here. At a deeper level, we can only explore agency against a backdrop of structure, not just medieval and Renaissance structures, but normative structures of twentieth century scholarship.

It is certain that the respective identities of Cromwell and Leicester are expressed in different ways. There is little of the insistent repetition of heraldry, emblems, and badges of office at Kenilworth, though Leicester himself was a very senior figure in the Elizabethan state from the 1570s until his death. Leicester lacked the opportunity for emblematic cross-referencing between castle and church, and no observer would fail to note that the livery upon the bodies of his servants and other staff was only there through Royal consent. Leicester did not fail to utilize heraldic cross-referencing when it was available; his own and his last wife's tomb in a medieval side-chapel in Warwick church, six miles away, is a combination of Gothic, Classical, and vernacular style combined with heraldic motifs. What was important for Leicester was elaboration of the surface of the body through his dress and through the depiction of that dress in contemporary portraits. In contrast, Cromwell's body is almost unknown to us; traditions of "realistic" portraiture were rare in fifteenth-century England and his funerary brass in Tattershall church has been defaced. It would not in any case have compared to Leicester's image in any way, whether as a focus of attention or in its elaboration and attention to detail in clothing and likeness.

Much of the symbolic vocabulary of identity is shared by Cromwell and Leicester. At both sites, the visitor is impressed with the marks of elite identity at least partly through movement. Passages through gatehouses, themselves marked with heraldry, and across artificially created moats and other bodies of water are important. It is the temporal succession and juxtaposition of pieces of architecture that impresses the visitor. However, the meanings of elements of this vocabulary have, in part, changed. Leicester's gatehouse may look similar to earlier gatehouses, but its meanings have changed utterly. And of course, most fundamentally, where for Cromwell cross-reference to royal power merely underpins prevailing notions of patriarchy, such a reading is intrinsically problematic for a man like Leicester, the subject of a female king. At Kenilworth, images of a patriarchal order are simultaneously stable and unstable, ordered and yet implicitly contradictory.

So we return to the start of my argument: we cannot apply a "recipe-book" approach, whether such a recipe is the unthinking application of methodological individualism or structuration theory. Maneuverings such as those at Tattershall and Kenilworth were part of a much wider and deeper historical process that involved the deepening of a sense of self. Put very crudely, to be an elite man in the fifteenth century can be seen as a relatively simple affair: to subscribe to a masculine honor code, to be loyal to one's king, and in particular to fight on his behalf when called upon. By the beginning of the seventeenth century, masculinity was more problematic; it also involved values of literacy, of civility, and in particular a deepening consciousness of the "other" and of cultural difference; as such, the self was tied in to emergent notions of empire. This last element is implicit at Kenilworth. Elizabeth's Protestant knights fought in Ireland; Spenser's chivalrous fantasies were implicated in the birth of colonialism (Maley 1997). Agency, therefore, was constructed in different ways.

In place of a recipe book, I think we need closer attention to the context and form of the archaeological material we are working with. A purely archaeological consideration of the detail and aesthetics of structures at Tattershall and Kenilworth forms the meat of this analysis, even if Cromwell and Tailboys, Elizabeth and Leicester add spice. At Tattershall, the tower is extraordinary enough, but what throws its meanings into relief is a consideration of the related structures at South Kyme and Wingfield. At Kenilworth, the gatehouse, stables and visitors' block are not in themselves remarkable structures; their context – the fact that they are found next to one another – is.

Such close attention to context leads us also to form. We cannot get very far towards agency through a quantitative analysis. Kenilworth is the largest castle in England, but this tells us nothing. It is the formal detail that tells us of the conscious anachronism of the gatehouse, the link between stable and heraldry. I therefore suggest that one technique to get us closer to agents – though I would prefer to talk of women and men in the past – is to write narratives, of people moving through buildings, rebuilding, and reconstructing their material environment. I think Tringham (1991) has shown the way here, though I think we should go further.

Both Tattershall and Kenilworth stage and re-stage the identities of the individuals that strut and fret across their spaces. The metaphor of staging is not an idle one. The metaphor was an obsession of sixteenth-century polite culture though it had medieval roots. The Renaissance stage was more than simply a platform; the theater itself was circular, and as such represented a microcosm of the world. It was also ordered socially, with tiers of seats graded from the lower orders in the pit to the gentler sort in the upper stories. The Renaissance theater stands in the middle of a genealogy that looks back to the medieval tower and forward to the Enlightenment panopticon (Belsay 1985: 19). It is also an arena that is *important*, important enough to cause an anxious State to throw playwrights such as Ben

Jonson into prison, and important enough to produce Puritan anxiety over boys playing women and the sublimated eroticism this involves (Butler 1997; Jardine 1983: 9–37).

I suggest, therefore, that archaeologists should be very careful about cross-cultural models of agency. A considered appreciation of Tattershall and Kenilworth leads us away from such models, towards a more nuanced and particular appreciation of their context. This is not to say that generalizations cannot be achieved or that all is endlessly particular; there are clearly generalities that can be discussed here. In another situation and given a different intellectual purpose, I could have written a paper stressing the generalities of elite politics, factional competition, links between patriarchy, property systems and lineages in "mature" State or feudal societies, the politics and economics of estate management, or processes involved in emergent colonialism, to name a few general processes and structures at random.

I do feel, however, that close and careful attention to the context of agency must precede any attempt to abstract general propositions from particular cases. The past is valuable, and above all deserves a more subtle approach.

Acknowledgments

I thank Marcia-Anne Dobres and John E. Robb for asking me to write this chapter and for providing critical comment. The comments of the Medieval Discussion Group at the University of Durham were extremely useful. The theoretical analysis offered here could not have been written without the benefit of the detailed empirical scholarship of Anthony Emery; though we have never met my arguments owe a great debt to his analysis of Tattershall and Lord Cromwell. Philip Dixon discussed Tattershall, South Kyme, and other buildings with me and I owe the observation that other castles kept their visitors cold to him. Any errors and misperceptions that remain are mine alone.

Bibliography

Belsay, C. 1985. *The Subject of Tragedy: Identity and Difference in Renaissance Drama.* Methuen, London.

Bermingham, A., and J. Brewer 1995. *The Consumption of Culture 1600–1800: Image, Object, Text.* Routledge, London.

Binford, L. R. 1983. *In Pursuit of the Past.* Thames and Hudson, London.

Breitenberg, M. 1996. *Anxious Masculinity in Early Modern England.* Cambridge University Press, Cambridge UK.

Butler, J. 1997. *Excitable Speech: A Politics of the Performative.* Routledge, London.

Deetz, J. 1977. *In Small Things Forgotten: An Archaeology of Early American Life.* Anchor Press, New York.

Dollimore, J., and A. Sinfield (eds) 1991. *Political Shakespeare.* Routledge, London.

Emery, A. 1985. "Ralph, Lord Cromwell's Manor at Wingfield (1439–c.1450): Its Construction, Design and Influence." *Archaeological Journal* 142: 276–339.

Evetts, D. 1994. *Literature and the Visual Arts in Tudor England.* Oxford University Press, Oxford.

Friedman, A. T. 1997. "Wife in the English Country House: Gender and the Meaning of Style in Early Modern England," in *Women and Art in Early Modern Europe: Patrons, Collectors and Connoisseurs,* ed. C. Lawrence, pp.111–25. Pennsylvania University Press, University Park.

Gaimster, D., and P. Stamper (eds) 1997. *The Age of Transition: The Archaeology of English Culture AD 1400–1600.* Oxbow, Oxford.

Gent, L., and N. Llewellyn 1990. *Renaissance Bodies: The Human Figure in English Culture c.1540–1660.* Reaktion, London.

Giddens, A. 1979. *Central Problems in Social Theory: Action, Structure, and Contradiction in Social Analysis.* Macmillan, London.

Goffman, E. 1959. *The Presentation of Self in Everyday Life*. Anchor, New York.

—— 1971. *Relations in Public: Microstudies of the Public Order*. Penguin, Harmondsworth.

Goldberg, J. (ed.) 1994. *Queering the Renaissance*. Duke University Press, London.

Greenblatt, S. 1980. *Renaissance Self-Fashioning: From More to Shakespeare*. University of Chicago Press, London.

Hill, C. 1964. *Society and Puritanism in Pre-Revolutionary England*. Secker and Warburg, London.

Hunt, L. (ed.) 1989. *The New Cultural History*. University of California Press, Berkeley.

Hutton, R. 1994. *The Rise and Fall of Merry England: The Ritual Year 1400–1700*. Oxford University Press, Oxford.

Jardine, L. 1983. *Still Harping on Daughters: Women and Drama in the Age of Shakespeare*. Barnes and Noble, New Jersey.

—— 1995. *Worldly Goods*. Routledge, London.

—— 1996. *Reading Shakespeare Historically*. Routledge, London.

Johnson, M. H. 1989. "Conceptions of Agency in Archaeological Interpretation." *Journal of Anthropological Archaeology* 8: 129–211.

—— forthcoming a. *Building Histories: Castles at the End of the Middle Ages*.

—— forthcoming b. "Archaeology and Social Theory," in *Approaches to Archaeology*, ed. J. Bintliff. Blackwell, Oxford.

Maley, W. 1997. *Salvaging Spenser: Colonialism, Culture and Identity*. Macmillan, London.

Marks, R. 1984. *The Stained Glass of the Collegiate Church of the Holy Trinity, Tattershall*. Garland, London.

McNay, L. 1992. *Foucault and Feminism*. Polity, Oxford.

Moore, H. L. 1985. *Space, Text and Gender*. Cambridge University Press, Cambridge UK.

Morley, B., P. Brown, and T. Crump 1995. "The Elizabethan Gardens and Leicester's Stables at Kenilworth Castle: Excavations between 1970 and 1984." *Birmingham and Warwickshire Archaeological Society Transactions* 99: 72–116.

Rosenthal, J. T. 1996. *Old Age in Late Medieval England*. University of Pennsylvania Press, Philadelphia.

Tait, H. 1997. "The Great Divide?" in *The Age of Transition: The Archaeology of English Culture* AD 1400–1600, ed. D. Gaimster and P. Stamper, pp. 1–8. Oxbow, Oxford.

Thompson, E. P. 1963. *The Making of the English Working Class*. Gollancz, London.

Tringham, R. E. 1991. "Households with Faces: The Challenge of Gender in Prehistoric Architectural Remains," in *Engendering Archaeology: Women and Prehistory*, ed. J. M. Gero and M. W. Conkey, pp. 93–131. Blackwell, Oxford

Williams, T. 1990 "'Magnetic Figures': Polemical Prints of the English Revolution," in *Renaissance Bodies: The Human Figure in English Culture, c. 1540–1660*, ed. L. Gent and N. Llewellyn, pp. 86–110. Reaktion, London.

15 Craft to wage labor

Agency and resistance in American historical archaeology

Paul A. Shackel

Introduction

Examining the meaning and uses of material culture and recognizing the role of agency is a relatively recent phenomenon in American historical archaeology. This approach has been developed since the 1980s (see, for instance, Leone 1984) and is influenced by several key works including those by Ian Hodder (1982a, 1982b, 1987) and Michael Shanks and Christopher Tilley (1987). While recognizing it as a logical alternative to positivism, many have resisted this change and American historical archaeologists continue to struggle and debate over how to interpret the archeological record. Much of the interpretation in American historical archeology does not go beyond particularistic endeavors and trickle-down theory, and those studying the industrial era often ignore the way people consciously manipulated material expressions to show their dissatisfaction with their new wage labor situation.

Recognizing individuals, households, or other small units of a cultural system as active agents that contribute to the archaeological record is one way to go beyond the particularism and positivism that dominate historical archeology. Under the premise of agency, actors know the way society operates, and individuals act within a pre-existing structure. They make sense of cultural practices that become routine in their daily activities within this structure (Bourdieu 1977; Giddens 1979). Actors think and act in a certain way, they interact with each other, and they may reproduce the existing structure. During this interaction, agents may also express power relations through material consumption and the production of goods. The choices they make are made with reference to others, and their actions, pursued within the parameters of social structures, may lead to tension and conflict. These differences require some sort of resolution, which may mean conformity, or change, depending upon one's position in the social order (see, for instance, Dobres 1999). Observing subtle variations in the archeological record and placing them within a historic and social context is one way to observe and interpret the choices that agents made.

Power, muted groups, and double consciousness

Power facilitates agency and it is essential to my work in the industrial town of Harpers Ferry (Figure 15.1). It is important for analyzing and understanding the archaeology of class relations (see also Foucault 1979; Miller and Tilley 1984, Paynter 1989; Tilley 1982). In the following analysis of industrial-era domestic sites, I examine how workers and their households responded to the new technology of the industrial revolution and resisted the imposed industrial ideology. Domestic consumption became an arena in which agents constructed social identities and in which they could either accept or reject the new industrial ethos.

Figure 15.1 Location of Harpers Ferry, West Virginia (drawn by Prashant Kaw)

Bourdieu's (1977) concept of habitus is important for this analysis. The everyday mundane acts of production at work and consumption at home codified social categories upon which expressions of people's self interests can be found. Searching for subtleties in the archaeological record allows us to see how people responded to and resisted new or changing power structures, in this case, the imposition of industrial labor. While most groups in industrial society have limited choices (for example, they all buy ceramics to set their tables), it is the choices that they make (the designs, such as feather edged, plain or transfer printed) that shows social agency in action. The kinds of objects chosen, and the way they are used in specific contexts, indicate power relations and the different and changing meanings associated with this material culture.

In the nineteenth-century arms manufacturing town of Harpers Ferry, Virginia (now West Virginia), workers operated in a rigid class structure based on power differences. Conflict between labor and capital often arose as workers (craftsmen, pieceworkers, and wage laborers) resisted managers. When the United States government imposed a wage labor system upon the armory craftsmen and pieceworkers, they reacted to this changing power structure in various ways. Individuals searched for, resisted, and negotiated power within the manufacturing system and on the domestic front.

In one case, the resistance was extremely obvious when, in 1830, an armory worker murdered a superintendent who tried to enforce time discipline in the factory. After this incident the armorers were allowed to maintain their craft ethos for over a decade. In other cases, the resistance was much more subtle and these reactions can be seen in the archaeological record. Some workers and their households had the power to resist change by manipulating and transforming the cultural rules of the new industrial order. Their everyday material culture played an active role by shaping their social relations with fellow agents within the workforce and in the community (Shackel 1996).

As I show in the case study to follow, material culture became the medium and the outcome of specific power relations (see also Johnson 1989: 189–93; Kirk 1991: 108–11). While some managers and unskilled workers accepted the new industrial order and the wage labor system as they became major players in its implementation, craftsmen and piece-workers resisted both at work and at home. Although there seem to be only slight differences between the domestic archaeological assemblages of workers' families who resisted the new order, and those of managers who accepted it, a closer, contextual examination of the local history and of specific social interactions shows that they reflect disparate attitudes by families toward a new wage labor system.

When searching for variability in the archaeological record, archaeologists must learn to interpret these artifact assemblages that do not "fit" expectations as something meaningful rather than just "noise" (Dobres 1995). The recognition of competition between groups and individuals amplifies the need to consider the composition, strategies, and constraints of subgroups. Some complexities of material culture expression and the role of agency are noticeable when I turn to questions related to class. Placing the material record in the framework of historical context helps show that the variability in the archaeological record is a product of agency, and peoples' reactions to power relations.

Barbara Little (1994, 1997) uses the concept of muted groups as a way to look at expressions of non-dominant groups in the archaeological record that may otherwise be seen as "noise" (see, for instance, Ardener 1975a, 1975b). For instance, dominant groups create and control the meanings and uses of material culture. If other groups wish to be understood by the dominant group, they must express themselves through the goods controlled by the dominant group. "Muted groups remain so because their models of reality and world view cannot be expressed adequately through the modes and ideologies accepted by dominant groups" (Little 1997: 227). The dominant group has power over social settings and structural power over social labor (Wolf 1990). Those that are muted have powers limited to interpersonal situations and to actions of resistance.

Also important in understanding the struggle for controlling the meaning and uses of material goods among members of a subordinate group is W. E. B. Du Bois' (1994: 5) concept of double-consciousness. Paul Mullins (1996) finds this notion useful to understand the idea of muted groups from the viewpoint of the subculture. Writing in the Jim Crow era, a time when laws increasingly segregated African-Americans from white America, Du Bois noted that African-Americans saw themselves through the eyes of Others, or the dominant white society. "One even feels his two-ness – an American, a negro; two souls, two thoughts, two unreconciled strivings; two warring ideals in one dark body, whose dogged strength alone keeps it from being torn asunder" (Du Bois 1994: 5). The history of the African-American, according to Du Bois, is this conflict of operating in two worlds. The concept of double consciousness allows for a complex understanding of material culture within the context of a muted group (see also Mullins 1996). It creates a framework to understand how a subordinate group may use and read material culture.

Searching for and understanding variability in the archaeological record from the beginning of the industrial revolution creates a challenge to understanding subordinate group behavior. While alternative views can be expressed in a mass-produced culture, the types of goods found often impose an appearance of consistency and sameness. They often hide the inequality and alternate expressions of subaltern groups. It becomes the challenge of historical archaeologists examining a group in a mass consumer society to decipher the complexities of alternative expressions and the role of agency (see Little 1997).

An archaeology of the industrial era

As more historical archaeologists turn their attention to industrial era sites, the interpretation of workers' domestic households will be recognized as contributing to understanding the development of a working-class society (see, for instance, Hardesty 1988; Shackel 1996). Recognizing the relationship between domestic and industrial sites is important for understanding the development of capitalism and the impact of industry on our daily lives. Examining the archaeology of the early industrial era is an exciting task since it provides insights into the roots of our mass consumer and mass producer society. Some scholars see the eighteenth century, and even earlier, as an era in which to trace the development of capitalism (Johnson 1996; Leone 1988, 1995; Shackel 1993a). I feel that examining the early industrial era in nineteenth-century America provides a more in-depth picture and can show how capitalism was implemented, operated, and/or resisted by different interest groups and individuals (see Shackel 1996). Recognizing the role of agency becomes a valuable tool for understanding any variability in the archaeological record.

Robert Paynter's (1989) synthesis on the archaeology of inequality is important when looking at the development of ideologies related to modernizing industrial conditions and the formation of a working-class society (also see McGuire and Paynter 1991). A new factory discipline was imposed by owners and managers and it was sometimes resisted by workers. Tensions that developed "between cores and peripheries, civil and kin groups, rulers and ruled, merchants and lords, men and women, and producers and extractors evoke an unwieldy tangle of processes" (Paynter 1989: 558).

The introduction of industrial capitalism meant a new work discipline, abandonment of craft work relations, and adherence to a new factory discipline. As Paynter (1989: 386) has shown, resistance by workers in a capitalist world could take on several forms, including malingering, sabotage, and even murder (see also, for instance, Juravich 1985; Scott 1985, Shackel 1996; Smith 1977). Sometimes these acts of resistance are visible in the archaeological record, although the extent of their defiance varies from place to place. Workers' acceptance of the new factory discipline varied between different workers and factories. Michael Nassaney's and Marjorie Abel's (1993: 251) analysis of the material remains at the John Russell Cutlery Company in the Connecticut River Valley describes discontent over the new factory system. Following James Scott's (1990) analysis, they recognize that discontented workers can challenge the existing power structure through a "hidden transcript." Nassaney and Abel (1993: 263–74) found a large quantity of artifacts related to interchangeable manufacturing along the riverbank near the former cutting room and trip hammer shop. These discarded materials consisted of inferior or imperfect manufactured parts. While these workers labored in a modern factory, Nassaney and Abel suggest that the discarded materials might be a form of defiance against the implementation of the new system.

The Harpers Ferry Brewery serves as another example of resistance in the work place. The brewery workers in late nineteenth- and very early twentieth-century Harpers Ferry subscribed to the national average of fourteen to eighteen hour workdays, six days per week and six to eight hours on Sunday (Schulter 1910: 92–3). Between 1890 and 1910, unions gradually decreased the work day to ten hours. Brewery workers, including those at Harpers Ferry, were constantly exposed to radical temperature changes and breathed contaminated air (Hull-Walski and Walski 1993: 17.34–5, 1994). In the first decade of the twentieth century, brewery-related accidents were almost 30 percent higher than those of other trades. This rate increased over the decade, probably due to the "higher speeding of machinery." The excessive use of alcohol by workers under the "free beer system" aided this high casualty rate (Schulter 1910: 259–63).

Some form of the free beer system existed in the Harpers Ferry Brewery, although it was probably a form of covert action. Workers drank the owner's profits while they operated machinery. For instance, more than a hundred beer bottles were found between walls of the bottling works and more than a thousand were found down the building's elevator shafts during the renovation of the beer bottling works in 1995/96. All of the bottles date to between 1893 and 1909, when beer bottling occurred in the building (Shackel 1993b).

These data, empirical and contextual, suggest that workers probably drank the owners' profits and concealed their subversive behavior by disposing of the bottles out of the view of supervisors. The conflagrations in the brewery in 1897 and 1909 may have been a coincidence, or may also be related to some general discontent among the workers (Shackel 1993b).

Changing republican ideologies during the industrial era

Understanding the historical context and the changing republican ideologies of the late eighteenth and early nineteenth centuries is one way of understanding the changing material culture found among workers' households during the industrial era. The classical republicanism of mid-eighteenth-century America condemned the spread of consumerism (Gilje 1996: 172). In the later eighteenth century, this criticism became popular among many colonial Americans as they resisted British imperial regulations and the many forms of consumerism that developed in England. However, the conditions of the American Revolution, based on Renaissance ideals, fostered the development of liberal republicanism ideals and the growth of capitalism among many Americans (ibid.: 173). Liberal republicanism encouraged the individual to act as an independent citizen. The change in ideologies, from resisting to embracing consumerism, did not proceed without contest, and the debate between the ideals of classical and liberal republicanism continued into the early nineteenth century among Americans. Thomas Jefferson and Benjamin Franklin proposed a new republican technology sensitive to human perfection and classical republican ideals; others like Alexander Hamilton and Tench Coxe supported liberal republican ideals and argued that industrialization would strengthen America (Shackel 1998).

Early-nineteenth-century American craftsmen, including those at Harpers Ferry, subscribed to classical republicanism. They believed that government would act as an arbitrator if any inequities existed between labor and capital. Their beliefs encouraged craft consciousness and inhibited the growth and implementation of industrial discipline. In the 1830s and 1840s, manufacturers consciously deskilled artisans throughout America, including those at the Harpers Ferry Armory. The factory system contradicted classical republican ideology, since the wage laborer was at the mercy of the capitalist. Workers lost their ability to be truly independent citizens (Ross 1985: 13). The US federal government and managers transformed the Harpers Ferry Armory from a system based on equality between labor and capital (known as craft-based production) to a factory system that depended not on skilled and independent citizen-workers, but unskilled laborers and "machine tenders" (Shackel 1998).

Resistance to the new industrial order in the domestic sphere: on ceramics, gender, and agency

A comparison of tablewares found in workers' (pieceworkers and wage laborers) and in managers' households shows how they responded differently to the change from classical to liberal republican ideology. While both increasingly participated in a consumer society, the different types of ceramics that they bought and used were subtly, but meaningfully, different. The variability I describe below provides empirical clues about how these differently situated households were active social agents in their response to industrialization. Since I examine reactions to the new industrial order in a domestic context, it is important to recognize the central role women played in reacting to the new social order.

In the early nineteenth century, women increasingly purchased and displayed domestic material culture. They were in charge of refinement within the home and they became responsible for promoting their home among friends and acquaintances (Wall 1994: 147–58). Promoting the home included ritualizing family meals. Creating specific times for meals changed middle-class home life (ibid.: 111). As Foucault (1979) argues, when the meal was held on a regular and timely basis, and when all family members participated, meal rituals taught and reaffirmed the values and body discipline of "punctuality, order, neatness, temperance, self-denial, kindness, generosity, and hospitality" (Sedgwick, quoted in Wall 1994: 112).

Ceramics became more elaborately designed and the types of dishes became more varied and played an important role in the new ritualization process. By the 1820s, the number of separate courses increased as did the ceramics on which to serve them. Serving more specialized foods became part of this elaboration and ritualization within the home (Wall 1994). De Cunzo (1995: 140–1) notes the importance of the various uses for different sets of dinner wares. An 1828 etiquette book, for instance, noted that proper households need to have three sets of dinner services: one for company, one for ordinary use, and the third for servants (Wall 1994: 147–58).

A review of the existing store ledgers from Harpers Ferry shows that women from working-class households became participants in the new consumer society by the 1830s, if not earlier. They increasingly purchased the finer earthenware tablewares for their households (see Lucas 1993: 8.33–8.35). They became active agents who expressed their anxieties about the new industrial technology within the world that they controlled: the domestic sphere. A fine-grained analysis of the specific sorts of domestic material culture under their control, tablewares, provides insights into not only their material choices and strategies, but the agential intentions motivating them. The tableware assemblages of the master armorers' (managers) households, and the armory workers' (pieceworkers and wage laborers) households provide an example of subtle differences in material culture of two types of households with varying views on industrialization.

For the purpose of comparison, I look at two master armorer refuse assemblages, one early (1821–30) and one later (1830–50), then compare these with a representative sample from pieceworkers' (ca. 1821–41) and wage laborers' (1841–52) households (Figure 15.2). Examining these assemblages within the local context of industrial development shows how they all participated in the new consumer ethic, but the variation in the assemblages shows agency at work.

The managerial class

One site examined belonged to the master armorer's household. The master armorer was responsible for the daily operations of the gun factory. While the earliest master armorer, Armistead Beckham, subscribed to a craft ethos, by 1830 a new master armorer, Benjamin Moor, became committed to industrializing the enterprise, despite protests from the armory workers. Moor became dedicated to new time-saving machinery, the division of labor, and the wage labor system (Smith 1977).

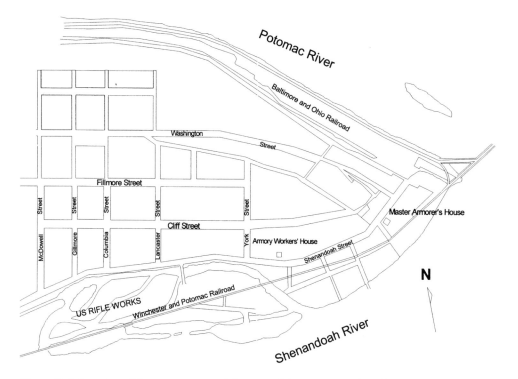

Figure 15.2 Location of the master armorer's house and the armory worker's house within Harpers
Ferry (drawn by Prashant Kaw)

A random excavation strategy retrieved a representative sample of the master armorer's
backyard area. Using the information gathered from this initial testing, additional excavation
units were placed in areas that could retrieve the greatest amount of information related to the
daily life of the master armorer's household. A larger concentration of excavation units was
placed near the rear of the house and next to the kitchen, creating a large block excavation
(Figure 15.3). This area contains continuously undisturbed deposits from the earliest armory
occupation around 1821, through the twentieth century. The stratigraphy consists of distinct
occupational layers interspersed with layers of flood silt. Since the town floods on average every
thirteen years, and all of the floods in town are well recorded in armory correspondences, documenting the diachronic change in material culture and attributing the archaeological record
to specific households is straightforward (Shackel 1996: 117–18, 1998: 11–13).

Armistead Beckham's household assemblage dates from 1821 through 1830. This is a period
when the town, 60 miles from the nearest port towns of Alexandria and Georgetown (just
outside Washington, D.C.), received consumer goods at a relatively slow rate. 86 percent of the
Beckham household tablewares consist of creamwares and pearlwares (Table 15.1). The
creamwares tend to be undecorated, while the pearlwares are relatively more expensive and
contain some type of design or pattern such as shell edged, painted, and undecorated ceramics
(85.7 percent) (Table 15.2). Both pearlware and creamware were fashionable for the time,
although pearlwares dominated the market by the 1820s (Miller 1980; Shackel 1996: 118).

The later master armorer's tableware assemblage (1830–50) belonged to Benjamin
Moor's household, and it consists almost exclusively of pearlwares and whitewares (98
percent). Creamwares were no longer fashionable and their use disappears from most

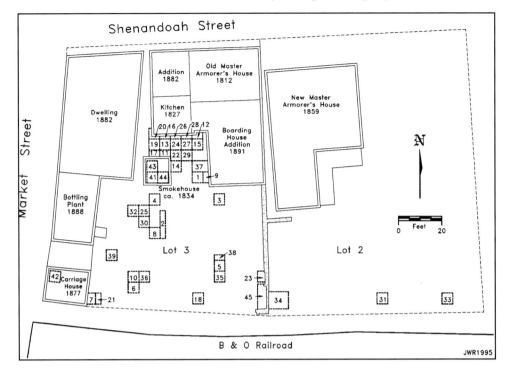

Figure 15.3 Excavation plan for the master armorer's house (drawn by John Ravenhorst)

American households by this era, including Master Armorer Moor's household. The most common design in the assemblage was transfer-printed patterns (41.9 percent), a very popular tableware design from the late 1820s through the 1850s (Shackel 1996: 119) (Table 15.2). These data show that between 1830 and 1850, Master Armorer Moor's household acquired the most fashionable consumer goods available on the market: transfer printed patterns as well as painted and edged designed tablewares.

Pieceworkers and laborers

Comparing the master armorers' assemblages with a pieceworker's and a wage laborer's assemblages shows some similarities and some slight differences in the patterning of

Table 15.1 Ceramic vessels by refined ware for two master armorer households, ca. 1821–30 and 1830–50 (from Lucas 1993: 8.15)

Ware type	ca. 1821–30		1830–50	
	no.	%	no.	%
Whiteware	—	—	—	—
Pearlware	14	—	36	35
Creamware	10	50	66	63
Porcelain	3	36	—	—
Unid. refined	—	—	—	—
Earthenware	1	3	2	2
Total	28	100	104	100

Table 15.2 Refined ware vessels by decoration from two master armorer households, ca. 1821–30 and 1830–50 (from Lucas 1993: 8.16; Shackel 1997: 120, 135, 1998)

Decoration	(ca. 1821–30)		(1830–50)	
	no.	%	no.	%
Dipped	2	7.1	5	4.8
Shell edged	6	21.4	34	32.4
Transfer print	1	3.6	44	41.9
Painted	7	25.0	14	13.3
Enameled	3	10.7	2	1.9
Undecorated	9	32.1	4	3.8
Other	0	0	2	1.9
Total	28	100	105	100

material culture (Figure 15.4). Excavation of an armory worker's domestic site provides some clues about how pieceworkers' and wage laborers' families reacted to the new industrial order, the imposition of wage labor, and the deterioration of classical republican ideology. Excavations yielded a plethora of information from the household occupations. Flood deposits were not as clearly marked in the stratigraphy as in the master armorer's backyard, but clear distinctive occupational zones are still visible. We can discern the archaeological materials before and after 1841. An 1841 construction phase of a house addition left shale spalls throughout the entire site. There is thus tight chronological control of the archaeological record that allows us to compare two different eras in the armory, dating before and after 1841. The year 1841 is significant at the Harpers Ferry Armory, since that is when the military took control of the armory and forced all workers to follow a wage labor system. Therefore, the pre-1841 context, when armorers living in the excavated structure tended to be pieceworkers and had some control over their labor, can be compared to the post-1841 context, when they became wage laborers (Shackel 1996: 132–3, 1998: 13–14).

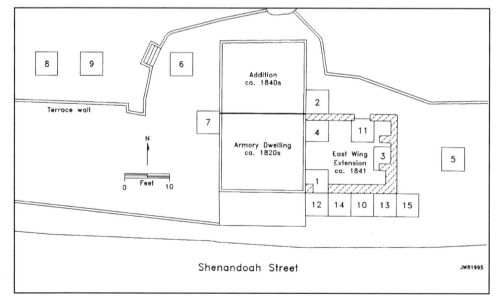

Figure 15.4 Excavation plan for the armory worker's house (drawn by John Ravenhorst)

The pieceworker (ca. 1821–41) and wage worker (1841–52) households from the two eras participated in consumerism in very different ways (Table 15.3, Table 15.4). The pre-1841 pieceworker's assemblage has a small percentage of creamwares (7 percent) and the largest group of wares consists of transfer printed pearlwares (38.8 percent). There is also a large representation of shell-edged (14 percent) and painted tablewares (23.1 percent). In contrast, there is an unexpected pattern in the post-1841 wage laborer household assemblage. First, the proportion of creamwares, which are no longer fashionable by the 1830s, doubles (14 percent). Second, though transfer printed wares were popular from the late 1820s through the 1850s, their proportion decreases substantially (from 38.8 percent to 27.5 percent). Third, though the popularity of shell edged wares decreases, their representation in the later assemblage increases from 14.0 percent to 21.1 percent (Lucas 1994).

Between 1820 and the late 1850s, armory workers' wages declined some 20 percent (Barbour 1851; Lucas and Shackel 1994; Stubbelfield 1821; Symington 1846). This reduction coincided with a decrease in prices of consumer goods attributed to the growing transportation infrastructure and the mass manufacture of products. For example, in a study of English pottery prices, George Miller (1980) shows that the cost of the production of ceramics decreased by 25 to 50 percent during this era, and he assumes that the cost savings were passed along to the consumer. I think it is all too easy to settle for an economic explanation when interpreting the changing material culture patterns at the wage laborer's

Table 15.3 Ceramic vessels by ware for the pieceworker's household (1821–41) and the wage-laborer's household (1841–52) (from Lucas 1994: 5.11)

Ware	Pieceworker's household (ca. 1821–41) no.	%	Wage-laborer's household (1841–52) no.	%
Pearlware	92	76	83	76
Creamware	9	7	15	14
Whiteware	1	1	2	2
Porcelain	19	16	9	8
Total	21	100	109	100

Table 15.4 Refined ceramic vessels by decoration for the pieceworker's household (1821–41) and the wage laborer's household (1841–52) (from Lucas 1993: 8.16; Shackel 1997: 120, 135; 1998)

Decoration	Pieceworker's household (ca. 1821–41) no.	%	Wage-laborer's household (1841–52) no.	%
Shell edged	17	14.0	23	21.1
Transfer print	47	38.8	30	27.5
Painted	28	23.1	29	26.6
Enameled	14	11.6	5	4.6
Dipped	7	5.8	5	4.6
Sponged	0	0.0	1	0.9
Moulded	1	0.8	2	1.8
Undecorated	7	5.8	14	12.8
Total	121	100	109	100

house. Why did they purchase ceramics that were cheaper and no longer in fashion? It is easy to think that since their wages had decreased, wage laborers had to acquire cheaper material goods. This type of economic explanation buys into the mechanistic ecosytemic framework and ignores the agency of each household. We need to look at other explanations when describing anomalies in the archaeological record, including the role of the active agent.

Explaining variability

In Harpers Ferry both men and women had their arenas of protest. Men rebelled in the work place, women protested on the domestic front. The differences of material culture patterning may be attributed to the very different outlooks on labor and the industrialization process at the armory. For instance, craftsmen resisted the implementation of time discipline that managers imposed upon them. In one case, a superintendent tried to enforce industrial discipline and was assassinated by a worker whom he had fired for not obeying the manufacturing regulations. In another case, in 1842, pieceworkers protested that they had to work ten-hour days like wage laborers. The armorers left their jobs, rented a canal boat, and marched to President Tyler's office in Washington, D.C. The armorers, still holding on to their belief in classical republicanism, hoped that the government would act as an arbitrator between capital and labor. Much to their chagrin, Tyler suggested they go back to Harpers Ferry and "hammer out their own salvation" (Barry 1988: 32). Throughout the next decade, workers continually protested by slowing production and destroying products and machinery (Shackel 1996: 169–70; Smith 1977; see also Scott 1985, 1990).

Women's roles changed in the industrial era as they were charged with purchasing consumer goods for their household. In the case of Harpers Ferry, some armory households, like the managers and the early pieceworkers, increasingly participated in the consumer culture that became synonymous with industrialization. Others households, like the wage laborers, became reluctant to adopt the newly fashionable mass-produced goods. In the above case, the tablewares found in the domestic sphere of an armory wage laborer's household did not change as expected when compared with a manager's household assemblage. It is likely that the wage laborer workers' wives were active agents who showed discontent with the new industrial era. While they were probably not protesting the wage labor system, they did protest their role in changing domestic production and their decreasing relations with markets. In this new relationship they were relegated less control and power overall. Therefore, they registered their protest through the use of a material culture whose meaning and use they could control, one that had been fashionable generations earlier, when they had some control over their everyday lives beyond the domestic sphere. They used these unfashionable goods even though the new consumer material culture was easily accessible and affordable through town merchants. These women did not purchase the same goods as those conforming to liberal republicanism and the ideology of mass production and mass consumption. They actively made choices about what types of goods they should purchase. In a mass-production industrial culture, the choices may be very subtle because they are limited. Every armory household placed ceramics on the table, but it was the types of ceramics acquired that allowed women from the wage laborers' households to protest their new roles in industrial society. The armory households examined used tableware to show their obligation, or conversely their lack of commitment, to the new consumer culture of the industrial era.

The concept of agency in historical archaeology

Under the premise of the New Archaeology, which pays considerable attention to function and systems, data that do not fit into predetermined patterns are seen as anomalies. In this view, humans play a limited role in determining culture change. The system is the focus, not the "social actor" (see Dobres and Robb, this volume; see also Brumfiel 1992: 551–2). In particular, elites are the only active components of ecosystem models. They have the power to impose their decisions upon subordinate groups who are usually seen as invisible and incoherent. Managerial theories do not allow subordinate classes the power to influence the system (Brumfield 1992: 555–6).

Brumfiel (1992: 559) also notes that we should not look at cultural systems as homeostatic, but rather as something that is contingent and negotiated, a product of human action. Human actors are the agents of culture change, and agency theory allows us to explain material culture differences in terms of tensions and social conflict within a society. It allows us to see the role of agents in creating their material world and expressing their discontent or resistance to the dominant culture.

Barbara Little (1988, 1997) has also suggested that traditional economic and systemic "rational man" models of culture change are overly simplified because they ignore those segments of a society that are outside the "mainstream" of the male, white, urban middle or upper class. The questions asked of the archaeological record are becoming much more complex, especially in historical archaeology where documentary material adds rich context. By looking at muted groups and examining the concept of double consciousness, historical archaeology is well-equipped to address the relationships between culture change and agency.

In the case of the armory households and their archaeological assemblages, they all had tablewares, but the type of tablewares they chose and what these choices meant can be seen as an expression of resistance to the new industrial culture and social position. Consumers, and in this case women, were making choices about what types of goods they should purchase (see also McCracken 1988; Miller 1987, 1995). In an industrial culture, the different choices one makes may be very subtle because the consumer is limited to culturally acceptable, manufactured forms. In this case study of domestic choices at the Harpers Ferry Armory, the choices that the households made conformed to mass manufactured products, but there are some noticeable subtleties regarding the choices they made in relationship to changing political ideologies.

The use of out-of-date materials that were fashionable generations earlier when classical republicanism dominated the work place shows the consumers' discontent with the new modern culture. It was not merely an economic decision. The armory wage laborers' households may have longed for the good old days, when craftsmen still had some control over their means of production and their daily lives and women may have also shown their discontent of their decreasing power in the market system (Lucas and Shackel 1994; Shackel 1996).

What happens when new technologies confront traditional values and norms? Historian Sean Wilentz (1984) observes that resistance can take on very conservative forms. For instance, in New York City's pre-Civil War era, craft workers struggled to maintain their craft traditions by referring to republican rhetoric. Historian David Montgomery (1979) suggests that other workers struggled to preserve their identity by fighting in political arenas. The family is "seen as a bulwark of resistance and change" (Kessler-Harris 1990: 175). As suggested in the forgoing analysis at Harpers Ferry, some craftsmen became contented laborers and their families willingly subscribed to the new consumer culture. Other workers' families found subversive ways to express discontent, albeit through the medium of mainstream products, both at work and at home. At times, the entire family unit expressed their anxieties over the changing power structure introduced with the implementation of industrial capitalism. The family became the "bulwark of resistance and change."

This examination of how different households reacted to the imposition of industrial capitalism does not pretend to decode the complexities of nineteenth-century domestic consumption. It should raise some questions about how a muted group, such as wage laborers' households, could – and can – reject specific tenets of the dominant ideology. They can actively express their identities and attitudes through the things they choose to buy and use.

Although the expressions of material culture were muted through the medium of mass manufactured household items, subtle variations expressed people's concerns about the new industrial era. In spite of the sameness of mass manufactured household items imposing a conformity of sorts on all consumers, these subtle variations (in context, presence/absence, and the like) provide a means of identifying their "ruled" practices of dissatisfaction and resistance. One of the challenges of archaeology is to search for the range of such expressions.

Acknowledgments

I thank Marcia-Anne Dobres and John E. Robb for inviting me to participate in this volume. They also provided many useful comments that helped improve the essay. Barbara Little also provided helpful suggestions.

Bibliography

Ardener, E. 1975a. "Belief and the Problem of Women," in *Perceiving Women*, ed. S. Ardner, pp. 1–17. Dent, London.
—— 1975b. "Belief and the Problem of Women Revisited," in *Perceiving Women*, ed. S. Ardner, pp. 19–27. Dent, London.
Barbour, A. 1851. Letter to Henry Craig, 24 December 1851, on file, Harpers Ferry, West Virginia: Harpers Ferry Library, Harpers Ferry National Historical Park, Microfilm reel 27, 2, 131.
Barry, J. 1988 [orig.1903]. *The Strange Story of Harpers Ferry With Legends of the Surrounding Country.* Shepherstown Register, Inc., Shepherstown, West Virginia.
Bourdieu, P. 1977. *Outline of a Theory of Practice.* Cambridge University Press, Cambridge UK.
Brumfiel, E. 1992. "Distinguished Lecture in Archaeology: Breaking and Entering the Ecosystem: Gender, Class, and Faction Steal the Show." *American Anthropologist* 94(3): 551–67.
De Cunzo, L. A. (ed.) 1995. "Reform, Respite, Ritual: An Archaeology of Institutions; The Magdalen Society of Philadelphia, 1800–1850." *Historical Archaeology* 29.
Dobres, M.-A. 1995. "Gender and Prehistoric Technology: On the Social Agency of Technical Strategies." *World Archaeology* 27: 25–49.
—— 1999. "Technology's Links and *Chaînes*: The Processual Unfolding of Technique and Technician," in *The Social Dynamics of Technology: Practice, Politics, and World Views*, ed. M.-A. Dobres and C. R. Hoffman, pp. 124–46. Smithsonian Institution Press, Washington, D.C.
Du Bois, W. E. B. 1994 [orig.1903]. *The Soul of Black Folk.* Gramercy Books, New York.
Foucault, M. 1979. *Discipline and Punish.* Vintage Books, New York.
Giddens, A. 1979. *Central Problems in Social Theory. Action, Structure and Contradiction in Social Analysis.* Macmillan, London.
Gilje, P. A. 1996. "The Rise of Capitalism in the Early Republic." *Journal of the Early Republic* 16: 159–81.

Hardesty, D. L. 1988. *The Archaeology of Mining and Miners: A View from the Silver State*. Special Publication Series, no. 6. Society for Historical Archaeology, California and Pennsylvania.

Hodder, I. (ed.) 1982a. *Symbolic and Structural Archaeology*. Cambridge University Press, Cambridge UK.

—— 1982b. "Theoretical Archaeology: A Reactionary View," in *Symbolic and Structural Archaeology*, pp. 1–16. Cambridge University Press, Cambridge UK.

—— 1987. *The Archaeology of Contextual Meanings*. Cambridge University Press, Cambridge UK.

Hull-Walski, D. A., and F. L. Walski 1993. "Brewing and Bottling in Harpers Ferry, West Virginia," in *Interdisciplinary Investigations of Domestic Life in Government Block B: Perspectives on Harpers Ferry's Armory and Commercial District*, Occasional Report no. 6, ed. P. A. Shackel, pp. 17.1–17.53. US Department of the Interior, National Park Service, Washington, D.C.

—— 1994. "There's Trouble A-Brewin': The Brewing and Bottling Industries at Harpers Ferry, West Virginia," in "An Archaeology of Harpers Ferry's Commercial and Residential District," ed. P. A. Shackel and S. E. Winter, *Historical Archaeology* 28: 106–21.

Johnson, M. 1989. "Conceptions of Agency in Archaeological Interpretation." *Journal of Anthropological Archaeology* 8: 189–211.

—— 1996. *An Archaeology of Capitalism*. Blackwell, Cambridge, Mass.

Juravich, J. 1985. *Chaos on the Shop Floor*. Temple University Press, Philadelphia.

Kessler-Harris, A. 1990. "Social History," in *The New American History*, ed. E. Foner, pp.163–84. Temple University Press, Philadelphia.

Kirk, T. 1991. "Structure, Agency, and Power Relations 'Chez les Derniers Chasseurs–Cueillers' of Northwestern France," in *Processual and Postprocessual Archaeologies: Multiple Ways of Knowing the Past*, ed. R. W. Preucel, pp.1–16. Center for Archaeological Investigations, Occasional Paper no. 10, Southern Illinois University, Carbondale.

Leone, M. P. 1984. "Interpreting Ideology in Historical Archaeology: Using the Rules of Perspective in the William Paca Garden in Annapolis, Maryland," in *Ideology, Power, and Prehistory*, ed. D. Miller and C. Tilley, pp. 25–35. Cambridge University Press, Cambridge UK.

—— 1988. "The Georgian Order as the Order of Mercantile Capitalism in Annapolis, Maryland," in *The Recovery of Meaning: Historical Archaeology in the Eastern United States*, ed. M. P. Leone and P. B. Potter Jr., pp. 235–62. Smithsonian Institution Press, Washington, D.C.

—— 1995. "A Historical Archaeology of Capitalism." *American Anthropologist* 97: 251–68.

Little, B. J. 1988. "Craft and Culture Change in the Eighteenth Century Chesapeake," in *The Recovery of Meaning: Historical Archaeology in the Eastern United States*, ed. M. P. Leone and P. B. Potter Jr., pp. 263–292. Smithsonian Institution Press, Washington, D.C.

—— 1994. "'She was . . . an Example to her Sex': Possibilities for a Feminist Historical Archaeology," in *The Historical Archaeology of the Chesapeake*, ed. P. A. Shackel and B. J. Little, pp. 189–204. Smithsonian Institution Press, Washington, D.C.

—— 1997. "Expressing Ideology without a Voice, or, Obfuscation and the Enlightenment." *International Journal of Historical Archaeology* 1: 225–41.

Lucas, M. T. 1993. "Ceramic Consumption in an Industrializing Community," in *Interdisciplinary Investigations of Domestic Life in Government Block B: Perspectives of Harpers Ferry's Armory and Commercial District*, Occasional Report no. 6, ed. P. A. Shackel, pp. 8.1–8.38. US Department of the Interior, National Park Service, Washington, D.C.

—— 1994. "An Armory Worker's Life: Glimpses of Industrial Life," in *An Archeology of An Armory Worker's Household: Park Building 48, Harpers Ferry National Historical Park*, Occasional Report no. 12, ed. P. A. Shackel, pp. 5.1–5.40. US Department of the Interior, National Park Service, Washington, D.C.

Lucas, M. T., and P. A. Shackel 1994. "Changing Social and Material Routine in 19th-Century Harpers Ferry," in "An Archaeology of Harpers Ferry's Commercial and Residential District," ed. P. A. Shackel and S. E. Winter, *Historical Archaeology* 28: 27–36.

McCracken, G. 1988. *Culture and Consumption: New Approaches to the Symbolic Character of Consumer Goods and Activities*. Indiana University Press, Bloomington.

McGuire, R. H., and Paynter, R. (eds) 1991. *The Archaeology of Inequality*. Blackwell, Cambridge, Mass.

Miller, D. 1987. *Material Culture as Mass Consumption*. Basil Blackwell, New York.

—— 1995. "Consumption Studies as the Transformation of Anthropology," in *Acknowledging Consumption: A Review of New Studies*, ed. D. Miller, pp. 264–95. Routledge, London.

Miller, D. and C. Tilley 1984. "Ideology, Power, and Prehistory: An Introduction," in *Ideology and Power in Prehistory*, ed. D. Miller and C. Tilley, pp. 1–15. Cambridge University Press, Cambridge UK.

Miller, G. L. 1980. "Classification and Economic Scaling of 19th-Century Ceramics." *Historical Archaeology* 14: 1–40.

Montgomery, E. H. 1979. *Workers' Control in America: Studies in the History of Work, Technology, and Labor Struggles*. Cambridge University Press, New York.

Mullins, P. R. 1996. *The Contradictions of Consumption: An Archaeology of African America and Consumer Culture, 1850–1930*. Unpublished Ph.D. dissertation, Department of Anthropology, University of Massachusetts, Amherst.

Nassaney, M. S., and M. R. Abel 1993. "The Political and Social Contexts of Cutlery Production in the Connecticut Valley." *Dialectical Anthropology* 18: 247–89.

Paynter, R. 1989. "The Archaeology of Equality and Inequality." *Annual Review of Anthropology* 18: 369–99.

Ross, S. J. 1985. *Workers on the Edge: Work, Leisure, and Politics in Industrializing Cincinnati, 1788–1890*. Columbia University Press, New York.

Schulter, H. 1910. *The Brewing Industry and the Brewery Workers' Movement in America*. International Union of United Brewery Workmen of America, Cincinnati, Ohio.

Scott, J. 1985. *Weapons of the Weak: Everyday Forms of Peasant Resistance*. Yale University Press, New Haven, Conn.

—— 1990. *Domination and the Arts of Resistance: Hidden Transcripts*. Yale University Press, New Haven, Conn.

Shackel, P. A. 1993a. *Personal Discipline and Material Culture: An Archaeology of Annapolis, Maryland, 1695–1870*. University of Tennessee Press, Knoxville.

—— 1993b. "Prospects for an Archaeology of the People without History," in *Interdisciplinary Investigations of Domestic Life in Government Block B: Perspectives on Harpers Ferry's Armory and Commercial District*, Occasional Report no. 6, ed. P. A. Shackel, pp. 18.1–18.22. US Department of the Interior, National Park Service, Washington, D.C.

—— 1996. *Culture Change and the New Technology: An Archaeology of the Early American Industrial Era*. Plenum, New York.

—— 1998. "Classical and Liberal Republicanism and the New Consumer Culture." *International Journal of Historical Archeology* 2: 1–20.

Shanks, M., and C. Tilley 1987. *Reconstructing Archaeology*. Cambridge University Press, Cambridge UK.

Smith, M. R. 1977. *Harpers Ferry Armory and the New Technology: The Challenge of Change*. Cornell University Press, Ithaca, N.Y.

Stubblefield, J. 1821. Letter to George Bomford, 6 April 1821, on file, Harpers Ferry, West Virginia: Harpers Ferry Library, Harpers Ferry National Historical Park, Microfilm Reel 21, 4, 404–6.

Symington, J. 1846. Letter to George Talcott, 29 June 1846, on file, Harpers Ferry, West Virginia: Harpers Ferry Library, Harpers Ferry National Historical Park, Microfilm reel 23, 6, 57–60.

Tilley, C. 1982. "Social Format," in *Symbolic and Structural Archaeology*, ed. I. Hodder, pp. 85–125. Cambridge University Press, Cambridge UK.

Wall, D. 1994. *The Archaeology of Gender; Separating the Spheres in Urban America*. Plenum, New York.

Wilentz, S. 1984. *Chants Democratic: New York City and the Rise of the American Working Class, 1788–1850*. Oxford University Press, New York.

Wolf, E. 1990. "Distinguished Lecture: Facing Power – Old Insights, New Questions." *American Anthropologist* 92: 586–96.

Part 4

Commentary

16 On the archaeology of choice

Agency studies as a research stratagem

Elizabeth M. Brumfiel

The papers in this volume cover the length and breadth of human history. They examine archaeological contexts from the Palaeolithic and Neolithic of the Old World to Precolumbian America, Renaissance England, and nineteenth-century America. What could this miscellany of archaeological cases share in common? Very little, except to provide evidence that agent-centered perspectives have much to offer archaeology.

The nature of agency

The contributors to this volume share an impressive core of agreement concerning the nature of agency. They all agree that agency refers to the intentional choices made by men and women as they take action to realize their goals. All would agree that these actors are socially constituted beings who are embedded in sociocultural and ecological surroundings that both define their goals and constrain their actions. All would agree that a dynamic interaction exists between actors and structures: actors are rooted in social and ecological contexts, and these contexts are transformed by the actions of individuals (although not always in the ways that the individuals intended). All the contributors share the conviction that archaeological accounts that recognize structurally-constrained human agency are better than those that do not.

However, this cheerful unanimity quickly dissolves in the effort to define the agents who peopled the archaeological past. Did these agents work toward goals that are in some way cross-culturally predictable, or were their goals defined by unique culturally and historically specific logics and values? A majority of the contributors (Wobst, Joyce, Clark, Pauketat, Walker and Lucero, Sassaman, and Shackel) argue the former case. These contributors share a Marxist sense that the goals of individuals in a given society are defined (in Cowgill's words) by "socially constructed interests," that is, goals that are determined by the position that individuals occupy within the social structure. Struggles over power and resources generate efforts to dominate or resist, compete or seek allies, exclude or include, accommodate or deceive. In this view, societies with similar social structures generate similar types of tensions, creating similar goals for actors who occupy analogous social positions. This view highlights struggles between groups of social actors as an important source for social change. No account of the past would be complete without an analysis of these struggles and how they were negotiated by individuals operating within their particular ecological and social circumstances.

A smaller group of contributors (Gero, Cowgill, Barrett, Chapman, Sinclair, and Johnson) argue for actors whose subjectivity is unique to their cultural and historical moments. These contributors argue that goals are determined not just by socially constructed interests, but also by deeply embedded cultural values, commitments, and "projects" (to use Ortner's 1984 term). Agents design strategy according to culturally specific patterns of cognition, logic, and meaning that shape the actor's understanding of reality. Particularly influential in determining agency is the actor's sense of identity, that is, the actor's ideas about what kind of person he or she is and how people like that ought to act. In this view, there is no assurance that people will pursue their interests in any predictable way since actors with different subjectivities will have different responses, even when confronted with identical circumstances.

In contrast to the other contributors, Hodder argues that studies of agency should focus on the individual. He is critical of studies of embodiment and practice (such as those presented by Chapman and Sinclair) because they omit consideration of individual lives. Hodder argues that individuals are important to archaeologists for three reasons. First, structure and system are never fully determinative of choice; second, in the absence of the individual as a unit of analysis, all variability must be dismissed as "noise" as opposed to the "situated construction of difference;" and third, the contradictions and conflicts generated by structure are worked out at the level of the individual.

Hodder's emphasis on the individual is provocative, opposed both to postmodern efforts to deconstruct the individual (see Dobres and Robb, Gero; also Johnson 1989) and to archaeological pronouncements that individuals cannot or should not be the focus of archaeological research (Cowgill, Sassaman). However, the fine chronologies that archaeologists now employ means that they can, in fact, identify the projects of individual leaders (Clark, Walker and Lucero), and in historic archaeology particular structures can often be linked to individuals (Johnson; also Leone 1984). In Hodder's own analysis, individuals are firmly rooted in structures and, in the case of the Ice Man, yield an effective archaeological narrative. In this analysis, Hodder recounts the structural circumstances that would have made decisions to undertake solitary journeys into the Italian Alps fairly common, which in the Ice Man's case resulted in death.

Research agendas

These contrasting conceptions of social actors highlight quite different problems for archaeological research. For those who see actors' goals as determined by socially constructed interests, much is already given. Presented with evidence of social inequality, these archaeologists are likely to presume the existence of competition within the emerging dominant group and struggle between dominant and subordinate strata. Consequently, the most pressing questions for these archaeologists concern strategy: how did some actors accumulate power while others tried to resist their efforts (Joyce, Clark, Walker and Lucero, and Shackel)?

However, Sassaman, Wobst, and Pauketat pose some other types of research questions that emerge from this Marxist, internal-conflict perspective. One such question deals with the identification of social cleavages other than class. While emerging rank and class inequality leave fairly obvious hallmarks in the archaeological record, other forms of social division do not. These other divisions (age, gender, ethnicity, lineage, locality) are sometimes important components of the social field within which agents operate. Sassaman's approach highlights technological variation and change. Observing that humans use material culture to define the boundaries of social groups, Sassaman suggests that the adoption of new technologies and styles define emerging cleavages in past societies. Similarly, Wobst suggests that artifact style is used to promote group unity in the presence of internal contest and unresolved stress. Thus, the degree of stylistic elaboration signals the intensity of conflict within the group. Other efforts to empirically determine social groups and interests include Saitta's (1994) focus on the extraction and use of surplus and Ensor's (in press) discussion of the mode of production.

Pauketat argues that social change comes not just from competition and conflict but also from the rare occasions when the interests of opposing groups coincide. Such a coincidence of interests produces only temporary cooperation, but it permits the realization of large-scale projects with unanticipated and irreversible outcomes. For example, Pauketat suggests that Mississippian mound-building was a joint consequence of leaders' search for power and commoners' efforts to create meaning, order, and identity through mound construction. Mound-building forged the otherwise divergent interests of leaders and followers into a stable social structure.

For those who see agents as deeply embedded in unique cultural circumstances, the research agenda focuses on developing methods to recover unique cultural definitions of identity. Chapman suggests that culturally specific identities might be defined in the dimensions of variation in burial programs that distinguish men and women, different age groups, members of different families, and so forth. (Joyce (in press) also considers how burial programs permit the definition of culturally significant criteria of social identity). Sinclair uses the skills and character traits required to produce specific types of artifacts to reconstruct the social values of the tool-makers (Keightly (1987) makes a similar effort for Shang-period pottery). Johnson inspects changes in architectural form to document the emergence of a new social identity, a "new" man, in Renaissance England.

The theoretical importance of agency studies

What does the study of agency contribute to our understanding of traditional problems in sociocultural evolution, and what new perspectives on the past does it introduce?

At a minimum, an agent-centered perspective provides an argument for the internal origins of at least some social change. In older, processual views of cultural evolution, cultures responded (adaptively) to stresses brought about by external forces such as climatic change or population growth. An agency perspective argues, however, that the impetus for at least some social changes was the desire of men and women to realize their (socially-determined) goals. Furthermore, an agency perspective argues that the timing of cultural change may be determined by evolving social circumstances rather than ecological conditions.

Beyond that, an agency perspective on individual lives reveals much about how social change occurs. In the manner of Hodder's Ice Man narrative and Johnson's description of Robert Dudley, we can ask how particular individuals embodied existing social trends and contradictions, and how the contradictions were worked out at the level of the individual and the event. Why did these individuals produce changes while others did not? Did they occupy unique positions within the social structure that posed unique problems or opportunities for them as social actors? Did evolving circumstances in other social spheres present them with access to resources that others lacked, and if so, how did these resources alter the processes of social reproduction? Did these individuals set forth new ideologies; if so, whose loyalties were influenced? Did they create new social institutions and, and if they did, how did the redistribution of social roles and resources affect the existing balance of power?

Beyond explaining social change, agent-centered analyses can add texture to descriptive narratives of the past. Agent-centered analyses incorporate all the variables that have entered into archaeology's grand narratives, but an agent-centered account encourages archaeologists to examine how these variables affected different categories of people. Rather than generalizing about the effects on the population as a whole, an agent-centered analysis could examine the range of consequences that a single variable might produce for individuals differently positioned within the social system. For example, warfare could result in death for one individual, in glory for a second, in the profits from the arms trade for a third, and in the loss of household labor for a fourth. An agent-centered analysis can examine the long-term changes in resource use and social structure that result from the consequences experienced by these different actors. Thus, agent-centered archaeology can provide more nuanced and varied understandings of events and processes.

Agent-centered analyses also promote the study of cross-cultural variation in social institutions and practices. For example, in this volume, Joyce explores how the power of rulers in Formative Oaxaca rested upon local notions of reciprocity and sacrifice between humans and their gods. These particular ideas provided both opportunities for rulers seeking to enhance their power and constraints impinging on their actions. Elsewhere, Gillespie (1999) attempts to reconstruct the prehistoric Olmec rulers' notions of "power" and "agent" through the analysis of two classes of material culture, colossal stone heads and massive stone altars. She also suggests how these concepts might have influenced the way that social inequality was perceived by Olmec subjects and how Olmec rulers and subjects negotiated the issue of social inequality.

Agent-centered archaeologists might also want to go beyond questions of power. As Gero and Pauketat observe, power is not the only prize capable of generating social transformation. Other projects can inspire collective action and irreversible change. Potentially, the exploration of other types of cultural "games" (see Holland 1998; Ortner 1996) would provide new narratives for archaeology beyond the well-told stories of human evolution, ecological adaptation, and evolving political hierarchy.

Finally, an agent-centered archaeology can supply new perspectives on our own lives. To the extent that archaeologists can recover the experiences, values, and commitments of past populations, they can broaden our conceptions of "the meaning of things." For example, the meaning of warfare is defined both by its practical consequences and by its place within a framework of cultural values and associations (retribution, masculinity, etc.). Today, the point of much of cultural anthropology (and much public archaeology) is to provide critical self-reflection upon our own assumptions and values by examining the assumptions, values, and experiences of others. As archaeologists become more expert at reconstructing the situations faced by humans in the past, they can participate more fully in critical examinations of the present (Leone *et al.* 1987; Wilkie and Bartoy in press).

The methodological importance of agency studies

In the history of archaeology, new theoretical approaches have frequently increased the range of data brought into analysis. For example, the cultural reconstruction approaches of the 1940s and 1950s stimulated interest in the functional and technical attributes of artifacts as well as the stylistic attributes previously analyzed by time-space systemicists. The New Archaeology introduced the chemical analysis of raw materials and artifact residues. Post-processual archaeology enhanced our appreciation of archaeological context. Agency theory encourages its own expansion of what is relevant in the archaeological record.

The contributors to this volume emphasize the importance of context and variation in asking about agency. Wobst points out that context can define the social frame (i.e., the

social situation) in which artifact use occurred. Context provides clues to the social identities of artifact makers and users, the messages and claims involved in artifact manufacture
or use, and the likely audience for these messages. Walker and Lucero show that an analysis
of context enables archaeologists to reconstruct the "life history" of an artifact or structure,
which in turn helps to define how the artifact or structure was used and the purposes of the
agent(s) who made and used it.

Variation in the archaeological record is very important to an agent-centered analysis. In
processual or structural archaeologies, certain kinds of variation, such as the differences among
artifacts assigned to the same "type" or the unique attributes of burials or structures, have been
treated as "noise." Such variation was not considered suitable for analysis; on the contrary, it
was regarded as hindering the definition of culturally meaningful patterns. In contrast, agent-
centered approaches are founded on the premise of social heterogeneity, which can only be
identified through variation in material culture. Therefore, agent-centered archaeologists are
predisposed to seek out variation and to explore its meaning.

As Shackel observes, variation indicates the existence of viable choices for individual
actors, or "the ability to have done otherwise," to quote Clark. Because variation implies
choice, Shackel can use variation or difference in the ceramics of managers and their
workers to suggest that some factory workers chose not to embrace the cultural practices of
the industrial order (for other examples of resistance defined through contrasts in material
culture, see Brumfiel 1996; Ferguson 1991). The presumption of choice also grounds
Sassaman's argument that technological and stylistic variation between contemporaneous
groups is evidence of ethnic diversity as a strategic choice made by social actors (also see
Barth 1969; Schortman and Nakamura 1991).

Variation also enables archaeologists to gauge of the degree of social conformity
demanded by past societies, as observed by Wobst and Chapman (also Dobres 1995). Low
coefficients of variation would imply strict adherence to social norms; high coefficients of
variation would imply a more relaxed social atmosphere.

The study of agency in archaeology: problems and prospects

While the prospects for an agent-centered archaeology are encouraging, agent-centered
studies must be strengthened in two ways. First, they must confront the issue of ethnocentrism, and second, they must concentrate on presenting strongly supported arguments.

Gero raises the issue of ethnocentrism in a critique that goes unanswered by the other
contributors. Particularly in studies of political development that postulate the existence of
political aggrandizers (e.g., Clark and Blake 1994; Flannery 1999; Hayden 1995), the agents
of cultural change are assumed to have qualities that are remarkably masculinist (Gero) and
capitalist (Saitta, personal communication 1993) in nature. Agents are portrayed as oppor-
tunistic, innovative, self-interested, decisive, and assertive. It is true that political leaders
often possess these qualities. As Earle (1987: 294) observes, political leadership is an inherently competitive, pragmatic process that may require a maximizing strategy. However,
more corporate leadership strategies are certainly conceivable (Blanton *et al.* 1996;
Gillespie 1999). Given this possibility, the presence of aggrandizers in the archaeological
record should be demonstrated rather than assumed.

The trap of ethnocentrism is not solely of concern to those who focus on political
competition; it is a danger even to those who attempt to recover the culturally-specific
values, commitments, and projects of prehistoric agents. For example, Sinclair suggests a
link between the techniques of biface manufacture in Solutrean culture and the

(re)creation of qualities that were particularly valued in Solutrean hunters: perseverance, boldness, and adaptability. Who was endowed with these characteristics? Given the evidence for game drives at the type site of Solutré, and given the ethnographically-known foraging societies where both men and women participate in game drives, we might expect Sinclair to conclude that these qualities were admired in both men and women. Thus, Sinclair's declaration that a separation existed between hunting and other non-hunting activities comes as a surprise. It seems to reserve the valued qualities of Solutrean hunters for men only, an unfounded inference but one that conforms to our own association of hunting and men.

Agent-centered analyses seem as vulnerable as other modes of archaeological interpretation to the projection of our own values onto past societies. Although an emphasis upon the embeddedness of agents in their sociocultural and ecological surroundings should prevent this sort of thing, it apparently does not. And agency theorists have simply not responded to this critique when it has been levelled at their work. However, as alternative models of cultural change are developed, models that ascribe different cultural principles to past actors (corporate models of state formation, for example), archaeologists continuing to employ ethnocentric assumptions will be forced to defend these assumptions. It will be an interesting discussion.

Agency theorists must also concentrate on presenting strongly supported arguments. Several presentations in this volume are intriguing, but not totally compelling. For example, more than any other contributor, Joyce embeds the stratagems of emerging leaders in Oaxaca in culturally specific commitments, in this case, the covenant of interdependence between the people and their deities. But his model would be stronger if he could show that the idea of the covenant motivated leaders as well as being used by them to attain more wealth and power. Why would leaders be any more cynical about this idea that commoners were? Likewise, Pauketat might supply more details on how Mississippian commoners found meaning, order, and identity through mound construction. Walker and Lucero successfully demonstrate that ritual activity was removed from the household to special facilities in the Southwest, but in the Maya area, ritual activity continues in households even after elites introduce more elaborate forms. How, then, did Maya leaders appropriate traditional rituals to perform "social alchemy" and promote "collective misrecognition"? Shackel's argument for resistance in nineteenth-century America would benefit from a conclusive demonstration that workers' adoption of unfashionable cream wares was not forced upon them by poverty.

Sinclair's analysis of technology offers a promising methodology for exploring what Cowgill calls palaeopsychology; however, this method needs to be verified through ethnographic testing. Does an inspection of the technologies of ethnographically known peoples actually demonstrate that culturally-valued skills and character traits can be read from production techniques of material culture?

Agent-centered archaeology clearly has its work cut out for it. But the diversity and originality of the analyses collected in this volume suggest that agency studies have made and will continue to make important theoretical and methodological contributions to archaeology. Agent-centered archaeology expands the questions we ask about the past and the data we use to try to answer these questions.

Humans, because of their intelligence, are able to contemplate a wide array of variables as they decide what to do next. But even with their expanded awareness, humans are often at a loss as they contemplate their options. Information is never complete, optimal strategies are rarely evident, moral choices are often ambiguous, and discursive spaces are difficult to find. Perhaps because agent-centered studies attempt to fit all of the complexities of daily life into their frame of analysis, they can render past actors more believable and supply accounts of the past that are more true, relevant, and interesting than studies where humans are the passive victims of dumb luck or circumstance.

Bibliography

Barth, F. (ed.) 1969. *Ethnic Groups and Boundaries*. Little, Brown, Boston.

Blanton, R., G. Feinman, S. Kowalewski, and P. Peregrine 1996. "A Dual-Processual Theory for the Evolution of Mesoamerican Civilization." *Current Anthropology* 37: 1–14.

Brumfiel, E. M. 1996. "Figurines and the Aztec State: Testing the Effectiveness of Ideological Domination," in *Gender and Archaeology*, ed. R. P. Wright, pp. 143–66. University of Pennsylvania Press, Philadelphia.

Clark, J. E., and M. Blake 1994. "The Power of Prestige: Competitive Generosity and the Emergence of Rank Societies in Lowland Mesoamerica," in *Factional Competition and Political Development in the New World*, ed. E. M. Brumfiel and J. W. Fox, pp. 17–30. Cambridge University Press, Cambridge UK.

Dobres, M-A. 1995. "Gender and Prehistoric Technology: On the Social Agency of Technical Strategies." *World Archaeology* 27(1): 25–49.

Earle, T. K. 1987. "Chiefdoms in Archaeological and Ethnohistorical Perspective." *Annual Review of Anthropology* 16: 279–308.

Ensor, B. E. in press. "Social Formations, *Modo de Vida*, and Conflict in Archaeology." *American Antiquity*.

Ferguson, L. 1991. "Struggling with Pots in Colonial South Carolina," in *The Archaeology of Inequality*, ed. R. H. McGuire and R. Paynter, pp. 28–39. Blackwell, Oxford.

Flannery, K. V. 1999. "Process and Agency in Early State Formation." *Cambridge Archaeological Journal* 9: 3–21.

Gillespie, S. D. 1999. "Olmec Thrones as Ancestral Altars: The Two Sides of Power," in *Material Symbols: Culture and Economy in Prehistory*, ed. J. E. Robb, pp. 224–53. Center for Archaeological Investigations, Southern Illinois University, Carbondale.

Hayden, B. D. 1995. "Pathways to Power: Principles for Creating Socioeconomic Inequalities," in *Foundations of Social Inequality*, ed. T. D. Price and G. M. Feinman, pp. 15–86. Plenum, New York.

Holland, D. 1998. *Identity and Agency in Cultural Worlds*. Harvard University Press, Cambridge, Mass.

Johnson, M. H. 1989. "Conceptions of Agency in Archaeological Interpretation." *Journal of Anthropological Archaeology* 8: 189–211.

Joyce, R. in press. *Gender and Power in Prehispanic Mesoamerica*. University of Texas Press, Austin.

Keightly, D. N. 1987. "Archaeology and Mentality: The Making of China." *Representations* 18: 91–128.

Leone, M. P. 1984. "Interpreting Ideology in Historic Archaeology: Using the Rules of Perspective in the William Paca Garden in Annapolis, Maryland," in *Ideology, Power, and Prehistory*, ed. D. Miller and C. Tilley, pp. 25–35. Cambridge University Press, Cambridge UK.

Leone, M. P., P. B. Potter, Jr., and P. A. Shackel 1987 "Toward a Critical Archaeology." *Current Anthropology* 28: 283–-302.

Ortner, S. B. 1984. "Theory in Anthropology Since the Sixties." *Comparative Studies in Society and History* 26: 126–66.

—— 1996. "Making Gender," in *Making Gender: The Politics and Erotics of Culture*, pp. 1–20. Beacon, Boston.

Saitta, D. J. 1994. "Agency, Class, and Archaeological Interpretation." *Journal of Anthropological Archaeology* 13: 201–27.

Schortman, E., and S. Nakamura 1991. "A Crisis of Identity: Late Classic Competition and Interaction on the Southeast Maya Periphery." *Latin American Antiquity* 2: 311–36.

Wilkie, L. A., and K. M. Bartoy in press. "A Critical Archaeology Revisited." *Current Anthropology*.

Part 5

Epilogue

17 Ethics and ontology

Why agents and agency matter

Henrietta L. Moore

> The self that is liberated is obliged to live its life tied to the project of its own identity.
> (Rose 1990: 244)

Agents and their relations

Attempts at definition very often produce more problems than they solve, but the attempt is ostensibly the very purpose of intellectual life. There are times when, as a social scientist, I envy natural scientists, in the sense that whatever problems their investigations throw up they are imagined to be potentially solvable, given enough time, money, equipment, imagination and so on. I doubt, of course, whether this halcyon view of natural science is accurate, but I am clear that it is born of a mixture of frustration and envy. Whatever the critiques of science and objectivism over the last several decades, there is still a lingering sense that natural scientists are less restricted in their endeavors by the limits imposed by their sense of themselves. Whether or not phenomena are affected by observation, and although interpretations are constrained by conceptual frames and academic politics, the one thing that stands out is that the objects of natural science inquiry are predominantly not sentient beings engaged in social relationships. Leaving aside the debates about higher primates and animal rights, one thing that can be said of atoms, for example, is that (whether or not they are socially constructed) they do not normally speak or, as far as we know, hold views about the scientists who study them.

The issue, of course, is not really that people have views about the social scientists who study them, but that social scientists are both enabled and constrained by the fact that social science inquiry is a form of social relationship, that the self of the enquirer is implicated with the selves under study. This point has been made forcibly in recent literature in social anthropology, but is not so frequently discussed in relation to archaeology. One reason for this is that archaeologists are rightly cautious about anachronism and forms of theoretical imperialism; that is, about assumptions of similarity and/or continuity between the past and the present. The influence of Foucault in all the social sciences and humanities has produced a formal commitment to the notion that the self is not ontologically prior to the relations in which it finds itself; it is therefore culturally and historically constructed and formed. It follows from this point that the selves of individuals living in the distant past are not likely to be the same as the selves of present day archaeologists. This may readily be acknowledged, as many papers in this volume evidence, but the larger problem concerns the pre-theoretical assumptions behind the concept of agency and the various debates about its relevance and specificity.

There are various ways to trace the intellectual genealogy of the term agency (see Dobres and Robb, this volume; see also Archer 1988; Emirbayer and Mische 1998; Joas 1996; Taylor 1985), and citations frequently cover social thinkers and philosophers from Aristotle and St Thomas Aquinas to Anthony Giddens and Pierre Bourdieu. What is most generally apparent from recent work on agency, however, is its implicit and explicit orientation towards creativity, innovation, and resistance. It is commonplace to find practice theorists – such as Giddens and Bourdieu – criticized for being overly "reproductive" and neglecting the potential for social change. The overall emphasis has tended to be on individual variation and intervention, and on the capacity for individuals to destabilize social systems creatively and inaugurate social change. The result in many contexts has been to conflate agency with the actor (Alexander 1992: 1), and thus to assume that evidence of agency is the same thing as evidence for individuals or subjects or selves. This confusion is an understandable one, and in archaeology its origins would seem to lie in the wholly necessary and laudable attempt to think about the concrete attributes of individuals in the past and their role in social and cultural change. It is thus the notion of action that links actors with agency, but although agency is a socially significant quality of action it is both more and less than mere action. These and related points are made by Cowgill, Barrett, and Clark in their chapters. However, many social actions result in nothing of any great significance, and to conflate agency with actors produces social actors who are always making choices, who always act creatively when faced with novel situations, and are thus perennially over-active or hyper-active. These actors are clearly abstractions, imaginary beings, and not concrete individuals, and their particular conceptualization is the result of defining agency as the opposite of structure. The effect is to reinforce the dichotomy between structure and agency rather than to reflect upon it critically and rethink it. In short, the problem of the relationship between structure and agency cannot be solved by making agents over-active, over-interventionist, and over-creative.

Why should this have happened in the first place? There are a number of ways in which this question might be answered, but one form of response should surely focus on the ethics of archaeology as a discipline and as a practice; that is, on the nature of the social engagement between archaeologists and the people they study. This might at first sight seem a strange statement because, ethnoarchaeology aside, all the people archaeologists study are by definition dead. However, Clark opens the way in his chapter when he argues that the social scientist's commitment to a certain mode of explanation precedes and is typically independent of any data set. The social engagement archaeologists have with the people they study is through the ethical spaces created by the pre-theoretical assumptions and values that make the discipline and its practice possible. These assumptions might better be termed the very conditions of possibility of archaeology itself. They include, for example, the idea that people in the past had societies and social relations.[1]

One such value, or pre-theoretical assumption, is that individuals in other times and other places were endowed with human characteristics, and thus archaeologists cannot reconstruct their lives or social systems without assuming that people in the past were competent social actors. This is part of the ethics of contemporary archaeology and it creates a space in which certain kinds of theories and ways of theorizing are legitimate and others are not. It also accounts in very large part for the popularity of agency theories in archaeology. The same kind of argument applies equally well to socio-cultural anthropology and feminist scholarship. The question of what constitutes a competent social actor is, of course, given by experiential, philosophical, popular, and academic discourses available to contemporary archaeologists. In spite of all the talk of the importance of not assuming that individuals, persons, selves, and subjectivities are constant or consonant across space and time, it does indeed turn out that agency is crucial in the past because it is significant in the present. But the past has never been just about the past; it has always been what makes the present able to live with itself. And we could not live with ourselves if our archaeology produced accounts of individuals, cultures, and societies that left no space for individuality, freedom of choice, will, self-determination, creativity, innovation, and resistance. No archaeologist could live with such a view because humans would then have no role, or very little, in the making of their own history. What then would be the point of being human?

Ontology versus epistemology

The point of discussing agents, actors, selves and subjectivities in the past, as many contributors to this volume point out, is not merely to implant certain social characteristics or individual capabilities in the past and then derive them analytically. Archaeology as a discipline and as a practice is definitively against anachronism. Consequently, many of the chapters in this book allude to the fact that agents and selves are not ontologically prior to relations of power and can therefore only be understood within socially and culturally patterned contexts. This is a commitment to understanding things – events, systems, people, artifacts – in their proper context(s). Several contributors comment that agents or selves cannot be assumed to be constant in their nature over time, and that the relationship between structure and agency cannot be presumed the same across time and space. While this commitment to historicism is part of the pre-theoretical assumptions of archaeology, it has also received a particular inflection from recent post-structuralist and deconstructionist critiques within the social sciences and humanities. That inflection emphasizes the exclusionary practices and sanctioned ignorances of "grand theory" and questions not just the substance of theories, but the nature of the theoretical project itself. The influence of Foucault on this critique has emphasized that selves are not natural, fixed, or unchanging entities, but the products of social, cultural, and historical circumstance. The determined view of much writing in the social sciences and the humanities is that entities and/or notions such as agent, actor, self, identity, and person are to be understood as having rhetorical rather than essential capacities and/or attributes: rhetorical in the sense that they are discursive constructions, situated reifications, that make sense experientially, socially, philosophically, and intellectually. They thus act not just as points of orientation and location, but as categories that help to make sense of a diverse range of social experiences and encounters, from embodiment to political citizenship. This point is true, of course, not just for the people being studied, but for those doing the studying, both for social actors in the past and for contemporary archaeologists.

Entities or notions such as self, person or social actor are not foundational categories, but this does not mean that they are not experienced categorically by individuals and groups. The notion of "imagined communities" in the social sciences has made not one whit of difference to ethnic cleansing in Europe in the 1990s, and the idea of the fragmented and processual self has apparently done little to undermine the sense of self of the famous academics who propound such theories! However, we should not lose sight of the fact that although we and others may experience the categorical effects of constructions such as self or person, such entities or notions are better understood as concept-metaphors (see Moore 1997). Their use within the discipline requires rigorous critical practice, part of which entails close attention both to how they worked in the lives of people in the past and how they work in the lives of contemporary archaeologists. By discussing notions of self, actor, person and so on that differ from one's own understandings, and analyzing how these notions may be operationalized in social relations of power, their historically and culturally determined nature is made evident. This move simultaneously interrogates the pre-theoretical assumptions and values regarding notions such as self, person and actor that underpin disciplinary practices and theories, including those held by contemporary archaeologists. In other words, a critical archaeology would inevitably hold the selves of archaeologists and past others in the same ethical space because not to do so would be to refuse the possibility of examining the theoretical foundations of the discipline. This, then, is the ethical position that underpins any critical examination of epistemology, and it is something that has been usefully inherited from post-structuralist and deconstructionist debates.

However, this inheritance, like many others, has not been without its complications. One part of the post-structuralist/deconstructionist critique has insisted that the universalistic pretensions of grand theories must be abandoned, and in some strong forms it maintains that all forms of generalization must be eschewed because they ignore differences and promote sanctioned ignorances. The discriminatory nature of much western theorizing is not in doubt, but we should not run away with the idea that we have abandoned universalisms in our theories, leave alone generalization. Many of our theories do make universalistic claims or contain universalistic assumptions, but these are of an ontological rather than epistemological nature (Moore 1997).

Many such assumptions relate to conditions for humanity. In the context of the discipline of archaeology and its related fields, it might be more accurate to say that they relate to the capacities of *homo sapiens*. When we say that the unconscious monitoring of social action is at the basis of human agency, or that all humans have the capacity for agency or that symbolism is a feature of human cognition, for example, we are making assertions that we imagine to be universally true, in that they apply to all humans. These are, effectively, conditions for humanity, and they are not just epistemologies or theories of the nature of humanity, but ontologies: conditions of and for humanity (Moore 1997: 137). In order to be critically aware of our own theorizing and its effects on others (past or present), we have to recognize that theories are composite. In other words, we have to distinguish between those parts of a theory that are context dependent, related to a specific time and place, and to particular disciplinary practices and bodies of data, and those that incorporate forms of ontological thinking. This is particularly true when we utilize higher order propositions or concept-metaphors, such as self, person, individual, and subject or notions such as agency, intentionality, identification, and subjectivity.

The work of higher order propositions in theorizing is two-fold. First, they serve to delineate domains of enquiry; they are domain terms. We use them as a kind of disciplinary shorthand, to indicate the area of human life, capacity, and relations we are referring to. They are at the basis of comparisons, but their boundaries and contents are frequently fuzzy, overlapping, and mutually implicated and defining. What, for example, is the difference between actor, agent, self, person, individual, and subject? We can differentiate between these terms and specify temporary boundaries for analysis, but we cannot irrevocably separate them from each other. This is equally true of intentionality, motivation, subjectification and a host of other related terms. This draws attention to the fact that while one feature of these terms is to serve an integratory or rhetorical function, to provide positions and reference points both for analysis and for living, they have another equally important function. Recent theorizing has emphasized that selves, individuals, subjects and so forth are categories in process: they are never finished or complete. This must be the case since they are the effects of discursive engagement with relations of power. This draws attention to the second role of concept-metaphors in academic theorizing and that is to create spaces, to open things up for analysis, and to maintain ambiguity. It is in asking the question "what is the difference?", for us as theorists and for people in the past, between selves and persons, or between subjectification and identification, that we create the spaces in which we can work, formulate research questions, and subject data to analysis. In one sense then agency matters not because we can define it completely or irrevocably, but because we cannot and this failure of specification is at the root of intellectual creativity, as well as disciplinary ethics.

Notes

1. See Moore 1999 for a discussion of this argument in relation to socio-cultural anthropology.

Bibliography

Alexander, J. 1992. "Some Remarks on 'Agency' in Recent Sociological Theory." *Perspectives* 15: 1–4.

Archer, M. S. 1988. *Culture and Agency: The Place of Culture in Social Theory*. Cambridge University Press, Cambridge UK.

Emirbayer, M. and A. Mische 1998. "What is Agency?" *American Journal of Sociology* 103(4): 962–1023.

Joas, H. 1996. *The Creativity of Action*. University of Chicago Press, Chicago.

Moore, H. L. 1997. "Interior Landscapes and External Worlds: The Return of Grand Theory in Anthropology." *Australian Journal of Anthropology* 8(2): 125–44.

—— 1999. "Anthropological Theory at the Turn of the Century," in *Anthropological Theory Today*, ed. H. L. Moore. Polity Press, Cambridge UK.

Rose, N. 1990. *Governing the Soul: The Shaping of the Private Self*. Routledge, London.

Taylor, C. 1985. *Philosophical Papers Vol. I: Human Agency and Language*. Cambridge University Press, Cambridge UK.

Index